ISBN 978-0-260-30494-0
PIBN 10986153

THE ANTIENT

Kalendars and Inventories

OF THE

TREASURY OF HIS MAJESTY'S EXCHEQUER,

TOGETHER WITH OTHER

DOCUMENTS ILLUSTRATING THE HISTORY OF THAT REPOSITORY.

VOL. II.

THE ANTIENT
Kalendars and Inventories
OF THE
TREASURY OF HIS MAJESTY'S EXCHEQUER,
TOGETHER WITH OTHER
DOCUMENTS ILLUSTRATING THE HISTORY OF THAT REPOSITORY.

VOL. II.

COLLECTED AND EDITED BY
SIR FRANCIS PALGRAVE, K.H.
OF THE HONOURABLE SOCIETY OF THE INNER TEMPLE, BARRISTER AT LAW,
KEEPER OF THE RECORDS IN THE AFORESAID TREASURY.

PRINTED BY COMMAND
OF
HIS MAJESTY KING WILLIAM IV.
IN PURSUANCE OF AN ADDRESS OF
THE HOUSE OF COMMONS OF GREAT BRITAIN;
AND UNDER THE DIRECTION OF
THE COMMISSIONERS ON THE PUBLIC RECORDS OF THE KINGDOM.

1836.

COMMISSIONERS

ON

THE PUBLIC RECORDS OF THE KINGDOM,

APPOINTED BY

HIS MAJESTY'S COMMISSION

OF THE

12th of March 1831.

HIS GRACE THE ARCHBISHOP OF CANTERBURY.
THE RIGHT HONOURABLE LORD BROUGHAM AND VAUX.
THE RIGHT HONOURABLE THE SECRETARY OF STATE FOR THE HOME DEPARTMENT.
THE RIGHT HONOURABLE THE SPEAKER OF THE HOUSE OF COMMONS.
THE RIGHT HONOURABLE THE CHANCELLOR OF THE EXCHEQUER.
THE RIGHT HONOURABLE THE MASTER OF THE ROLLS.
THE RIGHT HONOURABLE THE LORD CLERK REGISTER OF SCOTLAND.
THE RIGHT HONOURABLE EARL SPENCER, K.G.
THE RIGHT HONOURABLE THE EARL OF ABERDEEN, K.T.
THE RIGHT REVEREND THE LORD BISHOP OF LLANDAFF.
THE RIGHT HONOURABLE THOMAS GRENVILLE.
THE RIGHT HONOURABLE CHARLES WATKIN WILLIAMS WYNN, M.P.
THE RIGHT HONOURABLE SIR JAMES MACKINTOSH.
THE RIGHT HONOURABLE HENRY HOBHOUSE.
THE RIGHT HONOURABLE LORD DOVER.
THE RIGHT HONOURABLE MR. BARON PARKE.
THE RIGHT HONOURABLE MR. JUSTICE BOSANQUET.
SIR ROBERT HARRY INGLIS, BART., M.P.
LOUIS HAYES PETIT, ESQUIRE.
HENRY BELLENDEN KER, ESQUIRE.
HENRY HALLAM, ESQUIRE.
JOHN ALLEN, ESQUIRE.
EDWARD PROTHEROE, ESQUIRE.
EDWARD VERNON UTTERSON, ESQUIRE.
WILLIAM BROUGHAM, ESQUIRE.

CHARLES PURTON COOPER, ESQUIRE, SECRETARY.

CONTENTS

CONTENTS.

		Page.
Memoranda of the Treasury	1 Ric. II.	1, 2
	2 Ric. II.	2, 3
	3 Ric. II.	3—7
	4 Ric. II.	7—10
	5 Ric. II	10—12
	6 Ric. II.	13
	6 & 7 Ric. II.	14, 15
	8 Ric. II.	16, 17
	8 & 9 Ric. II.	17—20
	9 & 18 Ric. II.	46—52
	10 Ric. II.	20—22
	11 Ric. II.	22—26
	12 Ric. II.	26—29
	12 & 13 Ric. II.	29—35
	14 Ric. II.	35—41
	15 Ric. II.	41—43
	16 Ric. II.	43—45
	17 Ric. II.	45, 46
	19 Ric. II.	52, 53
	20 Ric. II.	53
	20 & 21 Ric. II. 1 Hen. IV. &c.	54—59
	1 Hen. IV.	59—63
	2 Hen. IV.	63, 64
	3 Hen. IV.	65
	3 & 4 Hen. IV.	66, 67
	5 Hen. IV.	67—69
	6 Hen. IV.	70—72

CONTENTS.

		Page.
Memoranda of the Treasury	7 Hen. IV.	72, 73
	8 Hen. IV.	74—76
	9 Hen. IV.	76, 77
	10 Hen. IV. &c.	77—79
	1-5-11, 12, 13, 14 Hen. IV. &c.	79—87
	1 & 2 Hen. V.	87—93
	3 Hen. V.	93—95
	3 & 7 Hen. V.	99—101
	4 & 5 Hen. V.	95—97
	6 & 7 Hen. V. &c.	97—99
	9 Hen. V.	101—104
	10 Hen. V.	104—108
	1 Hen. VI.	109—113
	2 Hen. VI. &c.	113—120
	2 & 9 Hen. VI. &c.	120—122
	3, 4, 5, 6 Hen. VI. &c.	122—128
	6 Hen. VI.	128—131
	7 & 8 Hen. VI.	131—133
	8 Hen. VI.	133—137
	9 & 10 Hen. VI.	137—147
	12, 13, 14, 15 Hen. VI. &c.	147—153
	13 Hen. VI.	153—155
	14 Hen. VI.	155—158
	15 Hen. VI.	159—168
	16 Hen. VI.	169—175
	16, 17, 18, 19 Hen. VI.	175—189
	19 Hen. VI.	190, 191
	20 & 21 Hen. VI.	191—194
	22, 23 Hen. VI.	194, 195
	24 Hen. VI.	195, 196
	25 Hen. VI.	196, 197
	26 Hen. VI.	197—200
	27 Hen. VI.	200—203
	27 & 28 Hen. VI. &c.	203—221
	29 Hen. VI.	221—224
	30 Hen. VI.	224—227

		Page.
Memoranda of the Treasury	31 Hen. VI.	227, 228
	32, 33 Hen. VI. &c.	228—230
	33 Hen. VI.	230, 231
	34 Hen. VI.	231, 232
	35 Hen. VI.	232, 233
	36 Hen. VI.	233—235
	37 Hen. VI.	235—238
	38 Hen. VI.	238—240

Inventory of the Regalia, Crown Jewels, &c. of Henry VI. deposited in the Treasury. .... 241—258

Inventory of the gold plate of Henry VIII., jewels of gold garnished with precious stones and pearls, and others ungarnished. .... 259—267

Crucifixes of gold, certain of them garnished with precious stones and pearls, and others ungarnished. .... 267—270

Chalices, cruets, and holywater sprinklers of gold, some garnished with precious stones and pearls, and certain ungarnished. 270, 271

Images of gold, some of them garnished with precious stones and pearls, and others ungarnished.... 271—273

Paxes, tablets, tabernacles, and corporas cases of gold, garnished and ungarnished..................... 273—275

Cups, bowls, and cups of assay of gold, garnished and ungarnished. .... 275—284

Candlesticks of gold for the chaundry. 284

Goblets of gold, whereof one garnished with precious stones and pearls. 285

Salts of gold. .... 286—292

Spoons of gold garnished with stones and pearl, and certain ungarnished. .... 292—294

Layers, ewers, and basons of gold garnished and ungarnished. .... 294—297

Glasses garnished with gold and cruises of gold. ... 297

Flagons and casting bottles of gold. 298

Inventory of the Regalia, &c. of James I. — Jewels remaining in an iron chest in the secret jewel house within the Tower of London. .... 299—306

CONTENTS.

Page.

Jewels of the secret jewel house in the Tower given by the King's Majesty's own hands to the Queen at several times .... 306—309

The Compendium of the Records in the Treasury, compiled and digested by Arthur Agarde, Esquire, 1610. .... 311—335

THE ANTIENT

Kalendars and Inventories,

&c.

All the proof sheets of this Volume have been compared, collated, and examined by me with the original records or documents; and the printed text, allowing for accidental errors, is a true and faithful copy of such originals, save only as to the introduction of the headings, dates, &c., and as to the substitution of capitals for minuscules when required, and vice versa.

FRANCIS PALGRAVE.

The text is given as it appears on the face of the record or document, with the addition of the following denoting marks: —

|| Doubtful readings; and also words which are apparently clerical errors in the originals.

† Readings evidently errors in the original.

* Apparent deficiencies in the original.

[ ] Interlineations.

" " Words written on erasures, or otherwise apparently added to the text after it was first written.

✝ ✝ Cancellations.

THE ANTIENT

KALENDARS AND INVENTORIES, &c.

OF THE

TREASURY OF THE EXCHEQUER.

MEMORANDA OF THE TREASURY,

1 Ric. II. to 38 Hen. VI.

(p. 17.) 1 Ric. II.

1 Md' qđ *xxv.* die *Januar̃* anno r̃ R *Ric̃i scđi primo* Dñs *Robtus Muskhᵃm* libavit in Thes̃ quandam lr̃am de papo sigillo Dñi de *Coucy* sigillat̃ p quā idem Dñs de *Coucy* renunciavit Dño Regi p̃dc̃o, fidem homag̃ ⁊ ‖garteram que quiđm lr̃a in ‖quodam ‖tillo inclusa pōitʳ in cista supᵃ Reᵗᵃᵐ titulat̃

Coucy.

{Coucy.}

"nō trahitʳ."

2 Md' qđ *xxvii°* die *Febr̃* anno r̃ R *Ric̃i scđi primo* Dñs *Petrus de Bartoñ* unus Magr̃oꝝ de Cancellar̃ libavit in Thes̃ quandam indenturam sigillo *Johis* Reg̃ *Castelle* ⁊ *Legionis* Ducis *Lancastr̃* sigillat̃ de confirmac̃oe cujusdam "carte" de quibusdam t̃ris ⁊ teñ eidem *Johi* nup assignat̃ p Dñm *E.* nup Regem *Angl̃* avū Reg̃ hujᵘˢ in escambiū p comitatu *Riche-*

Lancastre.

"*Riche-*"
"*mond.*"

mund̄ nuꝑ in mañ ejusdem *Joh̄is* Reḡ existent̃ ⁄ lib̄at̃ *Joh̄i* Duci *Britann̄* ad hoc signū

{**Lancastre.**}

---

2 Ric. II.

1 Med' qđ . *ix*°. die *Julii* anno r̃ ℞ *Ric̃i scđi* : *secund̄* . *Thomas Durant* unus nuꝰatoꝝ de Re[ta] lib̄avit in Thes̃ vidȝ . duas cōmissiones unam acquietanc̃ ⁊ unam lr̃am de salvo conductu [" magno "] sigillo Cancellar̃ ℞ sigillat̃ . quequid cōmissiones acquiet̃ ⁊ lr̃a ꝑdict̃ sunt resident̃ in " Thes̃ ꝑdc̃a " in hanapio ad t̄le signū

Durant.

{**Durant.**} " nō trahit[r]."

(p. 17 b.)

✚ Bulla Dñi P'p[e] de lib̄a eleccōne faciend̄ in ec-c[lis] Cathedr̃ *Angl̄*. ✚

2 ✚ Med' qđ . *xi*. die *Marcii* anno regni Reḡ *Ric̃i scđi scđo* . lib̄ fuit *Joh̄i Fordh[a]m* c̄lico de p[i]vato sigillo una bulla . qđ *Eccl̄ie Cath̄* ꝑ totam *Angl̄* h̄eant ✚ veram ✚ [lib̄am] el̄ccōem.

" Et postea *xvi*°. die *Marcii* eođ anno ‖restitut̃ ꝑ " eundē . ⁊ posit̃ in cista Cam̃e comp̃ in quodā " hanaper̃ ad [" tale "] signū "

H

" Delib̄at[r] eid̄m *Joh̄i* ead̄m Bull̃ *xviii*°. die *ejusdē* " *mens̃*." ✚

[✚ Pꝰea restituit[r] *xxvi*. die *Maii* a° r̃ ℞ *Ric̃i scđi scđo* ꝑ *W*. ‖*Dyton̄*. ✚]

Bulla ne aliquis t[a]hat se ex[a] regnū cont[a] p[i]vilegiū *Dño Regi* indult̃.

3 Med' qđ est una Bull̃ [*Innoc̃* P'p[e] *quarti*] in cist̃ Cam̃e comp̃ Ne aliquis t[a]hat[r] ex[a] regnū cont[a] p'vilegiū *Dño Regi* indultū. Et ponit[r] in i. pixide ad tale signū

Gillme ||*Saus* Sire de *Pomiers.*

4 Med' de sentencia t pcessu *Gillmi* ||*Saus* Sire de *Pomiers* põit in cista Carîe comp̃ . *xx*mo *die April* anno r̃ R *Rici scdi scdo.*

5 ♣ Med' qd *septimo* die *Junii* aº *scdo* regni R *Rici scdi* põitr in cista Carîe comp̃ una Bulla que

Bulla.

continet litam R. *Jotiis* p quam cõcessit qd libe ||eleccõs possint fieri in quibзcũq, ecclis regni sui imppptuũ t confirmacõem sup hoc *Innoc* Pape *tcii.* Et põitr in quodã hanapio ad tale signũ ♣

H

" q, alibi intᵉ memorand tempe Reg *Henr quarti.*"

Inquis capte p *Robm de Asshetoñ* in ptibз *Hibñ.*

6 Med' qd *xxvii.* die *Julii* aº *scdo* R *Rici scdi* *Wills de H'mesthorp* lib *Rico Lescrop* Canc *Angl* vi. Rolos cont inquisicões capt p *Robm de Asshtoñ* [in ptibз *Hibñ*] t unũ Rolũ cont ♣ con ♣ eand maᵗiam.

7 Med' qd venit pr *T.* Epus *Exoñ* Thes *Angl* libavit *xxvi*to. die *Julii* . aº *scdo* Reg *Rici scdi* . in Thesaurar R. salvo custod , quand acquietanc fcam

Acquiet ||Canonic *Robesart.*

p Canonic *Robesart* Dño nro Regi *Rico scdo* de quibuscũq, sũmis denar p ipm ♣ recept de ♣ exact de dco Dño Reg sive de Dño R *E.* avo Reg hujᵒ racõe debiti seu alia quacũq, de causa t ponitr in ||quod pixide in quad cista supa Retam ad tle signũ

(p. 18.)

3 Ric. II.

1 Med' qd *xxvii*º. die *Augusti* aº regni Reg *Rici scdi tcio* . Dñs *Wills Burstalle* Capital clicus Rotuloꝝ Cancell . libavit in Thes p manᵒ *Thome Org*a*ve* unam

Bulla.

Bullā continētem gr̃am sp̃ealem videlicȝ qđ p̃dc̃us Dñs Rex ‖pt "autoritate" Bulle p̃dc̃e una vice dumtaxat in singul̃ tam cathedralibȝ ⁊ metropolitanis quā collegiat̃ ecc̃liis secularibȝ Regni sui *Anglie Ibernie* ⁊ Principat⁹ *Wallie* duabȝ psonis idoneis quas idem Rex duxerit nominandos singulis videlicȝ ex psonis eisdem singulos canonicatus eccl̃iaꝝ ip̃aꝝ cū plenitudine juris canonici conferr̃. Et ponitr in i. pixide infa cistam supa Receptam ad tale signū ⌐

{Urbanus papa sextus.}

2 Med' qđ *xiii*o die *Sept̃* anno regni Rḡ *Ric̃i* [*scđi*.] *t̃cio*. lib̃ata fuit p man⁹ *Thome* [*Orgave*] in Thes̃ Reḡ salvo custođ quedā obligac̃ō p quā *Rob̃tus Knolles Joh̃es Fillipot Rob̃tus Launde* ⁊ *Adam Chaungeo*r tenentr Dño Regi in xvii. ml. marcaꝝ solvenđ in festo Sc̃i Mich̃is anno *t̃cio* Rḡ supadc̃i. It̃m alt̃a pars cuj⁹dam lit̃e indentate facte int̃ p̃dc̃m Dñm Regem ex pte una ⁊ p̃dc̃os *Rob̃tm Joh̃em Rob̃tm* ⁊ *Adam* ex alt̃a pte in qua continentr c̃ta jocalia Reḡ invadiata eisdem *Rob̃to Knolles Joh̃i Rob̃to* ⁊ *Adam* supadc̃is p. iiiiml. ciijxx. v. l̃i. x. s̃. viii. đ. mutuat̃ de *Joh̃e Sandes* ⁊ *Ric̃o Craddok'* p vađ c. hōinū ad arma ⁊. c. sagitt̃ sub c̃ta forma in eađm indentra content̃. Et ponūtr in una pixide infa cistam supa Receptam ad tale singnū ⌐

Obligacio fc̃a Dño Regi.

{Knolles Philippot Launde.}

3 Med' qđ *xxii*o. die *August̃* ✻ *Thomas Orgave* lib̃avit in Thesaurar̃ Reḡ salvo custođ unā acquietanciā Comitis de *Ormonđ* factam Dño Regi de om̄ibȝ acc̃onibȝ querel̃ ⁊ demanđ.

"Acquietancia Comitis de *Ormonđ*."

It̃ duas al̃ lit̃as patentes sigillat̃ magno sigill̃ Reḡ

Yberñ ꝛ ponūtʳ in . i. pixide infᵃ cistam supᵃ Receptam ad tale singnū

{**Comes de Ormond'.**}

(p. 18 b.) 4 Medʳ qđ . *xvᵗᵒ* die *Februar̃* anno t̃cio Reg̃ *Ric̃i scđi Thomᵃs Orgᵃve* lib̃avit in Thes̃ salvo custođ c̃ta

Berkᵃmstede. ‖munimēt̃ tang̃ oĩa terras ꝛ teñ cū ptiñ [in *Berkᵃmstede*] que fuerūt *Witti* [fit] ꝛ heredis *Johis Hunt* in halimota pquisit̃ dño Regi supᵃdc̃o de *Dionisia* que [fuit] uxor *Witti de Suttoñ.* Et ponūtʳ in quodā hanapio infrᵃ cistam supᵃ Receptam . ad tale signū

{**Berkᵃmstede.**}

5 Medʳ qđ *xiiiiᵒ* die *Febr̃* anno regni Reg̃ *Ric̃i scđi t̃cio* facta est indentʳa int̃ *Thomā* Ep̃m *Exoñ* Thes̃ *Angl* ꝛ *Johem de Hermesthorp̃* * *Johem Bacon* Camar̃ Scᵃcii dc̃i Dñi Reg̃ ex una pte :' ꝛ *Roblm Rous* , *Bernard Brocas* milit̃ ꝛ *Johem* ‖*Godford* ex alt̃a pte , de recepc̃oe cujusdam obligac̃ois de viii. mˡ. francoꝝ ꝛ alt̃ius obligac̃ois de . l. mˡ francoꝝ , ac triū instrumentoꝝ public̃ sup sūmis p̃dc̃is fc̃oꝝ sigillo

" *Franc̃.*" Dñi Comit̃ de *Sc̃o Paulo* sigillat̃ Et ponuntʳ una cū indentʳa p̃dc̃a *anno* ꝛ *die supᵃdc̃is* in cista supᵃ Recept̃ in quodam cofino ad tale signū

{**Comes Sc̃i Pauli.**}

" Et delib̃antʳ *xiᵒ*. die *April* aᵒ *quarto Johi Fordhᵃm* custodi privati sigitt p man⁹ *T. Orgᵃve* Et

"nō trahitʳ" " ‖restittuūtʳ *xxiiiᵒ* die *Ap'l px' seq'nt.*"

6 Medʳ qđ *Johes de Walthᵃm* c̃licus Cancett R̃ lib̃avit *xxvᵗᵒ die Febrū* aᵒ r̃ . R̃. *Ric̃i t̃cio* in Thesaurar̃ Reg̃ salvo custodienđ . unam indenturam fact̃ int̃ p̃dc̃m Dñm nr̃m Reg̃ ex una pte ꝛ ‖*Nichm Sharneffeld*

ex alt̃ de custodia Cast[i] Ville ⁊ Parc̃ de *Devyses* ⁊ de Forest̃ de *Melkesh*[a]*m* ⁎ *Chippeh*[a]*m* cū ptiñ ⁊ al̃ p̃dc̃o *Nicho* dimissis ad firmā tota vita sua. Et pōit[r] in quadā cista sup[a] Receptam in i. pixide ad tale signū

{ Cast[m] de Devyses
Nich'o Sharneffeld'. }

7 Med' qđ. *v*[to]. [die] *Marcii* [a°. r̃ R̷ *Ric̃i scđi tcio*] carta *Thome Larchier* de Mañiis de *Templehurst Templeneusom Flaxflete Deneye* ⁊ *Strode* jux[a] *Raucestre* libata fuit in Thes̃ salvo custođ ex p̃cepto Dñi R̷ *Ric̃i* in pliamento suo' ap[d] *Westm̃ a°* ⁊ *die* [*sup*[a]*dc̃o*] ibm tent̃ ⁊ pōit[r] in i. cista sup[a] Receptam in quodam hanapio ad tale sig[m]

« Strode. »

{ Templehurst Templ'nu'. }

(p. 19.)

8 Med'. qđ die *Jov'. vii°* die *Marcii*. a°. r̃ R̷ *Ric̃i scđi tcio* Magr̃ *Johes Bouland* delib in Thes̃ Reg̃ salvo custodienđ unā acquietanciam de octingent̃ florenis ac unā genalē relaxac̃oem de om̃ibs acc̃oibȝ cū q°dā inst[u]ment̃ sup ‖hm̃⁹ fact̃ p *Baptistam* ‖*Lazaro* mercatorem *Janue* dc̃o Dño nr̃o Rege factis. Et ponūt[r] in quadam cista sup[a] Receptam ī quodā coffino ad tale signū

{ Baptistam Mercatorem
de Janua. }

9 Fait a remembrer q̃ le *p*[i]*mer* jour de *Marz* l an *tiercz* nr̃e S[r] le Roy *Richarđ seconđ* la liance fait pentre nr̃e dit S[r] le Roy et le Duc de *Bretaigne* fust delivre en la Tresorie nr̃e dit S[r] le

La liance *dEngleterre* ⁊ *Bretaigñ*.

Roy pur sauvement garder ꝰ ⁊ fust mys en un cofre sur la receypt en un coffyn m̃chez ove tiel signe

10 " Et ‖exᵃ *vi*ᵗᵒ die *Novembr̃* anno *xi*ᵒ Regis
" *Henr̃ quarti* unam magnā indentʳam sub sigillo
" ꝑdc̃i *Ducis* ⁊ lib̃at̃ in Cam̃am ꝑdc̃i Dñi Reg̃ ꝰ Dño
" de *Gray* ꝑ ꝑcept̃ *Joh̃is* ‖*Tiptott* militis tunc Thes̃
" *Angl̃.*"

11 Medᵈ' qd̃ *pⁱmo* die *Juñ* anno r̃ R̃ *Ric̃i scd̃i* t̃cio

Tuderic̃ Vandale. lib̃ fuit quedam relaxacio gen̄alis *Tuderici Vandale* fc̃a Dño Regi ꝑdc̃o. Et ponitʳ in ‖uno pixide in cista supᵃ Reᵗᵃᵐ cū tⁱbȝ ceruris ad istud signū

{Vandale.}

12 Medᵈ' qd̃ *die Jov' xiiii*ᵒ die *Junii* [aᵒ. r̃ R̃. *Ric̃i scd̃i t̃cio*] *Joh̃ Muskehᵃm* cl̃icus Cancell̃ Reg̃ delib̃avit in Thes̃ Reg̃ salvo custodiend̃ duas relaxac̃oes fact̃ ꝑ

Claryngdoñ. *Rog̃m de Claryngdoñ* dño Regi de ꝑpositurᵃ vocata *dentre deux mares* et de Balliva de *Creoñ* cū ptiñ in *Vascoñ.* Et ponūtʳ in una cista supᵃ Receptam in i. skibett̃ ad tale signū ꝰ

{Claryngdon.}

---

4 Ric. II.

(p. 19 b.) 1 Medᵈ' qd̃ *Rog̃us de Kyrketoñ* unᵒ Justic̃ Dñi Regis *undecimo die Julii* anno regni Rg̃ *Ric̃i scd̃i quarto* lib̃avit in Thes̃ Dñi Reg̃ ꝑdc̃i div̄s rotulos ac b̃ria div̄saꝝ assiaꝝ in div̄s Comit̃ [ꝑ ip̃m] captaꝝ de div̉s̃ annis tempe *E. t̉cii*. ⁊ Reg̃ *Ric̃i scd̃i*. sicut pleniꝰ continet^r^ in q^a^dam indent^r^a confecta de delib̃acõe p̉dc̃a queq^i^dem indentura põit^r^ in ‖fine cujꝰdam ciste sup^a^ Recep^a^m.

2 Me^d'^ qđ anno *t̉cio* Regis *Ric̃i scd̃i*. *Hugo Caluilegh̃* ⁊ *Rob̃tus Wyngh^a^m* fecerũt duas ‖relaxassiones Dño nr̃o *E*. R̷ *Angl̃ t̉cio* ⁊ Dño nr̃o *Ric̃o* Regi *Angl̃ scd̃o* de c̉tis sũmis pecunie eisd̃m *Hugoni* ⁊ *Rob̃to* ‖debite Et ponũt^r^ in una cista sup^a^ Receptam in ‖uno pixide ad tale signũ

{Calutlegh'. Wyngh^a^m.}

Crull. 3 Me^d'^. qđ *xii^o^* die *Octob̃* anno *quarto* Reg̃ *Ric̃i scd̃i Rob̃ Crull̃* capital̃ cl̃icus naviũ Dñi *E*. Reg̃ *t̉cii* delib̃ in Thes̃ R̷ *Ric̃i scd̃i*. salvo custodienđ unã indenturam continent̃ div̉sa noĩa creditoꝝ p̉dc̃i Regis *E. t̉cii* ꝑ navibꝫ ejusdem R̷. temp̃ quo p̉dc̃us *Rob̃tus* extitit custos eaꝝdem naviũ et ponit^r^ in una cista sup^a^ Receptam in una alba baga ad tale sig^m^

{Crull.}

4 Me^d'^ de una indent^r^a fact̃ int̉ ven̉abil̃ Patrem dñm *Thom^a^ Exoñ* Ep̃m Thes̃ *Angl̃* et Dñm *Joh̃em de Hermesthorp* ⁊ *Joh̃em Bacun* Cam̉ar̃ Sc^a^cii Dñi nr̃i Reg̃ *Ric̃i scd̃i* ex una ꝑte et Dñm *Alanũ de Stokes* Custodem magne Garderobe ip̃ius Dñi Reg̃

A. Perriers. ex alt̉a de div̉s̃ pl̃ de jocal̃ *Alicie Perers*. ꝑ *Simonem de Burgh̃* Armig̉ũ et *Willm̃ Blakamore* s̉vientem Reg̃ ad arma arestat̃. Et põit^r^ p̉dc̃a indent^r^a salvo custođ in una cista sup^a^ Recep^t'^ in ‖quodã pixide ad tale signũ.

{A. Perers}

5 Med' qđ *sexto* die *Octobr̃* anno r̃ R̷ *Rič̃i* [*scđi*] *quarto* posita est in magna cista in capella int̃
R. Pelegryn. ||minument̃ *Scocie* una baga contiñ tres libros ⁊ unū pokkettū cū lr̃is que fuer̃ Magr̃i *Reimundi Pelegryn.*

6 Med' de una obligacōe ii^c. li. fc̃a Dño Regi
Leget. *R'.* p *Helminū Leget* ⁊ *Gaut̃ de Barges* ⁊ posita in quadam cista sup^a Re^tam. in ||quodam pixide ad tale signū

{**Leget.**}

(p. 20.) 7 ✝ Md' qđ *xii°* die *Maii* anno *quarto* Reg̃ *Rič̃i scđi* delibant^r in Thesaur̃ salvo custodienđ obligacōes ⁊ lr̃e pcuratoȓ fc̃e int̃ Regem *Ro^anoꝝ* ⁊ *Bohemie* ⁊ Dñm *Rič̃m* Regem *Angl* de alliganciis
" q. infe- " rius." eoꝝdem ⁊ ponunt^r in quadam cista sup Re^tam in quodam hanapio ad tale signum

{**Rex Ro^anor'.**}

8 " Que quidem obligac̃ ⁊ lr̃e delibant^r Magr̃o " *Johi Profet* Clico *xv°* die *Aprit* anno *t̃cio* Reg̃ " *H.* " *quarti* " p m^9 Magr̃ *Johis Oudeby* uni^9 Camarioꝝ " de Re^ta Sc^acii " " Restituit^r *xvii.* die *Ap^lt* px̃ " seqñ p m^9 *Prophete.*"

✝ Restitut̃ *x°. die Julii* px̃ seqñ p m^9 pdc̃i *Rič̃i.* ✝ 9 " Postea . *xi.* die *Maii* " *px' seqñ*" delibant^r ext^a " dc̃m hanapiū Magr̃o *Rič̃o Deram* Capett̃o Reg̃ " due lr̃e pcuratorie una sigillata cū sex diṽsis sigil- " lis ⁊ alt̃a sigillata cū uno grosso sigillo." ✝

10 Med' de una quietaclamancia fact̃ Dño nr̃o
Sandyk de la || *T^une.* Regi p *Sandic de la* ||*Trane* de . cc. scutis annuis sibi concess̃ ad t̃m vite sue p Dñm Principē Pr̃em dc̃i Dñi R̷ : ⁊ est data ejusđ quieteclamancie *London̄* . *xxiii.* die *Maii* . a°. Dñi *mitt̃o ccc^mo*. *octogesimo*

p'mo. Et ponit^r in quadam cista sr̃ Re^tam in ||quodam pixide ad tale signũ

{Sandyk de la T^ane.}

5 Ric. II.

1 ✠ Med' qđ *Magna Corona* Reg̃ ⁊ una aƚ Corona [vocaƚ *ẞcia Corona*] ejusđm R̃ ponũt^r inf^a *T^rrĩ Londoñ* sub salva custođ *xv^o*. die *Julii* a^o. r̃ R̃ *Ric̃i scđi v^to*. "Postea *ix. Augusƚ*. . a^o. r̃ R̃ *Ric̃i* " *scđi . vi^to*. *ẞcia corona* sup^adc̃a ext^a p Cam̃ar ⁊ " invadiat^r." ✠

Corona R̃.

2 Med' qđ *Thomas Org^ave* Cƚicus . liƀavit in Thesaurariam Reg̃ . *xix^o*. die . *Novembr̃* . anno *quinto* Reg̃ . *R'*. *scđi* . quandam cartam fc̃am p *Thomam de Holanđ* Comitem *Kanc̃* Dño Regi . in dc̃a Thes̃ salvo custodienđ ad hoc signũ in ||quodã pixide.

{Holand' Com' Kanc'.}

3 Med' de una relaxac̃one facƚ p *Edmũdũ* Comitem *Canƚ* Dño nr̃o Regi *Ric̃o scđo* ac executoribȝ testamenti Reg̃ *E. ẞcii* de om̃ibȝ sũmis deñ eiđm Comiti p p̃dc̃os debiƚ de daƚ *quarti* diei *Maii* anni *q^arti* Reg̃ *Ric̃i scđi* ✠ *q^arƚ* ✠ Et põit^r sup^a Receptam in quadã cista . in ||uno pixide ad tale sig^m

Cantebr̃.

{Cantebr'.}

4 Med'. qđ *Magna Corona* Reg̃ ⁊ una aƚ Corona vocaƚ *ẞcia Corona* ejusđm R̃ ponũt^r inf^a *T^rrim Londoñ* sub salva custodia *xv^o*. die *Julii* . a^o. r̃ R̃ *Ric̃i scđi* . *quinto*. " Et postea . *ix^o*. die *Augusƚ* . a^o. " *vi^to*. ejusđm R̃ *Corona ẞcia* sup^adc̃a ex^ait^r p Cam̃ar

Lumbard. " ⁊ invadiatʳ ||*Matheo Cheyne* Lumbard una cū tall
" jocal R'gis . ꝑ . "iiii ᵐˡ" ⁊ cc. marc̄ *Dn̄o nr̄o Regi*
" mutuand sicut patꝫ p unam indentʳam fact̄ int̄
" Cam̄ar̄ Scᵃcii ⁊ *Mattm̄* supᵃdc̄m. Et pōitʳ in ||uno
" pixide in quadā cista supᵃ Recept̄ ad tale sigᵐ ⁓"

{Lumbard'.}

(p. 20 b.) 5 Medʳ qd *vi*ᵗᵒ die *Februar̄* anno r̄ R *Ric̄i scdi quinto* lib fuit quedam lr̄a de alligancia fc̄a p
Rex *Roᵃnoꝝ.* ||*Vinceslauū* Regem *Romanoꝝ* ⁊ ꝓdc̄m Dn̄m Regem *Ric̄m.* Et ponitʳ in uno hanapio supᵃ Reᵗᵃᵐ ad istud signū

{Rex Romanor'.}

6 Medʳ qd *xii*ᵒ die *Febr̄* anno r̄ R *Ric̄i scdi quinto Jōhes de Leyre* Rector ecclie de *Dodyngtoñ*
Maiia de *Morende Burle.* libavit Thes̄ ⁊ Cam̄ar̄ cartas ⁊ ||munimenta tangent̄ escambiū cast̄ de *Morende* ⁊ al Mañioꝝ in Com̄ *Norht* ⁊ Mañii de *Burle* in Com̄ *Rotel.* Et ponūtʳ in quadam cista supᵃ Recept̄ in ||uno pixide cū lr̄a feoffament̄ Dn̄e *Anne le Despens̄* fact̄ Dn̄o *E.* R *Angl* de ꝓdc̄o Mañio de *Burle* ad tale sigᵐ.

{Man'ia de Morende Burle.}

7 ♣ Medʳ qd *Jōhes* ||*Wenhyngburgh* senior libavit *xx* die *Febr̄* Thes̄ ⁊ Cam̄ar̄ unā indenturam fact̄ int̄ *Thom̄* Comit̄ de *Bukyngh*ᵃ*m* ex una pte ⁊
Thomas Hunt. *Thom̄ Hunt* ex alt̄a pte de div̄sis victualibꝫ receptis p ꝓdc̄m *Thom̄ Hunt* p manus *Willi Caboʳne* Clici Comitis supᵃdc̄i ꝑ castro de *Chirburgh* ⁊ ponitʳ in cista supᵃ Receptam in ||uno pixide ad tale signū ♣

{Thom' Hunt.}

" Quia lib̄atr *Thome* "Com̄" *Buk' x°*. die *Julii* . a°.
" *vi*to p̄ man᷒ *Thome de Ferriby* Cl̄ici p̄dc̄i Comit̄."

8 Med' de indentura fact̄ int̄ excellentissimū Principem Dn̄m *Ric̄* Reḡ *Angl̄* ex una p̄te et Priorem ⁊ Cōventū *Sc̄e Trinitat̄ de Hundeslowe* ex alt̄a de domibȝ et clausis apud *Hatton̄ Grange* p̄dc̄o Dn̄o nr̄o R̄ ad firmā temp̄e vite sue dimissis Et pōitr in quadam cista supa Recept̄ in . i. coffino ad tale signū ☞

Hundeslowe.

{**Hundeslowe.**}

9 Med' de quad̄ relaxac̄oe fact̄ int̄ excellentissimū P'ncipem Dn̄m *Ric̄m* Regem *Angl̄* ex una p̄te et Dn̄m *Joh̄em* Ducem *Lancastr̄* ex alt̄a de om̄imodis vadiis ⁊ regard̄ eidem *Joh̄i* p̄ p̄dc̄m Dn̄m nr̄m Regem debit̄ usqȝ diem confecc̄ōis ejusdem relaxac̄ōis. Et pōitr in quad̄ cista supa Recept̄ in ||uno pixide ad tale signū

Dux *Lancastr̄.*

{**Dux Lancastr'.**}

(p. 21.)

10 Med' de quad̄ relaxac̄one fact̄ int̄ excellentissimū Pincipem *Ric̄m* Regem *Angl̄* ex una p̄te et *Will̄m fitz Wauter* Chivaler ⁊ *Aliciam* uxem ejus executricem testamenti *Rob̄ti Hokelynḡ* ⁊ *Thom̄ Walton̄* coexecutorem p̄dc̄e *Alicie* testamenti p̄dc̄i ex alt̄a de om̄iodis acc̄oibȝ ⁊ demandis que h̄ent v̄sus p̄dc̄m Regē p̄ p̄dc̄o *Rob̄to* ab origine mundi usqȝ diem confecc̄ōis relaxac̄ois p̄dc̄e ⁊ ponitr in quadā cista supa Recept̄ in i pixide ad tale signū

Rob̄tus Hokelyng.

{**Rob'tus Hokelyng.**}

6 Ric. II.

1 Med' de una indentura sub sigillo Dñi *Robi Knolles* conc̃. MMDCClxxixli. xi. s̃. vi. d̃ accomodat̃ *Knolles.* Dño Regi ꝛ conc̃ ꝯta jocalia q̃ lib̃antr dc̃o Dño *Knolles.* *Rob̃to* ꝑ securitate ejusd̃ sũme et dc̃a indentura lib̃at̃ fuit hic custodiend̃. *xvi.* die *Julii* anno *sexto.*

2 Med'. qd̃ *xxvii°.* die *Octobr̃* anno *vito.* regni Reg̃ *Ric̃i scd̃i* delib̃ate fuer̃ in Thesaurar̃ ejusdem Regis salvo ⸸ conductu ⸸ custodiend̃ sex obligac̃oes fc̃e ꝑdc̃o Dño nr̃o Regi vidȝ †u una de duobȝ mille ꝛ ducent̃ marc̃ monete *Anglic̃* fact̃ ꝑ xii gub̃natores ville Obligac̃oes fc̃e Dño Regi. *Bevꝰlacy* ꝛ alia de ml cctis libr̃ argenti fact̃ ꝑ ballios ꝛ burg̃ ꝛ cõies ville de *Scardeborw* ꝛ alia de ml marc̃ sterling̃ fact̃ ꝑ majorẽ ꝛ cõitatẽ civitatis *Ebor̃* ꝛ alia de xlta libris fact̃ ꝑ *Wilłm Meltoñ* Chr ꝛ *Joh̃em* [*del*] *Wod* de *Madhowe* ꝛ alia de xlta libr̃ fact̃ ꝑ quatuor hoĩes de ‖*Scrdeborw* et alia de xlta libr̃ ꝑ *Steph̃m Lescrop̃* [Chr] fact̃ ꝛ *Rob̃tum de Plumptoñ* Chr. Et ponũtr in qadam cista sr̃ Retã in uno cofino ad tale signũ

{ Ebor' Scardeburgh Bev'laic'. }

(p. 21 b.) Relaxac̃o tang̃ Maner̃ de *Kirketoñ* in *Lyndes̃.* { Felton }

3 Med' qd̃ *xx.* die *Febr̃* anno r̃ R̷ *Ric̃i scd̃i sexto*. Dñs *Johes de Walthạm* Clicus Rotuloꝝ Cancellar̃ lib̃avit in Thes̃ custodiend̃ unã relaxac̃oem sigillat̃ sigillo *Johanne* q̃ fuit ux̃ *Thome de Feltoñ* Milit̃ fact̃ Dño Regi ꝛ Dñe Rne de Maner̃ de *Kirketoñ* in *Lyndeseye.*

Acquiet̃ executoꝝ testam̃ *Thome de Feltoñ.* 4 Itm lib̃avit *eod̃ die* unã acquietanciã quam executores testamenti dc̃i Dñi *Thome* fecerunt dc̃o Dño Regi de omnimod̃ actionibȝ ꝛ debit̃.

6 & 7 Ric. II.

Arundett. 1 Me^d^' qđ *xvii*°. die *Julii*. a° r̃. Reḡ *Ric̃i* ⁎ *septĩo*. *Joħs Walth^a^m* C̃licus [Rotuloꝝ] Cancellar̃ R̃. lib̃avit in Thes̃ custodienđ duas indentur̃ fact̃ int̃ Dñm Reḡ ⁊ *Ric̃m* Comit̃ *Arundett* tanḡ advocacõem P^i^oratus de *Arundett* ⁊ Mañiū de *Sevenhamtoñ* in Coñ *Som̃s̃*. It̃m aliā indentur̃ ꝑ quā ꝓdc̃us Comes concessit Dño. R̃. x. li r̃cipienđ de Mañio suo de Thortyngtoñ Et ponūt^r^ in uno coffino in i. cista sup^a^ Recept̃ ad tale signū

" Advocacio " Prioratus " de *Arun-* " *dett.*"

Tortyngtoñ.

{Arundell'.}

2 Me^d^' qđ *xviii*°. die *Julii* a° r̃ Reḡ. *Ric̃i scđi vi*^to^. lib̃ata fuit ꝑ man⁹ *Thome Orgrave* in Thes̃ Dñi R̃ salvo custodienđ una obligacõ fact̃ ꝑ Dñm de *la Sparre* Dño nr̃o R̃ de trib; millib; ⁊ quingñtis marc̃ ||starlinḡ solvenđ *Witto le Scrop̃* in ꝑtib; *Aquitañ*. Et ponit^r^ in i. cista sup^a^ Recept̃ in uno coffino ad tale signū

Dñs de *Lesperre* *Witts Scrop̃*.

{D'n's de le Sperre.
W. le Scrop'.}

(p. 22.) 3 Me^d^' qđ *v*^to^ die *Nov*' anno regni Reḡ *Ric̃i scđi vii*° Dñs *Witt de Wykh^a^m* Ep̃us *Wynt̃* lib̃ Thes̃ ⁊ Cam̃ar̃ salvo custođ. unā cart̃ de t̃ris ⁊ teñ adquis̃ de *Joħe Brokaz* Milite in Coñ †*Bek*' que q^i^đ carta pōit^r^ in cist̃ sup^a^ Recept̃ in ||quodam pixide ad tale sig^m^

{Buk' Brokoz.}

4 Me^d^' qđ *vi*^to^ die *Decembr̃*. a°. r̃ R̃ *Ric̃i scđi*. *vii*°. Thes̃ ⁊ Cam̃ar̃ v^i^tute cuj⁹dam b̃ris eisdem di-

rect̃ et int' ligul breviũ de t'mio *Mich* anni *sup^a^dc̃i* remanent̃ libaver̃ *Henr̃ de Percy* Comiti *Northumbr̃* ⁊ *Johi de Nevill* de *Raby* oĩa lr̃as obligatorias ⁊ indentatas ac inst^u^menta publica redempc̃oem *David de Bruys* de *Scoc̃* defuncti conc̃nencia ut pat; p indentur̃ de huj'modi lib fact̃ int' p̃dc̃os Thes̃ ⁊ Camar̃ [ex] una pte ⁊ p̃dc̃os *Henr̃* ⁊ *Johem* ex alt'a queq^i^dem indentur^a^ sigilloꝝ p̃dc̃oꝝ *Henr̃* ⁊ *Johis* sigillat̃ pōit^r^ in quadam cista sup^a^ Recept̃ in uno cofino ad tale signũ ⸗

Redemp-c̃oem *David de Bruys* ℞ *Scoc̃.*

{ Redempc̃oem David de Bruys R' Scoc'. }

5 Me^d'^. qd ix^o^ die *Decembr̃* a^o^ regni Reg̃ *Ric̃i scdi septĩo Johes Bacoñ* custos jocall Reg̃ lib in Thes̃ Dñi Reg̃ salvo custodiend duas naves deaur̃ "p oblac̃" Dñi *E.* Reg̃ *t'cii* fact̃ ut pat; p indentur̃ int' Dñm Thes̃ ⁊ *Johem de H'mesthorp* Camar̃ ex una pte ⁊ *Johem Bacoñ* "custod" jocal Dñi Reg̃ de delib fact̃ ex alt'a. Et ponũt^r^ p̃dc̃e naves una cũ indentur̃ p̃dict̃ in mangna Thes̃ infr^a^ claust^m^ Abbtis *Westm̃* in duob; gross̃ cofinis cũ tali subsc^i^pc̃oe

Un nief dor.

{ Un nieff dor. }

6 Me^d'^ qd . *xiiii^o^* die *Junii* . a^o^ r̃ ℞ *Ric̃i scdi . vii^o^* facta fuit quedã indentura int' Thes̃ ⁊ Camar̃ ex una pte ⁊ *Robtm Knolles* ex alt'a de div's jocalib; de p̃dc̃o *Robto* r̃cept̃ que ||fuerũt eidm *Robto* p q^a^dam sũma pecunie invadiat̃. Et ponit^r^ in quadam cista sup^a^ Recept̃ in q^a^dam pixide ad tale signũ

"Indentur^a^ "*Knoll*."

{ Indentur^a^ Knoll'. }

8 Ric. II.

1 Me^d' qđ *xxiiii^to* die *Junii* . a^o. r̃ R̷ *Riči sđi* . *viii^o*. quedam fuit indentura fact̃ int̃ Thes̃ ⁊ Cam̃ar̃ ex una p̱te . et *Gautroñ de Bardes* ex alt̃a de div̄s jocalibȝ eiđm *Gautroñ* ꝑ quadam sum^a pecunie invadiat̃ Et pōit^r in quadam cista sup^a Recept̃ in q^odam coffino ad tale sig^m

{ Indentur^a
Gautron' de Bardes. }

(p. 22 b.) 2 Me^d' quod Magr̃ *Johes Bouland* lib̃avit in Thes̃ Dñi Reg̃ *xxix^o* die *Julii* a^o r̃ R̷ *Riči* [*scđi*] *viii^o* quođam inst^ument̃ de x^ml. marč franč solvenđ Dño Regi sigillo *Johis Schakutt* " Armig̃i " sigillat̃ recipienđ de Comite de *Foix* de redempcõe Comit̃ de *Dene* ac acquietanč sigill̃ p̃dči *Johis* sigillat̃ de p̃dča sūma recipienđ ⁊ ponūt^r in [quodam] coffino in quadā cista sup^a Receptam ad tale signū

Schakutt Dene.

{ Schakull Dene. }

Acquietancia *Witti de Latimer*. 3 Me^d' de quađ generali acquietanč Dñi *Witti de Latimer* fact̃ Dño Reg̃ p̱ executores ejusđm *Witti* anno r̃ R̷ *Riči scđi vii^o*. et ponit^r in quadā cista sup^a Recept̃ in quodam coffino ad tale signū ⁊

{ Acq^ietancia
Will'i de Latimer'. }

4 Relaxacio *Robti Tresilian* Militis fča Dño Regi de c. m^arȝ p̱ ipm Dño relaxat̃ [sub condič si ipe aliqua alia feoda seu vadia de dčo Dño Reg̃ p̱cepit] ꝑ eo qđ ipe est retent^9 cū dčo Dño Rege

Relaxacio *Robti Tresilian.*

⁊ de essend̄ occupat̄ ad consiliū ad totā vitā s̄ capiend̄ anñ c m^a r3 ꝑ consil̄ p̄dc̄o. Et ponit^r eadem relaxacio in uno ꝑvo pixide . ad signū

---

8 & 9 Ric. II.

Obligac̄o Impatoris libat^r *Michi de la Pole* Canc̄ *Angl*. *xx^o*. die *Sept*. a^o. *ix^o*.

1 Me^d' qd̄ *xxii^o*. die *Junii* a^o r̄ R̄ *Ric̄i scd̄i* "*nono*" libat̄ fuit in Thes̄ Dñi R̄ salvo custodiend̄ quedā obligac̄o Impatoris fact̄ *Michi de la Pole* Cancell̄ *Angl* de vii^ml florenoꝝ solvend̄ eidem *Michi* in ‖fēo *Sc̄i Georgii* a^o Dñi *m^o c^o c^o c^o* ‖*octuagesimo* Et pōit^r in ‖qua cista sup^a Recept̄ in ‖quodo pixide [ad] tale signū

{Mich's de la Pole.}

Acquietancia *Johis Palays*.

2 Me^d' de quadam acquietanc̄ fact̄ Dño nr̄o Regi *Ric̄o* ꝑ *Johem Palays* Militem de om̄ib3 arreraḡ eidm *Johi* debit̄ usq3 fēm *Pasch* a^o. *viii^o*. Et pōit^r in quodam hanepio de ꝑmīo *Pasch* a^o *viii^o*.

Le Counte *dO'mond* ⁊ *Johan Sleygh*.

3 Fait a remembrer q̄ Sr *William de Dyghton̄* ad delive le *sisme* jo^r de *Decembre* [l an *ixme*] . i. lr̄e patent ✠de✠ [p^r le] Conte *dOrmond* ꝑ quele le dit Conte ad g^a nte . xl. li. ꝑ an queux il prist a ꝑme de sa vie de la ferme de la Cite de *Watreford* a mon̄ S' *Phe de Courteneye* . p^r le temps qil s̄ra Lieutenant p^r nr̄e S^r le Roi en *Irland*.

4 It̄ *Johan* ‖*Sclygh* Boteller nr̄e S^r le Roi ad g^a nte au dit S' *Phe* p^r le temps qil s̄ra ensi Lieutenant touz les ꝑfitz sourdantz del manoir de *Cromlyn* quel il ad

a terme de vie. Et mesmes les lr̃es sont mises en un coffyn al tiel signe

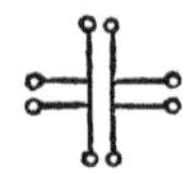

(p.23.) 5 Fait a remembrer d une obligacioũ de. D. m^a^rcz desouz les sealx Monsr̃ *Will̃ Beauchamp̃* ꝛ Mons̃ *Th̃ P̱cy* quele sõme ils sont obligez a paier a la fest de *Nowell̃* l an *noefisme* ꝛ mesme la obligacioũ est mys en un coffyn a tiel signe ☞

6 Et fait a rem̃ q̃ mesmes ✝ les D. m^a^rc ✝ la obligac̃on est deliv̾e al dc̃e Mons̃ *Thomas* s^r^ ses gages de *Brest* come appiert en la peel de la receite del Escheqer. le *vii.* jo^r^ de *Decembr̃* l an *ix^e^*.

7 Fait a remembrer d une obligacioũ faite p̱
Fiennes. Mons̃ *Robt* Sires de *Fiennes* Constables de *F^a^nce* a
Dalton. Mons̃ *Johan de Daltoñ* Chivaler ꝛ *Daiquin de Haytoñ* Englois de viginti ꝛ sex milibꝫ multonũ auri Et ponit^r^ in Thes̃ [in uno cofino] custod̃ *xxii.* die *Febr̃* anno regni Reg̃ *Ric̃i scd̃i nono* ad tale sig^m^

8 Itm̃ de una copia cujusdam indenture fc̃e int̾ Dñm Regem [*E. t̾ciũ*] ex una p̱te et quendã
Daykyn Hetoñ. *Daykyn de Hetoñ* ligiũ suũ ex p̱te alt̾a tangente dc̃m *Robtum Fenes* ☞ Ac etiam [de] quadã lr̃a p^i^vati sigilli tangente p̾dc̃m *Daykyn de Hetoñ* existentibꝫ in eod̃ cofino.

"nõ trahit^r^."

9 Fait a remembrer de deux endent^r^es ꝛ deux instrumentes faitz p̱ entre nr̃e S^r^ le Roy *Ric̃ scd̃e* et

Conte *Seint Poule.* le Counte de *Seint* † de *Seint* ‡ *Poule* . mys en un box rounde le *sisme* jo^r de *Marcz* l an du n̄re dit S^r le Roy *noefisme* a tiel signe

Portingat. 10 Me^d' qđ . *xxiii.* die *Maii* a^o regni Reḡ *Ric̄i scđi nono* . quoddam ꝑcur^ato^m Reḡ *Portingalie* cū sigillo plumbato delibat̄ fuit ad Recept̄ ꝑdc̄i Dñi Reḡ custodienđ ⁊ ponit^r in q^adā cista sup^a Recept̄ [" Ducat^9 *Lanc̄* "] in q^odā cofino ad tale sig^m

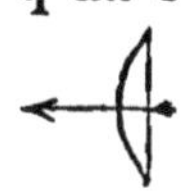

Dux *Lanc̄.* 11 Me^d' qđ *xx^mo*. die *Maii* a^o regni Regis *Ric̄i scđi nono* q^oddā ꝑcur^ato^m Regis *Castell* ⁊ *Leḡ* tangens viagiū *Hispanie* delibat̄ fuit ad Re^tam Sc^acii custodienđ ⁊ ponit^r in cista sup^a dc̄a Re^tā in q^adam pixide ad tale signū

(p. 23 b.) 12 Me^d', qđ *xxii^do*. die *Maii* a^o regni Reḡ *Ric̄i scđi nono* quedā indent^ra fc̄a int^9 *Johem* Ep̄m *Dunolm̄* Thes̄ *Angl* ⁊ Camar̄ Sc^acii ex pte una et *Gauterū de Barde* ex alt^9a de quibusdā vasis [eidē] *Gaut^9us Barde.* delibatis ⁊ invadiat̄ ꝑ c^9ta sūma pecunie ꝑ eosdē a ꝑdc̄o *Gautero* recept̄ delibata fuit ad Re^tā Sc^acii *Mathus Cheny.* custodienđ, ⁊ ponit^r in cista sup^a Recept̄ in q^adam pixide una cū alia indent^ra consimili tangente *Matheū Cheny* ad tale signū

13 Me^d', qđ *xxviii^o* die *Maii* anno regni Reḡ *Ric̄i nono* libate fuer̄t qued^am indent^re in Thes̄ fc̄e int^9 *Willm le Scrop̄* locūtenent̄ Dñi R̄ apud *Chirburgh*

⁊ *Johem Sandes* Milit locut Comit de *Kent* de delibacōe victualiū ⁊ attilioꝝ existenc in dca Villa remanent ad tale signū

Will's Scrop' Sandes Chirburgh.

14 Med' qd *xxviii°* die *Maii* anno regni R *Rici*
Portyngal. *nono* libat fuit in Thes q°dd^a^m instrument de tractatu Ambassatoꝝ Regis *Portugalie* de decem galeys m'tend in obsequiū Regis *Angl* ad tale signū in q°d coffino

"Restituitr." ✝ " Et libar Dño *J. Wellyngbo*r*ne xvi°* die *Junii* a° " *xi°* ex^a^ Re^tam^." ✝

15 " M^d^' qd *viii°* die *Maii* anno ℓcio Regis *H.* " *quarti* pdcm instrumentū libatū fuit *Robto Frye* " p m⁹ Magr *J. Oudeby* uni⁹ Camar Re^te^ " " Restituitr *xii°* die *Maii* px sequen p m⁹ pdci *Johis.*"

10 Ric. II.

1 Med' qd . *x*^mo^. die "*Julii*" anno regni Regis *Rici*
Hispania. *decimo* quedā alligancia fca int Dñm nrm Regem
Angl. *Angl Ricm scdm* et *Johem* Regem *Castell* ⁊ *Legionis Toleti* ⁊c de confirmacōe pacis ⁊ t^a^nquillitatis [ut^i^usq; regni] int eosdem inita ⁊ t^a^ctat, delibat fuit ad Re^tam^ Sc^a^cii custodiend . ⁊ ponit^r^ in quodā hanapio ad tale sig^m^

(p. 24.) 2 *Johes* pmissione divina *Bangoren* Epus Decan⁹ ⁊ Capitlm ecclie *Bangoren* concesserunt p se ⁊ suc-

cessorib; suis p̱ salubri statu Regis [*Rici*] dum vixit
Bangorieñ. ꝛ p̱ aĩa ejusdem cū ab hac luce migᵃverit [ꝛ aĩab;]
p̱genitoꝝ *Missam* " *B'e* " *Virginis Marie* " cū "
[nota] in Eccĺia p̃dc̃a ppetuis temporib; celebrare
cū orõnib; *Prã quesumꝰ O'ipotẽs D's ut famĺs tuus*
Rex Ric̃us ꝛc̃ ꝛ *Inclina* ut p; in quodā cophino ad
tĺe sigᵐ int̃ alia memorand̃ supᵃ Reᵗᵃᵐ

" Alliganc̃ " int̃ Regẽ " *Ric̃m* ꝛ "*Januenses.*" 3 Meᵈ' qd̃ . *xxvi.* die *Octobr̃* anno regni Regis
Rici scd̃i [*decimo*] delĩbatū fuit quoddā p̱curatoriū
tangens alligānciam int̃ Regē *Angĺ* ꝛ *Januens̃*
" Restituitʳ. *vii.* die *Nov' aᵒ supᵃdc̃o.*"

4 Meᵈ' qd̃ *xxiiii* die *Novembr̃* anno regni Regis
Rici scd̃i. *xᵒ*. quedam lr̃a de pⁱvato sigillo delĩbata fuit
Thes̃ ꝛ Camar̃ de Scᵃcio Reg̃ ad delĩband̃ Majori
Vic̃ ꝛ Aldermanis Civitat̃ *London̄* quandam Coronā
apparat̃ cū gross̃ lapidib; p̃cios̃ ut p; in eadē lr̃a noĩe
ypotece p̱ c̃ta sūma auri ꝛ ponitʳ in quadam pixide
ad tĺe sigᵐ

 {Rex}

5 Meᵈ' qd̃ . *xii.* die *Julii* . anno *xᵐᵒ*. Reg̃ *Rici*
scd̃i quedā acquietanc̃ fc̃a eidem Dñō Regi p *Rog̃ū*
Dñm [de] *Clifford̃* dc̃is *die* ꝛ *anno* delĩbat̃ fuit ad
Retᵃᵐ Scᵃcii ejusdē R ꝛ ponitʳ in quodā coffino
supᵃ Reᵗᵃᵐ p̃dc̃am ad tale signū

(p. 24 b.)

6 Mᵈ' qd̃ *xxviᵗᵒ*. die *April̃* anno r̃ R *Rici scd̃i* . *xᵒ*.
Alliganc̃ Reg̃ *Ispañ.* *Jo̅hes* Ep̄us *Hereford̃* restituit manu sua p̱pⁱa ad Retᵃ
Scᵃcii duas allegancias Reg̃ *Petri de Hyspania* .

sigillat̃ sigill̃ aureis rem̃ in [quadã] cista supª Retã. in quodam hanapio ad tale signũ

7 Md' qđ *xvi°*. die *Juñ*. anno. *x°*. r̃ ℞. *Ric̃i scđi Joħes Walthªm* Custos pivat̃ sigilli liƀavit ad Retª Scªcii quamdam indentʳam fc̃am ✝ int̃ ✝ p̃dc̃o Dño Regi p *Henr̃* ✝*H*✝ *Asty* Chivaler de quodam ‖anuo redditu c mªrȝ anñ pcipienđ de Mañio de *Burwell* cũ ptiñ in Com̃ *Linc̃*, et ponitʳ eadem indentʳa in quađ cista supª Retã in uno cophino. ad tale signũ

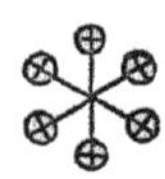

8 Med'. qđ *xxi.* die *Juñ Joħes Waltham* Cl̃icus [†Costos] pivati sigilli deliƀavit ad Retã Scªcii diṽsas

Gellerie. ⁎ de homagio fc̃o p *Will̃m* Ducem *Gelerie* excellentissimo Regi *Ric̃o* Regi *Angl* videl̃t unũ pcurªm̃, quandam indenturã *Georgii Felbrigg̃* ⁊ *Joħis H'mesthorp̃* ⁊ al̃ ex pte p̃dc̃i *Ducis* ⁊ quatuor diffidac̃ões ⁊c̃. Et ponuntʳ in quadã pixide ad tale signũ

---

11 Ric. II.

1 Med' qđ †qđ. *xvii* die *Julii*. anno regni Regis *Ric̃i scđi*. *xi°*. quedã indentura fc̃a int̃ p̃dc̃m Dñm

Lascels. Regem et *Joħem Lascels* de *Bristuyt* de mineris auri ⁊ argenti in Com̃ *Gloucestr̃* ⁊ *Som̃s̃* inventis ⁊ eidem *Joħi* concess̃ a festo Pasche px̃ p̃cedent̃ [añ dat̃ p̃dc̃am] usq; finẽ septem annoȝ extunc subseqñ delibat̃ fuit in "Thesaurariã Reg̃" custodiend̃. ⁊ ponit' in quadam pixide ad t̃le signũ

2 Med' qd̃. *xvii.* die *Julii* anno regni Regis *Ric̃i scd̃i. xi°.* quedã indentur̃ fc̃a int̃ p̃dc̃m Dñm Regem et *Joh̃em Crane* de *Cranebrok'* de Com̃ *Kanc̃* de Crane. subsidio pannoȝ cõmisso, ⁊ ad firmã dimisso [eidẽ *Joh̃i*] in p̃dc̃o Com̃ p manucapc̃oem *Joh̃is Somer* Draper de *London̄* ⁊ *Simonē Atte More* de ead̃. delibat̃ fuit ad Retam Reg̃ custodiend̃ ⁊ ponit' in quad̃ pixide ad t̃le signũ

(p. 25.) 3 Visis ⁊ inspectis pellibȝ memorandoȝ de Reta Scacii billis indentatis ⁊ aliis memorandis recepc̃ones ⁊ soluc̃ones factas ⁊ intratas in eisdem pellibȝ p *Joh̃em de Haddeley* ⁊ *Nich̃m Exton̄* assignat̃ receptores uni⁹. xve. ⁊ xe. ⁊ medietatis unius. xve. ⁊. xe. a laicis anno *ix°* conc̃ necnõ recepc̃ones ⁊ soluc̃ones de dc̃is. xva. ⁊. xa. ⁊ medietate. xve. ⁊ xe. ad dc̃am Retã p Thes̃ ⁊ Camar̃ de dc̃o Scacio fact̃ plenar̃ contenent̃ p̃textu mandati huic cedule consuti, comptum est in eisdem pellibȝ qd̃ recepc̃ones ⁊ soluc̃ones p p̃dc̃os receptores de dc̃is. xva. ⁊ medietate. xve. fc̃e se extendunt ad ɑ xxxi ml'. iii c. v. li. xi s. iiii. d̃.

Et recepc̃ones ⁊ soluc̃ones p Thes̃ ⁊ Camar̃ p̃dc̃os de xva ⁊ medietate xve. añdc̃is fc̃e se extendũt ad ɑ xxiiiml. DLxi. li. x. s̃. i. d̃. ob̃.

Et ulta recepc̃ones ⁊ soluc̃ones fc̃as in forma

p̄dc̄a adhuc debentʳ p̱ collectores qui nondum computarunt p̱celle subscripte videlicet.

P̱ collectores . xvᵉ. ⁊ medietate . xvᵉ. in Comitatu *Northumbr̃* ꝯ iiiiᶜ. iiiiˣˣ. v. li̇. vˢ. xiᵈ. qᵃ.

P̱ coll̄ . xvᵉ. ⁊ medietate . xvᵉ. in Com̄ *Westm̄l*
ꝯ cclxxvi. li̇. iiiˢ. iiiiᵈ. ob̄ . qᵃ.

P̱ coll̄ xvᵉ. ⁊ med̄ xvᵉ in Com̄ *Cumbr̃*
ꝯ ccclx. li̇. x. s̄.

P̱ coll̄ . xvᵉ. ⁊ med̄ xvᵉ. in Villa *Novi Castri sup̱ Tynā* ꝯ cc. li̇.

(p. 25 b.) 4 ♣ Medᵈ' qd̄ . *vi.* die *Oct̄* anno r̃ R̷ *Ric̄i scd̄i . xi.* "restituta" fuit quedā indentʳa p̱ man⁹ *Joh̄is* [*atte*] *Roulles* . fc̄a int̄ *Georgiū Felbrigḡ* Militem ⁊ *Joh̄em de H'mesthorp̄* Cl̄icum p̱curatores illustrissimi Principis Reḡ *Angl̄ Ric̄i* †*sci scd̄i* et ven̄abilem *Henr̃ de Steenbergen̄* P̄positū ⁊ Archidiaconū eccl̄ie *Sc̄i Salvatoris Traiecten̄* consanguineū nobil̄ Principis *Will̄i* ||primogeniti *Juliacen̄* [⁊c̄] Duc̄ *Gelrie* de homagio faciend̄ ⁊c̄. salvo ||custodie in Recepta Dn̄i Reḡ. Et ponitʳ in quodā cophino ad tl̄e sigᵐ ♣

Duc̄ *Gelrie* alligancia.

5 Fait a remembrer q̃ le *xv*ᵐᵉ. jour de *Marz* lan nr̃e Sʳ. le Roi *Ric̄ second̄* puis le conq̃ . *xi*ᵐᵉ. *Arnald̄ Brocas* Chaml̄ein de lEschequer nr̃e dit Sʳ. le Roi ad liv̄ee hors de la Treszorie a Sʳ *William Dyghton̄* la liance faite pentr̃ nr̃e dit Sʳ. le Roy ⁊ le Duc de *Bretaign̄* . en un coffyn m̄chez a teil signe

La liance *dEnglet̄re* ⁊ *Bretaign̄.*

6 Fait a remembrer . q̃ le . *xiiii*ᵐᵉ. jorʳ de *Aprill̄* l an du regne nr̃e Sʳ le Roi *Richard̄ second̄ . xi*ᵐᵉ.

une chartre de feffement d un mees ⁊ deux shopes queux furent a Monš *Johan Beauchaump̃* [a *Wodewharf* de *Londr̃s*] fust delivre as Tresorer ⁊ Chamƀleins pur garder al oeps nr̃e dit S[r] le Roi ⁊ est mys en un coffyn a tiel signe ⁊ deux autres munimentes

{J. Beauchamp de Holt.}

7 Fait a rem̃ q̃ . le *xxii*[e] jour *dAv̄ill* l an du regne le Roi *Ric̃ second* puis le conq̃ . *xi*[me]. xvii. obligacions p queux div̄ses Chirs ⁊ auts sont

Brembre. obligez a *Nichol Brembr̃* Chir en div̄ses sõmes furent delivez as T'szorier ⁊ Chamƀleins ⁊ mys en un hanap a tiel signe N

8 Fait a remembrer q̃ le *viii*[e] jour de *Maii* l an du regne le Roi *Richard second* puis le conq̃

L alliance le Duc de *Gelre*. *xi*[o]. la alliance pentr̃ nr̃e S[r] le Roi av[a]ntdit ⁊ le Duc de *Gelre* fust delivez as T'szorier ⁊ Chamƀleins .⁊ mys en un hanape a tiel signe

" Cancellat[r] car il remeynt en une cofre en le " *Sterre Chambre* ⁊ illoqe fust trovez le *xvi.* jo[r] de " *Juyn* l an nr̃e S[r] le Roy *Richard xxii.*"

9 Fait a remembrer q̃ le . *xx*[me]. jour de *Juyn* l an du regne le Roi *Richard second unzisme* une endenture faite pentre *Johan* Evesq de *Hereford* Tresorer *dEngl* Mestre *Arnald Brocas* ⁊ autres

Exton. *F[a]nceys.* d une pte . et *Nicholas de Exton̄* Mair de *Londres* ⁊ *Auneys* nadegaires la fem̃e *Adam F[a]nceys* d autre pte des c̄teins jueaux delivrez as ditz *Nicholas* ⁊ *Auneys* en gage p les ditz Tresorer ⁊ autr̃s fust delivre mesme le jo[r] as ditz Tresorer ꝛ Chambleins ꝛ est mys en un box. a tiel sign̄

---

12 Ric. II.

1 Fait a rem̄ q̃ le *xvii*[me]. jour de *Juyll* l an *xii*[e]. une endenture fait ꝑentr̃ nr̃e S[r] le Roi *Ric̃*.

R. B. ꝛ *Richard Bukyngh*[a]*m* d aunage des d[a]ps vendables en le Countee de *Norht* fuist delive al T'szorie. ꝛ mys en un coffin a tiel signe

R. B.

2 Fait a rem̄ q̃ le *p*[i]*m̄* jour de *Decembr̃* l an du regne le Roi *Richard second* puis le conq̃. *xii*[me]. deux obligacions ꝑentr̃ Madame le P[i]ncesse ꝛ le Duc de *Bretaign̄* de ꝯteines sōmes en quell la dc̃e Madame fuist obligez a le Duc suisdit.. les quell sōmes mesm̄ le Duc ad ꝑdonez a nr̃e [dit] S[r]. le Roi d estr̃ paiez de. cc. li. [xxxiii. li. vi. s̃. viii. d.] en tout furent delivez a T'szorier ꝛ Chambleins ꝛ sont mys en. i. coffin a tiel signe

La Pincesse
Duc de Bretaign'.

" Et ponit[r] sup[a] Recept̃ Duc̃ *Lanc̃* cū ||all."

3 " Fait a rem̄ q̃ le *xxvii.* die *Octobr̃* l an de " regne le Roi *Henr̃ quart* puis le conquest *p*[i]*mer* la " alliance ꝑentre nr̃e S[r] le Roi ꝛ le Duk de *Gelre* " fust delivez hors de la Tresorie ꝑ les maynes de

Gelre. " *Janico* [*Dartasso*] Esquier a *Henr̃ Percy* Conte de

" *Northumbr̃* cestassavoir un box ⁊ un hamper a tiel
" signe"

(p. 26 b.) 4 Fait a remembrer q̃ * *xxvi*me. jour de *Novembr̃* l an du regne le Roi *Richard second* puis le conq̃ *xii*e. le trete entr̃ le Roi de *Castille* ⁊ de *Leons* ⁊ Duc de *Lanc̃* Lieutenant le Roi *dAquitaign̄* ⁊ div̾ses aut̃ psones de *Baion̄*, et le Roi de *F*ance ⁊ le Duc de *Berry* fuist liv̾ee as T'szorier ⁊ Chamb̄leins de lEscheqier ⁊ mys en un coffin a tiel signe come desus

{**Franciscus Florymundꝰ.**}

5 Fait a rem̄ q̃ le *xix*me. jour de *Fev̾er* l an du regne le Roi *Richard second* puis le conq̃ . *xii*e. le t̾srev̾ent Pier en Dieu l Erchesvesq̄ *dEv̾yk* Chanceller *dEngl* . deliv̾a en la T'srorie nr̃e dit Sr. le Roi " trois " coffins contenͣtz div̾ses munimentz touch̄ Mons̃ *Simond de Beurley* ⁊ sont mys en un bage a tiel signe

Simond de Beurley.

" Et lib̄antr exa Thes̃ *xi*o. die *Maii* anno r̃ R
" *Henr̃ quarti viii*o. *Ric̃o de Arundell* Chlr Custodi
" *Joh̄is de Burley* consanguinei ⁊ h̄edis ip̄ius *Simonis*
" *de Burley* infa etatem existent̃ virtute cujusdam
" br̃is folio *xii*o. seqn̄ consut̃."

(In sched p.41.) 6 *Henricus* Dei gr̃a Rex *Angl* ⁊ *Franc̃* ⁊ Dn̄s *Hib̄n* Thes̃ ⁊ Cam̾ar̃ suis salt̄m. Mandamꝰ vob̄ qd om̄ia cartas scripta ⁊ alia munimenta man̾ia t̾ras ⁊ ten̄ que fuerunt *Simonis de Burley* Chivaler tangencia seu quovismodo conc̾nencia in Thesauraria nr̃a sub custodia vr̃a existencia nob̄ in Cancellar̃ nr̃am [*Ric̃o de Arundell* Chivaler custodi] *Joh̄is de Burley* consanguinei ⁊ heredis ip̃ius *Simonis* [infra etatem existentis] ibidem lib̃and̃ sine dil̃one mittatis. T. me ip̃o apud *Westm̃ quarto* die *Maii* anno r̃ ñ *octavo*.

Kirkeby.

(p. 26 b.) 7 Fait a rem̃ q̃ le *xx*^me^ jour de *Fev̾er̃* l an du regne le Roi *Ric̃ second̃*. *xii*^me^. fuist deliv̾e a la T'szorie nr̃e S^r^. le Roi un escript enseale desouth le seal le Conte *dArondell* d une sõme de. ccc. li. p lui resceuz p voie dap̾st jeosq̃zs a un c̾tein jour ⁊ mys en un coffin a tiel signe

Arondell.

{Arondell'.}

8 Fait a rem̃ q̃. *xxiiii*. jour de *Marcz* l an du regne le Roi *Ric̃ second̃*. *xii*^me^. ✝ fut ✝ *Rog̃ Juyl* deliv̾a en la T'szorie c̾teines Chr̃es ⁊ autr̃s munimentz p queles mesm̃ le *Rog̃* p^r^chacea c̾teins terr̃ ⁊ teñz en le Countee de *Cornewaill* de *Rog̃ Lowys* les quel terr̃ ⁊ teñ * dona a *Rob̃t T'silian* en fee ⁊c̃. et sount mys en un coffin. a tiel signe

{Rog' Juyl' Rog' Lowys.}

" Que quid̃m carte ⁊ munim̃ta p r̃cept̃ *Joh̃is* " *H'mesthorp̃* uni⁹ Cam̾ar̃ de Re^ta^ lib̃ant^r^ *Joh̃i* " *Hawele* de ||*Dertem̃ xviii*° die *Oct*. anno r̃ ℞ *Ric̃i* " *sc̃di*. *xiii*°."

(p. 27.) 9 ✝ M^d^' qd̃ Thes̃ ⁊ Cam̾ar̃ lib̃av̾ũt *die Pasceues* a° *xii*° *Lamb̃to Fermer* Receptor̃ Cam̾e ℞^is^. p man⁹ *Will̃i Hugh̃loc* unam *Coronam* nup. *E*. ℞. fil̃. ℞ *H*. p illa h̃enda apud *Langele* f̃o *Pasche* seqñ ✝

"Restituit^r^" " ⁊ Restituit^r^ in Re^tam^. *ix*° die *Junii* anno regni ℞ " *R' sc̃di* post conq̃. *xiiii*°. p dc̃m *Lamb̃tm Ferm̾*."

10 M^d^' qd̃ *Will̃s Fulbo^r^ne* Cl̃icus *ult̃io die Marcii*. anno r̃ ℞ *Ric̃i sc̃di* post conq̃ *xii*° lib̃avit Thes̃ ⁊

Camar̃ de Reta Scacii Dñi R̃is p indentr div̾s bull̃ ⁊ pcess̃ tang̃ statū ⁊ psonam dc̃i Dñi R̃is in div̾s coffinis ⁊ pixid̃ . que ponūtr in una baga ad tale signū

{Rex Ric'us.}

11 Md' qd̃ *Jolines Wellyngburgh* senior Clic9 *xiiii*°. die *Maii* a° r̃ R̃ *Rici scdi* post conq̃ . *xii*°. libavit in Thes̃ unū hanapiū ⁊ . i. skippett̃ cont̃ div̾s munimta tang̃ Man̄ de *Pva M'lawe* ad tale signū

{Maner'iu' de P'va M'lawe.}

☞ " Postea ||restituntr *Nicho Salesby* Clico v̾tute " cuju9d̃ bris Thes̃ ⁊ Camar̃ Rte direct̃ cuj9 dat̃ est " *quarto* die *Febr̃* a° *xiii*° R̃ *Rici scdi* . . ⁊ huic fol̃ " consut̃."

12 Md' qd̃ *Johes Notyngham* Clicus libavit in Thes̃ R̃ . quandam relaxc̃ *Johis Cressewell* fact̃ Dño Regi *Rico* a°. *x*°. ejusd̃ R̃ ⁊ ponitr in quod̃ coffino ad tale signū

{Joh'es Cressewell'.}

13 Md' qd̃ *Johes Innocent* Clicus *xvi*° die *Junii* a° r̃ R̃ *Rici scdi* post conquest̃ . *xii*°. libavit in Thes̃ unam indentur̃ Comitis *Northumbr̃* de relaxac̃oe c̃toꝝ debitoꝝ p septingentis libris dc̃o Comiti p Dñm Regem conces̃ anno *x*mo ejusd̃ R̃ . ⁊ ponitr in qad̃ pixide ad tle signū

{Comes Northumbr'.}

---

12 & 13 Ric. II.

1 Md' qd̃ idem *Johnes Innocent xxii*do. die *Jun̄* a°. *xiii*°. r̃ R̃ *Ric̃* libavit in Thes̃ [duas] ✝unam✝ re-

laxacões fact̃ p̱ *Johem Symme* de ꝉde *Wrytelmersh* in Com̃ *Kanc̃* Excellentissimo Principi Regi *Ric̃o* supᵃdc̃o de sex acr̃ ⁊ dimid̃ t̃re jac̃ in pc̃ R̷ de *Elthᵃm* et ponitʳ in qᵒd̃ coffino ad tale signũ

{Joh'es Symme Elthᵃm.}

(p. 27 b.) 2 [" Mᵈ' qd̃ Ep̃us *Lond̃* cepit it̃ suũ penes *Calis̃* " ad tᵃctand̃ cũ *Francig̃ xx* die *Febr̃*. aᵒ r̃ R̷. *E.* " t̃cii *E. xlvi*ᵗᵒ."

" ¶ Itm̃ Dñs *Rog̃us de Bello Campo* cepit it̃ suũ " penes *Calis̃* p̃dc̃am *xxii.* die *Febr̃*.

" ¶ Itm̃ Dñs *Guido de Brian* p̱ eod̃m viag̃. *xxii.* " die *Febr̃*.

" ¶ Itm̃ Magr̃ *Johnes Branketr̃*."]

3 Fait a remembrer q̃ le *xxvii*ᵉ. jorʳ de *Juyl*. l an du regne le Roi *Richard̃ second̃* puis le conq̃ *xiii*ᵉ. Sʳ. *Johan H'mesthorp̃* un des Chamb̃leins de la Receite deliṽa en le T'szorie les trieves prises pentr̃ nr̃e Sʳ le Roi *E. tierz* l an de son regne *xlix*ᵐᵉ et mys en un hanap. a tiel signe

Angl. Franc̃.

{Angl' Franc'.}

4 Fait a rem̃ q̃ *mesm̃ le jo*ʳ ⁊ *an* le dit Sʳ *Johan* deliṽa en la dc̃e T'szor̃ l alliance prise pentr̃ nr̃e dit̃ Sʳ. le Roi *E.* ⁊ *Johan* Duc de *Bretaign̄*. l an nr̃e Sʳ. *mill ccc. lxxii.* et mys en un coffin a tiel signe

{Alliganc' Ducis Britainne.}

5 Mᵈ' qd̃ *xx* die *Maii* anno r̃ R̷ *Ric̃i scd̃i* post conq̃ ‖*xii*ᵒ. *Robtus Bolton̄* Clicus libavit in Thes̃ Reg̃ duas cistas cũ diṽs cartis script̃ ⁊ al̃ muni-

Pole. ment *Michis de la Pole* Comi *Suff'*. int que muniint repiunt[r] quatuor carte tangent tras ⁊ ten que dcus *Mich de la Pole* pquisivit de *Hugone de Normanton* que quidm carte mittunt[r] in Cancellar ℞ *xxiii*° *die*. *Novembr*. a°. r ℞ *Rici* sup[a]dci. *xiii*°. virtute cujusd bris Thes ⁊ Camar inde direct "tenores "cuj⁹ bris ⁊ cartaꝝ pdcaꝝ "‖sequnt[r]" ut pꝫ inferi⁹."

Ricus Dei gra Rex *Angl* ⁊ *Franc* ⁊ Dns *Hibn* Thes ⁊ Camar suis, Saltm. Mandam⁹ vob qd (p. 28.) omimoda cartas scripta ⁊ alia munimenta tangencia tras ⁊ ten que *Michael de la Pole* nup Comes *Suff'* *Normanton.* *Nott.* pquisivit de *Hugone de Normanton* in *Weston* ⁊ *Normanton sup Trentam* ⁊ que in custodia vra in Thesauraria nra existunt ut dicit[r] nob in Cancellar nram omi dilone postposita mitti ⁊ deferri fac. T. me ipo apud *Westm*, *quarto* die *Novembr* anno r n *tciodecimo*.

6 Sciant psentes ⁊ futuri qd ego [*Hugo*] *fil Johis fil Hugonis de Normanton* dedi concessi ⁊ hac psenti carta mea confirmavi Dno *Michi de la Pole* Militi hedibꝫ ⁊ assignatis suis una culturam tre arabil sicut jacet in longitudine ⁊ latitudine in Campo de *Normanton* apd *Dalthorndik'* int Campu de *Gresthorp* ex parte aust[a]li ⁊ tram *Rici Basset* ex pte boriali cu omibꝫ suis ptin. H'end ⁊ tenend pdcam cultura tre cu omibꝫ suis ptin pdco Dno *Michi de la Pole* her ⁊ assign suis libe quiete integre bene ⁊ in pace de capitalibꝫ dnis feodi illius p svicia inde debita ⁊ de jure consueta. Et ego vero pdcus *Hugo* ⁊ heredes mei pdcam cultura tre cu omibꝫ suis ptin pdco Dno *Michi de la Pole* hed ⁊ assign suis contra omes gentes warantizabim⁹ imppm. In cuj⁹ rei testiom huic psenti carte sigillu meu apposui hiis testibꝫ *Willo de Bacheley de Musch*[a]*m Johe fil Willi de Weston Robto*

de Cam͛a de Normantoñ Robto fil Hug̃ de eadē *Georgio Pye* ⁊ aliis Dat̃ apud *Normantoñ* die *Lune* ꝑx̃ *ante fm̃ Sc̃i Petri in Cathedra*. anno regni Regis *Edwardi* ͛*cii* post conquest̃ Anglie *quadragesimo* ͛*cio.*

7 Sciant ꝑsentes ⁊ futuri qđ ego [*Hugo*] *fil Joh̃is de Normantoñ* dedi concessi ⁊ hac ꝑsenti carta mea confirmavi Dño *Mich̃i de la Pole* Militi h̃edibȝ ⁊ assigñ suis om̄ia ͛tras pata ⁊ teñ redditus ⁊ ͛svicia ⁊ rev͛siones om̄imodas "que h̃eo in Villa ⁊ t͛tretorio de "*Westoñ in ye Clay*" h̃nđ ⁊ tenenđ om̄ia ꝑdc̄a ͛tras pata ⁊ tenementa redditus ⁊ ͛svicia ⁊ rev͛siones om̄imodas cū oĩbȝ suis ꝑtiñ ꝑdc̄o Dño *Mich̃i* her̃ ⁊ assigñ suis lib̃e quiete bene integre ⁊ in pace de cap̃ dñis feođ illius ꝑ ͛svicia inde debita ⁊ de jure consueta. Et ego vo ꝑdc̄us *Hugo* ⁊ h̃edes mei om̄ia ꝑdc̄a ͛tras pata ⁊ teñ redditus ⁊ ͛svicia ⁊ rev͛siones om̄imodas cū om̄ibȝ suis ꝑtiñ ꝑdc̄o Dño *Mich̃i* her̃ ⁊ assigñ suis conta om̄es gentes warantizabimꝰ impp̃m In cujꝰ rei testiõm huic ꝑsenti carte sigillū meū apposui hiis testibȝ *Francisco de Meryng̃ Joh̃e de* ||*Glancestre de Suttoñ Joh̃e fil Witt̃i de Westoñ Nich̃o fil Witt̃i* de eadē *Joh̃e Cock'* de eadem *Joh̃e del Birkes* de eadē *Witt̃o fil Ric̃i* de eadē ⁊ aliis. Dat̃ apud *Westoñ* die *Martis* ͛*cio* die mens̃ *Apil* anno regni Regis *Edwardi* ͛*cii* post conquestū *quadragesimo nono.*

8 Sciant ꝑsentes ⁊ futur̃ qđ ego *Hugo fil Joh̃is fil Hugonis de Normantoñ* dedi concessi ⁊ hac ꝑsenti carta mea confirmavi Dño *Mich̃i de la Pole* Militi her̃ ⁊ assigñ suis quinqȝ decem solidos tres denarios ⁊ obolū ||anui redditꝰ ad ꝑcipienđ annuatim de div͛sis tenentibȝ meis in *Westoñ in ye Clay* videlcȝ de *Elizabeth̃ Palm͛* octo solidos septem denarios ⁊ obolū ꝑ

novem acris t̃re arabil̃ quas de me in feodo tenet de (p. 28 b.) *Witto fil Henrici* quatuor solidos ⁊ duos denarios ꝓ quatuor acris una roda ⁊ dimid̃ rod̃ t̃re arabil̃ quas de me in feodo tenet ⁊ de *Isabella* quond̃ Ux̃e *Ric̃i Magotsoñ* duos solidos ⁊ sex denar̃ ꝑ una placea ⁊ trib; acr̃ t̃re arabil̃ vocat̃ *Squiercroft* quas de me tenet ad t̃minū vite sue simul cū reṽsione escaetis ⁊ dominio dc̃aꝝ placee ⁊ t̃raꝝ cū om̃ib; aliis ꝓficuis ⁊ ptinenc̃ suis. hend̃ ⁊ tenend̃ p̃dc̃os quinq̧decim solidos tres denarios ⁊ obolū ‖anui reddit⁹ sim̃l cū reṽsione escaet̃ ⁊ dominio dc̃aꝝ placee ⁊ t̃r̃ cū om̃ib; aliis ꝓficuis ⁊ ptiñ suis p̃dc̃o Dño *Michi* hered̃ ⁊ assigñ suis lib̃e quiete bene integre ⁊ in pace de capit̃ dñis feod̃ illius p s̃vicia inde debita ⁊ de jure consueta. Et ego vero p̃dc̃us *Hugo* ⁊ her̃ mei p̃dc̃os quinq̧decim solidos tres denar̃ ⁊ obolū anui reddit⁹ sim̃l cū reṽsione escaet̃ ⁊ dominio dc̃aꝝ placee ⁊ t̃r̃ cū [om̃ib;] aliis ꝓficuis ⁊ ptiñ suis p̃dc̃o Dño *Michi* her̃ ⁊ assigñ suis cont^a om̃es gentes warantizabim⁹ impp̃m. In cuj⁹ rei testiōm huic p̃senti carte sigillū meū apposui hiis testib; *Johe fil Witti* de *Westoñ Nicho fil Witti* de ead̃ *Johe Cock'* de eadē *Johe de Birkes* de eadē *Witto fil Ric̃i* de eadē *Francisco de Meryng̃ Johe de* ‖*Glancestr̃* de *Suttoñ* ⁊ aliis. Dat̃ apd̃ *Westoñ in ye Clay* t̃cio die mens̃ *April* anno regni Regis *Edwardi* t̃cii post conqū *quadragesimo nono*.

9 ¶ Hec indentura fc̃a int̃ Dñm *Michem de la Pole* Militē ex una pte ⁊ *Hugonē de Normantoñ* de Coñi *Notyngh* ex alt̃a parte testat^r qd̃ dc̃us *Hugo* dedit ⁊ concessit dc̃o Dño *Michi* her̃ ⁊ exec̃ suis ꝓ quadā summa pecunie quam idem Dñs *Michael* solvit eidē *Hugoni* p̃ manib; quandā pasturā vocat̃ *Le*

Soutdykes que jacet ex parte australi ꝑpe t͛ras dc̄i Dn̄i *Mich̄is* vocat̄ *Le Longlondes* ⁊ ex ꝑte occidentali dc̄a pastura abuttat suꝑ regiam stratā vocat̄ ‖*Ryholmestrete*. ⁊ ex ꝑte orientali juxᵃ *Normanton̄ mersshe.* Et ex parte boreali juxᵃ cōem *Outegong*ꝭ de *Normanton̄* h̄end̄ ⁊ tenend̄ ꝓdc̄am pasturā cū om̄ibꝫ suis ꝑtin̄ ꝓdc̄o Dn̄o *Mich̄i* her̄ ⁊ execut̄ suis a dat̄ ꝓsenciū usqꝫ ad finē decem annoꝝ ꝑx̄ sequent̄ plenar̄ complet̄. Et ego vero ꝓdc̄us *Hugo* ⁊ hered̄ mei ꝓdc̄am pasturā cū om̄ibꝫ suis ꝑtin̄ ut ꝓmittitʳ ꝓfato Dn̄o *Mich̄i* her̄ ⁊ execut̄ suis durante t͛mino ꝓdc̄o contᵃ om̄es gentes warantizabimꝰ ⁊ defend̄. In cujꝰ rei testiōm hiis indent'is ꝑtes ꝓdc̄e sigilla sua alt͛natim apposuerunt. hiis testibꝫ *Will̄o fil̄ Henr̄ Nich̄o fil̄ Will̄i* ⁊ *Joh̄e fil̄ Will̄i de Normanton̄* ⁊ multis aliis. Dat̄ apud *Gressethorp̄* in *vigil̄ Sc̄i Martini in Yeme* anno regni Regis *Edwardi* t͛cii post conquestū Anglie *quadragesimo octavo.*

(p. 29.) 10 Mdʼ qd̄ *xxiii*ᵒ die *Februar̄* aᵒ r̄ R͛ *Ric̄i sc̄di xiii*ᵒ Rev͛end̄ Dn̄s Ep̄s *Wynton̄* Cancellar̄ *Angl̄* lib̄avit in Thes̄ Reḡ salvo custodiend̄ div͛sa munimenta tangencia heredit̄ *Pembroch̄* ⁊ ponūtʳ in quod̄ hanaꝑio ad t̄le signū

{Comes Pembroch'.}

11 Mdʼ qd̄ *eodem die* lib̄ fuer̄ in dc̄am Thes̄ R͛ div͛se lr̄e tangent̄ Comitem de *Foitz* ⁊ ponūtʳ in quod̄ hanaꝑio ad tale signū

{Comes de Foitz.}

12 Mdʼ qd̄ *xiiii*ᵒ die *Maii* anno *xiii*ᵒ R͛. *Ric̄i sc̄di Joh̄es de Catesby* ⁊ *Rob̄tus Burguyllon̄* Justic̄ de pace

Warr. " in Com̃ *Warr̃* " lib̃averũt in Thes̃ R̃ ✝ extract̃ ✝ [record̃ ꝯvic̃] ab a° *p'mo* Reg̃ *Ric̃i* usq, annũ . *x*^m^. ejusđm Dñi Reg̃ . et ponũt^r^ in quađ baga de alb̃ coreo. ☞ Et ext^a^cte de eisđ annis lib̃ant^r^ in Sc^a^cm.

---

14 Ric. II.

1 M^d'^ qđ *xix*° die *Ocł* a° r̃ R̃ *Ric̃i sc̃di xiiii*° lib̃ fuit in Thes̃ R̃ una relaxac̃õ fc̃a dc̃o Dño Regi p Ducem *Lancastr̃* eo qđ ip̃e fuit retent⁹ ꝯs⁹ Dñm Regem pfectur̃ ꝯs⁹ *Aquitañ* cũ m^l^. hoĩb3 ad arma . ⁊ m^l^. sagittar̃. Et ponit^r^ in quađ pixiđ ad tł̃e signũ

{Relaxac'o Ducis Aquitan'.}

" nõ trahit^r^."

2 M^d'^ qđ . *xxiiii*^to^. die *Ocł* anno *xiiii*°. R̃ *Ric̃i sc̃di* quedam lr̃e patentes sub magno sigillo direct̃ fuerũt Thes̃ ⁊ Camar̃ de Sc^a^cio . ad vadianđ ex pte dc̃i Dñi R̃ . quandam *sellam* cũ duob3 scansilib3 ⁊ unũ *gladiũ* de *Ispañ* p . iii^ml^. ⁊ ||quadringent̃ marcis. in Camam Dñi R̃ solvenđ , ⁊ eandem sũmam in mense *Pascħ* px̃ futur̃ " eisđ Thes̃ ⁊ Camar̃ " restituenđ Et ponũt^r^ in pvo viridi coffro salvo ib̃m custodienđ ⁊ indorsat̃ tł̃i sigñ

3 M^d'^. qđ " *xxviii*° " die *Ocł* a°. r̃ R̃ *Ric̃i* . *xiiii*°. virtute lr̃aꝝ p^i^vat̃ sigill̃ Thes̃ ⁊ Camar̃ [Sc^a^cii] direct̃ , sub dat̃ . *xxviii*°. die . *Ocł* a°. s^a^dc̃o . lib̃averũt Dño *Thome Pcy* subcamar̃ Reg̃ unũ palettũ garnis̃ cũ pł ⁊ pre sicut in dc̃is lr̃is pleni⁹ p3 ad vadianđ p ꝯta sũma p^c^cunie ad opus Dñi Reg̃. Et ||po-

nūt^r in viridi coffro salvo custodienđ indorsat̃ tł̃i signo

(p. 29 b.) sub tali signo

4 ♣ M^d'. qđ *Roƀtus Cotum* recepit ad Receptā Sc^acii quatuor cartas sigilł aur̃ sigillat̃.

Itm̃ unā cartam Reg̃ *Angł* sig̃ cū cera viriđ.

Itm̃ unū instrumentū sig̃ sub sigillo ‖plumbio.

Itm̃ unū instrumentū sig̃ ♣ sub ♣ cū duob₃ sigilł de cera rubea vid₃ *t̃cio* die *Januar̃* a^o *xiiii^o* Reg̃ *Ric̃i sc̃di.* ♣

[“ Me^d' qđ om̃ia p̃dc̃a scripta restitut̃ fuer̃ in Thes̃
“ Reg̃ vid₃ *xviii^o* die *Januar̃* anno *xiiii* R̷ *Ric̃i sc̃di*
“ ꝛc̃.”]

5 M^d'. qđ *sc̃do* die *Octobr̃* anno r̃ R̷ *Ric̃i sc̃di* post conq̃. *xiiii^o*. liƀat̃ fuit in Thes̃ quedam acquietancia sub sigillo *Colynet Arnaud* Attorñ Com̃ “*Sc̃i Pauli*” de cent̃ libr̃ recept̃ de “revenc̃oib₃” ꝓvenient̃ de Prioratu de *Okebo^rne* Et ponit^r in quađ pixide ad tale signū ⁊

“Comes *Sc̃i* “*Pauli.*”

{Okebo^rne.}

“ nō trahit^r.”

6 M^d' qđ *x^o*. die *Aprił* anno r̃ R̷ *Ric̃i*. *xiiii^o*. Thes̃ ꝛ Camar̃ Sc^acii R̷ virtute bris R̷ eisđ direct̃ cuj^9 dat̃ *xviii^o* die *Febr̃* a^o *s^adc̃o* rem̃ int̃ manđ de t̃mio *Mich* a^o *s^adc̃o* liƀavūt *Joħi Scarburgħ* ex^a Thes̃ viii cartas ꝛ munimenta tangenc̃ cert̃ terr̃ ꝛ teñ que fuer̃ *Mich de la Pole* nuꝑ Com̃ *Suff'* in *Southwhetlee Strettoñ* ꝛ ‖*Southwodehous* ꝑ ip̃m *Joħem Scarburgħ* “de” Dño Rege ꝑquisit̃.

Scarburgħ.

* * * * *

7 Prim̃ement une lr̃e obligatoire du Roy de *Castell* Don *Petro* faite au dit *Prince* de lvi. m^l. floryns paiez au Roy de *Navarre* p le dit *Prince* p^r le dit Roy Don *Petro* a paier la dc̃e sōme en le Chastel de *Bordeux* p le dit Roy Don *Petro* devant la feste de *Seint John Baptiste* alors pschein avenir Et est la date de la dc̃e lr̃e a *Lybo^rne* le *xxiii* jo^r de *Septembr̃* l an de nr̃e S^r *mil ccc lxvi.*

8 Item une autr̃ lr̃e obligatoire du dit Roy Don *Petro* p la quelle il est obligez au dit *Prince* en xi^c. ⁊ ix ^ml. floryns de la chambre ⁊ deux centz iiii^xx. ⁊ x. fortes p^r les gages ⁊ regardz du dit Prince ⁊ de ses gentz p^r iii. moys comensantz le *x*^e jo^r de *Janver* lors darrein passez ⁊ en les avantditz lvi^ml. floryns d or de la chambre. Lesquelx le dit *Prince* paia p^r le dit Roy Don *Petro* au Roy de *Navarre.* Et est la date de la dc̃e lr̃e en le Mouster de ||*Olgis* jouste la Cite de *Burges* le . *vi.* jo^r de *Maii* l an de nr̃e S^r. *m^l ccc lxvii.*

9 It̃m une autr̃ lr̃e obligatoire du dit Roy Don *Petro* faite au dit *Prince* d un million de floryns d or a paier a c̃teins t̃mes ⁊ sur c̃teines peines en la dc̃e lr̃e contenuz Et est la date de la dc̃e lr̃e en le dit Mouster de *Olgis* de la Cite de *Burges.*

10 Item une autre lr̃e obligatoire du dit Roy Don *Petro* faite au dit *Prince* de v^c. l. m^l' floryns d or de coign de *Florence* a paier au dit *Prince* en recompensac̃ōn de les g^andes custages q̃ le dit *Prince* avoit s^r li mesmes ⁊ le Comtes ⁊ aut̃s S^rs de son Host outre lo^r fees ⁊ gages ⁊ p^r aut̃s causes exp̃ssez en la dc̃e lr̃e. Et est la date de mesme la lr̃e a *Lybo^rne* le *xxiii.* jo^r de *Septembr̃* l an de nr̃e S^r *m^l. ccc lxvi.*

(p. 30.) 11 Itm̃ un autr̃ lr̃e obligatoir du dit *Roy* faite au dit *Prince* le *sc̃de* jo^{r} de *Maii* l an de nr̃e S^{r}. *m^{l}. ccc lxvii* en l esglise Cathedral de *Burgis* de mesmes les v^{c}. l. m^{l} floryns.

12 Itm̃ une lr̃e obligatoir du dit Roy Don *Petro* ꝑ la quelle il confesse ‖li avoir resceu du dit *Prince* en ꝯteines monies d or tanqꝫ a la sōme de. v^{ml}. floryns ⁊ soy oblige a les repaier au dit *Prince* dedeins ꝯtein t̃me en la dc̃e lr̃e contenuz.

La some totale de les obligac̃ons avantditz ꝯ deux millions vii^{c}. xx. m^{l}. floryns ⁊ cciiii^{xx}. x. fortz d or.

13 Itm̃ une autr̃ lr̃e du dit Roy Don *Petro* faite a *Lybo^{r}ne* le *xxiii^{e}* jo^{r} de *Septembr̃* l an de nr̃e S^{r} *m^{l}. ccc lxvi.* cont̃ les articles treiteez ⁊ acco^{r}dez entr̃ le dit Roy ⁊ le Roy de *Navarr̃* touchant le viage *d Espaigne.*

14 Itm̃ deux lr̃es du dit Roy Don *Petro* faites a *Lybo^{r}ne* le *xxiii^{e}* jo^{r} de *Septembr̃* l an de nr̃e S^{r} *m^{l}. iii^{c}. lxvi.* ꝑ les quelles le dit Roy Don *Petro* g^{a}nta q̃ a q̃conq̃ temps q̃ le Roy *d Englet̃re* ⁊ son eisne filz ou lo^{r} heirs ⁊ successo^{r}s Roys *d Englet̃re* ⁊ lo^{r} eisnez filz q̃ p^{r} le temps s̃roient vorroient venir en lo^{r} ꝑpres ꝑsones a la guerre q̃ le dit Roy Don *Petro* ou ses heirs Roys de *Castille* aṽont contr̃ le Roy de *Gernade* ou aut̃s enemys de la foy, les ditz Roy *d Englet̃re* ⁊ lo^{r} eisne filz eient le p^{r}m̃ bataille ⁊ l avangarde. Et ꝑ meisme la lr̃e le dit Roy Don *Petro* g^{a}nta q̃ toutz les gens nobles pelegrins du Royalme *d Englet̃re* ⁊ de la Principalte de *Guyene* s̃ront f^{a}nches a touz jours de tout peage custume maletote ⁊ aut̃s imposic̃ons ⁊ exacc̃ons q̃conqes im-

posez ou a imposer dedeins les Royalmes du dit Roy Don *Petro*.

15 Itm̃ une autr̃ lr̃e de mesme la foᵣme faite a *Burgis* le *iiᶜ*. joʳ de *Maii* l an de nr̃e Sʳ. *mˡ*. *iiiᶜ*. *lxvii*.

16 Itm̃ une autr̃ lr̃e du Roy Don *Petro* faite au dit *Prince* en la Cite de *Burgis* †de *ii*. joʳ de *Maii* l an de nr̃e Sʳ. *mˡ*. *iiiᶜ* *lxvii*. en la quele lr̃e sont contenuz les articles ⁊ covenantz accordez entr̃ les ditz *Roy* ⁊ *Prince* a cause du dit viag̃ *d Espaigne*.

17 Itm̃ . iii. lr̃es du dit Roy Don *Petro* fc̃es au dit Prince a *Lyboʳne* le *xxiii*. joʳ de *Septembr̃* l an de nr̃e Sʳ *mˡ*. *iiiᶜ* *lxvi*. ꝑ quelles le dit Roy dona au dit Prince ⁊ a ses heirs ⁊ assignez le chastel ⁊ lieu de *Vermeo* ⁊ les lieux de *Bilbau* ⁊ de la ||*Queyte* ⁊ toutes les t̃res ⁊ s̃ʳies de *Biscaie* ⁊ de *Castre d Ordialis*.

18 Itm̃ . une lr̃e du dit *Roy* faite a *Burgis* le *sc̃de* joʳ de *Maii* l an de nr̃e Sʳ. *mˡ* *iiiᶜ* *lxvii*. en la quelle le dit Roy dona ⁊ conferma au dit *Prince* ⁊ a ses heirs ⁊ assignes les ditz *Castel* ⁊ lieu de *Vermeo* ⁊ les lieux de *Bilbau* ⁊ de la ||*Queyte* ⁊ toutes les t̃res ⁊ s̃ʳies de *Biscaie* ⁊ de *Castre d Ordialis*.

19 Itm̃ . une lr̃e du Roy *Petro* direct̃ a touz juges alcaides scabynes mairs ⁊ aut̃s ministres ⁊ vassalx de mesmes les t̃res ⁊ s̃ʳies pʳ obeier au dit Prince ⁊ a li fe homag̃ ⁊ touz aut̃s s̃vices ⁊ devoirs cōme a loʳ. Sʳ. selonc le pʳpoit du dit doū.

(p. 30. b.) 20 Itm̃ une autr̃ lr̃e semblable du dit Roy Don *Petro* de mesme la foʳme.

21 Itm̃ troys lr̃es du dit Roy Don *Petro* executoires s^r mesme le don dont les deux sont dirc̃es a Mons̃ *John Chaundos Thomas de Feltoñ Rog̃* S^r de la *Ware* Mons̃ *Guychard d Angle* ⁊ *Gerard de Turcays* S^r de *Poyane* ⁊ la tierce lr̃e est dirc̃e au dit S^r de *Poyane* ⁊ a *Roderik' Petir de Soto* p^r mettr̃ le dit Prince en possession de mesmes les terres ⁊ seign^ries.

Ely. Seint David. Saz.

22 Fait a rem̃ q̃ ces lr̃es mises en deux grosses hanaps furent delivez as T'srorier̃ ⁊ Chamb̃leins de l Escheqier le q^int jour de *Maii* l an du regne nr̃e S^r. le Roy *Richard second* puis le conq̃ . *xiiii^e*. p *Johan* Evesq̃ *d Ely* en p̃sence de *Johan* Evesq̃ de *Saz* ⁊ *John* Evesq̃ de *Seint David* a *Westm̃* p^r y demorer en la T'srorie de nr̃e dit S^r le Roy. Et "——" sont mys en les ditz hanaps ove une bille signee ove teil signe ☞

{Ely Seint David Sar'.}

"Kerm̃dyñ." "Cardikan."

23 Fait a rem̃ q̃ le *xme*. jour de *Maii* l an du regne le Roi *Richard second* puis le conq̃ *xiiii^e* la bagge de la session del Conte *dArundell* en *Kerm̃dyn* ⁊ *Cardikan* en *Gales*. fuist delive hors de la T^rsrorie en la Chauncellerie p vtue d un brief dont la date [est] le *xme*. jour de *Maii* susdc̃e reto^rnes [⁊ envoiez] en dc̃e Chaunc̃ ovesq̃ la bagge av^antdit.

Dux Eboz.

24 Fait a rem̃ q̃ le *darrein* jour de *Maii*. l an du regne le Roi *Ric̃ second*. *xiiii^e*. une obligacioñ ove la defesance p quele le Duc *dEṽwik'* est obligez a nr̃e S^r. le Roi en . m^l. m^l. m^arz delivez p Mons̃ *Thomas Gerberg̃* Chr a T'srorier ⁊ Chamb̃leins de lEscheqer. Et sont mys en une box a tiel signe

{Dux Ebor'.}

(p. 33.) 25 Memod' qđ *xxviii*° die *Octobr̃* anno *xiiii*° Regis *Rič̃i sc̃di* libat̃ fuit ext^a Thesauraȓ dc̃i Dñi Regis Dño *Thome Percy* Militi Subcam̃ar̃ Dñi Regis quoddam palett̃ voc̃ *Le palet de Spayne* ornat̃ div̄s̃ lapidibȝ p̄ciosis virtute cujusdam bȓis Thes̃ ꝛ Cam̃ar̃ de Sc^acio direct̃ filat̃ int̄ bȓia de t̄mino *Micħis* anno dc̃i Dñi nȓi Regis *xiiii*°. sup^adict̃.

Percy.

---

15 Ric. II.

(p. 31.) 1 M^d' qđ *xiiii*° die *Jul* a° r̃ R̸ *Rič̃i . sc̃di* * . libat̃ fuer̃ . ♣ quedam ♣ in Thesaur̃ Dñi Reg̃ salvo custodienđ queđ carta Dño nȓo Regi fact̃ de quodam teñ in villa *Westm̃* p *Thom̃ Astoñ Joħem Thurstan* ꝛ *Joħem Kynbell* dc̃o Dño R̸ fact̃. Aceciam unam lȓam attornat̃ sigill de magno sig̃ Reg̃ direct̃ *Bernardo Brocas* Militi ꝛ *Joħi H'mesthorp̃* . ad recipienđ noīe dc̃i Dñi nȓi Reg̃ seisinā ꝛ possessionē in teñ p̄dc̃o ꝛ ponit^r in quađ pixide ad hoc signū

Brocas. H'mesth.

{Brocas H'mesth'.}

" ‖Qua carta libat^r *Joħi Burrewell* Monacho Abbie " *Westm̃ xxi*° die *Novembr̃* anno regni Reg̃ *Rič̃i sc̃di* " . *xv*°."

2 M^d' qđ *xxix*° die *Novembr̃* anno r̃ R̸ *Rič̃i* . *xv*° Thes̃ ꝛ Cam̃ar̃ R̸ virtute bȓis R̸ eisdem direct̃ cuj̄ dat̃ *xxiii*. die *Nov'* a°. p̄dc̃o rem̃ int̄ manđ de t̄mīo *Micħis a*°. *sup^adc̃o* libv̄unt *Joħi de Nevill* Militi ex^a Thes̃ †due †carte ꝛ al munimenť tang̃ c̄tas t̄r̃ ꝛ teñ que nup fuer̃ *Micħis de la Pole* in Com̃ *Lincolñ* p ip̄m *Joħem* p̱quisit̃ de Dño Reg̃.

Nevill.

3 M^d' qđ *xi*°. die *Decembr̃* . anno r̃ R̸ *Rič̃i sc̃di* *

Thes̃ ⁊ Camar̃ Dñi Reg̃ libaverunt *Baldewyno Radyngtoñ* Militi . xvi. sigilla ordinat̃ ꝑ pann̄ ven-

Surr̃. dibil in Com̄ *Surr̃* ⁊ *Sussex'* sigilland̃ ꝑ indenturā

Sussex'. int̃ eosd̃ Thes̃ ⁊ Camar̃ ⁊ ꝑdc̄m *Baldewinū* inde

Radyngtoñ. fc̄am Et ponit^r in quadam pixide in cista sup^a. Re^tam ad tale signū

4 M^d' qd̃ . *xx*°. die *Januar̃* . a°. r̃ R̃ *Ric̃i sc̄di* . *xv*°. libat̃ fuerunt in Thes̃ R̃ quedam obligac̄o " cccc " m^arz . ꝑ quam *T. Gerberge* Miles *T. Wroghtoñ Ric̃ Gedyngtoñ* ⁊ *Wills Galandre* Clici obligant^r

Dux *Ebor̃.* Excellentissimo P^incipi R̃ *Ric̄o* . ⁊ Dño Thes̃ *Angl*

Thom̃ Gerberg̃. noīe Ducis *Ebor̃* cū defesanc̃ sr̃ eand̃ ⁊ quad̃ acquietanc̃ sub sigillo dc̄i Ducis sigillat̃. Et ponūt^r in quad̃ pixide . ad tale signū

{Dux Ebor'. T. Gerb'ge.}

(p. 31 b.) 5 Fait a rem̃ q̃ le *xxvi*^me. jour de *Fev̄er* l an du regne le Roy *Ric̃ second̃* puis le conquest̃ *xv*^me. un seal app^rten^ant a l office du Seneschall ⁊ Receivour de *Haverford̃* contenant deux foilles l un foille g^ave des armes le Roy ⁊ l autr̃ foille g^ave du

Hav'ford̃. Roy chivachant tout armez estoit livez ꝑ indentur̃ faite ꝑentr̃ *Johan* Evesq̃ de *Saresbirz* T'srorer *dEngl* ⁊ *Thom̃ Lagherñ* ⁊ auts ꝑdhōmes de la ville de *Hav̄ford̃* le quel seal mesm̃ les ꝑdhōmes ount receu p^r le deliver a *Morys Gwyn* Seneschall de la dc̄e ville. Et est mys en une box a tiel signe

{Haverford'.}

6 Fait a rem̃ q̃ le *xxi*^e. jour *dAprill* l an du regne le Roy *Richard̃ second̃* puis le conquest̃ *xv*^me. furent delivez en la T'szrorie ꝑ Sr *Thomas*

Angl. Fnc. Scoc. Cales. *Stanley* Clerc de la Chauncelrie . vi. roules ⁊ iiii. enquestes ensemble filez touchantz diṽses tretez de pees pentr̃ les Roys ✝ du ✝ *dEngletre* ⁊ de *Franc̃* . ⁊

“ Alligãcia “ Ducis “ *Britanñ.*” alliance de Duc de *Bretaigñ* ∗ *dEscoce.* Et ponũtr in qadam baga ad ponend̃ in cista juxa ‖gad̃ supa Retam. ad tle signũ

{𝕿. 𝕾𝖙𝖆𝖓𝖑𝖊𝖞.}

Ducat⁹ *Aquitañ.* *Fylongley.* 7 Fait a rem̃ q̃ mesm̃ le *xxi*e jour *dAprill* furent deliṽez en la T'szorie p *Richard̃ Fylongeley* Esquier ii. roules touchantz les rents ⁊ pfitz de la Duchee *d Aquitaigñ* Et sont mises en une bage enclose en une ciste sr la Receite a tiel signe

{𝕱𝖞𝖑𝖔𝖓𝖌𝖊𝖑𝖊𝖞.}

“ Libatr ✝ Thes̃ ✝ *x.* die *Maii Johi Northbury* “ Thes̃ *Angl* †*Angl* ao r̃ ℞ *Henr̃ primo.*”

8 ‖Feat a rem̃ q̃ mesm̃ le *xxi.* jour *dAp'll* furent deliṽez en la dc̃e Trszorie une lr̃e p quele le Prior ⁊ le Convent de *Cantirbirz* soi obligerunt de chaunt̃ pr l alme . ‖du *Edward̃* le ̃tsnoble Prince de *Gales* ⁊ pr l estate du Roi qore est ⁊ del *Anne* la Roigne. Et est mis en un box a tiel signe

{𝕻𝖗𝖎𝖔𝖗' ⁊ 𝕮𝖔𝖓𝖛𝖊𝖓𝖙⁹} 𝕮𝖆𝖓𝖙𝖚𝖆𝖗'.}

---

16 Ric. II.

Libantr Cancellar̃ . iii. bull.

(p.32.) 1 Md' qd̃ *xv*o die *Febr̃* anno r̃ ℞ *Ric̃i scd̃i* post conq̃ *xvi*o unũ hanapiũ in quo ponũtr tres bulle

P'p^al libat^r ex^a Thes̃ Dño Archiepõ *Eboȝ* Cancellar̃
Bulle. *Angl* quaȝ una de liberis eleccõnibȝ ⁊ ✝ una ✝ [al] qd omes patroni infra regnū *Angl* possint libe conferre bñficia sua. Et iii. ✝ de ✝ tang̃ *Dñm Regem* ⁊ jus suū.

2 M^d' de "xiiii." obligacõibȝ. in quibȝ certe psone obligarunt se Dño *Michi de la Pole* Militi. Et ponunt^r in hanapio ad tle signū

{Michael de la Pole.}

simplex. 3 i. oblig̃ [simplex] p quam *Johes Pounde* fil *Ade Pounde* de *Kyng̃ sr̃ Hull* tenet^r eid *Mich de la Pole* in ♂ lx. li.

simplex. i. oblig̃ [simplex] p quā *Joh de Middeltoñ* de ead obliga^r eid *Mich* in ♂ DCClxi. li. vi. s̃. viii^d.

i. oblig̃ [simplex] p quā *Joh Janne* Capellan⁹ tenet^r eid *Mich* in ♂ c. li.

i. oblig̃ [statut mcatoȝ] p quā *Joh de Faxflete* de *Bartoñ sr̃ Humbr̃* tenet^r eid in iiii^xx. li.

i. oblig̃ [statut mcatoȝ] p quā *Ricus fil Johis* de *Strettoñ* tenet^r eid *Mich* in ♂ lxvi. li. xiii^s. iiii^d.

Pole. i. oblig̃ [in dupl.] p quā *Ricus Wilkokes* de *Mersh* tenet^r eid *Mich* in ♂ lx. li.

i. oblig̃ [simplex] p quā *Johes de Wyngefeld* Miles tenet^r eid *Mich* in ♂ iiii^ml. li.

i. oblig̃ [in duplo] p quā *Johes Staple* tenet^r eidem *Mich* in ♂ x. li.

i. oblig̃ [simplex] p quā *Joh Boteler* Miles tenet^r eid *Michi* in ♂ c. s̃.

i. oblig̃ [simplex] p quā *Wills de Nessefeld* tenet^r eid *Michi* in ♂ iiii^xx. li.

i. oblig̃ [simplex] p quā *Joh Sherborne* Civis *Londoñ* tenet^r eid *Michi* in ♂ vi. li.

i. oblig̃ [in dupl] p quā *Johes Frere* de *Blakenay* tenetr eid *Michi* in ☌ xl. li.

i. oblig̃ [simplex] p quā *Gerardus de Grymeston̄* Miles tenetr eid *Michi* in ☌ l. li.

i. oblig̃ [simplex] p quā *Rob Butt* ⁊ *Joh de Yngh'm* de *Fryseby* tenēr eid *Mich* in ☌ l. li.

" Md' qd iste obligacōes libat̃ fuer̃ Dn̄o *Walt'o*
" *Malet* Remori. ex pte R̨ in Scacio p execucōe de
" eisd faciend ao R̨ *Ric̃i . xviio.*"

---

17 Ric. II.

1 Md' qd *xiiiio.* die *Ocl* anno r̃ R̨ *Ric̃i sc̃di xviio.* libat̃ fuerūt . iiii ferr̃ equoꝝ cū ||cl ⁊ . ii. cultell exa Scacm in Retam p *Johem* ||*Dautre* salvo custodiend.

Franc̃. 2 Md' qd *xiiiio* die *Novembr̃* anno r̃ R̨ *Ric̃i sc̃di xviio.* libat̃ fuerūt Thes̃ ⁊ Camariis p consiliū quatuor rotuli tangent̃ div's ||tractus int' Regem *Angl* ⁊ adv'sariū suū *Franc̃.*

Et eciam al memorand tangenc̃ Ducem *Aquitann̄* ⁊ ponuntr in quad bagg̃ canab ad tal signū

(p. 32. b.) 3 Memod' . qd *quarto* die *Decembr̃* anno r̃ R̨ . *Ric̃i sc̃di . xviio.* libat̃ fuit qued ||acquitanc̃ Thes̃ ⁊ Camar̃ fact̃ p *Mathēū de Gournay* ⁊ *Pham* uxem ejus ⁊ *Willm Tarent* execut̃ *Robti dAsshton̄* dc̃o Dn̄o Regi de lix. li. vii. s̃. viii. d. ⁊ de quibȝcumqꝫ aliis sūmis accōibȝ seu demand , quas erga dc̃m Dn̄m Reg̃ exig'e seu vendicar̃ pot'int ⁊ ponitr in quadam pixide supa Retam Scacii ad hoc signū

{Gornay.}

4 Memorand̄ qd̄ *xiiii*° die *Januar̄* anno r̄ R̷ *Ric̄i sc̄di xvii*°. lib̄at̄ fuerūt quidam tractatus cū una obligac̄oe sub sigill̄ div̄s Dn̄oꝝ *Angl̄* ꝑ quam obligati fuerūt ad restituend̄ Castrū ꝛ Villam de *Chirburgh̄ Karolo* Regi *Navarr̄* vl̄ ejus ꝑcu^a^ribꝫ ad hoc certe deputat̄ ꝛ cū [una lr̄a ꝑcu^a^ria ꝛ. i. acquietanc̄ ꝛ] al̄ lr̄is dc̄am restōem tangentibꝫ Et ponunt^r^ in quodam hanapio ad tl̄e sign̄

Karolus Rex *Navarr̄*.

5 M^d'^ qd̄ *x*°. die *Januar̄* anno r̄ R̷ *Ric̄i sc̄di xvii*° lib̄at̄ fuit Thes̄ ꝛ Camar̄ quedam confirmac̄o treuḡ ♣ int̄ ♣ ꝑ Regem *Castelle* ꝛ *Legionis* fact̄ int̄ Reges *Angl̄* ꝛ *Francoꝝ* Et ponit^r^ in quad̄ pixide ad tl̄e signū

" *Ispannia.*"

{Angl' ꝛ Franc'.}

6 M^d'^ qd̄ *ix*°. die *Marcii* anno . *xvii*°. R̷ *Ric̄i sc̄di Margareta* que fuit ux̄ ꝛ executrix test̄i ejusd̄m. *Laurencii* relaxavit dc̄o Dn̄o Regi . l. li. vii. s̄. ꝑut patet ꝑ lr̄as acquietanc̄ ip̄ius *M'garete* remanent̄ in quadam pixide in Re^ta^ Sc^a^cii ad tl̄e signū

Laurenc̄ Seybrok'.

{Seybrok.}

---

9 & 18 Ric. II.

1 M^d'^ qd̄ *xi*° die *Augusti* anno *xviii*° Reḡ *Ric̄i sc̄di* lib̄at̄ fuit Thes̄ ꝛ Camar̄ "quedam" indent^r^a cujusdam composic̄ois int̄ Dn̄m Regem ꝛ Abb̄em ꝛ Conventū *Westm̄* ꝑpe *London̄* ꝑ quodam anniv̄sario *Anne* nuꝑ Regine *Angl̄* singul̄ annis celebrand̄ aceciam ꝑ anniv̄sario ꝑdc̄i Dn̄i Reḡ post obitū suū singl̄is

[annis] ꝛ̃ celebranđ remanent̃ in quadam pixide in Reᵗᵃ Scᵃcii ad tale signū

(p. 33.) 2 Memoᵈ' qđ *x*ᵒ. die *Februar̃* anno *nono* Regis *Ric̃i sc̃di* lib̃at̃ fuit extᵃ Thesaurar̃ dc̃i Dñi Regis

Rex *Ermonie.* Regi *Ermonie* unā navem argenteam deaurat̃ ꝛ ∥emełł virtute cujusdam bñs de privat̃ sigillo Thes̃ ꝛ Cam̃ar̃ de Scᵃcio direct̃ filat̃ inꝰ bñia de ꝰmino *Mich̃is* anno dc̃i Dñi nr̃i Regis *nono* supᵃdict̃.

" non trahitʳ."

3 Memoᵈ' qđ *viii*ᵒ die *Octobr̃* anno *xviii*ᵒ Regis *Ric̃i sc̃di Henr̃ Malpas* Cłicus de Cancełł Dñi Regis lib̃avit in Thesaurar̃ dc̃i Dñi Regis unā relaxacõem gen̄alem fc̃am dc̃o Dño nr̃o Regi p *Rog̃m de Boys Thomā Moore* ꝛ alios exec̃ testamenti *Wiłłi de Uffordđ* nup Comitis *Suff'* de om̄ibȝ ꝛ quibuscūqȝ accõibȝ quas ab ip̃o Dño Rege exigᵉre vel vendicare poꝰunt a pⁱncipio mundi usqȝ in diem confeccõis ꝑsent̃ Et ponitʳ in quadᵃm pixide in quadᵃm cista resident̃ supᵃ Reᵗᵃᵐ. ad tale signū

{Ufford.}

4 Memoᵈ' qđ eođ *viii*ᵒ die *Octobr̃* anno *xviii*ᵒ Regis *Ric̃i sc̃di* dc̃us *Henr̃ Malpas* lib̃avit in Thesaurar̃ dc̃i Dñi Reg̃ unā cartam fact̃ Dño *Edwardo* ꝰcio nup Regi *Angł* p *Joh̃em Bykenore de Claveryng̃*

Coldhᵃm. dictū *la Veele* ∥dñm Man̄ii de *Coldhᵃm* in Com̃ *Essex'* consanguineū ꝛ heredem *Rob̃ti de Bykenore de Dertefordđ* in Com̃ *Kanc̃* de Man̄io de *Portebrig̃* cū ptiñ in Com̃ *Kanc̃* Et ponitʳ in quađ pixide in quađ cista resident̃ supᵃ Reᵗᵃᵐ ad tale signū

(p. 33 b.) 5 Md' qd̄ . *xx*°. die *Octobr̃* anno r̃ R̷ *Ric̃i sc̃di xviii*°. lib̃at̃ fuit qued̄ acquietanc̃ fact̃ dc̃o Dño Reg̃ ex p̱te *Thome* Duc̃ *Glouc̃* sigillat̃ sigillo dc̃i Duc̃ de cxxv. li. xvi. d̄. p dc̃m Ducē recept̃ p̱ unam tall̄ levat̃ ad Re^tam^ Sc^a^cii . " *xii*°. die *Febr̃* " anno r̃ R̷ dc̃i Dñi Reg̃ *xii*°. de arrerag̃ Abbatisse de *Cadomo* existent̃ in manibȝ *Joh̃is de* ||*Browych̄* Milit̃ ⁊ ponit^r^ in quad̄ pixid̄ resident̃ ad Re^tam^ Sc^a^cii . salvo custodiend̄ ad tale signū

6 Md' qd̄ *primo* die *Maii* anno r̃ R̷ *Ric̃i sc̃di xviii*° Dñs *Joh̃es Innocent* Cl̃icus lib̃avit in Thesaur̃ quasdam indenturas ac unam cartam ⁊ alia munimenta in quadam pixide posita int᷑ *Rob̃m* Ep̃m *London̄* *Reginaldū* *Breybrok* Cl̃icum *Gerardum* *Braybrok* p̃rem ⁊ ||*Grererdum Braybrok* filiū et *Joh̃em Pauele* " *Ric̃m Stury* Militem " *Lodewycum de Cliffor̄d* Militem *Edwardum Dalyngrege* Militem *Joh̃em Cheyne* Militem *Hugonem de Annesley* *Joh̃em Warrewyk* *Will̃m Brauncepeth̄* *Jacobum Foliambe* ⁊ alios [fc̃a] Mañiū de *Byngham* tangencia ac advocac̃oem eccl̃ie ejusdem Mañii p̱ut in eisdem munimentis in dc̃a pixide positis plenius apparet residente in Re^ta^ Sc^a^cii ad tale signū

Byngham.

London̄.

7 " Md' qd̄ *vii*° die *Februar̃* anno r̃ R̷ *Henr̃* " *quarti primo* virtute b̃ris Dñi Reg̃ huic folio con- " sut̃ om̃es p̃dc̃as indent^r^as cartam ac alia muni- " menta Mañiū de *Byngh^a^m* in Com̃ *Not̃* ac advo- " cac̃oem eccl̃ie ejusdem Mañii tangenc̃ delib̃avimꝰ " *Thome de Rempston̄* Chr p manus *Ric̃i Wakefeld̄* " Cl̃ici."

(In sched p.33.) 8 *Henricus* Dei gr̃a Rex *Angł* ⁊ *Franc̃* ⁊ Dñs *Hibñ* Thes̃ ⁊ Camar̃ suis saltm. Cum Dñs *R'* nup Rex *Angł sc̃dus* post conquestum p finem in Cur̃ nr̃a levatum concesserit *Thome de Rempstoñ* Chivaler qđ Mañiũ de *Clipstoñ othe Hitt* juxta *Plumptre* cum ptiñ triginta ⁊ duo mesuagia triginta ⁊ tres virgate t̃re quinquaginta acre prati ⁊ centum solidate redditus cum ptiñ in *Clipstoñ othe Hitt* juxta *Plumptre Codegrave Kynalton Outhorp̃* ⁊ *Neutoñ* que *Isabella* que fuit ux̃ *Witti de Byngham* tenet ad vitam suam de hereditate p̃dc̃i nup Regis ac Mañiũ de *Byngham* cum ptiñ quod *Johanna* que fuit ux̃ *Johis Pauely* Chivaler tenet ad vitam suam de hereditate ejusdem nup Regis ⁊ quod quidem Mañiũ de *Byngham* post mortem ip̃ius *Johanne* ad *Wittm de Arundell* ⁊ *Agnetem* uxem ejus si iidem *Witts* ⁊ *Agnes* p̃dc̃am *Johannam* supvix̃int remanere debet . tenenđ ad vitam eoꝝdem *Witti* ⁊ *Agnetis*. reṽsione inde ac dc̃oꝝ Mañii de *Clipstoñ othe Hitt* juxta *Plumptre* ⁊ teñ ad p̃dc̃m nup Regem ⁊ heredes suos spectante.post mortem eoꝝdem *Isabelle Johanne Witti* ⁊ *Agnetis* p̃dc̃o *Thome* ⁊ heredibꝫ suis remaneant . Jamqꝫ p̃fatus *Thomas* nob supplicaṽit ut cum qᵃmplura carte scripta ⁊ alia munimenta mañia ⁊ teñ p̃dc̃a tangencia in Thesaurar̃ nr̃a sub custodia vr̃a existant , Velimꝰ cartas scripta ac alia munimenta p̃dc̃a sibi delibari jubere. Nos supplicac̃oi p̃dc̃e annuentes de avisamento Consilii nr̃i Vobis mandamꝰ qđ scrutatis cartis scriptis ⁊ aliis munimentis p̃dc̃is eadem cartas scripta ⁊ alia munimenta p̃fato *Thome* seu ejus in hac parte attornato delibetis T. me ip̃o apud *Westm̃ primo* die *Februar̃* anno r̃ ñ *primo*.

P. Consilium. *Byllyngford.*

(p. 33 b.) "Cantia" *Lincolñ.*

9 Md' qđ *xiii°* die *Maii* anno r̃ ℞ *Ric̃i sc̃di xviii°* libat̃ fuit p quenđ vallectum Dñi *le Warre* ||quadam carta p quam Abbas ⁊ Conventus de *Valle Dei* in Com̃ *Lincolñ* obligant^r Dño Regi de inveniendo quendam capellanũ secularem impp̃m fundatum p Dñm *le Warre* in eccl̃ia pochiali de *Edenham* sub ista condic̃one qđ si defec̃int in inveniendo dc̃m capellanũ p duodecim septimanas qđ tunc teneant^r solvere Dño Regi *Angl̃* ⁊ her̃ suis centum solidos tociens quociens, remanens in quadam pixide in Re^ta Sc^acii ad tale signũ.

{Lincoln.}

(p. 34.) 10 Md' qđ *xxviii°* die *Augusti* anno r̃ ℞ *Ric̃i sc̃di xviii°* Dñs *Johes Innocent* Cl̃icus libavit in Thesaur̃ alt̃am ptem cujusdam indent^re fc̃e int̃ Dñm Regẽ ex una pte ⁊ Magr̃m *Henr̃ Yevele* ⁊ *Stephm Lote* latomos ex alt̃a pte p una tumba marmorea facienđ ⁊ repanđ p *Anna* nup Regina *Angl̃* ⁊ p dc̃o Dño Rege ⁊ It̃m p̃dc̃us *Johes* libavit *eodem die* in p̃dc̃am Thes̃ alt̃am ptem cujusdam indent^re fc̃e int̃ dc̃m *Dñm Regem* ex una pte ⁊ *Nichm Broker* ⁊ *Galfr̃m Prest* copsmythes de *Londoñ* ad faciēđ duas ymagines ad similitudines Reg̃ ⁊ Regine de cupro ⁊ latoñ deaurat̃ sup dc̃am tumbam ||marmoriã cũ aliis clausulis infra dc̃am indent^ram cont̃ ⁊ It̃m cont̃ i. patroñ ad similitudĩes Regis ⁊ Re~n~^e sub q^a forma iidem tenent^r dc̃m opus pfic̃e Et ponunt^r in quodam hanapio resident̃ in Re^ta Sc^acii salvo custodienđ ad tale signũ

11 Md' qđ *xxviii°* die *Augusti* anno r̃ R̷ *Ric̃i sc̃di xviii°* dc̃us *Joħes Innocent* liƀavit unam cartam ꝑ quā Magr̃ ⁊ Capeƚƚi *Novi Collegii* sive *Cantarie* in cimit̓io juxᵃ eccƚiam cathedralē *Menevens̃* obligantʳ ad unū obitū facienđ ꝑ quoƚt a° ꝑ *Anna* nuꝑ Reⁿᵃ *Angƚ* ⁊ ꝑ Dñо nr̃o Rege cū ab * luce migᵃverit ⁊ ponitʳ in quođ hanaꝑio de virgis residenť in Reᵗᵃ Scᵃcii salvo custodienđ ad tale signū

12 Md' qđ *xxviii°* die *Augusti* a° r̃ R̷ *Ric̃i sc̃đi xviii°* dc̃us Dñs *Joħes Innocent* liƀavit unam lr̃am obligator̃ cū una defesancia fc̃am ꝑ *Adam Fᵃunceys* Militē ⁊ *Joħem Parker* Civem *Londoñ* ꝑ ꝯta sūma in qua *Joħes Slegħ* Dño Regi tenetʳ ꝑ offic̃o pinꝯne Reg̃ ⁊ ponitʳ in quođ hanaꝑio de virgis residenť in Reᵗᵃ Scᵃcii salvo custodienđ ad tale signū

13 Md' qđ *xxviii°* die *Augusti anno supᵃdc̃o* dc̃us Dñs *Joħes Innocent* liƀavit alt̓am ꝑtem cujusdam indentʳe fc̃e int̓ J. Eꝑm *Saꝫ* Thes̃ *Angƚ* ex una ꝑte ⁊ Aƀƀem ⁊ Conventum *Sc̃i Augustini Cantuar̃* ex alt̓a ꝑte de vendic̃oe uniꝰ bosci voc̃ *Hobbesgrove* ad opus Reg̃ ⁊ ponitʳ in quadam [pixide] ✠hanaꝑio de virgis ✠ residenť in Reᵗᵃ Scᵃcii salvo custodienđ ad tale signū.

14 Md' qđ ꝓdc̃o *xxviii°* die *Aug̃ anno supᵃdc̃o* dc̃us *Joħes Innocent* liƀavit alt̓am ꝑtem uniꝰ carte indentate ꝑ quam Dñs nr̃ Rex *Ric̃us* concessit Aƀƀi

⁊ Conventui *Westm̃* cc li p annū p uno anniv̾saȓ quolt anno tenendo p aĩa *Anne* nup Re[ne] *Angl* ⁊ p dc̃o Dñ̃o Rege cum ab hac luce mig[a]v̾it cū al condic̃oib₃ in eadem carta contenť ⁊ ponit[r] in quodam hanapio ad tale signū

(p. 34 b.) 19 Ric. II.

1 Me[d'] qđ *ultimo die Februaȓ* anno ȓ R̷ *Ric̃i sc̃di xix* Magist̾ *Radulphus Selby* Clic̾ libavit in Thesauraȓ Regis unū rotulū tria instȓ ⁊ alia munim̃t tang̃ Ducať *Aquit* Et ponunt[r] in quadā baga in una cisť sup[a] Recepť ad tale signū.

{Guyen.}

2 Me[d'] qđ *xii* die *Marcii* anno regni Reg̃ *Ric̃i sc̃di xix. Rog̃us Walden̄* Thes̃ *Angl* libavit in Thesauȓ unū cofphinū conť oblig̃ de div̾s̃ sūmis in quib₃

J. Bloys. *Johes Bloys* tenebat[r] *Robto de Veer* nup Duci *H'bñ* in quib₃ modo tenet[r] Dñ̃o Regi p̾dicť rõne forisfc̄uȓ *Robti* Ducis p̾dicť ⁊ ponit[r] in quadam cista magna infra Thesauȓ p̾dicť.

3 M[d'] qđ *die* ⁊ *anno p̾dc̃is Blanchia* Dña de

B. Dña de Ponyng̃. *Ponynges* inpignoravit p̾dc̃o *Dño Regi* in dc̃a Thesauȓ ii. ciph auri in ii. cophiñ de coreo p xl. li. p ip̃am recepť. *xiiii.* die *Dec̃.*

4 Me[d'] qđ *xix* die *April* anno ȓ R̷ *Ric̃i sc̃di xix Rogerus Walden̄* Thes̃ *Angl* libavit in Thesauȓ duas

Comes Preguort. lr̃as missas † missas dc̃o Dñ̃o Regi p Comitē de

Preguort Et ponūt^r in quodam pixide cum tali intitulacōne in una cista sup̃ Recept̃ Sc^acii

"nō trahit^r"

5 M^d' qđ. *xxix.* die *Julii* anno *xix^o.* r̃ R̷ *Rīci scdi* libat̃ fuit *Rogo Walden̄* Thes̃ *Angl̃* quoddam sigillū sub isto titlo

Magnū Sigillū Cancellar̃.

Magnu' Sigillu' Edwardi t'cii
cu' stilo Franc' & Angl' &
cu' armis Franc' et Angl'.

Quod quidem sigillū Dn̄s Rex libar̃ manđ ext^a Thes̃ ad carianđ secū v̄sus ptes *Cales̃.*

---

20 Ric. II.

1 Sont delivez hors de la Tresorie a S^r "*Guy Mone*" le *tiers* jo^r *dAust* lan *xxme.* un *cerkil de la scđe corone* garnesse od peirs & pee

Itm live mesme le jo^r a dit Sr *Guy* le *Spey* de *Spayne* od le seynt^re de le dit *Spey* garnesse od peirs & pee.

2 M^d' qđ *ix* die *Maii* anno Reg̃ nunc *xx^o* libata fuer̃ tria bri̅a de magno sigillo Regis p Dm̄ Thes̃ unū p *Thoma Oldecastell* de essendo coram Consilio aliud p *Johe* ||*Manus* de essendo silit coram Consilio & tciū p *Thoma Walwen̄* de essendo & c̄ *Jacobo Assh.*

(p. 35.) 3 M^d' qđ *x.* die *Junii* videlt in festo *Pentecost̃* a^o Regis *Rīci scdi xx^o Corona* dc̄i Dn̄i R̷ de *Ispania* libat̃ fuit p *Rogerum Walden̄* Thes̃ R̷ & ejus Camar̃ *Guidoni Mone* Custodi privati sigilli & jocaliū pdc̄i Dn̄i R̷ de pcepto Dn̄i Regis pdc̄i ext^a Thes̃ pdc̄am.

---

21 & 22 Ric. II. 1 Hen. IV. &c.

1 Med' qđ *xx* die *Maii* anno Reḡ *Riĉi sc̄di xx°* *p^i mo Guido Mone* Ep̄us *Menev'* Theš *Angl̄* lib̄avit unā indent^r am int̄ dc̄m *Guidonē* Theš ⁊ *Joh̄em de* Clyntoñ. *Clyntoñ* Ch̄r fc̄am de expenš fc̄is p̄ p̄dc̄m *Joh̄em* de tempe quo fuit custos Castri de *Warrewyk'* que indent^r a remanet in quođ cophino in q^a dā cista sup^a Receptā Sc^a cii ad tale signū

2 Med' qđ *die Marł vii* die *Juñ* anno r̄ R̄ *Riĉi sc̄di xxi°* lib̄at̄ fuit Theš ⁊ "———" Camar̄ una geñalis acquietanc̄ Duc̄ *Britanñ* p̄ quā idē Dux remisit ⁊ relaxavit dc̄o Dño Regi om̄imođ acc̄oes quas idem Dux h̄et h̄uit sive h̄ere pot̄it de Com̄ *Richemonđ* a p^i ncipio mundi usq; diē *xxiii* die *April̄ anno ejusd̄m* Dñi Reḡ *xxi°* que acquietancia sive relaxac̄o remanet in quadā cista cū trib; seruř. sup^a Re^tā in quadā pixide ad tl̄e signū

3 Med' qđ *p^i mo* die *Marc̄* anno *xxii°* sex indent^r e ♣ lib̄ant^r ♣ una lr̄a patens sup̄ acceptac̄oe treuga₰ cū copia cuj⁹dā appunctuac̄ōis in p̄camino lib̄ant^r in Theš Reḡ p̄ m⁹ *Joh̄is Bussy* ⁊ *Laur̄ Drwe* ⁊ mittunt^r in uno hanap̄io ad tale signū

{Scocia.}

4 Med' qđ *ix°* die *Ap^i l̄* anno *xxii°* Reḡ nūc p̄dc̄e sex indent^r e una lr̄a patens sup̄ acceptac̄oe treuga₰ " cū copia cujusdā appunctuac̄ in p̄cameno [una cū

" uno hanapio] libant^r ext^a Thes Dnis de Consilio.
" p m^9 *Johis Innocent*" Postea restituunt^r.

5 ♣ "Inde lib^r Epo *Bathe quarto* die *Marcii* anno " *sexto* Reg *H. quarti* duas indenturas ⁊ unā ap- " punctu . . . put p3 p quand indent^ram sigill sigillo " dci Epi ♣ q3 restituunt^r v3 *p^imo* die *Maii* . . . . " . . . . ."

6 ♣ " Inde lib *Robto Umfravill* unā indent^ram " sigill cū iiii^or sigill p bre de p^iv sig huic fol " consut ♣ quia restituit^r *vii* die *Junii* anno *x^o* p " man^9 *Willi Massy*."

7 *Henri* par la grace de Dieu Roy *d Engleterre* ⁊ de *France* ⁊ Seignur *d Irland* as Tresourer ⁊ Chamblains de nre Eschequier saluz. Por ce q nous avons . . . . ⁊ assignez noz chs ⁊ foiaux Chivalers *Rauf de Euere Richard* "*Redmayn*" *Robt Umfravill* ⁊ *Johan de Mitford* eux "quatre" ou trois de eux noz cōmys . . . . pur treter ovesq3 certains commys ⁊ deputez pur la ptie *d Escoce* sur certaines trieues pticulers ou genalx. selonc ce q nous lour en avons done . . . . Si volons de l assent de nre Counsail ⁊ vous mandons. q les trieues originalx parentre nre tsch S^r ⁊ pe qi Dieux "assoill" ⁊ certains autres q . . . . de nre tresch Seignur ⁊ cousin le Roy *Richard* qi Dieux pdoint. d une pt. et certains cōmissairs pur la ptie *d Escoce* d autre pt. prises . . . . le *seszisme* jour de *Marz* l an de grace *mill troiscens quatrevyntz dys* ⁊ *sept*. facez liv^er p endenture ales s^9ditz noz commys ⁊ deputez . . . . . de l avantdit *Rob Umfravill*. au fin q par l inspection de mesmes les trieues. puissent yceux noz cōmys ⁊ deputez mieux lour . . . . . . traitie

s⁹dit. Doñ souz nr̃e prive seal a *Westm̃* le *tierz* jour de *May*. I an de nr̃e regne *disme*.

(p. 35.) Scocia.

8 Med' qđ *xviii* die *Novembr̃* anno r̃ ℞ *Henr̃ primo Laur̃ Drwe* libavit in Thes̃ Reg̃ quatuor cōmissiones quaꝝ una de pace int̃ Regē *Angl* ⁊ Regē *Scotoꝝ* tractanđ alia de treug̃ int̃ eosđm ⁊ due de attemptat̃ emendanđ siml̃ cū una cōmissione ejusđm Reg̃ *Scotoꝝ David* Duc̃ *Rothesaye* fact̃ una cū quadā instruccōe sigillat̃ cū magno sig̃ pⁱvato sigill ⁊ signet̃ Reg̃ *Ric̃i* ⁊ ponūtʳ in unō hanapio ad tle signū

9 ♣ Inde lib Ep̃o *Bathoñ quarto* die *Martii* anno *vi*ᵗᵒ Reg̃ *Henr̃ quarł* dict̃ cōmissiones ♣

"Quia restituuntʳ."

"‖Sex p̃dc̃a ‖instrum̃ta libātʳ p dc̃m Ep̃m Magr̃o *Joh̃i Shepey* ⁊ una instruccio put p indenturam dc̃o Ep̃o supius allegatam."

"Itm p̃dc̃us *Laur̃* restituit in Thes̃ Reg̃ *p̃dc̃is die* ⁊ *anno* sex indentʳas ⁊ unū appūtuamentū sub magno sigillo pⁱvat̃ sig̃ ⁊ signet̃ [sigillat̃] *Ric̃i* nup Reg̃ *Angl* ⁊ ponūtʳ in eođm hanapio."

"Postea t̃cio die *Decembr̃* anno regni Reg̃ *Henr̃ quarti primo Joh̃es Innocent* libavit *Robto Fry* Clico Consilii Reg̃ p̃dc̃m hanapiū cont̃ p̃dc̃as sex indentʳas ⁊ unū appunctuamentū ⁊ p̃dc̃as quatuor cōmissiones ⁊ om̃ia alia munimenta tangenc̃ treug̃ int̃ *Ric̃m* nup Regē *Angl* ⁊ Regē *Scocie*."

(p. 35 b.)

Arundell.

10 Med' qđ die *Sabbi xxvi* die *Januar̃* anno regni Regis *Ric̃i sc̃di* post conq̃ *vicesimo primo* libat̃ fuer̃

in Thes̃ due indenture una int̃ *Ric̃m* nup̱ Comitem *Arundell̃* et *Ric̃m Talbot* Chr̃ de m^l' ⁊ DC. li. alt̃a int̃ eundm̃ nup̱ Comitẽ ⁊ *Thomam Ponynges* S^r de *Seint John̄* ⁊ alios de iiii^c. li. Itm̃ vii lr̃e obligatoȓ fc̃e eidẽ nup̱ Comiti una p̱ *Ric̃m Talbot* Chr̃ ⁊ al̃ de cc li. Itm̃ alia p̱ *Thomam de Ponynges* Chr̃ ⁊ al̃ de. lx. li. Itm̃ t̃cia p̱ *Thomam Ponynges* Chr̃ ⁊ al̃ de iiii^c. li. It̃ quarta p̱ *Willm̃ d Arundell̃* Chr̃ de iiii^xx. li. Itm̃ quinta p̱ *Robm̃ Seman de Duryngton̄* de xx. li.

11 Itm̃ vi p̱ *Ric̃m Talbot* Chr̃ de . m^l DC. li. It̃ vii p̱ *Johem̃ Harpeden̄* Chr̃ de cc. li. ⁊ ponunt^r in quadã pixide in cista sup^a Recept̃ . cũ trib3 seruris . ad tale signũ

" Virtute bȓis sub magno sigillo Dñi Regis de " dat̃ *xvi*^o die *Febȓ* a^o *ix*^o ȓ R̸ *Henȓ q^arti* Thes̃ " ⁊ Camaȓ direct̃ libat̃ fuit [ext^a Thes̃ p̃dc̃am] in " Cancellaȓ ip̃i^9 Dñi Reg̃ ⁊ ibm̃ libat̃ Custodi " Rotuloꝝ in Cancellaȓ p̃dc̃a p̱ m^9 *Simonis* ||*Gau-* " *sted̃* unam p^ixidem continent̃ p̃dc̃as indent^ras ⁊ " obligac̃oes sup^adc̃as *xvii*^o die *Febȓ* ⁊ *a*^o *sup^adc̃o.*"

12 Me^d' qd̃ *viii* die *Junii* anno regni Regis *Ric̃i sc̃di* post conq̃ *vicesimo primo* libata fuit Thes̃ ⁊ Camaȓ quedam cart̃ sigillis Abbis ⁊ Conṽ mon̄ *B'e Marie de Graciis* jux^a *Turrim London̄* sigillata p̱ quam p̃dc̃i Abbas ⁊ Conṽ obligant^r ad celeb^and̃ annuatim anniṽsaȓ grõse memorie Dñe *Anne* nup̱ Regine *Angl* necnon anniṽsaȓ Dñi nȓi Regis nunc ✠ ac ✠ post ejus obitũ ac *Simonis Burley Jacobi Berners* ⁊ *Johis Salesbury* Militũ in eccl̃ia Abbie

p̃dc̃e Et ponit[r] in cista sup[a] Receptā Sc[a]cii in quadā pixide cū tali signo

13 Med' qđ una relaxacio fc̃a p̱ *Wilłm Vannere* de *Londoñ* de Manlio de *Northalle* ponit[r] in cista cū iii ceruſ̃ sup[a] Receptam in quadam pixide.

14 Med' qđ testamentū Dñi nr̃i Regis *Ric̃i scđi* ponit[r] in quodam hanap̱io cū quadā cedula . ⁊ tali signo

⁊ ponit[r] in cista [" grossa ferro ligata"] ♣ sup[a] Receptā cū trib3 ceruſ̃ ♣ infra Thesauraſ̃ in Abbia *Westm̃.*

" iii m[l] " m[a]rc3 " *Constan-* " *tinople.*"

15 ♣ Med' qđ unū instr̃m ⁊ una endent[r]a fact̃. Dño nr̃o Regi *Ric̃o* p̱ quatuor M'catores de *Janua* . de trib3 milib3 marcaȝ st̃lingoȝ bone monete *Angł* solvenđ Imp̱atori *Constantinopolitane* Ponunt[r] in quodā cophino ⁊ ponunt[r] in cista sup[a] Receptā ad tale signū ♣

 {**Lopham.**}

" q̧ ext[a]."

" Et postea *xiiii* die *Marc̃* anno *sc̃do* Reg̃ " *Henr̃ quarł* . libāt[r] *Joh̃i Norbury* Thes̃ *Angł* dc̃m " instr̃m ⁊ indent[r]a apud *Westm̃* ♣ in cophino ♣ una " cū cophino."

Homag̃ Archiep̃i *Coloneñ.*

16 Med' *xxvi.* die *Octobr̃* anno *xxi*[o] Reg̃ *Ric̃i sc̃di* ‖libata fuerunt sex lr̃e patent̃ " de homag̃ " Archiep̃i *Colonieñ* ‖*Wynanđ* de ‖*Holtzhein* Milit̃ Comit̃ de ‖*Muerse* ⁊ *Hug̃ de Heruorst* ‖p̱thonotoř Pape in

Thes̃ Dñi Reg̃ ꝑ *Thom̃ Stanley* Et "ponūtʳ in" quodā cophino ⁊ ponuntʳ in cista supᵃ Retᵃ "Principatus *Watt*" ad tale signū

(p. 36.) 17 Medʼ qđ *xxvi* die *Octobr̃* anno *xxi*° R̷ *Ric̃i sc̃di* lib̃at fuer̃ in Thes̃ Reg̃ ꝑ *Thom̃ Stanley* Custodē Rot̃loꝝ Cancell̃ Reg̃. diu̾se lr̃e tangent̃ tᵃctat̃ h̃itū ꝑ *Thom̃* Ep̃m *Karl̃ Edward̃* Comit̃ *Rotel̃* ⁊ *Thom̃*
Ruptus *Not̃* [nunc̃ Dñi Reg̃ miss̃ ad tractand̃] cum *Rupto*
Comes Palatin⁹ Dux Juniori Comite Palatino *Reni* ⁊ *Bavarie* Duce ⁊ al̃
Bavar̃ ⁊ al̃. lr̃e homag̃ ejusđm *Rupti* [al̃ lr̃a] Dñi *Rupti* señ p̃ris sui *Joh̃is Hirtz Horñ* Milit̃. *Nich̃i Burgman* de ‖*Congov̾*. *Friderici de* ‖*Mit*ᵃ ‖*Thalpini Knebill̃* Milit̃. *Joh̃is* ‖Cam̾er̃ de *Dalburgh̃* ⁊ ponūtʳ in cophino. ⁊ ponūtʳ in cista supᵃ Retᵃ ad tl̃e signū "in quodā "cophino"

18 Medʼ qđ die *Dñica xvi* die *Apˡl̃* anno *xxii*° due pixides cont̃ lr̃as indentʳas ⁊ al̃ muniment̃ tangenc̃
Hib̃nia. t̾re *Hib̃nie* submissiones ꝑlat̃ ⁊ al̃ de t̾ra *Hib̃ñ* ad ‖nu̾ū lxx. lib̃at fuer̃ [*Willo Scrop̃*] Thes̃ *Angl̃* ꝑ m⁹ *Joh̃is Innocent* extᵃ Thesaur̃.

---

1 Hen. IV.

1 Medʼ qđ *xx* die *Octobr̃* anno *pⁱmo* Reg̃ *Henr̃ quarti pⁱmo*. unū *Espiceplate* empt̃ apud *Parys* fuit lib̃at *Joh̃i Elwet* Custodi jocaliū Reg̃.

2 Mᵈʼ qđ una indentʳa fc̃a apᵈ ‖*Haudenstauk' xiiii.* die *Maii* a° Dñi *mˡ*. *ccc° nonagesimo nono*. int̾ Dñm *Dđ*. pⁱmogenitū Reg̃ *Scottoꝝ* et Ducem *Albemarlie*

ꝰ al ꝑ pte Reḡ *Angł Ric̃i scđi* de treugis ꝓgat̃ intͣ dc̃a duo regna ponitʳ in cista, cū iii. ceruř in Recepta comp̃. in quadā ♣ cophino . ⚜ pixide ad tale signū

{**Angl' & Scocia.**}

♣ " Et liƀ Ep̃o *Bathoñ quarto* die *Marcii* anno *sexto* " Reḡ *Henř*. ꝓut pȝ p quanđ indentuř dc̃i Ep̃i sigillo " s̃ signat̃ " ⚘ " quia restitʳ *pͥmo* die *Maii eođm anno*."

3 Medᵈ' qđ *Johes Northbury* Thes̃ *Angł* liƀavit in Thes̃ Reḡ apud *Westm̃ xxviii.* die *Novembř* anno *Henř* [Reḡ] *quarti primo* unū trussyng coffre in quo continebantʳ c̃ta munimenta tangenc̃ maritaḡ *Ric̃i* [nuꝑ] Reḡ *Angł* ꝰ *Isabelle* filie *Karoli* Reḡ *Franc̃*. ꝰ alia munimenta tangenc̃ treugas intͣ eosđm Reges ꝰ. ponitʳ in quadā cista cū tribȝ ceruris in qua ponitʳ membrana ad tłe signū ☞

" Liƀantʳ *xx°* die *Februař* Dñis de Consilio Reḡ " anno *pͥmo* Reḡ *H. ✝pͥmi.*"

" Postea restituuntʳ *xxi.* die *Febř* anno *pͥmo* Reḡ. " *H. quarti.*"

" Et postea *xxiiii*ᵗᵒ die *Maii eodē a°* liƀantʳ eisdē " Dñis de Consilio ꝑ manꝰ *Johis Oudeby* uniꝰ Cam̃ař " Eodē die liƀabantʳ in Thes̃ ubi supᵃ."

Coket. 4 Medᵈ' qđ sigillū vocat̃ *le Coket* liƀat̃ in Thes̃ ꝑ *Thomā* ‖*Bedumeny* liƀatʳ. *xi.* die *Decembř Johi Hertham* Contᵃrotulatori custume in portu Ville *Bristołł* ꝑ manꝰ *Johis But* Cłici ejusdē *Johis.*

5 Medᵈ' qđ sigillū vocat̃ *le Coket* liƀat̃ fueř in Thes̃

Coket. Reḡ ꝑ *Johem Chaddesley* Collect̃ custume ꝰ subs̃ Reḡ in portu Ville de *Melcombe*. Et postea . *vi.* die

Febr̃ anno r̃ R̷ *Henr̃ primo* lib̃ata fuerũt p̃dc̃a sigilla "*Joh̃i Hoke*" Custm̃ in portu de *Melcombe* p manus *Thome Barbo*r ꝯvient̃ ejusdẽ *Joh̃is Hoke.*

(p. 36 b.) 6 Med' qđ confirmacio treugaꝝ sub sigillo Regis *Franc̃* consign̄ tempore Regis *Henr̃ quarti* post conq̃ lib̃atr Dñis de Consilio *xxiii* die *Maii* a° *p*i*mo* dc̃i Reg̃ *Henr̃* in quadã pva pixide. Et px̃ die immediate seqñ lib̃abatr in Thes̃ eadem confirmacio et ponitr infa cistam supa Scacm̃ comp̃tor̃ ad hoc sign̄ {**Treuga Franc'.**}

Franc̃.

✝ "Lib̃atr Ep̃o *Roffeñ* in Cam̃a Stellat̃ *vi.* die "*Mart̃ quarto* die *Julii* a° t̃cio Reg̃ *Henr̃ q*a*rti.*" ✝

7 Med' qđ *Witt̃s Lescrop̃* Thes̃ *Angl̃* libavit in Thes̃ Reg̃ ["qᵬ rest̃. *quarto* die *Maii* anno r̃ R̷ *Ric̃i xx*"] c̃tas cartas ꝛ indentras p quas Dñs *R.* nup Rex *Angl̃* dedit c̃ta maṇ̃ia t̃ras ꝛ teñ in diṽsis Com̃ Monast̃io *Westm̃* p anniṽsar̃ ejusđm Reg̃ h̃endo singl̃is annis Et ponũtr in ‖quodã pixide ad tl̃e signũ

{**Abbas Westm' Anniv'sar' Reg' Ric'i.**}

8 Med' qđ *viii.* die *Junii* anno r̃ R̷ *Henr̃ p*i*mo*. confirmac̃o treugaꝝ int̃ *Henr̃* Regẽ nr̃m *Angl̃* ꝛ Regẽ *Franc̃* lib̃ata fuit [*Joh̃i Scarle*] Dñi Cancellar̃ *Angl̃* p manus *Ph̃i Burtoñ* Cl̃ici exta Thesaur̃ Reg̃. ✝ Que quiđm confirmac̃o restituitr in Thes̃ R̷ p mañ *Thome Dunolm̃.* Ep̃i *p*i*mo* die *Julii* anno *viii*° Reg̃ *Henr̃ q*a*rti* Et ponitr in quodam hanapio * hoc signo

{**Confirmac'o treugar' Francie.**}

Treuge int̃ *R'* Regē *Angt̃* ꝛ Regē *Francͥ.*

9 Itm̃ *eisdm̃ die* ꝛ *anno* treuge int̃ Dñm *Ricm̃* nup Regē *Angt̃* ꝛ Regē *Francͥ* capte sub sigillo [dc̃i] Reg̃ *Francͥ* signat̃ libate fuerunt eidm̃ Cancellar̃ p manus dc̃i *Phi Burton̄.* ♆

"q̃ inferius."

10 ♆ Med' qd̃ div̾sa carte ꝛ munimenta tangencia maritagiū *Rici* nup Regis *Angt̃* ꝛ *Isabelle* fil̃ Regis *Francͥ* ꝛ pcelle tractat⁹ pacis int̃ p̾dc̄os Reges ponūtʳ in cista supᵃ Scᵃcii Comp̃ . ad hoc signū ♆

{Rutland' Notyngham Scrop'.}

11 Med' qd̃ div̾sa munimenta tangenc̃ c̾tas convencōes matⁱmonii int̃ *Fil̃ Comil̃ Marescall̃* ꝛ *Nottyngh̃* ꝛ *Filiam Comil̃ Huntyngdon̄* libat̃ fuerunt in Thesaur̃ Reg̃ *xii* die *Julii* anno r̃ Ꝝ *Henr̃ quarti primo* ꝛ poʳ in cista cū trib3 cerur̃ ad tle signū

{Marescall' ꝛ Huntyngd'.}

Scocia.

12 Med' qd̃ die *Jovis xv*° die *Julii* a° r̃ Ꝝ *Henr̃ quarti pⁱmo* libat̃ fuer̃ exᵃ Thes̃ *Johi Norbury* Thes̃ *Angt̃* ad deferend̃ secū ꝛ monstrand̃ dc̄o Dño Regi quedā pva cista depicta cū div̾sis arm̃ *Angt̃* ꝛ *Scocie* cū div̾s̃ cart̃ ꝛ munimen̄t tangent̃ regnū *Scoc̃* . cū uno pvo qᵃt̾no pgam̃ cont̃ xviii. fol̃ script̃ . in quib3 continentʳ div̾sa memorand̃ tangent̃ homagiū fc̄m div̾s̃ Regib3 *Angt̃* p div̾sos Reges *Scottoꝝ.*

"Dc̄a xviii fol̃ fuer̃ capti exᵃ ♆ quandā ♆ quendā "magnū librū cū div̾s̃ med̃ jac̃ in magna cista "infᵃ Receptᵐ [camar̃]."

13 "Itm̃ *die Sabbi xvii.* die *Julii* . *px' seqn̄* libat̃ "fuer̃ extᵃ Thes̃ infra *Turrim London̄* una cista "cont̃ div̾sa munimenta tangenc̃ subjeccōem Reg̃

" *Scottoꝝ* cū aƚ međ ꝛ unam bag̃ cū diꝰsis cronic̃ ꝛ " liƀat̃ *Joħ Norbury* Thes̃ *Angƚ* defer̃ Reg̃ *Henr̃* " in viagio suo existeñ ꝰsus *Scotos* ♣de♣ divina gr̃a " devincendos."

(p. 37.) 2 Hen. IV.

1 Med' qđ *viii* die *Octobr̃* anno *sc̃do* Reg̃ *Henr̃ quarti* lr̃a confirmac̃ treugaꝝ ꝑ parte *Franc̃* liƀat̃ fuit in Thes̃ Reg̃ ꝑ manus *Joħis Innocent* Et ponitʳ [in quadā pixide] in cista cū tribꝫ seruř ad tƚe signū

" ———————— "

2 ♣ Med' qđ acquietancia Impatoris de *Constantinoble* de mˡ mˡ mˡ marc̃ sibi soluť in recompensac̃oem tante sūme sibi concesse ꝑ Dñm *Ric̃m* nuꝑ Regem *Angƚ* ꝛ *Reginaldo Griƚƚ* M'catori de *Janua*. liƀat̃ ponitʳ in quodam cophino in cista cū tribꝫ ceruris supᵃ Scᵃcm Comp̃ ad tale signū ♣

" ———————— " " nō trahitʳ."

3 Med' qđ una indentʳa fc̃a intꝰ Thes̃ ꝛ Cam̃ar̃ Dñi Reg̃ ꝛ *Thomam Erpyngham* Cħr de liƀac̃oe triū cistaꝝ cū carť ꝛ aƚ muniment̃ concernentibꝫ her̃ ꝛ ꝰras ꝛ teñ que fuer̃ *Joħis de Monte Acuto* nuꝑ Com̃ *Saꝝ*. ponitʳ ī ꝑva viriđ cista cū ‖foƚ ‖conꝰvanđ. Comes *Saꝝ*.

4 Med' qđ quoddā warant̃ de pⁱvato sigillo *J. Norbury* Thes̃ ꝛ Cam̃ar̃ direct̃ de assignac̃oe facienđ Justic̃ S'jeant̃ Baroñ ꝛ Cam̃ar̃ ꝛ aliis ꝰtis ꝑsonis in dc̃o waranto specificat̃. de iiii ᵐˡ' ix ᶜ xlviii ƚi. vi. s̃. x. đ oƀ. de xvᵃ ꝛ xᵃ. Dño Regi anno

scđo conc̃. q^a^m sūmā dc̃e ꝑsone ꝓstiterunt Regi ⁊ hoc [waranť] libať fuit Thes̃ ⁊ Camar̃ [*xvi.* die *Maii* anno *sc̃do* Reg̃ *Henr̃ quarti*] ⁊ ponitʳ in quodā cophino ad tle signū

5 Med' qđ Dñs *Walťus* Dei gr̃a Ep̃us *Dunolm̃* libavit Thes̃ ⁊ Camar̃ de Sc^a^cio Reg̃ [*xviii.* die *Aug̃* anno *sc̃do* Reg̃ *Henr̃ quarť*] septē lr̃as Reg̃ *Gallici* ac *Isabelle* Regine *Angl* necnon *Biturie Burgundie Aurilianens̃* ⁊ *Bourbonie* Ducū sigillis sigillať quaꝝ *pⁱma* erat acquietancia ꝓfať Reg̃ suꝑ restitucõe dc̃e Regine jocaliū ⁊ bonoꝝ suoꝝ *secunda* erat licencia ⁊ auctoritas dc̃i Reg̃ *Gallici* dc̃e Regine attⁱbuta ad quietanđ Dñm nr̃m Regē ⁊ alios ꝑceres suꝑ restitucõe sua *ťcia* est acquietancia ip̃ius Regine suꝑ restitucõe ꝓdc̃a ac instr̃m puᶜᵃ continens ‖juriū ip̃ius Regine *quarta* erat Ducis *Biturie quinta* Duc̃ *Burgundie sexta* Duc̃ *Aurilianeñ septima* Duc̃ *Burbonnie* Et ponūtʳ in quodā hanaꝑio ad tle signū

{Isabella Regina.}

6 Lega de *Fryse.*

Fryse.

Med' qđ *xxiii*° die *Octobr̃* [a° *sc̃do*] ℞ *Henr̃ quarti* libata fuit Thes̃ ⁊ Camar̃ quedam carť sigillať sigilł de *Fryse* de amic̃ ⁊ concordiis [initis] inť ip̃m Dñm Regem ⁊ ilł de *Fryse* ⁊ ponitʳ in quadam [" rotunda "] pixide ad tale †sigillū

{Fryse.}

3 Hen. IV.

(p. 37 b.) 1 M^d' qđ *x*° die *Maii* anno t̃cio Reḡ *Henr̃ quarti* libat̃ fuit Thes̃ ⁊ Camar̃ ꝑ *Robm̃ Frye* Clicum quidam saculus in quo continent^r quatuor cōmissiones magno sigillo sigillat̃ quaꝝ *prima* est genat̃ rōne attemptatoꝝ tam ꝑ t̃ram q^am ꝑ mare . *Scđa* est rōne attemptatoꝝ ꝑ mare tm̃ . *Tercia* est ꝑ salvo conductu concedendo . *Quarta* est spāl ꝑ exaccōe ctaꝝ sūmaꝝ debit̃ ꝑ redempcōe recolende memorie *Johis* quondam *Francoꝝ* Reḡ. Itm̃ continet^r in eodem sacculo copia treugaꝝ int̃ regna *Angl* ⁊ *Francie* captaꝝ. Itm̃ quedam instruccio sigillis signeti privati ⁊ magni sigillata. Itm̃ continent^r in eodem due lr̃e de p^ivato sigillo. Itm̃ ultimū appunctuamentū indentatū †in Ambassiatores *Angl* ⁊ *Francie* Et ponit^r in quadam cista sup^a Re^tam Sc^acii ad tale signū

Int̃ Regem *Angl* ⁊ *Franc̃.*

2 " Memo^d' qđ *quarto* die *Julii a° sup^adc̃o* libat̃ " fuit dc̃us saculus cū ꝓfat̃ munimen̄t ꝑ m^9 *Rogi* " *Holdanby* Dn̄o *Johi* Dei gr̃a Ep̄o *Roffen̄* in con- " silio ext^a Thesaur̃ Dn̄i Reḡ."

3 M^d' " qđ " *xxvi*^to die *Junii* anno t̃cio Reḡ *Henr̃ quarti* libat̃ [" fuer̃ "] Thes̃ ⁊ Camar̃ due lr̃e ꝓcurator̃ tangenc̃ [tam] maritaḡ *Henr̃* Principis *Wall* q^am *Phe* fil Reḡ *Henr̃ quarti* ⁊ ponunt^r in quadam pixide in cista sup^a Receptam Sc^acii ad tale signū

3 & 4 Hen. IV.

1 Md' qđ *xviii*° die *Octobr̃* anno *iiii*to Reg̃ *H. iiii*ti lib̃at fuit Thes̃ ⁊ Cam̃ar̃ p *Robm Frye* divs̃ rol' ⁊ evidenc̃ fact̃ apd *Lollyngham* int̃ Ambassiator̃ *Angl* ⁊ *Franc̃* ⁊ ponuntr in quadam ✝ pixide ✝ [" pixide" ✝ " hanapio" ✝] ad tale signū

" Unde una indentra lib̃at fuit" ✝ tamen postea " p̃dict̃ Rot' ⁊ evident̃ [videlt iii. rotuli ⁊ i. inden- " tura] lib̃at fuer̃ ✝ p Magr̃m *Johem Oudeby* [Magr̃o " *Nicho Rixston*] ✝ Custođ pivat̃ sig̃ Dñi Reg̃ ✝ " vidȝ *x*°. die *Maii* anno *qarto* R̷ nūc. " Et postea " p̃dc̃us *Nichus* restituit p̃dc̃am indentram Thes̃ ⁊ " Cam̃ar̃ p̃dict̃ vȝ *x*°. die *Octobr̃* a° *qinto* r̃ nūc."

2 Md' qđ *vii*° die *Novembr̃* anno *iiii*to Reg̃ *Henr̃ qarti* lib̃at fuit Thes̃ ⁊ Cam̃ar̃ " quedam " indentura fact̃ int̃ Ep̃os "*Exoñ*" *Bathoñ* ⁊ *Welleñ* Com̃ *Northumbr̃* ⁊ *Thomam Langley* Cl̃icum ex pte una ⁊ Majorem ⁊ ‖Cōitatum *Londoñ* ex pte alt̃a ⁊ ponitr in q°dam coffino ad tale signū

{**London'.**}

3 Md' qđ *xiii*° die *Junii* anno *t̃cio* Regis *Henr̃ qarti* lib̃at fuit Thes̃ ⁊ Cam̃ar̃ salvo custođ obligac̃oes ⁊ pcurator̃ fact̃ int̃ Reg̃ *Romanoꝝ* ⁊ Reg̃ [*Ric̃m* nup R̷] *Angl* ⁊ eciam al obligac̃oes ⁊ pcurator̃ fact̃ int̃ p̃dc̃m Regē *R'* ⁊ Regem *Franc̃* tang̃ maritag̃ ⁊ alliganc̃ eoꝝđ ⁊ ponuntr in quodam coffino [" ⁊ quo- " dam hanaperio "] ad tale signū

{ **Rex Romanor' & Rex Franc'.** }

" Inde lib̃at^r Ep̃o [*Bangoreñ*] ✝ *Roffeñ* ✝ *vi*^to
" die *Marcii* a^o *sexto* Reg̃ p̃dict̃ ✝ quasdam lr̃as
" Inde r̃." " pat̃ ✝ [una lr̃a patens] de contractu mat^imonii
" sub sig̃ Reg̃ *Franc̃*." †

(p. 38.) 4 ✝ M^d' " qd̃ " *xxv*^to *Augusti* anno *q^arto* Reg̃ *Henr̃ q^arti* lib̃at̃ fuit Thes̃ ⁊ Camar̃ salvo custodiend̃ quodd^am coffinū continēs ult̃ appunctamentū indentatū int̃ Ambassiatores *Angl̃* ⁊ *F^anc̃* cū duobȝ aliis appunctament̃ non indentat̃ ⁊ ponit^r in quadam cista sup^a Receptam ad tale signū

{ Angl' & Franc'. }

" qȝ ponunt^r inf^s in ti^lo de *Angl̃ F^aunc̃* ⁊ *Flandr̃*."

✝ " Lib̃at^r *xxvii*^o die *Febr̃* anno *q^into* Regis *Henr̃*
" *q^arti Nicho* ||*Bubbewith* Clico Rotuloȝ Regis " ✝

✝ " qȝ idm̃ *Nichus* restituit in Thes̃ p̃dict̃ *ultĩo*
" die *Marc̃* ⁊ ponit^r ||ult^a Re^t' ut sup^a." ✝

5 " Et lib̃ant^r Magr̃o *Nicho Rixstoñ* utriusqȝ juris
" ꝓfessori *xxv* die *Novembr̃* anno *vi*^o Regis *Henr̃*
" *q^arti* qȝ ||restitunt^r in Thes̃ ꝑ eundm̃ Magr̃m *Nichm*
" *xxvi*^o die *Marcii* anno *vii*^o. *R̷ nunc* ⁊ ponunt^r in
" quod̃ coffino ad tale signū " †

---

5 Hen. IV.

1 Memorand̃ qd̃ *viii*^o die mens̃ *Octobr̃* anno r̃ R̷ *Henr̃ quarti quinto Robtus Frye* Clicus lib̃avit ꝑ manus ꝓpr̃ Thes̃ ⁊ Camar̃ Dñi Reg̃ quandam indent^ram fc̄am apud ||*Leulynghem xxvii*^o die *Maii* anno Dñi *m*^lo *cccc*^mo. *p^imo* int̃ Ambassiatores ꝑ ꝑte

Les appointementz de *F^a^nce.*

Angl̄ ꝛ Ambassiatores ꝑ pte *Francie* sigillis ꝛ subscripcionib; ipoꝝ Ambassiatoꝝ *Francie* roboratam.

¶ It̄ quandam aliam indentᵣam fc̄am *tcio* die *Octobr̄* anno r̄ dc̄i Dn̄i Regis *quinto* int̄ consiliū ejusdem Dn̄i Regis ex pte una ꝛ nuncios ꝑ pte T're *Prucie* ||int̄ regnū *Angl̄* destinatos ex pte alt̄a ¶ It̄ quandam aliam indentᵣam fc̄am *scd̄o* die mens̄ *Marcii* anno Dn̄i *m^mo^ cccc^mo^ secundo* int̄ consiliū dc̄i Dn̄i Regis ꝛ nūcios pciū *Flandrie* int̄ regnū *Angl̄* t^a^nsmissos ꝛ ponuntᵣ in quodam hanapio ad tale signū

{**Prucia.**}

2 ✝ M^d'^ qd̄ *Nichus Rixston̄* utriusq; juris ꝓfessor lib̄avit [ꝑ indentᵣam] v; *xiii^o^* die *Octobr̄* anno r̄ R̄ *Henr̄ quarti quinto* in Thes̄ Dn̄i Regis duos coffinos cont̄ indentur̄ cōmissiones ꝛ alias evidencias fact̄ apud ||*Leulynghem* int̄ Ambassiatores ꝑ pte *Angl̄* ꝛ Ambassiatores ꝑ ptib; *Franc̄* ꝛ *Flandr̄* sigillis ꝛ subscripcōib; ipoꝝ Ambassiatoꝝ p̄dc̄oꝝ [roborat̄] ꝛ ponuntᵣ in quod̄ saculo ad hoc signū

{**Angl' Franc' ꝛ Flandr'.**}

✝ " Lib̄antᵣ *xxv^to^* die *Octobr̄* a^o^ *sexto* Reḡ *Henr̄*
" *q^a^rti* eidem *Nicho* ꝑ c̄tis negoc̄ ip̄ius Dn̄i Reḡ
" specialit̄ conc̄" ✝

¶ ✝ " q; restituuntᵣ in Thes̄ p eund̄ Magr̄m *Nichm*
" *xxvi^to^* die *Marcii* a^o^ *vii* Reḡ nunc ꝛ ponuntᵣ in quod̄
" coffino ad tale signū ut p; " in " pticul̄ supiꝰ." ✝
" ¶ Quia plenius p; in quarto folio ꝓx̄ seqn̄."

3 . Med̄ qd̄ *Wills Esturmy* Miles ꝛ *Johes Kyngton̄* Clicus lib̄averunt ꝑ indentᵣam div̄s cart̄ ꝛ munimenta in Thes̄ [Dn̄i Reḡ] salvo custodiend̄ v; *xviii^o^* die *Nov'* anno *q^a^rto* Reḡ *Henr̄ q^a^rti* tangenc̄

maritagiū int̃ Dñam *Blanchiam* dc̃i Dñi Regis fil̃ seniorem ⁊ Dñm *Lodewycū* Com̃ ||Palatineñ *Reni* ⁊ Ducē *Bavarie* filium seniorem Dñi *Rupti Romanoꝝ* Regis sēp *Augusti* et ponūt' in quod'm cofino " sup'" Ret' ad tale signū

{Bavar'.}

(p. 38 b.) 4 ¶ Md' qđ *Nichus* ||*Bubwith* libavit in Thes̃ p manus ppr̃ *xix°* die *Febr̃* anno r̃ ℞ *Henr̃ quarti* , *quinto* Thes̃ ⁊ Camar̃ unam relaxacõem *Edwardi Hastynges* fact̃ eidm Dño Regi de ii. acr̃ t̃re cū ptiñ jacent̃ in *Suttoñ Scoteneye* in Com̃ *South* , et ponit' in quod'm cofino [" sup' Recept̃ "] ad tale signū

{Relax'cio E. Hastynges.}

5 Md' qđ *xvi°* die *Julii* anno regni Reg̃ *Henr̃ quarti quinto Nichus Bubwyth* libavit in Thes̃ Dñi Regis p manus ppr̃ unam lr̃am patent̃ sub sigillo Reg̃ *Scotoꝝ* fact̃ p Ambassiatoribȝ suis vȝ *Daviđ Flemyng̃* , ⁊ *Willmo Murehede* " ⁊ unam" indent̃am fact̃ int̃ Dñm Regem ⁊ p̃dc̃os Ambassiatores sub sigill̃ p̃dc̃oꝝ Ambassiatoꝝ sigillat̃ cont̃ treugas ||initaꝝ usq, festū *Pasche* px̃ futur̃ ⁊ ponunt' in quod'm hanapio ad tale signū

{Int' D'n'm Regē ⁊ Ambassiatores Scocie apud Pountfrept'.}

† " Et libant' Ep̃o *Bathoñ quarto* die *Marcii* " anno *sexto* Reg̃ *H.* put pȝ p quanđ indentur̃ sigillo " *dc̃i Ep̃i* signat̃." †

" q, restituunt' *p'mo* die *Maii* tunc px̃ seqñ."

6 Hen. IV.

1 M^d^ qđ *xxii*^o^ die *Oct̃* anno *vi*^to^. Reg̃ *H. q^a^rti*. qued^a^m bulla *Gregorii* P^a^pe *ix*. de revocando que alienat̃ [sunt] ✝fuerunt✝ cont^a^ dignitatem Corone.

It̃ i alia bulla ejusđm *Gregorii* direct̃ Legato de inducendo *Regem* ad revocanđ alienac̃oes fc̃as p Regem in p̃judiciũ Corone.

Bulle miss̃ usq̧ *Coventr̃* tempe Pliamenti ib̃m.

It̃ i alia bulla qđ Archiep̃us *Cant̃* Ep̃us *Norwic̃* ⁊ Thes̃ ecc̃lie *Eboꝝ* penit^9^ revocent statuta ordinac̃oes ⁊ colligac̃oes fact̃ p quosd^a^m Magnates *Angl̃* in diminuc̃oem potestatis regie, mittunt^r^ Dño de *Roos* Thes̃ *Angl̃* de mandato ejusđm Thes̃ ad Villam de *Coventr̃* tempe pliamenti ib̃m tenti.

2 Fait a remembre q̃ le *xvi*. jour de *Fevŕer* l an *vi*. du Roy *Henry quart* "*Guy*" *de Port* Lumbard ad delive as Tresorer ⁊ Chaumb̃leyns un tablet dore de la salutacion Nr̃e Dame pendant p un cheyne garnise de v bal̃. v. saphir̃. ⁊. xxv. gross̃ perl̃. pois de troye † la quele tablet a luy fuit mys en gage p^r^ un c̃teine sũme d argent p le tresrevent pier lEsvesq̧ de *Seint David* adonq̃s Tresorer *dEngletre* ⁊ est mys en un petit cofyn m̃chez ove tiel signe

{ **Un tablet de N're Dame dore.** }

" Liberat^r^ Dño de *Furnevale* Thes̃ *Anglie* p
" manus *Joh̃is Darell̃ xx*^o^ die *Febr̃* anno *vi*^o^."

Et postea *x*^o^ die *Marc̃ eođm anno* idem *Joh̃ Darell̃* restituit dict̃ tablet̃ in Thes̃ Reg̃ ib̃m custodienđ ⁊c̃. Et ponit^r^ in "Thes̃ Regis" in claustro " Abb̃ie *Westm̃*."

(p. 39.) 3 Medʼ qđ *primo* die *Marcii* anno r̃ ℞ *Henr̃ quarti sexto Robtus Frye* C̃licus lib̃avit Thes̃ ⁊ Camer̃ in Thes̃ Dñi ℞ diversa appunctuamēta int̃ regna *Angl̃* ⁊ *Scocie* apud ‖*Haudenstank* *octavo* die *Octobris* facta . videlt unū instrumēt̃ de prorogac̃oe treugaꝝ apud *Pomfreit* captaꝝ ✠ It̃ unam cōmissionē sub sigillo Reg̃ *Scotoꝝ* div̄sis Dñis de *Scocia* fact̃ ꝑ dicta pace tract̃ ✠ It̃ unam endentʳam fact̃ apud ‖*Haudenstank* "*xi.*" die *Octobr̃* . . de confirmac̃oe ‖trugaꝝ . apud *Pomfreyt* captaꝝ. Et ponuntʳ in quodᵃm hanapio ⁊ in cist̃ supᵃ Recept̃ . ad t̃le signū

{**Prorogacio trug' Scoc' apud Pomfr' capt'.**}

" Et lib̃antʳ Ep̃o *Bathoñ quarto* die *Marcii* anno " *sexto* Reg̃ *H. quarti* una cū hanapio ‖hujꝰ ꝑticle " ꝑut pȝ ꝑ quanđ indentur̃ sigillo dc̃i Ep̃i signat̃ " remañ in hanapio de t̃mino *Mich̃* dc̃o anno *sexto.* " Et postea restituuntʳ."

4 ✠ " Et lib̃antʳ *ultĩo* die *Januar̃* anno . *viimo*. ℞ " *H. quarti* Dño de *Fournyvall̃* Thes̃ *Angl̃* ꝑ mꝰ " *Alani Whytheueđ.*" ✠

" Quia ‖restituntʳ *scđo* die *Febr̃* eođm anno."

Scocia. 5 Medʼ qđ *pʳmo* die *Maii* anno *sexto* "Regis" *Henr̃ qᵃrti* Ep̃us *Bathoñ* lib̃avit in Thes̃ Dñi Regis unam comissionem Regis *Anglie* ꝑ tractatu *Scocie* tenenđ apud ‖*Haudanstank' xxiiiio*. die *Marc̃ eođm anno*: et unam instrucc̃oem dat̃ eiđm Ep̃o ⁊ al̃ ꝑ eođm tractatu ib̃m tenenđ. Et ponuntʳ in quodᵃm cophino ✠ult✠ supᵃ Retʼ. ad tale signū.

{**Bowet.**}

☩ " Et lib̄ant^r ultı̄o die *Januar̃* anno . *vii^mo*. ℞ . *H.* " *quarti* Dn̄o de *Fournyvall̄* Thes̃ *Angl* ꝑ m^9 *Alañ* " *Whythevèd.*" ☩

☩ " q̊ꝫ ‖restitunt^r *scd̄o* die *Febr̃* eod̄m anno." ☩

---

7 Hen. IV.

1 M^d' qd̄ *xxviii^o* die *Octobr̃* anno *vii^o* Reḡ *Henr̃* *quarti* ponebant^r ii carte ⁊ ii lr̃e attornat̃ de quod̄ hospicio in *Lumbardestrete* tangenc̃ *Joh̄em Holand̄* Comes " *Hunt̃.*" Comit̃ *Huntingdoñ* in quadam pixide sup^a Re^tam in una cista ꝑpe fenestram ad tale signū

aceciam quandam copiam lib̄tatuū Burgi de *Barstaple.*

(p. 39. b.) 2 M^d' qd̄ *xviii* die *Marcii* anno *vii^o*. Reḡ *Henr̃* *quarti* lib̄ant^r in custod̄ Thes̃ ⁊ Cam̃ar̃ due inquisi-Cornub. c̄oes facte apud ‖*Clyuelond̄* ⁊ *Lyskyrde* in Com̄ *Cornub̄* ad supplicac̃ nativoꝝ Reḡ ib̄m anno *vi^to* Reḡ *Ric̃i* *scd̄i* ⁊ ponunt^r in quad̄ cista sup^a Re^tam jux^a ostiū in quadam pixide ad tale signū

3 M^d' qd̄ *xxvi^to* die *Aprilis* anno *vii^o* Reḡ *Henr̃* *q^arti* lib̄at̃ fuit " in Thes̃ salvo custodiend̄ una carta ꝑ quaꝫ *Rob̄tus Lary*" Cl̄icus conc̃ Dn̄o Regi ⁊ her̃ suis unū mesuagiū quinqꝫ solidat̃ redditus in *Shakirstoñ* in Com̄ *Leicestr̃* ac eciam advocac̄oem

ecclie ejusdem ville de *Shakirstoñ* cū ptiñ ꝛ ponit^r in quadam pixide ad hoc signū

‖quequadam pixis ponit^r in cista sup^a Receptam.

4 M^d' qđ *xii°* die *Maii* anno *vii°* Reg̃ *Henr̃ q^arti* lib̃at̃ fuit quoddam sigillū cū duobȝ foliis in quadam bursa de albo corio sigillata ꝑ officõ cancellarie in dñio "*Dunolm̃*" sede vacante ꝑ br̃ibȝ ꝛ aliis itm̃ sigillanđ ꝑ Thes̃ ꝛ Camar̃ coram Baronibȝ de Sc^acio Dñi Regis "ꝑut patet" ꝑ recordū inde fact̃ in officio Reme^ris ex ꝑte Regis in Sc^acio ꝑdcõ. “ Dunolm̃.”

" Et ‖restuit^r ꝑ manus *Joh̃is Massy* in Thes̃ tꝑ
" patet ꝑ recordū inde fact̃ anno *vii°* Reg̃ *Henr̃*
" *quarti* videlt int̃ recorđ de t̃mīo *Pasche* R°
" *quarto* ex ꝑte Rem̃ ℞. Et ponit^r cū al diṽs
" sigill ꝛc."

5 M^d' qđ *xxviii^vo* die *Augusti* anno r̃ ℞ *H. iiii^ti* *septīo* . lib̃at̃ fuer̃ *Nicħo Bubwyth* Custodi privati sig̃ ꝑ man⁹ *Galfr̃i Rokell* scutiferi sui videlt quoddā instr̃m de ꝑrogacõib; treugaȝ apud *Pountfreit* captaȝ " una " indent^ra de lingua *Scotica* apud ‖*Houdenstang* fcã *xi°* die *Octobr̃* a° Dñi *m^mo cccc^mo iiii^to*. et alia indent^ra de eodē ydeomate *Scotico* fcã apud *Houdenstang xvi^mo* die *Marcii* a° Dñi *m^mo ccc^mo iiii^xx xvii^mo*.

Ꝑrogacio treug̃.

Bubwyth.

" In uno hanapio põit̃."

" qȝ alibi." ["ex Thes̃"]

8 Hen. IV.

1 M^d^ qđ "*vii*^o^ die" *Decembr̃* anno r̃ R̷ *Henr̃ q*^a^*rti* *octavo* virtute bр̃is [Dñi] Regis huic folio consut̃ om̃ia cartas ⁊ munimenta hereditat̃ carissime consanguinee *Matiƚƚ* que fuit ux̃ *Joħis Montagu* nuꝑ Comitis *Saꝫ* tangenc̃ liƀat̃ fuerunt *Ric̃o* . . . . *um* Armig̃o ⁊ attorñ ꝑdc̃e *Matiƚƚ* ut patet ꝑ lr̃as attorñ tam sub sigiƚƚ . . . . q^a^m sub sigillo *Thome* filii [⁊ ħedis] ꝑdc̃e *Matiƚƚ* ⁊ Com̃ *Saꝫ* ad hoc deputat̃ . . . . *die* ⁊ *anno* sup^a^dict̃ . . . . ꝑdict̃ ponunt^r^ in quadam pixide ⁊ ponit^r^ in cista sup^a^ . . . . signū.

(p. 40.) 2 M^d^' qđ *xvi*^o^ die *Febr̃* anno *viii*^o^ Regis *Henr̃ q*^a^*rti* liƀat̃ fuit Thes̃ ⁊ Cam̃ar̃ p *Roƀtum Fry* Cƚicum una lr̃a acquitanc̃ fact̃ Dño Regi ꝑ *Petrum Oliverū* de *Barselonia* in *Catelonia* nuꝑ possessorem ⁊ patronū ✝ ejusđ ✝ carrachę de *Barselonia* vocat̃ *Sanct̃ Mar̃* ⁊ *Sanct̃ Nichoƚ* de *Barselonia* ꝑ quam lr̃am ꝑdc̃us *Petrus* conc̃ eidē Dño Regi ꝑdictam carracham valoris quatuor miƚƚ marcaꝫ de donọ suo ⁊ ponit^r^ in quadam pixide ad hoc signū

{**Carracha de Berselon'.**}

⁊ ponit^r^ in cista sup^a^ Receptam ↄ que quiđm acq̃ liberat^r^ *xx*^o^ die *Febr̃* eođm a^o^ *viii*^o^. Magr̃o *Joħi* *Prophet* Custodi privati sigilli R̷^is^ ꝑ manus Magr̃i

"ex^a^." *Thome Feelde* ꝑcepto Dñi Reg̃.

"nō trahit̃."

3 M^d^' qđ virtute cujusdam bр̃is Thes̃ ⁊ Cam̃ar̃ directi huic folio consuti quidam saccus continens div̾sa cartas scripta ⁊ alia munimenta man̾ia t̾ras ⁊

Simon de Burley. teñ que fuerunt *Simonis de Burley* Chr tangencia libat̃ fuit exa ‖Thesauriam *Ric̃o Arundell* Chr custodi *Johis de Burley* consanguinei ꝛ heredis ejusdē *Simonis* infa etatem existentis videlt *vii*o die *Maii* anno *viii*o. ℞. *H. quarti.*

(In sched p. 41.) 4 *Henricus* Dei gr̃a Rex *Angl* ꝛ *Franc̃* ꝛ Dñs *Hibñ* Thes̃ ꝛ Camar̃ suis saltm. Mandamꝰ voƀ qđ om̄ia cartas scripta ꝛ alia munimenta manlia t̃ras ꝛ teñ que fuerunt *Simonis de Burley* Chivaler tangencia seu quovismodo concnencia in Thesaurar̃ nr̃a sub custodia vr̃a existencia noƀ in cancellar̃ nr̃am [*Ric̃o de Arundell* Chivaler custodi] *Johis de Burley* consanguinei ꝛ heredis ip̃ius *Simonis* [infra etatem existentis] ibidem libanđ sine dilōne mittatis. T. me ip̃o apud *Westm̃ quarto* die *Maii* anno r̃ ñ *octavo.*

Kirkeby.

(p. 40.) 5 Md' qđ *xxii* die *Junii* anno *viii*o Regis *Henr̃ qarti* quedam diffesanc̃ fact̃ sup qađm obligac̃oe continent̃ iiiiml'. p *Dños de Magno Consilio* Regis divsis *Mercatoribꝫ Angl* fact̃. libat̃ fuit in Thes̃ Dñi Regis salvo custodienđ ꝛ ponitr in quadam pixide in cista computatoꝝ ferro ligat̃ ad tale signū

{Condic'o oblig' d'nor' de Consilio R'.}

6 "Md' qđ quedam oblig̃ cont̃ ‖c iiiixx. vii. li. xvi. s̃. x đ oƀ. fact̃ p *Ric̃m Whityngtoñ* ꝛ *Henr̃* ‖*Londoñ* Cives ꝛ Merceres *Londoñ* Dño Regi ꝛc̃ p cust̃ ꝛ subs̃ divs̃ lanaꝝ ꝛc̃ rem̃ in hanapio de t̃mino *Pasch* anno *viii*o Reg̃ *Henr̃ qarto* Que quiđm oblig̃ libatr

"lib exa." ꝛc̃ Ep̃o *Londoñ* Thes̃ *Angl* ✝ p ⸸ ad mꝰ ppr̃ *xx* die *Julii* anno *viii*o."

" It͂ quedᵃm oblig̃ cont͂ mˡ mˡ mˡ li. fact͂ ꝑ *Dños de* " *Consilio Johi Norbury* scut͂ rem̃ in quadᵃm pixide " in viriđ coffř infᵃ Recept͂."

---

9 Hen. IV.

1 Fait a rem̃ q̃ le *xxiii*ᵒ " jorʳ " de *Januer̃* l an de regne le Roy *Henr̃ quart* puys le Conquest͂. *ix*ᵐᵉ. fuyt deliꝰe en le T'szorie ꝑ *Robt Fry* Clerc une box contenant l alliance de Duc̃ de *Bretaign̄* [" de la " trieux ‖prisez pʳ un an"] a tiel signe

{**L allianc' Duc' Bretan'.**}

2 ✝ Mᵈ' qđ *xxv* die *Maii* anno *xii*ᵒ Regis *Henr̃ quarti Johes Wakeryng̃* Clicus Roˡᵒꝝ Cancellar̃ Regis libavit in Receptā Scᵃcii ad salvo custodienđ ibm ꝑ manꝰ *Robti Watton̄* unam lr̃am ‖treugaꝝ intꝰ Regem

Bretañ. *Angl* ⁊ Ducem *Bretañ* ꝑ duobꝫ annis supᵃ mare du-

" . . . . iiiiᵗᵒ raturas tangentem incipient͂ *vi*ᵒ die *Julii* ꝑdc̄o anno

" fol seqñ." *xii*ᵒ que quidem lr̃a rem̃ in quodam cofino supᵃ eandem Receptam intꝰ alia munimenta in quadam pixide sub tali signo ⊕

" Libatʳ exᵃ Magr̃o "*Th*" *Felde* ꝑ mꝰ *Johis Skelton̄* " *ultīo* die *Oct* anno r̃ ℞ *Henr̃ qᵃrti xiii*ᵐᵒ."

" Postea ‖restituit vꝫ *xii.* die *Febr̃* ꝑx̃ seqñ."

" Libatʳ postea Dño Regi ꝑ mꝰ *Karoli de Holanđ* " valetti Camꝰe sue videlt *vii*ᵒ. die *Oct* aᵒ *pⁱmo* ℞ *H.* " *quinti.*" ✝

(p. 40. b.) 3 Mᵈ' qđ *viii*ᵒ die *Maii* anno *ix*ᵒ Regis *Henr̃ quarti* libat͂ fuit Thes͂ ⁊ Camꝰar̃ salvo custodienđ quoddam coffinū cont̃ duas lr̃as patent̃ treugaꝝ int̃ regna *Angl̃* ⁊ *Franc̃* apud *Pountfreyt* capt̃ sub sigill̃ Ambassiatoꝝ ex pte deputatoꝝ Reg̃ *Franc̃* p̃dict̃ initaꝝ usq₃ fm̃ *Sc̃i Michis* tunc px̃ seqñ ad tale signū

{ Int' Ambassiatores R' Angl' ⁊ Franc' apud Pountfreyt. }

4 Md' qđ *ixo* die *Maii* anno r̃ R *Henr̃ quarti ixo*. Magr̃ *Henr̃ Herburgh* lib̃avit in Thes̃ R salvo custodiend̃ " ||unū pixidem " cont̃ duas lr̃as progator̃ treugaꝝ int̃ regna *Angl̃* ⁊ *Fancie* apud *Gloucestr̃* capt̃ sub sigill̃ Ambassiatoꝝ ex pte Reg̃ *Fanc̃* deputatoꝝ usq₃ c̃tos dies progat̃ ⁊ ponitr supa Receptā Scacii ad tle signū

{ P'rogac'o treug' Fanc'e ap'd Gloucestr' ao ixo. }

---

10 Hen. IV. &c.

Treug̃ init̃ int̃ Reg̃ *Angl̃* ⁊ *Franc̃* p Magr̃m *Johem Catrik'* ⁊ *Hugoñ Mortimer.*

1 ✠ Md' qđ *xviiio* die *Octobr* anno r̃ R *Henr̃ quarti xmo Henr̃ Som̃s* lib̃avit in Thes̃ Reg̃ salvo custodiend̃ " duas lr̃as patent̃ treugaꝝ sigillat̃ cū rubia cera" sub noĩb₃ Ambassiatoꝝ Regis *Franc̃* ⁊ ponitr in uno hanapio titulato cū una cedula p Magr̃m *Johem Catrik'* Clicum ⁊ *Hugonē Mortimer* Armig̃ū Ambassiatores ex pte Regis *Angl̃*. Itm cont̃ in eođ hanapio [alias] duas lr̃as patent̃ tang̃ p̃dc̃as treugas sigill̃ cū diṽs sigill̃ ||rubie cere. ✠

" Lib̃antr *xxvii* die *Aug̃* anno *xiio Dño Principi* p " m *J. Burgh.*"

2 Md' qđ unū instrumentū fc̃m sup recognic̃oe fc̃a p [patronos ⁊] mercatores triū galeaꝝ de *Venecia*

in portu *London̄* aº *x*º Regis *Henr̄ quarti* existenciū. de ꝯta forisfc̄ura Regi ꝑ eosđm patronos ⁊ m̄catores ꝓ concellamento custumaꝫ Reg̃ fact̃ ꝑpt̄ quod iidē patroni ⁊ m̄catores Regi ⁊ gracie sue se submiserunt ⁊ fecerunt finem Dn̄o Regi de. m¹ m¹ li. libatʳ. ad Reᵗᵃᵐ Scᵃcii ꝑ *Henricū Somer* ⁊ ponitʳ in ||quodam pixide ad tale signū

⁊ ponitʳ in cista supᵃ Reᵗᵃᵐ cum tribꝫ seruris.

(p. 41.) 3 Ponder̄ ad tronanđ lanas in portu *London̄* de novo fact̃ videlt mens̃ *Marcii* anno *x*º Reg̃ *Henr̄ quarti*. *T. Tiptot* Thes̃ *Angl* existent̃.

viii. ponder̄ voc̃ qᵃrt̄iū quodlt ponder̄	xiii. cl
iii ponder̄ quodlt ponder̄	viii. cl
iii ponder̄ quodlt ponder̄	iiii cl
iii ponder̄ quodlt ponder̄	ii cl
iiii ponder̄ quodlt ponder̄	i cl
i ponđ	đi cl

Smᵃ	pec̃	xxii. ponđ
	ponder̄	c xlviii. cl đi

Que quidm̄ ponder̄ libantʳ *viii*º die *Marcii* anno r̄ ℞ *Henr̄ quarti x*º *Ric̄o Whityngton* ⁊ *Joh̄i* ||*Heud* custumar̄ ℞ in portu *London̄* unde iiđm debent responder̄.

(p. 41 b.) 4 Cont̃ in quadam pixide unam cartam ꝑ quam *Rogerus Yve* de *Leeton̄* Rector Capelle *Sc̄i Joh̄is Bapt̃e* de *Adbrygton̄ Husee* in Com̄ *Salop̄*. dedit Dn̄o Regi *Henr̄* post conquest̃ *q*ᵃ*rto* quandam placeam t̄re cū om̄ibꝫ supedificatis infᵃ Dn̄ium de *Adbryghton̄ Husee* juxta *Salop̄* jacentē in campo qui vocatʳ *Hateleyfelđ* in quo campo bellū int̄ ip̄m

ꝑ capella de novo construenđ juxta *Salop̄*

divina p̄ aīab3 ib̄m mortuoz impp̄m celebrand̄.

Regem ⁊ *Henr̄ de Percy* ||defuncti ||existit ⁊c̄ ad edificand̄ ⁊ construend̄ sup̄ eandem placeam t̄re quandam Capellam in honore *Sc̄e Marie Magdalene* divina singl̄is dieb3 in capella p̄dc̄a p̄ salubr̄ statu dc̄i Dn̄i Regis ⁊ bn̄fc̄oz dc̄e Capelle ⁊ aīab3 illoz in dc̄o bello int̄fectoz †existinct̄ ⁊c̄.

Et eciam cont̄ al̄ lr̄as patent̄ sub sigillo Dn̄i Regis direct̄ *Willo Walford̄* Chivaler ad delib̄and̄ seisinam de p̄dc̄a placea t̄re p̄dc̄o *Rogero* Magr̄o sive Custodi Capelle p̄dc̄e ||quequadam pixis ponitʳ in cista supᵃ R'ceptam ad tale signū

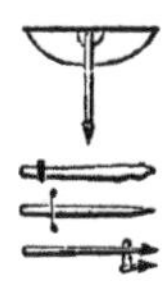

5 Mᵈ' qd̄ quoddam coffinū continens div̄sas indentur̄ div̄soz bonoz ⁊ jocaliū Regi *Henr̄ qᵃrto* forisfc̄oz anno regni sui *pⁱmo* una cum indentur̄ *Joh̄is Elvet* tunc custod̄ jocaliū dc̄i Dn̄i Regis de jocalib3 sibi p̄ Thes̄ *Angl̄* lib̄at̄ ponitʳ in quadam cista cum trib3 seruris supᵃ Reᵗᵃᵐ Scᵃcii juxta cistas p̄gameni ad tale signū

Remembraunces des biens forfaitz au Roy Henry. l an primer.

1–5–11–12–13–14 Hen. IV. &c.

1 Mᵈ' qd̄ ||quadam †pixidis continens div̄s̄ cartas ⁊ munimenta tangenc̄ c̄tas t̄ras ⁊ ten̄ in *Langeley* ⁊ alibi in Com̄ *Kanc̄* extᵃhitʳ de quadam magna cista existente in capella juxᵃ Receptam Scᵃcii *t̄cio* die *Februar̄* anno *xiii°* Regis *Henr̄ iiiiᵗⁱ* ⁊ ponitʳ

eodem die in quadam cista ad gradū Came supa dc̃am Retam ad tale signū

{Kanc' Langle.}

(p. 42.) {Angl' Franc' Flandr'.}

2 Md' qđ *Nichus Rixston̄* utriusq̃ juris ꝓfessor lib̃avit ꝑ indenturam vȝ *xiii.* die *Octobr̃* anno regni Regis *Henr̃ quarti quinto* in Thes̃ Dñi Regis duos coffinos cont̃ indentur̃ cōmissiones ⁊ alias evidencias fact̃ apud *Leulyngham* int̃ Ambassiatores ꝑ pte *Angl̃* ⁊ Ambassiatores ꝑ ptibȝ *Franc̃* ⁊ *Flandr̃* sigillis ⁊ subscripc̃oibȝ ip̃oꝝ Ambassiatoꝝ p̃dc̃oꝝ roborat̃ ⁊ ponuntr in quođ grosso coffino ad tale signū ut patet in capite

✠ "Inde lib̃antr "*Dño*" *Cancellar̃ Angl̃* ꝑ m⁹
" Mag̃ri *Joh̃is* ||*Oudeby vi* die *Maii* ✠ anno *xi*o Reg̃
" *H. quarti* una indentra ⁊ i. instrumentū" ✠
" q̃ restituuntr ꝑ m⁹ *Joh̃ Skelton̄ xi* die *Maii* ꝓx̃
" seqñ."

3 Md' qđ *xvii* die *Junii* anno *xi*o Regis *Henr̃ quarti* lib̃at̃ fuit in Thesaur̃ Reg̃ ꝑ manus *Henr̃ Som̃* quedam lr̃a patens sub sigillo Ducis *Alban̄* dat̃ apud ||*Fawlanđ vi*to. die *Maii* anno Dñi *m*l *cccc x*o. ab ip̃o Duce Gubernatore *Scocie* Dño Regi direct̃ de h̃endo treugas int̃ ||regnū *Angl̃* ⁊ *Scocie* a *xx*o die *Maii* ult̃ elaps̃ usq̃ eundem diem anni futur̃ [ad placitū Reg̃] Et ponitr in quodam cofino in cista sup Receptam ad tale signū

Scocia.

4 " Md' qđ *xxvii*° die *Octobr̃* anno *primo* Reg̃
Alligancie Ducis *Gelrie.* " *Henr̃ quarti* libat̃ fuerunt ext[a] †Theserar̃ Dñi " Regis alligancie fc̃e int̃ Regẽ *Angl* ⁊ Ducẽ *Gelrie* " *Henrico* Comiti *Northumbr̃* ⁊ *Witt̃o Styrkland* Ep̃o " *Karlioli* p man⁹ ||*Jenico Dartasso.*" " ext[a]."

(p. 42. b.) 5 Md' qđ *vii*° die *Junii* anno r̃ R̃ *Ric̃i sc̃di sc̃do* *Joh̃es Fordh[a]m* [tunc] Clicus Privati Sigilli libavit Thes̃ ⁊ Camar̃ tres bullas quaꝝ una est de eleccõib; Bulle. p̃latoꝝ *Angl*, sc̃da concessa Archiep̃is ⁊ Ep̃is *Angl* qđ libe possint conferr̃ bñficia ad eoꝝ collacõem spectant̃, t̃cia concessa patronis *Angl* qđ liceat eis p̃sentare ad ecclias suas cũ vacaṽint ⁊ ponũt[r] in

quođ hanapio sup[a] Re[tam] ad tale signũ

H

" Que quidem bulle libant[r] *Johi Wakeryng* Clico " Rotloꝝ Cancellar̃ Regis p m⁹ Mag̃ri *Johis* ||*Oudeby* " *xxii* die *Nov'* anno *xii*° Reg̃ *H quarti.*"

" Et postmodũ bulle p̃dc̃e restituunt[r] *xxv*[to] die " *Maii anno p̃dc̃o* p manus *Robti Watton̄* Clici " Cancellar̃ Reg̃ de mandato p̃dc̃i *Johis Wakeryng.*"

6 Md' qđ *xxviii*° die *Maii* anno r̃ R̃ *Henr̃ quarti xii*° *Joh̃es Wakeryng* Clicus Rotloꝝ Regis libavit in Thes̃ salvo custodienđ quand[a]m lr̃am patent̃ sigillo Fr̃is *Henr̃ de* ||*Plalvo* ordinis *B'te Marie* dom⁹ *Theutonice Irlmitanoꝝ* Mag̃ri Genal signat̃, conti-

Prucia. nent̃ treugas int̃ Dñm Regem *Angl* ⁊ ptes *Prucie*

p *Kyngton̄.* capt̃ p *Ric̃m* ||*Merlowe* Majorẽ tunc *London̄* ⁊ *Johem Kyngton̄* cuj⁹ dat̃ est ap[d] ||*Maienburgh xx* die *Decembr̃* anno Dñi *mitimo cccc*[mo] *x*[mo]. Et ponit[r] in quad[a]m [" pixide"] †hanapio† ad tale signũ in cista sup[a] Receptam Ducat⁹ *Lancastr̃*

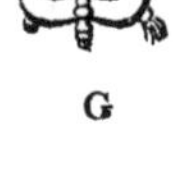

"Et postea *xxvi* die *Aprił* anno r̃ R̷ *Henr̃ sexti* " *xv*° eadem lr̃a patens *Prucie* lib̃at̃ [fuit] Ep̃ò " *Lincolñ*."

"Postea videłt *xiii*°. die *Junii* p̃x seqñ idem Ep̃us " restituit eandem lr̃am ⁊ remañ ut sup^a."

"De istis "evidenciis "plenius fit "mencio in "memorand "de anno "*xxix*°. R̷. "*H. vi*^ti."

7 " †Postodum vero videłt. *ultimo* die *Julii*. anno " r̃ R̷ *Henr̃ vi*^ti. *xxviii*°. de man^to Dñoꝝ de Consilio. " dc̃a lr̃a patens unde supra fit menc̃o lib̃at̃ fuit et " tradita Magr̃o *Thome Kent* Cłico Consilii Dñi nr̃i " Regis et *Joħi Stocker* m̃catori missis in ambas- " siata in partes [*Prucie*] cujus quidem lr̃e p̃fate " transcriptũ sub sigillo reṽ^mi in X° pr̃is Dñi " *Cantuar̃* Archiep̃i ac ✝ sigillo ✝ signo et sub- " scripc̃oe Magr̃i *Robti Kent* notarii pu^ci. tradit̃ " fuit dict̃ Thes̃ et Cam̃ar̃. p *Ric̃m Langport vi*^to. " die *Maii*. anno *xxix*°. ⁊c̃."

(p. 43.) 8 M^d' qđ quoddam hanapiũ in quo continent^r diṽse indentur̃ facte int̃ *Ric̃m Merlawe* nup Thes̃ ville *Cales̃* ⁊ colł subs̃ lanaꝝ [corioꝝ] ⁊ pelliũ lanut̃ in singulis portubꝫ *Angł* de međ ejusdem subs̃ lanaꝝ in portubꝫ p̃dc̃is p dc̃a villa [*Cales̃*] ⁊ m̃cħ ejusdem. annis *ix*°. ⁊. *x*°. R̷^is. *H. quarti* assignata remanet in quadam cista sup^a Re^tam Sc^acii int̃ alias evidencias ejusdem Regis ⁊ hoc nõine scribit^r in dica ejusđ hanapii

{**R. Merlawe.**}

9 M^d' qđ *viii*° die *Junii* anno *xiii*° Reg̃ *Henr̃ quarti* Thes̃ ⁊ †Camaraii lib̃averunt ex^a Thes̃ Magr̃o *Ric̃o Courteney* diṽs munimenta tangenc̃ alligănciã int̃ Regẽ *Angl* ⁊ Regem *Scocie*, "ac eciã" diṽs ał tangenc̃ *Flandr̃*, videłt ex^a quandam coffram oblongã intitulat̃ s^c **Hic continent^r obligac̃oes sup'**

" exa p " Courte- " nay." delibacoe 'tc. existent in cista sup quam solet ludere ad Scacm x. lras patentes sigill variis signat 't duo instra puca. ac unu quatnu de pgameno 't aliud de papiro put in quodam folio papiri inde ptictarit scripto rem in eadm coffr continetr. Itm exa aliam coffr existent in eadm cista signat cu . ✠ . xiiii al lras patentes sigill variis signat Itm exa al coffr [||sinat cu ✠] existent ut supa vi al lras patentes 't unu instrm pucu. 't al rotlm longu de pgameno 'tc. put ||patet in quadam indentur sigillat p dcm Magrm *Ricm* rem infa istu libru plenius ||apparet.

" exa."

10 Md' qd *xxv* die *Maii* anno *xiio* Regis *Henr quarti Johes Wakeryng* Clicus Rolor' Cancellar Regis libavit in Receptam Scacii ad salvo custodiend ibm p manus *Robti Watton* unam lram treugaz int Regem *Angl* 't Ducem *Bretan* p duob annis supa mare duratur tangentem incipient *vio* die *Julii* anno *xiio* pdco que quidem lra rem in quodam cofino supa eandem Receptam int alia munimenta in quadam pixide sub tali signo

Treuga int Regem *Angl* 't Ducem *Bretan* anno *xiio*. ✠ fact ✠ Reg *H. iiiiti*.

" libatr exa Magro *Thome Felde* p m9 *Johis Skelton* " *ultimo* die *Oct*. anno r R *H. iiiiti. xiiio*.

" Postea restituit v3 *xiio* die *Febr* px seqn."

" Libatr postea Dno Regi p m9 *Karoli de Holand* " valett Came sue v3 *viio* die *Oct* anno *pimo* Regis " *H. quinti.*"

(p. 43 b.) 11 Memorand qd *vicesimo* die *Julii* anno *xiiio* Regis *Henr quarti Nichus Wymbush* clicus *Johis*

Joħes Dux *Biturie* *Karolus* Dux *Aurelianeñ* *Joħes* Dux *Burboñ* ⁊ *Joħes* Comes *Alencoñ.*

Wakeryng Custodis Rotuloꝝ de Cancellar̃ Reg̃ liƀavit hic quatuor scⁱpta de ꝯtis appunctamentis intᵖ *Dñm nr̃m Regem* ex una ꝑte ⁊ *Joħem* Ducem *Biturie* ⁊ *Alverñ* [⁊] *Karolū* Ducem *Aurelieñ* *Joħem* Ducem *Burboñ* ⁊ *Joħem* Comitem de *Alencoñ* tangent̃ hereditatem Reg̃ de Ducatu *Acquitanñ* Et ponuntʳ in ‖quođ pixide signato tali signo

‖qui quiđ pixis pōitʳ infᵃ [qᵃndam] cistam supᵃ Recept̃ Scᵃcii ≈

" Extᵃ Magr̃o *Thome Feld̄ x*ᵐᵒ die *Maii* anno ꝯcio
" ℞ⁱˢ *Henr̃ quinti.*"

" Et postea vȝ eodem die dict̃ ‖pixidis liƀatʳ ꝑ
" eundem Magr̃m *Thomam* Venᵃabili pr̃i Ep̃o *Norwic̃*
" apud *Lambheth* in Camera Regis."

12 Memorand̄ qđ *xx*ᵐᵒ die *Maii* [anno *viii*ᵒ] Regis *Henr̃ quarti Joħes Rome* Cl̄icus ꝑliamenti Reg̃ liƀavit Thes̃ ⁊ Camᵃar̃ "duas" magnas lr̃as patentes sigillat̃ sigillo magno Regis ⁊ sigillis tam Dñoꝝ Sp̃ualiū qᵃm Temporaliū tocius Regni *Angl̄* tangent̃ successionē Corone *Angl̄* ⁊ ponuntʳ in quadam magna cista supᵃ Receptam Scᵃcii "——" in qua ponitʳ ꝑgamenū.

Successio Corone Regis *Angl̄.*

" Et postea videl̄t *xxii*ᵈᵒ. die *Maii* anno *pⁱmo*
" Regis *Henr̃ quinti* liƀantʳ dc̄e litᵉe patentes
" *Thome* Com̃ *Arundell̄* Thes̃ *Angl̄* ꝑ manus *Joħis*
" *Burgħ.*"

" Et postea dc̄us *Joħes* restit̃ dict̃ lr̃as *xxi* die

" *Julii* anno " *ƚcio* " R̷ *Henr̃ quinti* ⁊ remanent in " dc̃a cista ubi ponit^r p̱gamenũ."

" Et postea *scđo* die *Junii* anno *xxxi*° R̷ *H. vi*^ti " *Joħes* Comes *Wygorñ* Thes̃ *Angƚ* ħuit easđ lr̃as " Dñ̃o Regi monstranđ."

" Et postea vȝ *xxvi*^to die *Octobr̃* anno dc̃i Dñ̃i " R̷ *xxxii*° idem Thes̃ restituit dc̃as duas lr̃as."

(p. 44.)

Bona Comiƚ *Hunƚ.*

13 Međ qđ *vicesimo sexto Januar̃* a° r̃ R̷ *Henr̃ quarti* "*primo*" Dñ̃a *Johanna* Comitissa *Hereforđ* liƀavit [coram] Consilio Dñ̃i Regis p̱cellas subscripƚ de bonis *Joħis Holanđ* Com̃ *Hunƚ* tanq^am Reg̃ forisfacƚ Et iƀm p̱ idem Consiliũ cõmissa Thes̃ ⁊ Camar̃ salvo custodienđ.

14 In primis unũ par de trussyngcofres cordis ligaƚ ⁊ sigillaƚ. Iƚm unũ besagiũ conƚ div̾sa vessellamenƚ arg̃. Iƚm duo salaria argentea ⁊ deauraƚ [‖squarr̃] cũ coop̱culis arg̃ ⁊ deauraƚ pounsenez de ‖cheres de furment Iƚm unũ aquariũ arg̃ ⁊ deauraƚ †

15 **Acquietancia Joh'is Norbury de cccc. li.**

Memoranđ qđ *vicesimo ƚcio* die *Januar̃* anno *xiiii*°. Regis *Henrici quarti Henricus Somer* Cancellar̃ Sc^acii Dñ̃i Regis liƀavit in Receptã ejusdem Sc^acii quandam acquietanciã p̱ quam *Joħes Norbury* Armig̾ cognovit se recepisse de dc̃o Dñ̃o Rege *Henrico* cccc. ƚi. [sibi p̱ dc̃m Dñ̃m Regem debiƚ] Et ponit^r in quodam coffino signato tali signo ut patet in capite qui quidem cofinus ponit^r infra quandã cistam sup^a dc̃am Receptã existentem.

Vendom.

16 ♣ Mď qď delibať est p manus *Witti Kyn-welm̃cħ* ad "——" *Robtum Frye* videlt *xxvii*mo. diè *Februar̃* anno regni *H. quinti sexto* finanč Comit de *Wendū.* ♣

(p. 44 b.)

17 ¶ Fait a rembr̃ q̃ toutz les joalx desouz escriptz remañ en la Tresoury desouz le gand sale deins le *Tour̃ de Loundr̃* "queux feur̃" srveyez p les Tresorer ⁊ Chambleys de l Escheqer le *xxi*me jor de *Juñ* l an nr̃e Sr le Roy *Henry quart* puis le conq̃ *xii*me assavoir.

¶ ||ū joust d arg̃ enorrez sanz covcle

¶ Itm i autre joust d arg̃ enorrez ove les scochons des divses armes ove botons de curall ⁊ cristall ove un covcle rouge sur le sumet ||piš iiii li xiii š

¶ It i autre joust sanz covcle

¶ It i longe pot de cristall ove le covcle d argent enorrez le pee debrussez

¶ Itm i longe cruskyn de cristall le * d arg̃ enorrez

Jocalia infra *Turrim.*

¶ It i gobelet de cristall hernese d arg̃ saunz * pee brusee

¶ Itm i longe hanap d argent enorrez ove une pee saunz covcle q̃ poyse xi. marz di v ď

¶ Itm ii pees de hanaps d argent enorrez q̃ piš xxxii š

¶ It ii petitz barell de ||tamarye brussez l un saunz stopill hnesez en ptie d argent

¶ It iii cornettz d evye hernesez en ptie d argent

¶ It la *Rose* q̃ fuist * a Roy *Edward* fitz a Roy *Henry* p le *Pape*

¶ Itm i hanap de tamarye ove le pee d arg̃ pois vii š xi ď

¶ Itm i pott de cristall ove lez pee & covercle d arg enorrez ove le bordur pamont [garnie] dez garnetz.

¶ It i cornall d arg enorrez plein . q pois xx s

¶ It meyne p^r les tables ove i pair dys

¶ It i ||espor enorrez ove le ||tissewe vert

¶ It i pair sendals roials rouge

¶ It i pair sabatons de mesme le suyt

¶ It i pair sendals roialx roug

¶ It i pair sabatons de mesme le suyt

¶ It i sendall de rouge drap de sey

¶ It i pair sabatons de rouge drap de sey

¶ It i pair sandals de ♣ rouge ♣ drap blank de sey

¶ It i coyf de drap rouge de sey ove ribans d ore

¶ It i camyse i pair bracez & i coif en quele un auncien Roy *d Englet're* fuist anoyntez

¶ It i dalmatyk & i tunycle de blank drap de sey ove mantell de rouge drap de sey ||rebanye ento^r d ore p^r coronacioū d un ancien Roy *d Englet're*

¶ It i kirtill de satyn rouge furre de bys en quele *le Roy* fuist anointe

¶ Itm i furk de cristall debrusse

¶ Itm i autre furk d arg

¶ Itm i petit covercle d arg enorre

---

1 & 2 Hen. V.

Anno *primo* Reg *Henr quinti.*

(p.45.) 1 Md' qd *Robtus Fry* Clicus in officio privati sigilli libavit *xix*° die *Maii* anno *primo* Reg *Henr quinti* p m^9 *Johis Burgh* Thes & Camar unam lram patentem Regis *Castelle* ⁊ *Legionis* ·*Toleti* ✱ sigillo ‖plumbio sigillat̃ de tractatu pacis int̃ ip̃m Regem ⁊ Dñm *H* nup̱ Regem *Angl̃* p̃rem Dñi nr̃i Reg̃ nunc. Et ponit' in quodam cofino ad tale signũ

Ispãnia.

"Ext[a] Magr̃o *Thome Feld̃ xxvii°.* die *Juñ* a° *scd̃o* "℞ *H. quinti.*"

"Et postea ✝vil✝ videl̃t *x°.* die *Julii* p̱x̃ seqñ "✝idm̃✝ restituit' p̱ p̃dc̃m Magr̃m *Thomam Felde.*"

2 Acquietancia *Edwardi* Ducis *Ebo*ꝝ Dño *H* Regi *Angl̃ quinto* fc̃a in plenam soluc̃ oĩm denar̃ dc̃o *Duci* p̱ dc̃m Dñm Regem debit̃ usq; festũ *Pasche* anno t̃cio. Ponit' in quad̃ cista sup[a] Re[tam] Sc[a]cii cũ trib; seruris in pixide ad tale signũ

Acquietancia Ducis *Ebo*ꝝ.

{Dux Ebor'.}

Portugalia.

3 M[d'] qd̃ *decimo* die *Oct̃* anno *primo* Regis *H quinti* lib̃at̃ fuerunt Thes̃ ⁊ Camar̃ de Sc[a]cio videl̃t quedam cõmissio *Joh̃is* Regis *Portugalie* fact̃ *Joh̃i* ‖*Valesci* de *Almadana* ⁊ *Joh̃i Aluari* Decano ‖*Viseñ* legum doctori ⁊c̃. ad treugas ⁊ unionem int̃ Dñm *Ric̃m* nup̱ Regem *Angl̃ scd̃m* ⁊ p̃fatũ Regem *Portugalie* anno dc̃i nup̱ Regis *Angl nono* captas ‖stabiliend̃ ⁊ firmand̃ cuj⁹ quidem cõmissionis dat̃ est anno Dñi *mill̃o quadringentesimo t̃ciodecimo* aceciam unus quart̃nus papiri in quo om̃es convenc̃ões ⁊ circumstancie dc̃aꝝ treugaꝝ ⁊ unionum plenius continet' necnon una lr̃a creditoria dc̃i Regis *Portugalie*

Portugalia.

de papiro Dño *H.* Regi *Angl quinto* directa qui quidm cōmissio quatnus & lra simul ponunt[r] in quodam cofino signato cū hoc verbo

{Portugalia.}

Et ponit[r] in quad[a]m cista sup[a] Re[am] Sc[a]cii [" Ducat *Lanc*"] custodiend &c.

4 " Itm *xvi*° die *Maii* a° *xviii*° R Henr *sexti* " *Radus* Dns *Cromwell* Thes *Angl* libavit in Thes " R ||quēdam lram *Alfonsi* Regis *Portugal* de data " anno Dñi *millmo iiii[c] xxxix*°, et reman in cista " cum pdca cōmissione R *Portugalie* ut sup[a]."

" nō adhuc" " int[a]t"

5 M[d'] [qd] sup[a]dco *x*[mo] die *Octobr* anno *primo* libata fuit eisdm Thes & Camar p *Johem Burgh* quedam indentura continens divsa bona & catalla *Johis Oldecastell* Militis Dñi de *Cobham* existent infra manlia sua de ||*Covelyng* & *Cobeham* .& ponit[r] in quadam pixide signata cum hoc verbo

Indentura bonoz *Johis Oldecastell.*

{Oldecastell'.}

Et dict pixis ponit[r] " in viridi cofino de officio camar " infra Receptam R[is] ibm custodiend."

(p. 46.)

6 M[d'] qd *decimo* die *Octobr* anno *p[i]mo* Regis *H. quinti* libat fuit Dño Thes & Camar de Sc[a]cio videlt quedam cōmissio *Robti* Regis *Scocie* filii Ducis *Albanie* Comitis de *Fife* & de *Menteth* ac Regni *Scocie* gubnatoris fca *Patricio de Dunbar* de ||*Bele Willo de Hay* de ||*Lochorwart* & *Willo de Borthwyk'* Militib3 ad tractand & concordand cū cōmissariis Regis *Angl* sup treugis genalib3 p mare & pticularib3 p tram int Regna *Angl* & *Scocie* capiend & firmand cuj9 quidm cōmissionis dat est *vii*°. die mensis

Scocia.

Augusti anno Dñi *millio quadringentesimo ṫcio decimo* ꝛ gubnacõis ipius *Robti octavo* ꝛ ponitr in quadam pixide signat cū hoc verbo

{ **Scocia.** }

Et dict pixis ponitr in quadam cista sup Receptam Regis conservand ꝛc.

7 Med' qd libat fuit virtute bris Regis de magno sigillo suo dat *xiiii*o die *Febr* anno *p*i*mo* R *H. quinti* Thes ꝛ Camar *xviii*o die *ejusdem mensis* tunc px seqñ. recordum ꝛ pcessus assise nove disseïe que int *Henr* ||*Nansumer* Clicum *Johem Lannoy* ꝛ al sūmonita fuit ꝛ capta coram *Johe Colepeper* ꝛ soc suis Justiciar Regis ad assisas in Com *Somŝ* capiend assignatis. apud *Yeuelchestre* de teñ in *Yeuele* ad custodiend infra Thesaur "Ris." Qui quidem recordum ꝛ pcessus unacum brib3 dcam assisam tangent ponuntr in quadam baga canabi remanente in viridi cista infra eandem Retam ibm custodiend.

Recordum cujusdam assise de teñ in *Yeuele*.

(p. 46 Sched.)

8 *Henricus* Dei gra Rex *Angl* ꝛ *Franc* ꝛ Dñs *Hibñ* Thes ꝛ Camar suis saltm. Recordum ꝛ pcessum assise nove disseïe que int *Henr Nansumer* Clicum *Ricm Wyche* Clicum ꝛ *Johem Lannoy* et *Johem Botreaux* ꝛ *Elizabeth* uxem ejus *Henr Hemyrford Henr Belman Nichm Taillour* de *Yeuele* ꝛ *Emmam* uxem ejus ꝛ *Johannam* filiam eoꝝdem *Nichi* ꝛ *Emme* ꝛ *Willm Napper* ꝛ *Luciam* uxem ejus sūmonita fuit ꝛ capta coram dilco ꝛ fideli nro *Johe Colepeper* ꝛ sociis suis Justic nris ad assisas in Com *Somŝ* capiend assigñ apud *Yeuelchestre* p bre nrm de teñ in *Yeuele* cum omib3 ea tangentib3 que coram nob in Cancellar nra ctis de causis venire fecimus vob mittim9 psentib3 intclusa ut ea in Thesaurar

nr̃a poni fac̃ de recordo ibidem remansur̃ T. me ip̃o apud *Westm̃ xiiii* die *Februar̃* anno r̃ ñ *primo*.

Mapiltoñ.

(p. 46 b.)

Magnū Sigillū Dñi Regis.

9 Md' qđ *xxiii*o die *Januar̃* anno *primo* Regis *Henr̃ quinti* lib̃at̃ fuit in magnam Thes̃ p manus *Joh̃is Burgh̃* magnū sigillū argenti [" Cancellar̃ "] dc̃i Dñi Regis sigillat̃ in una baga de corio sub sigillo " *Thome* Comitis *Arundell̃* Thes̃ *Angl̃* " ib̃m salvo custodienđ videl̃t in quadam cista in qua ponitr Thesaurus Regis ib̃m.

10 Md' qđ lib̃at̃ fuerunt Thes̃ ⁊ Camar̃ p *Joh̃em Burgh̃* Cl̃icum Thes̃ *xxix*o die *April* anno *scđo* Regis *Henr̃ quinti* due lr̃e videl̃t una in Latino ⁊ alia in Gallico continentes treugas genales tam p t̃ram qam p mare int̃ dc̃m Regem *Angl̃* ⁊ adṽsarium suū *Franc̃* [" captas "] p eoꝝ t̃ris ⁊ dñiis subditis alligatis ⁊ confederatis citra ⁊ ulta mare p uno ao duraturas videl̃t ab ortu solis *diei Pur̃ Bl̃issime* ⁊ *Gl̃iose Virginis* ao dc̃i ℞is *Angl̃ primo* usq; ad occasum solis diei ejusdem *Pur̃* anno revoluto. quaꝝ quidem lr̃aꝝ dat̃ est *Londoñ xxiiii*to die *Januar̃* anno Dñi *millmo cccc*mo *xiii*o et regni dc̃i Regis *Angl̃ primo* Et ponuntr in quodam cofino ||lignio signat̃ cū hiis ṽbis.

Treuge [" genal "] int̃ Reges *Angl̃* ⁊ *Franc̃* ao *p*i*mo* ℞is *H. quinti* capte.

Treuge [" genales "] int̃ Reges *Angl̃ Franc̃* [" ⁊ *Castelle* ac Ducē *Britannie* "] anno *p*i*mo* ℞is *H. quinti* capte residente in quadam nova cista in capella juxta Retam existente.

(p. 47.)

Treuge int̃ Regem *Angl̃* ⁊ Regem *Castelle* †anno dc̃o anno *p*i*mo* capte.

11 Md' qđ lib̃ata fuit eisdem Thes̃ ⁊ Camar̃ p manus *Joh̃is Burgh̃ die* ⁊ *anno sup*a*dc̃is* una lr̃a cont̃ consĩles treugas genales int̃ dc̃m Regem *Angl̃* ⁊ *Joh̃em* Regem *Castelle* ⁊ *Legionis* [captas] p tempore p̃dc̃o duratur̃ cuj9 dat̃ est *Londoñ xxviii*o die mens̃ *Januar̃* anno Dñi *millmo cccc*mo *xiii*o et regni dc̃i

Regis *Angl* p^imo que quidem lr̃a simul ponit^r cum lr̃is sup^adc̃is in sup^adc̃o cofino salvo custodiend.

Ispannia.

(p. 47 b.)

Treuge genlal int Regem *Angl* ꝛ Ducē *Britannie* a° p^imo R̨^is *H. quinti* capte.

12 M^d' qd libat fuit Thes ꝛ Camar p *Johem Burgh* Clicum Thes *xix*° die *April* a° ‖sdo Regis *Henr quinti* una lr̃a continens treugas genlales tam p ꝰram q^am p mare intꝰ dc̃m Regem *Angl* ꝛ *Johem* Ducem *Britannie* captas ꝛ a ꝰcio die *Januar* anno *p^imo* dc̃i Regis [*Angl*] in x annos tunc px seqñ duraturas. et ponit^r in quodam cofino ‖lineo simul cum al treugis intꝰ Regem *Franc* ꝛ Regem *Castelle* ꝛ *Legionis* ac [dc̃m] Regem *Angl* signato cum hiis ꝰbis

Treuge gen'ales int' Reges Angl' Franc' ꝛ Castelle ac Ducem Britannie anno primo capte.

In quadam nova cista juxta Capellam Re^te remañ salvo custodiend.

"Libat^r Ep̃o *Dunolm* ꝛ aliis Dñis Consilii. *xxvii.* " die *Novēbr* anno ꝰcio Reg. *H. quinti* p manus " *Johis Skelton.*"

"Postea. *xxii.* die *Januar* libant^r pdc̃e lr̃e in " Recept Sc^acii Thes ꝛ Camar p *Robtum Frye* Clicū " ꝛ ‖ponūt^r in pdc̃a cista salvo custodiend."

13 **L'ra reformac' attempt' treug' int' Reges Angl' ꝛ Ducem Britannie nup' captar'.**

M^d' qd *xxi*^mo die *Maii* sup^adc̃o anno ‖*primo* libat fuit eisdem Thes ꝛ Camar p manus ejusdem *Johis* quedam lr̃a ✠ de ✠ de reformac̃oe attemptatoꝝ cont^a formam ꝛ effectum divsaꝝ treugaꝝ tam intꝰ *H. quartū* prem Regis nunc ꝛ dc̃m Regem nunc ac Ducem *Britannie* ante ꝰciū diem *Januar* a° *p^imo* dc̃i Regis nunc initaꝝ ⁊ captaꝝ Et ✣ in ✣ ponitʳ in †quodo cofino ligneo ✣ lineo ✣ signato cū v̄bis ut in capite hujꝰ ꝑcelle in cista supᵃdc̄a salvo remansur̃.

" Et lib̃atʳ eciam extᵃ dc̄is Ep̄o ⁊ Dn̄is eod̃m die " *xxviiᵒ* die *Novembr̃* ꝑ manus dc̄i *Joh̄is Skelton̄.*"

" Postea *xxii* die *Januar̃* lib̃antʳ ꝑdc̄e lr̄e in " Recept̃ Scᵃcii Thes̃ ⁊ Cam̃ar̃ ꝑ *Rob̃tū Frye* Cl̃icum " ⁊ ponūtur in ꝑdc̄a cista salvo custodiend̃."

---

3 Hen. V.

(p. 48.) 1 Mᵈ· qđ Thes̃ ⁊ Cam̃ar̃ delib̃averunt Magr̃o *Thome Feld̃* unam lr̄am tangentem allegan̄c [int̃] ✣ Regem de *Hispannia* ✣ *Edwardū* Regem *Angl̃* ⁊ *Petrum* Regem *Castelle* vȝ *iiiitᵒ* die *Maii* anno regni Regis *H. vᵗⁱ* post ✣ cō ✣ conquestū t̃cio . sigillat̃ sub sigillo ‖aurio [⁊] posit̃ in quodᵃm hanapio ad tale signū

" Et postea videl̃t *viiiᵛᵒ* die *Maii* ꝑx̃ seqn̄ ‖restituitʳ

Ispania. " ꝑ ꝑdc̄m Magr̃m *Thomā Feld̃.*"

" Et postea *xᵐᵒ* die *ejusdem mensis* lib̃atʳ eidem " *Thome* ꝑ *Rob̃tum Welton̄.*"

2 " Postea vȝ *xvii* die mensis *Junii* anno t̃*cio* Reg̃ " *H quinti* restituūtʳ ꝑ dc̄m Magr̃m *Thomam.*"

" Postea lib̃ata fuit *xixᵒ* die *Octobr̃* anno *ixᵒ* ℞ " *Henr̃ sexti* Magr̃o *Ric̃o* ‖*Cawedre* Cl̃ico in magna " Cam̃a Consilii de mandato Dn̄oꝝ de Consilio in " ꝑsenc̄ Dn̄i Ducis *Glouc̄* ad tᵃnscribend̃."

[" Postea restituuntʳ vȝ *xxiᵒ* die *Octobr̃* ꝑx̃ seqn̄."]

3 " It̃m lib̃atʳ ib̃m eidem. Magr̃o *Ric̃o* una alia

" alligancia ✠ Reg̃ ✠ *Alfonsi* Reg̃ *Castelle* sigillo aureo
" sigill̃ *eođ die* ad tᵃnscribenđ."

" Iste bulle supᵃdc̃e cū aliis bullis [sigillat̃ sigillis
" aureis] remañ in una baga de canabo supᵃ Recept̃
" Ducatus *Lancastr̃* ad tale signū "

4 Meᵈ' qđ *viii.* die *Octobr̃* anno *Henr̃* Regis *quinti tercio* libat̃ fuit Thes̃ ⁊ Camar̃ p manus Magr̃i *Thome Felde* quoddam hanapiū in quo continentur quatuor lr̃e de confirmac̃oe ⁊ progac̃oe treugaꝝ int̃ Regna *Angl* ⁊ *Castelle*, quaꝝ lr̃aꝝ due sigillate sunt sub plumbo ⁊ due cū cera ‖rubia .⁊ ‖ponūtur in quadᵃm cista existente in cam̃a supᵃ Recept̃ Ducatus *Lancastr̃* ad tale signū

Confirmacio ⁊ progacio treugaꝝ int̃ regna *Anglie* ⁊ *Castelle.*

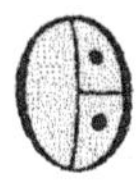

5 Meᵈ' qđ *xx* die *Decembr̃* anno ƥcio Regis *Henrici quinti* libantʳ extᵃ Recept̃ Regis p manus *Johis Burgh* unū hanapiū cont̃ unam cartam feoffamenti †

6 Exemplificat̃ alligancie *Alfonsi* Regis *Ispannie* facte *Henr̃* Regi *Angl* ƥcio heređ ⁊ successoribȝ suis ponitʳ in quođ hanapio residente in quađ sista supᵃ Reᵃᵐ Ducatus *Lancastr̃* ad tale signū

{ Ispannia. }

" Postea vȝ *xxii* "die" *Januar̃* libatʳ Magr̃o *Johi*
" *Stokes* legū doctori p m⁹ *Willi White* s̃vientis sui
" mᵈ' de quađ alliganc̃ ejusđ *Alphonsi* exemplific̃
" anno *xxxvi* R *E.* ƥcii Libatʳ *Johi Colvyll* Militi
" *xiiii* die *Febr̃* anno *vii* Reg̃ *H quinti*."

Stokes Colvyll.

(p. 48 b.) 7 Med' qđ *xx* die *Decembr̃*. anno t̃cio Regis *Henr̃ quinti* lib̃at̃ fuit Dño nr̃o [Regi] p Dñm Thes̃ ꝛ Camar̃ p manus *Rob̃ti Mortoñ* scutiferi quoddam hanapiũ cont̃ unam cartam feoffamenti fc̃am Dño Regi p *Hugonem Burnett* Militem Dñm de *Holgot* cũ una lr̃a fc̃a *Ric̃o Fox* ad lib̃anđ seisinam dc̃o Dño Regi de Manlio de *Hãme upp̃ Kyngeston̄* in Com̃ *Surr̃* cũ ptiñ suis.

Mañiũ de *Hãme up Kyngeston̄* in Com̃ *Surr̃*.

---

4 & 5 Hen. V.

1 Med' qđ *xxvi* die *Junii* anno *iiii*to Reg̃. *H. quinti* lib̃at̃ fuerunt Dño Thes̃ ꝛ Camar̃ in Recept̃ Scacii due lr̃e sigillate cũ sigillis Ambassatoꝝ Ducis *Burgundie* quaꝝ quidē lr̃aꝝ una est de abstinencia guerraꝝ p ptibus *Flandr̃* int̃ dc̃m Dñm Regem et dc̃os Ambassatores tractat̃ ꝛ concordat̃ a *xxiiii*° die *Junii* anno Dñi *millimo cccc xvi*°. usq; festũ *Sc̃i Mich̃is* quod erit a° Dñi *m° cccc xvii*° duratur̃. alia autem lr̃a continet div̾sas mat̾ias int̃ dc̃m Regē ꝛ dc̃os Ambassatores coĩcatas ꝛ eisdem Ambassatorib; p dc̃m Dñm Regem dat̃ in mandatis dc̃o Duci *Burg̃* dicenđ ꝛ sub sigillo dc̃i Ducis cũ oĩ festinac̃oe Capitaneo Ville *Cales̃* mittenđ. et ponũtur dc̃e due lr̃e in una pixide sup quam scripta sũt hec v̾ba

Abstinencia guerraꝝ *Flandr̃* anno *iiii*to R. *H. quinti* tactat̃.

{**Abstinencia guerrar' Flandr'.**}

ad tale signũ Et ponitr p̃dc̃a pixis cũ dc̃is lr̃is in quadā cista supa Recept̃ Ducatus *Lancastr̃* salvo custodienđ.

2 " Postea *scđo* die *Junii* anno *septimo* Regis " *Henrici quinti* lib̃antr dicte due lr̃e Magr̃o *Joh̃i* " *Estcourt* Cl̃ico ꝛ Magr̃o *Joh̃i Bray* Cl̃ico."

3 Med' qđ *xii* die *Junii* anno *quinto* Regis *Henrici quinti* Thes̃ ⁊ Cam̃ar̃ de Scᵃcio receperunt in recept̃ Scᵃcii unā indentur̃ ꝑ quam *Lodewicus de Burbon̄* Comes de *Vandom̃* recognoscebat se esse fidelem prisonariū dc̄i Dn̄i Regis ⁊ obligabat se solvenđ dc̄o Dn̄o Regi centū milia scutoꝝ ꝑ financia sua Et quoddam scriptū Ducis *Burbon̄* ꝑ quod idem Dux ꝑ majori securitate soluc̄ois ꝑ̄dc̄e obligabat se ad soluc̄oem dc̄e sūme in defectu dc̄i Comitis ||consanguinii sui.

Financia Com̃ de *Vandom̃.*

Vandom̃.

4 " Que quidem indentura ⁊ scriptū ante dc̄a " lib̃abantʳ extra dc̄am Recept̃ ꝑ Thes̃ ⁊ Cam̃ar̃ *xvi*° " die *Decembr̃* anno *scđo* Reg̃ *Henrici sexti* Dn̄is " Magni Consilii Dn̄i Reg̃ [ad instanciam] *Joh̄is* " *Cornewayle* militis."

(p. 49.) 5 Md' qđ *vii*° die *Maii* anno *quinto* Reg̃ *Henr̃ quinti Will̃s Kynwolmersh̃* lib̃avit in Thesaurar̃ Regis unam litt̃am de financia *Lodewici* Comitis de *Vendon̄* et unam aliam lr̃am de securit̃ Ducis *Burbonne* ꝑ eodem Comite ac quatuor obligac̃ fc̄as ꝑ *Joh̄em Victory* ⁊ *Gerardū Davy* ⁊ alios Mercatores de *Florencia* ⁊ ponūtʳ in quodam hanapio residente in quadam ||sista cū tribꝫ seruris existente in alta Cam̃a computatoꝝ supᵃ Reᵗᵃᵐ Ducatus *Lancastrie* ad tale signū ☞

Vendom̃.

{Comes de Vendon:}

" It̃m unam lr̃am testimonialem [de] capc̄oe ejus- " dem Comitis apud *Agyncourt* ˏ in ꝑtibꝫ de *Franc̃.*"

" D quibꝫ dict̃ quatuor obligac̄oibꝫ una obligac̄o " de . xxᵐˡ'. [⁊] i. scut̃ lib̃at̃ dc̄o *Joh̄i Victory septimo* " die *Junii* ꝑx̄o sequenti." ☞

⁊ Cam̃arii recepunt "in Receptā Scacii" unū longū cophinū ligni in quo continent^r div̾si evidencie tractatus ⁊ convencōes tangentes Reges *Anglie* ⁊ *Scocie* ⁊ Comitem *Flandr̃* "⁊ remanet in magna cista in "Cam̃a compo͡ꝝ ubi pargamenū ponit^r."

Anglia. Scocia. Flandria.

15 Me^d' qđ *xvi* die Julii anno regni Reg̃ *Henrici sexti* "*p^imo* [*Wiƚƚs Kynwolm̃sshe*]" Thes̃ ["*Angƚ*"] liƀavit in Receptā Scacii unū scriptū relaxacōis prioris eccƚie *Ederose* juxta Parcum de *Claryngdoñ* indentatū fc̃m Dño Regi de uno hoĩe vocat̃ *Stikker* colligent̃ ligna infra dc̃m Parcū ad opus dicti Prioris ꝑ eccƚia de *Upham* cū capella de *Cherltoñ* eiđ eccƚie annex̃ ꝓbenđ eccƚie catheđ *Saꝝ* p ip̃m Dñm Regem ꝓfat̃ Priori ⁊ Conventui concedenđ ⁊ remanet in cophino ad tale signū

Ede

in cista cū tribꝫ ceruris ad capud gradus dom̃us ||coputatoꝝ.

16 Scriptū Scabĩum ⁊ ꝓboꝝ hoĩm de *Duaco* fc̃m *Joħi* quondam Regi *Angƚ* ⁊ regno suo de fidelitate ⁊ securitate ||amisicie int̾ eosdem ⁊ ponit^r in quadam pixide in quađ cista sup^a Re^tam Ducatus *Wallie* ad tale signū

{**Duaco Prucia**}

---

2 Hen. VI. &c.

(p. 63.) ꝑ *Merstoñ*.

1 Me^d' qđ Magister *Joħes Staffordđ* Thes̃ *Angƚ* liƀavit ext^a Thesaurar̃ Regis *xiiii^o* die *Augusti* anno

Murra lib̄at̄ *Joh̄i Merston̄* c̄lico jocal̄ Regis. "nl'"

scd̄o Reḡ *Henr̄ sexti Joh̄i Merston̄* C̄lico jocaliū Regis unā ꝑvam murram cooptam ad modū uniꝰ olle garnisat̄ cum argent̄ deaur̄ ponder̄ ii unc̄ iii qartr̄.

Cornu lib̄at̄ *Joh̄i Hotoft* Thes̄ Hosp̄ Regis.

2 Itm̄ idem Thes̄ lib̄avit *Joh̄i Hotoft* eodem die unū ꝑvū cornu garnis̄ cū argent̄ deaur̄ ad delib̄and̄ D̄no Regi, quod quid̄ cornu nuꝑ fuit *Thome* nuꝑ Duc̄ *Glouc̄*.

" *Scrop̄* ꝑ " *Stokdale*."

3 " Md' qd̄ *xi°* die *Decembr̄* anno *xii°* R̄ *Henrici* " *sexti Thomas Stokdale* lib̄ ||Tes̄ ⁊ Camariis noīe " *Ric̄i Scrop̄* Milit̄ defuncti viȝ ✝ xiii discos de " argento ⁊ deaurat̄ cū uno salsario de argento de- " aurato pond̄ xxx l̄i v unc̄ pond̄ troge. Itm̄ xv " discos cavos cū uno salsario de argent̄ "sil̄" pon- " derant̄ ⁊c̄ xxx l̄i ꝑ pondus troge ✝ ⁊ postea lib̄ in " magnā Tesaur̄ ⁊c̄."

4 " Itm̄ unā ymaginē de *S̄co Georgio* existent̄ " suꝑ uno ||veridi t̄ragio cū una puella genuflectante " cū xiiii baleys viii saphers xvi troches qual̄t iii " perlys ponderant̄ lii unc̄ ⁊ postea lib̄ in magnā " Tesaur̄."

"Les esquils " de argent " dorres."

5 " Memorand̄ qd̄ disci suꝑius specificati cū " ꝑdc̄is salsariis ||dilib̄at̄ fuerūt *Joh̄i Merston̄* Cus- " todi jocaliū D̄ni Regis vidl̄t *xviii°* die *Aplis* anno " *xii°* R̄ *Henrici sexti* ꝑ indenturā int̄ dc̄m *Joh̄em* " ⁊ *Rad̄m* D̄nm de *Cromwell* factam ["ꝑ"] quam " indent̄ magnꝰ discus [elemosinaria], vocat̄ *gret* " *ship* de argent̄ deaurat̄ lib̄at̄ fuit eidem *Joh̄i* ⁊ que " quid̄ indent̄ ponitr in ||quodam pixide remanēte in " ||veredi cista."

(p. 63 b.)

6 Md' qd̄ anno r̄ R̄ *Henr̄ sexti* "*scd̄o*", quedam indentur̄ fact̄ fuer̄ int̄ Magr̄m *Joh̄em Stafford̄* Thes̄

Angl ꝛ Camar̃ de Scᵃcio ex una pte, Et *Henr̃* Epm *Wyntoñ* ex alt̃a pte, ꝑ divs̃ jocal dc̃i Regis p p̃dc̃os Thes̃ ꝛ Camar̃ eidem Ep̃o invadiat̃, ꝛ illa ps indentur̃ que debuisset remaner̃ in custod dict̃ Thes̃ ꝛ Camar̃ libat̃ fuit eidem Ep̃o p eundem Magr̃m *Johem* Thes̃, *anno supᵃdc̃o.*

(p. 64.) 7 Memorand qd *xxiii* die *Decembr̃* anno *scdo* Regis *Henrici sexti* Dñs Thes̃ libavit in Receptam Scᵃcii unam cartam indentat̃ p quam *Radus Cromwell* Miles *Johes Colvyle* Miles *Wills Bowes* Miles *Johes Martyñ Henricus Merstoñ* Clicus ꝛ *Jacobus Strang-*
Brestwyk'. *ways* tᵃdiderunt ꝛ dimiserunt *Robto* Dño de *Wylughby Thome Erpyngham Willo Bonevile Willo Crumwell* Militibꝫ *Thome Burges* Armigo ꝛ *Willo Thirwall* manliũ ꝛ dñium de *Brustwyk'* ꝛ castrum ꝛ manliũ de *Skipse* ꝛ al dñia ꝛ manlia, hend eisdem Dño de *Wylughby* ꝛ al ꝛc̃ usqꝫ ad finē quadraginta annoꝝ px̃ seqñ post dat̃ dc̃e carte post quem t̃miũ revsio õniũ dc̃oꝝ dñioꝝ ad dñm Regem spect̃ hend ꝛ ponitʳ in quadam pixide rem̃ in cista supᵃ capud gᵃdus domus computatoꝝ ad tale signũ

{ Holdirnesse. }

8 ♣ " Mᵈ' qd *Humf̃rus* Dux *Glouc̃* libavit in " Thesaur̃ Dñi Regis *xxiii* die *Februar̃* anno *viiº* " Reg̃ *Henr̃ sexti* unam lr̃am de elargac̃oe ꝛ deliba- " c̃oe *Johis* Ducis *Burboñ* cũ una lr̃a Ducis *Bedford* " de delibac̃oe ejusd Ducis *Burboñ* ꝛ ponuntʳ in quo- " dam hanapio in una cista supᵃ Receptam Princi- " patus *Wallie* ad tale signũ ♣ "

{ Burbon'. }

Burboñ.

" ‖qȝ postea vȝ *xii°* die *Novembr̃* anno *viii°*.
" dc̃i Reg̃ dc̃e lr̃e lib̃ate fuer̃ Dñis de Consilio
" ad sectam Magr̃ *Ric̃i* ‖*Leyot* Cancellar̃ dc̃i Dñi
" Ducis *Bedford̃* eo qđ dc̃us Dux *Borboñ* relib̃at^r ꝛ
" restituit^r."

(p. 64 b.) Oleū sc̃m. 9 Me^d' qđ *xvi* die *Januar̃* anno regni Regis *Henrici vi^ti* *scđo* Dñs Thes̃ ꝛ ‖Camar̃ receperunt salvo custođ in magnā ‖Thesarauriam dc̃i Dñi Regis unam tecam in qua continet^r [una alia teca in qua] *oleū sc̃m* [‖contenet^r] quo ungunt^r Reges in coronac̃oibȝ suis ꝛ duo paria armillaꝝ ꝛ unū ceptrū [in una teca correa] ꝛ unā tecam auri vocat̃ *le case p^r le treyfoyle* ꝛ ‖ponūt^r in quadam cista infra Thes̃ ꝑdc̃am ubi jocalia regia poni solebant. que qued^am teca cū reliquiis ꝛ jocalibȝ ꝑdc̃is ꝛ septrū delib̃abant^r ✝ *eodem* ✝ *eisdem die* ꝛ *anno* ꝑ indenturā int̃ dc̃os Thes̃ ꝛ Cam̃ar̃ ꝛ *Joh̃em Meerstoñ* Cl̃icum jocal̃ dc̃i Dñi Regis factam que quidem indentura ponit^r in quadam pixide ad tale signū

ꝛ remanet in quadam cista sup^a capud gradus Comp̃.

" Postea videl̃t *ult̃ die Febr̃* anno *quinto* dict̃ Regis
" ext^aunt^r de dict̃ teca ꝑ Ducē *Bedford̃* in *Cam̃a*
" *Stellat̃* in ꝑsencia Dñoꝝ de Consilio *Ampull̃ cū*
" ‖*olio bñdicto* ꝛ Virga *Aroñ* ꝛ ponunt^r in cophino in
" quo continet^r magna corona Regis ut plenius patet
" in t̃cio folio ꝓx̃ sequeñ."

[" Jocalia ꝑdc̃a lib̃ant^r *Joh̃i Merstoñ* die corona-

" cõis dc̃i Reg̃ p̱ br̃e de priṽ sig̃ int̃ mand̃ de t̃mīo
" *Mich̃* anno *viii*°.]

"Inde rec̃ "t̃mīo*Pasch̃* "a° *viii*°. "ix^c viii l̃i "ii^s i^d q^a." — 10 Me^d' qd̃ " Mag̃r " [" *Joh̃es Stafford̃*"] Thes̃ [" *Angl̃*"] lib̃avit extra magnā Thesaur̃ Dñi Reg̃ " *t̃cio* die *Marcii* [anno] *scd̃o* ". R̷ *H*. " *vi*^ti " ven̄abili [in Xp̃o] pr̃i Ep̃o *Wynton̄* jocalia subscript̃ p̱ iiii^ml l̃i a dc̃o Ep̃o mutuat̃ p̱ Consiliū Regis invadiat̃ vidl̃t "*p*^i*mo*" die "*Marc̃*" anno "*scd̃o* [ejusd̃]" Reg̃ *Henr̃ sexti*.

Aurū. — 11 Un grand tabulet d ore q̃ fuit a le Duc de *Lancastr̃* garnise de xvi baleys iii rubies ii saphires liiii perles pois̃ } xli lb̃ viii unc̃ p̃c en tout vi^c lxvi l̃i xiii. s̃ iiii d̃.

12 It̃m un tabulet d ore ⁊ argent enorrez de la salutac̃ de *nr̃e Dame* esteant sur un pee le quel fuit a le Duc de *Burgoyne* garnise de xxvi baleys xxii saphers cxxxviii perles pois̃ de troye } xlv lb̃ p̃c en tout .cc.x. l̃i.

13 It̃m ii paxbredes d ore l un de *nr̃e Dame* l autre enamell̃ de crucifix *Mary* ⁊ *John̄* pois̃ ensembl̃ de troy } xv unc̃ iii q^art̃ le unc̃ a xx s̃. xv l̃i x^s.

14 It̃m i tabulet cheyne d ore ovec un ymage *Seint Kat̃ine* garnise de viii bal̃ i. sapher i petit diamand̃ xvi. perles grosez ⁊ ix. petitz entour le corouñ pois̃ de troy } xi unc̃ i q^art̃ le unc̃ a xx s̃. xi l̃i v s̃.

(p. 65.) — 15 It̃m i hanap d ore coṽe del oṽage d un ||kyrymyry ⁊ iii scochons dez armes d *Englet̃re* ⁊ de *Fraunce* en le sumet pois̃ de troy } ii lb̃ x unc̃ iii. q^art̃ le unc̃ a xxv s̃ xliii l̃i. viii s̃. ix d̃.

Aurū.	16 Itm i croyse d ore esteant sur un pee d ore enameƚƚ dez cerfz blankez en un vert terage garnise de ii petitz diamandez en trochez sur le pee ꝛ aillours de diversez petit pers ꝛ perles de diverse sortez poiš	vi lb ii unc dĩ le unc a xx š lxxiiii ƚi x š.
	17 Itm i hanap d ore fait d ameƚƚ ‖applice garnise de iii diamandez sur le pee vii baƚ ꝛ de xxvii perles sur le pee ꝛ le coᵖcle poiš de troy	iii lb iii unc ꝑc en tout xx ƚi.

Smª auri ꝑc m¹ xli ƚi xii š i đ

Argentū deauraƚ.	18 Itm i hault tabulet enorrez de *nr̃e Dame* ovec *Seint John Bapƚ* en ƚ sumet poiš de troy	xxix lb viii unc.
	19 Itm i esqueƚƚ dalmoigñ del faisioñ d un nief veil ꝛ debruse ovec ii. facons ꝛ argent bruse poiš	xx lb ii unc i qªrƚ.
	20 Itm i payr basyns enorrez lez ‖founcez enameƚƚ dez cerfez blank d ore l ore esteme a iii unc du poise poiš en tout	xxi lb ii unc dĩ.
	21 Itm xiiii esquelx i saucer enorrez poiš ensemble	xxxviii lb viii unc.
	22 Itm iii esquelx enorrez ꝓfoundez ovec i saucer poiš ensembƚ	vii lb dĩ unc.
	23 Itm i veil potte poteller enorrez poiš de troy	iii. lb v. unc dĩ.

Argentū deauraī.

24 Itm i payr basyns ||suisorrez dez armez de *Lancastr* pois — xiiii lb x unc.

25 Itm i veil ||pece cov̄e ovec un ewer enorrez pois ensembl — ii lb ix unc.

26 Itm iiii saucers suisorrez de div̄se sortes pois ensembl — xix lb iiii unc.

27 Itm ii. chaundelers remuablez p gemews pois — xxvi lb.

28 Itm i crucifix del veil faision esteant sur un grand pee tout enorrez pois — xii li ii unc.

(p. 65 b.)

Argentū deauraī.

29 Itm i espiceplate veil & debruse enamell p tout de rosez pois — xvi lb xi unc.

30 Itm v ymagez enorrez i de *nr̄e Dame* i de *Seint Thomas* i de *Seint George* ii de *xi ml virgin* pois ensembl — xix lb v unc.

31 Itm i ymage de *Seint Edward* i petit crucifix tout enorrez pois ensembl — ii lb v unc di.

32 Itm i saler enorre saunce covercle & i cov̄cle gave & enorre ovec i sengle pece tout blank saunz cov̄cle pois ensemble — ii lb vii unc.

Argentū.

33 Itm xv esquelx d argent marchiez dez cignez pois ensembl — xxiiii lb i unc.

34 Itm iiii esquelx ꝛ v saucers d argent marchiez d armes *d Engl* ꝛ de *France* pois ensemble } viii. lb. iii. unc.

Sm[a] argenti deaurati ꝛ argenti in lb de troy cclxix lb le lb a xxx s iiii[c] iii li xi s x. d. ob.

Sm[a] utriusqȝ [pt] conjunct m[l] iiii[c] xlv li. iii s xi d ob.

---

2 & 9 Hen. VI. &c.

(p. 66.) 1 Me[d'] qd *xvi* die *Maii* anno *scdo* Reg *Henrici sexti* Dns Thes libavit in Receptā Scc[a]rii "divs" memorand ꝛ obligacōes [*Jacobi*] Reg *Scottoꝝ* ꝛ divsaꝝ villaꝝ regni sui *Scocie* ac tractatus "treugaꝝ" ꝛ abstinenc guerraꝝ int Cōmissar Regis *Anglie* ꝛ dcm Regem *Scottoꝝ* habit ꝛ "alia acta" ꝛ appunctuamenta sup delibacōe dci "Regis" *Scottoꝝ* ꝛ obsidum suoꝝ cū una indentura int dcos Cōmissarios ꝛ Magrm *Johem Stafford* Thes *Angl* sup delibacōe dcoꝝ memorand ꝛ appunctuament dco Thes *Angl* ꝛ ponunt[r] simul in "uno [grosso] cophino" ad hoc signū

rem in una cista cū tribȝ ceruris sup[a] domū Consilii principatus *Wallie*.

2 " M[d'] qd *Wills* Epus *Norwic* libavit in Re[tam] " Sc[a]cii *xvij* die *Januar* anno *ix*[o] Regis *H. sexti* " unam indentur de t[a]ctatu pacis int ipm Regem ꝛ

"*Jacobū* Reg̃ *Scocie* cuj⁹ dat̃ est *xv*° die *Decembr̃*.
"*a*° Dñi *millio quadringentesimo tricesimo* et unam
"lr̃am de potestat̃ Cōmissar̃ dc̃i Regis *Scocie* sigillat̃
"sigillo suo magno Et ponuntʳ in quad̃ quadrante
"pixide remanent̃ in quad̃ cista supª Retᵃᵐ Prin-
"cipatus *Wallie* ad tale signū

"ꝛ postea die †*M̃curie* p̃x ante festum Aploꝝ *Phi*
"ꝛ *Jacobi* anno *xii*° dicti [℞] ||idem pixis libat̃ fuit
"venabili in Xp̃o patri Archiep̃o *Cantuar̃*. ꝛ postea
"restituitʳ videlt die *Ven̄is* p̃x sequēt ꝛ ponitʳ in
"cista supªdict̃."

(p. 66 b.) Bulle tangent̃ ||previlegiis "ecclie "*Anglicane*."

3 Medʼ qd̃ *xxviii*. die *Maii* anno *scdo* Regis *Henrici sexti* Dñs Thes̃ ꝛ Camarii liberaverunt extª Receptā Scªcii Magr̃o *Johi Alnewyk'* Custodi privati sigilli quinq, bullas papales ["in uno hanapio"] quaꝝ una qd̃ Patroni ||eccliasti libe possint conferre bñficia ad eoꝝ donacõem spectancia sine aliqª contradiccõe Et al qd̃ Pr̃oni tempal eodem modo possint conferre bñficia sua It̃ al cū carta *Johis* quondam Regis *Angl* de liba electõe prelatoꝝ Itm al de confirmacõe juriū ꝛ usus Regis in eccliis Itm al de confirmacõe p̃vilegioꝝ ꝛ indulgenciaꝝ Regis in *Angl* ꝛ *Hibñ* videlt p manus *Robti Fry*.

"Restituūtʳ in dc̃am Recept̃ p manus ejusdem
"*Robti xxx* die *Octobr̃* anno *tcio* ejusd̃ Regis ꝛ rem̃
"in una cista supª capᵈ gªdus dom⁹ compot̃ "in
"[uno] hanapⁱᵒ" ad tale signū"

4 ♣ M^d' qđ *xii* die *Julii* anno regni Reḡ *Henrici sexti scđo* Dñs Thes̃ lib̃avit in Receptā Sc^a cii [p man⁹ *Ric̃i Bukland* Thes̃ *Cales̃* unā cōmissionē ⁊] sex inquisic̃ōes captas apud *Guynes* in *March Cales̃* ["virtute ejusđ cōmissionis"] anno *decimo* Reḡ *Henrici quinti* coram *Rađo Rocheforđ* ⁊ soc̃ suis ⁊ duos rotulos de clam̃ tenenciū ib̃m in uno cophino ad tale signū

remanent̃ in una cista sup^a domū Consilii principatus *Wallie*. ♣

"Postea vidl̃t *xxviii Junii px' seq'ñ* lib̃ant^r de "mandđ Magr̃i *Joh Staff'* Ep̃i *Bathoñ* Thes̃ *Angl̃* "*Willo Warde* rem̃ ex pte Reḡ p m⁹ *Th* ‖*Leuesh^am* "corā Baroñ de Sc^a cio."

3, 4, 5, 6 Hen. VI. &c.

Ducat̃ auri cuj⁹đ m̃catoris de *Vinicia.*

1 Me^d' qđ xx. ducat̃ auri lib̃at̃ hic in curia *xvii°* die *Febr̃* anno t̃cio Regis *H sexti* de bonis cujusdam m̃catoris de *Venicia* p custum̃ ⁊ subs̃ diṽsaꝝ m̃candis̃ suaꝝ non custumataꝝ lib̃at̃ p *Barth̃m Goldbeter* Magr̃m monete infra *Turrim Londoñ* ponderat̃ hic in cur̃ eodem die ponderant p pondus standardi *Turris Londoñ* ult^a cunaḡ ⁊ seignoraḡ lxvii s̃ ii đ.

2 Me^d' qđ *ultimo* die *Februar̃* a° *v^to* Regis *Henr̃ sext̃ Johes* Dux *Bedforđ* ⁊ alii Dñi de Consil̃ Dñi

Regis libaverunt Dño *Waltro Hungerford* Thes *Angl* ꝛ Camar de Scacio *Magnam Coronam* Regis nup existent in custod Venabil pris Epi *Wynton* ad salv ꝛ secur custod "que" quidm Corona residet in quadam cista cū tribȝ ceruris infra magnam Thesaur Regis apud *Westm* in quodam cophino de corio ferro ligato ꝛ sigillat cum signeto dci *Dñi Ducis* Et [ponitr] ✤ ponuntr ✤ in eod cophino ✤ aquila cū ‖olio benedco ꝛ virga *Aron* ✤ Et dict cophanus ceratr cū tribȝ ceruris unde una clavis remanet penes dict Dñm Thes in custodia *Johis* ‖*Pontrell* ꝛ cetre due claves penes Camar.

Magna Corona.

[✤ " Libatr *Johi Merston* die coronacois Reg " *Henr sexti.*" ✤]

" qȝ rest postea eisd Thes ꝛ Camar."

Relibaco custod Castri Ville *Berewici.*

3 Md' qd *viio* die *Februar* ao *vto* Regis *Henr sext Walrus Hungerford* Thes *Angl* libavit quandam lram sub sigill Dñi Ducis *Bedford* sigillat in Receptam Scacii custod facient mencoem de tradicone concessione relibacone ꝛ sursumreddicoe custodie Castri de *Berewico sup Twedam* ꝛ ponitr in quadam pixid remanent in cista camre ‖computoȝ juxta gradū ejusdm camre ad tale signū

{ **Dux Bedford'.** }

(p. 67 b.)

Tabula tunice inconsutilis.

4 Md' qd *xii* die *Decembr* anno *quarto* Reg *Henrici sexti* " Magr *Johes* [*Stafford*] Thes *Angl* " libavit in Receptā Scacii p manus *Robti Popyngeay* executoris testi *Katine Lardener* unā tabul auri cū *Trinitate* in sumitate ejusdem ꝛ decess gliose *Virgis Marie* subtꝰ ped *Trinit* ꝛ iii Reg *Colonie* in pede ejusdem tabule garnisat cū xxvii gross perul quaȝ [‖qualbt de] vii ‖appreciantr ad v marc ꝛ xx ad

xxx soliđ que quidem tabula quondam invadiat̃ fuit *Thome Duttoñ* Cħr ꝛ rem̃ in magna Thes̃ Dñi Regis ꝛ ponderat ꝑ pondus troge v lƀ i unc̃.

5 Med' qđ dc̃a tabula liƀat̃ [fuit] dc̃o Dño Thes̃ de mandato suo *ult* die *Decembr̃* dc̃o anno *quarto* ꝑt ii perule ejusdem tabule que rem̃ in una pixide in cista monete in cam̃a compotatoꝝ ad tale signū

" Que quidem tabula postea restituit^r in dc̃am
" Thesaurariam ꝑ dc̃m Thes̃ ac postea dc̃a tabula
" liƀata fuit ꝑ Dñm *Hungerforđ* Thes̃ *Angl* Aƀƀi
" *Westm̃ xxi* die *Aprilis* anno *viii*° Reg̃ *Henr̃ sexti*
" custodienda ꝑ una corona que nuꝑ fuit *Ric̃i* nuꝑ
" Reg̃ *Angl̃i scđi* ab eođm Aƀƀe recepta."

Jocalia restit.

6 Med' qđ *xxix*° die *Januarii* anno regni Reg̃ *Henrici vi*^ti *quarto* " Mag̃r [*Joħes Staffořd*]" Thes̃ *Angl* liƀavit in Re^tā Sc^acii unā ꝑvā pelvim de argento deauratā cū xviii bosis rotundis ꝛ uno ꝑvo anulo unū candelabrū argenti unū ewer ꝛ unā pelvim argenti cū *Sc̃o David* in fundo que quondam invadiat̃ fuerunt *Joħi Chenduyt* Armig̃o ꝛ ꝑ eundem in Sc^ac̃im ꝑdc̃m *dc̃o die* restit̃. Et rem̃ infra magnā Thesaur̃ Dñi Regis infra Aƀƀiam *Westm̃* in una cista ubi jocalia Reg̃ reponi solent.

7 " Md' qđ dc̃a ꝑva pelvis deaur̃ cū xviii bosis
" liƀat̃ fuit Dño [" *Walťo* "] ✠ *Galf r̃o* ✠ ‖*Hunger-*
" *gorđ* Thes̃ *Angl* ꝑ Cam̃ar̃ ꝑ man⁹ *Wiłłi Darel*
" Sub Thes̃ ꝑ ꝑceptū ip̃ius Thes̃ *xiii* die *Apriľ*
" anno " *quarto* " Reg̃ *Henrici vi*^ti ad portanđ usqꝫ
" *Leicestr̃* ꝛ iƀm liƀanđ Dño Regi."

(p. 68.) Baga cū divš sigillis.

8 Med' qđ *primo* die *Maii* anno *iiii*to Reg̃ *Henrici sexti* Dñs *Hungyrforđ* Thes̃ *Angl* cepit exa Retā Sc̃cii unā bagam continent̃ "unū magnū sigillū "argenti Cancellarie Regis *Ric̃i sc̃di*" ⁊ al pva sigill ad ||differenđ usq; *Leycestr̃* ⁊ ibm frangenđ corā Consil Dñi Regis.

9 Que quidem dampnantr ibm coram dc̃o Consilio ⁊ postea libantr p man9 *Robti Burtoñ* Camaȓ de Scacio salv̄ custodienđ ⁊ ponuntr in magna cista infra magnā Theseaur̃ Dñi Regis ubi jocalia dc̃i Dñi "Regis" resident custodienđ.

10 Et postea vidlt *xviii* die *Julii anno* p̃dc̃o libantr exta dc̃am Thesaur̃ p manus *Willi Darell* Sub Thes̃ *Joñi Merstoñ* Clico jocaliū Regis ad facienđ divsos ciphos ad usum dc̃i Dñi Regis ponderant̃ in toto p pondus de troye x lb vii unc̃ ⁊ iii qart̃.

11 Md' qđ Dñs de *Hungerford* Thes̃ *Angl* libavit in Recept̃ Scacii custodienđ *xxvi* die *Febr̃* anno *quinto* Regis *Henr̃ sexti* unū rotlm de valore pfic̃ Senescalcia3 Principatus *Aquitanie* Domino *Edwardo* nup Principi *Wall* ptinent̃ ⁊ ponitr in quadam cista existente in cam̃a supa domū Consilii Principatus *Wall* ad tale signū

{**Vasconia.**}

(p. 68 b.)

12 ✠ Med' qđ *xviii* die *Julii* anno *quarto* Regis *Henrici sexti Waltus* Dñs *Hungerforđ* Thes̃ *Angl* libavit in Retam Scacii salv̄ custodienđ c̃ta jocalia nup invadiat̃ *Joñi Durwarde* Armig̃o de Com̃ *Essex'* p unā indenturā int̃ *Thomam* ||*Chyttern̄* [nup] Clicum jocaliū Regis *Henrici quinti* ⁊ dc̃m *Joñem Durwarde* fc̃am vidlt un tabernacle d ore de *Nr̃e Dame* seant sur un vert tarage ovec *Adam* ⁊ *Eve* ⁊ iiii angels

Joñn Durwarđ.

a les iiii corners ꝰt i crucifix [le ymage esmaile de blank] sur la dit tabernacle ꝰt un eygle blank [le quel ||saut] en [le] sumet garnise de ii rubies iii diamandz iiii balyse iii saphirz lxxvii grose perles ꝰt xliii petitz perles [pois de troy v m^a^rz ꝰt i unc̃ ||ꝰt d or] Itm̃ un hanapp̃ de byrell̃ ovec un coṽcle d ore [garnise] ♣d ore♣ de xi. grosez perles ꝰt de l petitz perles [poisant xxii unces ꝰt dĩ] que quidem jocalia ponūt^r^ in magna [cista] infra magnā Thesauraȓ Reg̃ ubi jocalia Regis reponi solent in Abbia *Westm̃.* ♣

[" qꝫ libant^r^ *Johi Merstoñ* virtute bȓis de priṽ " sigillo rem̃ inṫ manđ de ṫmīo *Sc̃i Michis* anno " *viii°*."]

13 Med' qđ *xxvi°* die *Julii* anno *iiii°* Regis *Henȓ sext̃ Johes Shadworthe Robtus Teye* ꝰt *Johes Basset* execut̃ test̃i *Johis* ||*Heende* nuꝑ Civis ꝰt Aldermani *Londoñ* libaṽ ad Re^tam^ Sc^a^cii ꝯta jocalia nuꝑ dc̄o

||*Hende.* *Johi* ||*Heende* invadiat̃ ꝑ D marcz ab eo mutuat̃ ꝑ viag̃ Regis ṽsus pt̃ exṫas videlt un palet appell̃ l *Palet de Spayne* garniz d ore de xxxv baliz ꝰt rubiez bastardz iiii saphires xv gros esmeraudez ꝰt de ciii ||ṫspitz esmeraudez ꝰt de ccc petitz ꝑlez le pois de mesme le palet viii lb vi unc̃ de pois de

(p. 69.) troy le pris de mesme l palet cc. li Itm̃ un coronall̃ d ore garnise de x flours ||doore faitz al mañ de flourez de lice garniz dez baliz saphirez ꝰt esmeraudez ꝰt ꝑlez ovesqꝫ x oṽaignez square ||shoscun garniz d un baliz en mye lieu xii ꝑlez environ̄ pois̃ de troy xvii unc̃ i q^a^rt̃ ꝰt xx đ ||door tout entierment garniz q est de la value de c m^a^rcz.

It̃ un haut tabnacle ove iiii berillꝫ p^r^ le sacrement ovesqꝫ iii angelz esteauntz sur trois corners sur le pee dount d un aungell̃ faut i wynge pois̃ de troy x. lƀ ii unc̃ dĩ ♣pus♣ pris ł liƀ xl. s̃. sm^a xx. łi vi. s̃ viii đ.

Itm̃ i tablet d or garnie en mye lieu d un g^aunt saphir gravez d un ymage de la *Trinite* et envirou͂ la bordure de iiii balisez xi ꝑlez pendantz ꝑ i. cheine de wyre d or pois̃ de troy iii unc̃ ꝛ v s̃ de or pris xx marz.

It̃ ii novelz sensurez d argent enorrez pois̃ ensemble vii liƀ vi unc̃ ꝛ iii quart͛z pris de la liƀ xlvi s̃ viii đ Sm^a xvii. lƀ x s̃. It̃ ii chaundelerz d argent ꝑcell̃ enorrez dount de l un faut "le" bolle ꝛ le pike ꝛ de l aut^e i pike pois̃ ensemble xiii. liƀ ix unc̃ p^is de la liƀ xxx s̃ Sm^a xx. łi xii s̃ vi đ que quiđm jocał ponu͂t^r in magna cista infra magñ Thesaurar̃ Regis ubi jocał Regis reponi solent in Aƀƀia *Westm̃.*

14 M^d' qđ *xxviii* die *Maii* anno *quinto* R̷ *Henr̃ sexti Wiłłs Talbot* Ch̃r liƀavit Dño *Waltõ Hungerforđ* Thes̃ *Angł* c͛ta jocalia nuꝑ sibi invadiata ꝑ unā indent^ram int͛ ip̃m ꝛ *Ric̃m Courteney* nuꝑ Ep̃m *Norwiceñ* tunc Thes̃ Cam͛e R̷ *H.* "p̃ris Reg̃ [nu͂c]" fc̃am videłt ♣ ii bolles de auro ponderant̃ xxxi unc̃ i q^art̃ ♣ [liƀant^r *Joh̃i Merstoñ* ꝑ indent̃] ꝑc̃ unc̃ xxviii s̃. iiii. đ. Sm^a xliiii łi v s̃ Itm̃ ii cerfs

Talbot. d argent ennorrez pois̃ ensemble iiii. lƀ i unc̃ i q^art̃ p^ic̃ de liƀ xxx s̃ Et p^r le dorrure xx. s̃ Sm^a vii. łi iii s̃ i đ oƀ Itm̃ i tablet d argent ennorres ovesq; i. berell̃ ovesq; i esglise ꝑamount poisaunt xix unc̃ iii q^art̃ p^ic̃ la lƀ xxxiii s̃. iiii đ. Sm^a liiii s̃ vi đ oƀ q^a Itm̃ i petit burse d ore garnise d un balise i safire ꝛ de iiii perles ꝑc̃ de tout c s̃.

15 ¶ Itm̃ i broche d ore fait al man͛e de deux bracez al man͛ d un ||tronch̃ coronez garnes d un

emeraude ꝛ de xxi ꝑlez poiꝫ de trois iii q^a rt̃ d un
(p. 69 b.) unc̃ ꝛ dĩ Sm^a xl. s̃. les queux joialx sount misez
in l̃ Tresorie nr̃e S^r le Roy en un g^a unt ciste ovesqȝ
autre joialx ✠ de ✠ ꝑ le dit Tresorer *dEngleťe l an* ꝛ *jo^r suisditz.*

---

6 Hen. VI.

1 M^d' qd̃ "*Walťus*" Dñs *Hungreford̃* Theš *Angl̃* delibavit in Thesaurariam Regis ib̃m custodiend̃ *xxv* die *Novembr̃* anno regni Regis *Henrici sexti vi^to* ꝯta jocalia nuꝑ invadiata *Thome Chaworth̃* Militi ꝑut in quadam indentura inde inť *Ric̃m* nuꝑ Ep̃m *Norwiceñ* ꝛ dc̃m *Thomam* fc̃a continet^r ꝛ que ꝑticulariter "||sequitur" videlt. In p^i m̃ i tab̃nacle d argent ennorrez ovec un beryll "dedeinz" enmilieu ovec i. crucifix en la somet poiš de troye . v. lb̃. dĩ lb̃ ad xlvi š viii d̃ Sm^a xii li xvi š viii d̃. Itm i coupe d argent ennorez debrusez ovec i berill en mie lieu ꝛ i angel ꝑamont ovec i. g^a unt cheyne poiš v lb̃ iiii unc̃. ꝑc̃ unc̃ ut sup^a Sm^a x li xiii š. iiii d̃ ✠ It̃ i graunde almesdich̃ pee d argent [ꝑcelles] ennorrez
Cheyworth̃. ovecqȝ les armes de *Sr de Lovell* en le somite achatez dez executours [del] lErchevesqȝ de *Caunťbury* poiš xxii lb̃ iii unc̃ ✠ lb̃ ad xxx š. Sm^a xxxiii li. vii š. vi d̃ It̃ i. petit flaket de beryll garniš d or ꝛ [de] vi deamaundes de ix. balez ꝛ xxiii ꝑles ꝑc̃ de tout xvi li ✠ It̃m i petit paxbrede d or ["poisant
"qȝ libant^r v unc̃ iii q^a rt̃"] debrusez ovec ii coclers d or [poiš
"*Joh̃ Merstoñ* iii unc̃ i qȝ^a ꝛ i^d d or It̃m i chaundeler tout
"ꝑ indenť. d or debrusez ✠ poiš ensemble [poisant iiii unc̃ i q^a rt̃] xiii unc̃ dĩ ꝑc̃ unc̃ xxvi š viii d̃ Sm^a xviii
". . . . i flour li ✠ It̃ i braselet d or fait de ii dames enamelez de
"qui ꝑd . . in
"cam̃a R̃." blank chescuñ tenaunt en sa main un flour de

6 ♣ M^d' qđ *octavo* die *Febr̃* anno Regis *Henr̃*
D panno ℞. *quinti quinto Witts Kynuolmarcħ* [" lib̄avit in Thes̃ " Dñi Regis"] unū trapper̃ de panno auri in duabȝ peciis ib̄m custodienđ. ꝑ salva custodia ☌.♣

P Dñm de *la Sparr̃* Dño Regi *Angl.* " ‖Qui postea vȝ *xxiiii* die *Febr̃* anno *vii°* ejusđ ℞ " lib̄atū fuit *Rob̄to* ‖*Rellestoñ* Cl̄ico magne garde- " robe Reg̃ ad opus Reg̃ custodienđ."

---

6 & 7 Hen. V. &c.

(p. 49 b.) 1 Me^d' qđ lib̄at̃ est *Witto Kynuolmarcħ* una indentur̃ Comit̃ de *Vendom* cont̃ tresdecim milia . ccc.
Vendom̃. triginta ⁊ tres scut̃ boni ⁊ puri auri vidl̄it *decimo* die *Maii* anno *sexto* * *H. quinti* ⁊c̃.

2 M^d'. qđ . *xxvi^to* die *Novembr̃* anno *sexto* Reg̃ *H. quinti* lib̄ati fuerunt quinqȝ libri in Thes̃ Dñi Regis ꝑ *Witt̃m Kynwolmarcħ* locū tenentem Dñi *Henr̃ Fitzhugħ* Thes̃ *Anglie* custodiendi videl̄t i. ‖*Biblea* ⁊ unus liber [voc̃] *Paralipomenon* ⁊ alius liber de *Concepc̃ōe B'e Marie* ⁊ alius liber voc̃ *Compendiū Theologice Veritat̃* ⁊ alius liber vocat̃ *Libellus de emendacōe vite.* Qui quidem libri fuerunt †

Et ponūt^r in quadam cista [⁊] in quad^am baga de canabo remanent̃ in quadam cista cū tribȝ cerur̃ sup^a Recept̃ ad tale signū

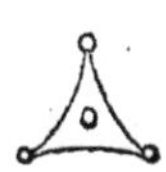

" Postea vȝ *xvi.* die *Nov'* a° *vii°* ‖lib̄ate fuer̃ dc̃i " quinqȝ libri domui *Sc̃i Salvatoris* jux^a *Shene* ꝑ m⁹ " *Henr̃ Chatertoñ* de mandato dc̃i *W Kynwolm̃ssħ.*"

3 M^d' qđ *Witts Kynwolmersshħ* lib̄avit in Re^am Sc^acii *t̃cio* die *Maii* anno *septimo* Reg̃ *H. quinti* duo instrumenta fc̃a videl̄t unū ꝑ *Arthurū de Britania*

filiũ quondam Ducis *Britañ* ⁊ aliud ꝑ *Carolũ de Artoys* Comitem de *Augo* de passag̃ suis maris versus Dñm nr̃m Regem in *Normañ* ꝑ ꝓvisione redempc̃onũ suaꝝ Et ponuntʳ in ||quodam pixide de salice remañ in quadam cista supᵃ Receptam Principatus *Walł* ad tale signũ

{Britannia.}

(p. 50.) 4 Mdʼ qđ *vi°* die *Maii* anno *septimo* Reg̃ *H quinti* libantʳ Dño Regi in ꝑtibꝫ ext̃is existenti ꝑ manus *Ric̃i Flemmyng̃* Cłici in ꝓ̃sencia Dñi Ducis *Bedforđ* ⁊ alioꝝ Dñoꝝ in domo Consilii Reg̃ existent̃ tres lr̃e patentes extra unũ longũ coferũ pictatũ armis *Franc̃* in quo continetʳ magna pax int̃ Regem *Edwardum* nuꝑ Regem *Angł* t̃ciũ ⁊ *Joħem* nuꝑ Regem *Franc̃* videłt una lr̃a patens ꝑ quam dc̃us *Joħes* nuꝑ Rex *Franc̃* confirmavit tractatũ magne pacis fact̃ apud *Brettigny* juxᵃ *Chartres* ꝑ *Karolum* primogenitũ dc̃i *Joħis* Dat̃ apud *Calais xxiiii°* die *Octobr̃* anno Dñi *m*ᵐᵒ *ccc*ᵐᵒ *lx°*.

Franc̃.

5 Itm̃ alia lr̃a patens ꝑ quam dc̃us *Joħes* quondam Rex *Franc̃* recitavit dc̃m tractatũ in parte ⁊ adjecit ||clasulam *cestassavoir*.

6 Itm̃ alia lr̃a patens ꝑ quam dc̃us *Joħes* quondam Rex *Franc̃* mandavit subditis suis de *Rupella* qđ obedirent Regi *Edwardo* ⁊ successoribꝫ suis impꝑp̃m Dat̃ *xxiiii die sup*ᵃ*dc̃o*.

7 " Medʼ qđ Dñs Ep̃us *Norwic̃* libavit in Reᵗᵃᵐ
" Scᵃcii *xvi* die *Novembr̃* anno r̃ R̷ *Henr̃ sexti nono*
" duas lr̃as de treugis captis int̃ Regem *Angł* ⁊
" *Joħem* Regem *Castelle* ⁊ *Legionis* anno Dñi *milłmo*
" *cccc xxx°* et ponũtʳ in ||quođ qᵃdrant̃ pixide cũ

" aliis evidenc̃ in quad̃ sista supᵃ Reᵗᵃᵐ Principat⁹ " *Wallie* ad tale signū "

{Ispannia.}

(p. 50 b.) 8 Meᵈ' qđ recepte sunt quatuor l̃re †

---

3 & 7 Hen. V.

(p. 51 b.) " Anno *vii*ᵒ."

1 Mᵈ' qđ *x*ᵐᵒ. die *Octobr̃* anno regni Regis *Henr̃ quinti ᵽcio* recepte fuerunt in Recept̃ Scᵃcii " quatuor l̃re unā l̃ram " pacis Ducis *Burgundie* sigillat̃ cū sigillo suo ⁊ aliam l̃ram *Caroli* Regis *Franc̃* sigill̃ suo sigill̃ Et unū tractat̃ guerr̃ int̃ Regem *Angl̃* ⁊ quatuor membᵃ *Flandr̃* Et unā l̃ram Dñi Regis *Angl̃* ⁊ ponūtʳ in uno ||cofano supᵃ Receptā ad tale signū

Abstinencia guerr̃ *Flandr̃.*

† " Lib̃ Dño " Cancellar̃ " *vi*ᵗᵒ die " *Febr̃* aᵒ " *xxxi*ᵒ." † " restituitʳ."

2 " Postea lib̃at̃ est unū tractatū *scđo* die *Junii* " anno *septı̃o* Regis *Henr̃ quinti* Magistro *Joh̃i Est-* " *court* ⁊ Magistro *Will̃o Bray* qui incipit. *A tous* " ⁊c̃. ⁊ t̃minatʳ *cccc* ||hinc."

3 Mᵈ' qđ *Will̃ms Kynwolmersh̃* Cl̃icus lib̃avit in Recept̃ Scᵃcii *xii*ᵒ. die *Octobr̃* anno *septimo* Regis *Henr̃ quinti* unam indentʳam fc̃am *Cales̃ xiiii*ᵒ die *Julii* anno Dñi *m*ˡ *ccc xix*ᵒ. p *Will̃m Bardolf* Militem ⁊ alios Ambassatores Regis de tᵃctatu pacis int̃ regnū *Angl̃* et partes *Flandrie* Et ponitʳ in quodam ||cofono infra cistam supᵃ Recept̃ Principat⁹ *Wallie* ad tale signū

{Angl' Flandrie.}

" Postea videlicet *xxii°* die ejusdem mensis dc̃a
" indentra lib̃ata fuit Magr̃o *Witt̃o Bray* ꝑ ꝓcept̃
" Thes̃."

✠ " Lib̃ Dño " Canc̃ *vi*lo. " die *Febr̃* " a° *xxxi*to" ✠ " restituitr."

" Et postea vȝ *xxiii* die *Januar̃* ꝑx̃ seqñ idem
" Magr̃ *Witts* restituit dc̃am indenturã Thes̃ ⁊
" Camar̃."

(p. 52.) 4 Md' qđ carta ꝑ quam *Bernardus* Dñs *de la Sparre* dedit Dño *Henr̃* Dei gr̃ia Regi *Angt quinto* villam castrũ dñium baroniam ⁊ castellaniam *de la Sparre* ⁊ *de la Sparrays* ; ponitr in cista cũ tribȝ seruris supa Retam Scacii ad tale signũ

{**Sparre.**}

5 Md' de diṽsis cartis ⁊ muniment̃ *Johis de Warrenna* Comitis *Surr̃* fact̃ Regi *Edwardo* t̃cio ; existeñ in uno hanapio rem̃ in cista supa Receptam R̷ juxta gradus comput̃ ad tale signũ

{**Comes Surr'.**}

" In eodem hanapio cont̃ vi script̃ ⁊ unã
" copiam " †

(p. 54 b.) Jocalia restituta.

6 Md' qđ *ultimo* die *Octobr̃* anno t̃cio Regis *Henrici quinti* . executores *Johis Attilbrigg* restituerunt in magnam Thesauriam Regis unũ gipsere de velvet de colore purpur̃ hernesat̃ cũ auro cũ uno anulo magno de auro in quo scribitur

en un sans plus

Restitucio cujusdam gipser̃ cũ quodã anulo ⁊ uno par̃ de pat̃ nr̃es ꝑ executores *Johis Attilbrigg.*

⁊ unũ par̃ de pater nr̃es de auro puro continent̃ in toto . xii. knoppes quodquidem gipsere cũ anulo ⁊ pat̃ nr̃es ✠ ꝓdict̃ ✠ ꝓdc̃us *Johes* h̃uit ꝑ vađ suis in itinere suo in viagio in comitiva Regis ṽsus *Harefete* . et ponuntur in quadam cista magna ; ferro

ligata in dc̃a magna Thesauria salvo custodienđ
" quodquidem gipser *Joħes* ‖*Rotheuale* Miles Thes̃
" *Angl̃* recepit in suam custodiam. ꝛ p̃dc̃os pat̃
" nr̃es. *xix.* die *Decembr̃* *anno* *p̃dc̃o* liƀavit *Thome*
" *Chitterne* Cl̃ico jocaliū ꝛc̃."

7 Itm. *xxvi*^to^. die *Novembr̃* *eodem* *anno* restitut̃ ꝛ liƀat̃ fuit Thes̃ ꝛ Cam̃ar̃ in Recept̃ Reg̃ p *Joħem Irby*. i. tablet de auro ħnes̃ cū. iiii. bał. xi. gross̃ ples cū. i. magno saphire de ymagine Dñi *Jħu Xp̃i.* quodquidē tablet p̃dc̃us *Joħes* ħuit p securitate vađ unius lanc̃ ꝛ. ii. sagitt̃. p viagio p̃dc̃o ꝛ pōit^r^ in p̃dc̃a cista magna ferro circūligata in dc̃a Thesauria salvo custodienđ.

Restitutio cujusdā tablet p *Joħem Irby.*

" Quod quidem tablet liƀat̃ fuit p dc̃m Thes̃
" p̃dc̃o *Thome* eodem [*xix*] die *Decembr̃* *anno* *sup*^a^-
" *dc̃o.*"

8 Memoranđ qđ *Wiłłs Kynwolmersshe* Deputatus Thes̃ *Angl̃* deliƀavit *xii* die *Maii* anno *vii*^o^ Regis *Henr̃ quinti* in Thesaurariam Regis custodienđ, unū trappour de panno †aurio continent̃ i. mantyłł ꝛ i. testyr.

Trappour.

Postea videłt *xxiiii*^o^ die *Febr̃* px̃ seqñ dc̃m trappour liƀatum fuit p p̃ceptū dc̃i *Wiłłi Roƀto Rolleston̄* Cl̃ico magne garderobe Dñi Regis in eadem garderoba custodienđ ad opus Regis ꝛc̃.

(p. 55.)

9 Hen. V.

1 ♣ Me^d^ qđ Dñs Thesaurar̃ ꝛ Barones de Sc^a^cio liƀav̄unt in Receptā ejusdem *xxiiii*^to^ *Aprił* anno *ix*^o^ Regis *Henrici quinti* unā ollam de beralle garnisat̃ ꝛ ligat̃ cū auro puro.

Jocał liƀat̃ in Thes̃ R̃.

2 Itꝫ *eodem die* unū ciphū de jaspyr auro inclusum cū coopculo qui quidem ciphus ⁊ olla pōiti fuerunt p Camar̃ *ix°* die *Maii eodem anno* in Thesaur̃ Dñi Regis ⁊ ibm rem̃ int̃ alia jocal dc̃i Dñi Regis. ✠

3 Medᵈ' qd Dñs Thesaurar̃ libavit in Receptā Scᵃcii *viii°* die *Maii* anno *ix°* Regis *Henrici quinti* unam acquietanciā fc̃am p illos qui ceperunt *Johem Olde-castell* Lollardum ⁊ ponitʳ in pixide hente tale signū

Lollardus Lollardoꝝ.

Acquiet' eor' qui ceperunt Joh'em Oldecastell.

Que ponitʳ int̃ alias rememoracões in ||veridi cista.

4 Itꝫ libavit in eandem Receᵃᵐ *xvi°* die *Maii eod anno* unā aliā acquietanc̃ dc̃oꝝ hoim remanent in eadem pixide.

(p. 55 b.) Jocal libat *Thome Chittern̄.*

5 Medᵈ' qd Dñs Thesaurarius libavit in Receptā Scᵃcii *xii°* die *Octobr̃* ["anno *ix°* Reg̃ *H. quinti*"] ||unum pelvim duos discos ⁊ unū ciphum argenteos hentes tale signū

rem̃ in una cista [in] domo compoꝝ.

Postea viꝫ *xxviii°* die *ejusdem mensis* px seqñ libantʳ *Thome Chyttern̄* p manus *Rog̃i Keston̄.*

nˡ *Radclyf.'*

Radclyf.

6 Medᵈ' qd *xxi* die *Novembr̃* anno *ix°* Regis *Henrici quinti Johes Radclyf'* Miles libavit in Recept Scᵃcii p manus *Alexandri Lasyngby* tayloʳ unū discū elimosinar̃ ad modū navis ibm custodiend.

["Delibatʳ *Robto Felton̄* Clico unus discus elemo-"sinar̃ Elimosinar̃ *Katine* Reⁿᵉ *Angl.*"]

Postea viȝ *xxiii°* die *ejusdem mensis eodem anno* lib̄atʳ *Rob̄to Feltoñ* Cl̄ico "elimosinario *Kat̃ine* Re-" gine *Angl̄*" p̱ Thesaur̃ ꝛ Cam̃arios dc̄i Scᵃcii.

Tractatꝰ ꝛ concorđ int̃ Reḡ *Angl̄* ꝛ Ducē *Januenš.*

7 Medʼ qđ "*Witts* [*Kynwolmersshe*]" Thesaurarius "*Anglie*" lib̄avit in Receptā Scᵃcii *xii°* die *Decembr̃* anno *nono* Regis *Henrici quinti* unum quat̃num continent̃ tractatum ꝛ concordiam h̄it̃ int̃ *Regem Angl̄* ꝛ Ducē *Januenš* sigillat̃ sub sigillo dicti Ducis ꝛ cōi sigillo Civitatis "*Januenš*" inclusis in quadam pixide ꝛ ponitʳ in quadam pixide habente tale signū

Januenš.

rem̃ in una cista supᵃ Receptā Principatus *Wallie.*

[" Lib̄ Custodi pivati sigilli p̱ Theš *Angl̄ iiii°* die " *Jul̄* a° *iido* ℞ *E. iiiiti* Et postea *vii°* die *Julii* " *eođ a°* idem Custos pivati sigilli lib̄avit quat̃nū " p̱dc̃m in Thesaurar̃ ℞."]

(p. 56.) 8 Medʼ qđ "*Witts* [*Kynwolmersshe*]" Theš ["*Angl̄*"] ꝛ Cam̃arii receperunt in Thesaurariam Dñi Regis *vii* die *Novembr̃* anno *ix°* Regis *Henrici* [*quinti*] unū ciphū auri garniš cū foliis de hathorne circa coop̱cl̄m ꝛ pedem ejusdem Et unū aliū ciphū auri chaced cū una perula in sūmitate ejusdem Et unū par pelviū argenti ꝛ deaurat̃ chaced cū uno sole ꝛ cū cervis in fundo eoꝝdem garniš cū xix parvis perulis Et unā ollam potellar̃ veter̃ deaurat̃ qui remanent in Theš int̃ al̄ jocalia Dñi Regis que quidem jocal̄ [nup̱] invadiat̃ fuerunt *Witto Haryngtoñ* Militi.

Jocal̄ quondā invađ *Witto Haryngtoñ* Ch̄r.

(p. 56 b.) 9 Medʼ qđ Theš ꝛ Cam̃arii receperunt in Thesaur̃ Dñi Regis *iiiito* die *Febr̃* anno *ix°* Regis *Henrici quinti* unū ciphū argenti [cū coopculo] deauraẗ chaced ⁊ ||stampes. Et unū parvū ewer argenti deauraẗ cū una alba ||aquilia in sūmitate ejusdem. Et quatuor discos ⁊ unū salsariū argenti sub ||cigno armoꝫ *Anglie* restituẗ p manus *Willi Redeston̄* rem̄ ibm int̾ alia jocał Dn̄i Regis que quidem jocał nup invadiaẗ fuerunt *Joh̄i Philip̄* Armig̾o.

Jocał quondā invadiaẗ *Joh̄i Philip̄* Armig̾o restiẗ p *Witt Redeston̄.*

10 Meᵈ' qđ Thes̄ ⁊ Cam̾arii receperunt in Thesaur̄ Dn̄i Regis *xvii*° die *Febr̄* anno *ix*° Regis *Henrici quinti* unum ||hauslyn̄ dc̄i Dn̄i Regis enbroudet ⁊ couchet cum pre ⁊ ał petris vocaẗ safers ⁊ balise restiẗ eisđ " die ⁊ . . . . p *Joh̄em Skydmore* Ch̄r sibi " libaẗ p *Joh̄em* "*Broune*" nup garcionem cam̾e " Dn̄i Regis."

Unū ||hauslyn Reḡ *Henr̄ quinti.*

11 Meᵈ' qđ Thes̄ ⁊ Cam̾ar̄ receperunt in Thesaur̄ Dn̄i Regis *vi*ᵗᵒ die *Marcii* anno *ix*° Regis *Henrici quinti* unū ciphū auri cū armis de ||*Navern̄* garnis̄ supᵃ cū ix pvis baleys iii pvis saphyres ⁊ xxx perles ⁊ unū paxbređ auri ||amelaẗ de blođ cū una ymagine *B'e Marie* alb̄ que quidem jocalia fuerunt in custodia *Ric̄i Courtney* nup Ep̄i *Norwic̄* nup Custodis jocaliū dc̄i Dn̄i Reḡ [⁊] hic restituuntʳ p *Walt̾um Beauchamp̄* Ch̄r.

Jocał quondam in custodia *Ric̄i Courtnay* nup Ep̄i *Norwic̄* exisẗ restiẗ p *Walt̾ū Beauch̄* Ch̄r.

---

10 Hen. V. &c.

(p. 57.) Acquiẗ Ambassiatoꝫ Comiẗ *Fuxi*
Comes de *Foitz.*

1 Međ qđ Dn̄s Thes̄ libavit in Reᵗᵃ Scᵃcii *x*° die *Junii* anno *decimo* Reḡ *Henrici quinti* unā acquietanc̄ " Ambassiatoꝫ Comitis *Fuxi* fc̄a Thes̄ *Anglie* " de c̾ta sūma dc̄is ābassiatoribꝫ p ip̄m Thes̄ soluẗ " de quodā appuncẗ int̾ Reḡ *Franc̄* ⁊ dc̄m [Comi-

"tem et]" unū instrumentū eandem solucōem testificans ꝛ affirmans que quidem acq̃ ꝛ instr̃m ponūtʳ in quandᵃm pixidem ad tale signū

remanent̃ in quadam cista supᵃ Reᵗᵃ Ducatꝰ *Lancastr̃.*

2 [" Mdʾ q̃d *xiiiᵒ* die *Marcii* aᵒ *xxᵒ* R̃ *Henr̃ viᵗⁱ*
" Ep̃us *Lincolñ* lib̃avit in Reᵗᵃᵐ Scᵃcii dc̃i Dñi R̃
" ꝑ mꝰ *Henr̃ Benet* duas lr̃as de tractatu ꝛ con-
" cordia fc̃a intꝰ Dñm *H* nuꝑ Regē *Angl̃ quintū*
" ꝛ *Joh̃em* Com̃ de *Foitz*, de dat̃ *xviᵒ* die *Marcii*
" aᵒ. Dñi *mill̃mo iiiiᶜ xxiᵒ* et rem̃ in una pixide cū
" aliis evidenc̃ ejusd̃ Com̃ ut supᵃ."]

Muniment̃ Comit *Hunt̃.* 3 Medʾ qd̃ Dñs Thes̃ lib̃avit in Reᵗᵃᵐ Scᵃcii *xxi* die *Julii* anno *decimo* Reg̃ *Henr̃ quinti* quamdᵃm bagam de canabo continent̃ cartas ꝛ monimenta *Joh̃is* Comitis *Hunt̃* sigill̃ sigillo *Will̃i Yerde* nuꝑ Locumtenent̃ *Turr̃ Londoñ* ꝛ ponitʳ in cista ad capud grad̃ camꝰe computatoꝝ ad tale signū

4 [" Postea vȝ *xii* die *Junii* anno *quarto* Reg̃
" *Henr̃. sexti* virtute br̃is huic folio consut̃ dc̃a
" baga cum cartis ꝛ aliis munimentis in eadem con-
" tent̃ lib̃ata fuit dc̃o Comiti ꝑ manus † ."]

(p.57 b.) 5 Medʾ qd̃ Dñs Thes̃ ꝛ Camꝰarii receperunt in Theseraur̃ Dñi Regis *penultīo* die *Maii* anno *xᵒ* Regis *Henrici quinti* certa jocalia [dc̃i] Dñi Regis vidȝ unū paxbrede auri enamelet cū albo ꝛ crucifixo cū ymag̃ *B'e Marie* ꝛ *Joh̃is Evangeliste* ꝛ unam ꝑvā tabulam auream factã ad modũ spectaculi garnisat̃ cũ trib; bat̃ ix perulis pendent̃ p unam cathenã auri ex una pte ‖amelat̃ cũ salutacõe *B'e Marie* ⁊ ex alt̃a pte spectacul̃ vitri ⁊ alia plura jocalia put continet^r in quadam indentura huic folio consuta que quidem jocal̃ restitut̃ fuerunt *eisdem die* ⁊ *anno* p *Radm̃ Shyrley* in uno calatho rem̃ int̃ alia jocalia dc̃i Dñi Reg̃ infra Thesaraur̃ in Abbia *Westm̃.*

(In sched p. 58.) 6 ♣ Cest endenture faite pentre *Richard Courtenay* l Evesq; de *Norwicz* Tresorer del Chambre du Roy nr̃e S'vaigne S^r ⁊ gardein de ces joialx d un part ⁊ mon Sr *Rauf de Schirley* Chr retenu ovec nr̃e dit S^r le Roy p^r luy s̃vir en ceo p̃sent voiage es pties d outre la mer p un an entier ovec vi launcez luy mesmes acompte ⁊ xviii arch d autre pt tesmoigne q̃ le dit *Richard* p vertu ⁊ comandement des lr̃es patentes du Roy seales de soun g^aunde seal ovec un bille seale du signet ⁊ signe p les mains du Tresorer *dEngletre* sur ceo a luy adrecez ad deliṽe au dit †dit Mons̃ *Rauf* primerment un paxbred d or esmaile blanc d un crucifix *Marie* ⁊ *John* pois̃ de troie v uncz p^is del unce xxvi s̃ viii d̃ la somme vi li vi s̃ viii d̃ Itm un tablet d or fait al manre d un merour garniz de iii bat̃ ix ples pendantz p un cheyne d or dount en l un coste esmaile de la salutacõn de *nr̃e Dame* ⁊ en l autre coste un mirour pois̃ vi uncz di ⁊ di q^artr̃ p^is de tout xii li Itm un corone d or garniz de iiii bat̃ vi saph ⁊ de xiiii ples pois̃ ii uncz di xx d̃ p^is de unce xl s̃ la somme c s̃ Itm iiii gros sonettes d or p^r faukenes ovec ii vertucles ⁊ i ‖warrek d or ⁊ xxxi autres sonettes d un ‖shap̃ d or pois̃ ensemble xii uncz xx d̃ p^is le unce xxvi. s̃ viii d̃ la somme xvi li xx d̃ Itm un corn garniz d argent enorrez le tussu de soy noier poiš ensemble ii lb v unc̃ di p's c š Itm ii colers d or dount le corps del un vert ꝛ de l autre noier poisantz ensemble xviii uncz di qartr dount abatez pr les tussuez ii uncz di qartr p's de unce xxvi š viii đ la somme xxi li vi š viii đ Itm ii cruettes de berill garniz d or pois ensemble xi uncz v š d ount abatez pr le berill iii uncz v š p's le unce xxvi š viii đ la somme x li xiii š iiii đ Itm un petit maser de jasp garniz d or ꝛ d un saph iii ples sr le somet pisauntz ensemble xxi unc̃ i qartr p's de or ꝛ pe xv li xiii š iiii đ pr la surte de iiii^xx vi li ii š viii đ la quele somme il doit pndre ꝛ receivoir pr le seconde qart entier de l an susdit solonc la forme ꝛ porport de les endentures sur ceo faitz pentre le Roy nr̃e Sovaigne Sr susdit ꝛ le dit Monsr *Rauf* d ount le jor de paiment a quele le Roy veolt ꝛ doit. . . . . . lez joialx avantditz p ces deputees ꝛ assignez ses heires ou executours serra le jor de *Circumcision* q̃ sra l an du grace *ml iiiic xvi* solonk le course ꝛ computacion de lEsglise *dEngletre* purveu toutfoiz q̃ le dit Monsr *Rauf* soit tenu de bien ꝛ loialment garder les joialx avantditz saunz debrusement ou empeirement d icelles en aucun manre tanq̃ au dit jor sicome il voelt ent respondre vers mesme nr̃e Sr le Roy ses heires ou executr En tesmoignance de quele chose a ycestes endentures les pties avantditz entrechaungeablement ont mys lour seales Don̄ a *Wyncestr* le *vi* jor de *Julet* l an du regne nr̃e dit Sr le Roy *Henry quinte* puis le conquest *tierce*.

(p. 58.) Indentura *Randolf.*

7 Medr qd Dn̄s Theš libavit in Recept Scacii *sexto* die *Julii* anno *x*o Regis *Henrici quinti* unam

indentur̃ de bonis ⁊ jocalibʒ Fr̃is *Joh̃is Randolf* invent̃ infra Domū *Fratrū Minoꝝ* in Villa *Salop̃* ⁊ ponit[r] in una pixide ad tale signū

rem̃ in viridi cista infra Receptā p̃dc̄am.

" Jocalia infra dc̄am "indenturā" content̃ lib̃ant[r]
" ext[a] dc̄am Thes̃ p Dñm [Ep̃m *Bathoñ*] Thes̃ *Angl̃*
" ⁊ Cam̃arios executoribʒ test̃i Reg̃ *Henrici quinti*
" p lr̃am de privato sigillo "⁊ de" mandato Magni
" Consilii vidl̃t *xix* die *Julii* anno *primo* Regis
" *Henrici sexti.*"

(p. 59 b.) 8 [Lib̃ac̄o bag̃ ꝑ Sc[a]cio Dñi R̷ t̃mīo *Mich̃*. a°. *xv°*. r̃ R̷ *Ric̃i scd̃i*.

ꝑ off̃o Cl̃ici ad extract̃ } i. bag̃. de . viii. / i. bag̃ de . vi. / iii. bag̃ . q̃ . de . iiii.

ꝑ off̃o Pipe iiii. bag̃ . q̃ . de . iii.

ꝑ. Privat̃ sig̃ . iii. bag̃ . q̃ . de . vi.

ꝑ. *Joh̃e Stav̾ton* . i. bag̃ de . ii. duodeñ.

ꝑ. off̃o Cl̃ici ad pl̃ita . i. bag̃ . de . xii.

ꝑ offic̄o *J. Stav̾ton* i. bag̃ cont̃ ii. duodeñ lib̃at̃ t̃io *Hill̃ a° s[a]dc̄o.*]

9 M[d] qd̃ *xxvii* die *Octobr̃* anno r̃ . R̷ . *H.* ||*quarti*. ||*decimo* [" lib̃at̃ fuit Thes̃ ⁊ Cam̃ar̃"] unū br̃e de c̃tiorari ꝑ *Henr̃ Bewemoūt* ⁊ aliis ꝑ expedic̄oe cujusdā scrutinii ꝑ [quodā] teñ inf[a] Civitatem *Londoñ* in parochia *O'i'm Sc̄oꝝ* parva sup solariū in *Tēmestrete.* *Bewemoūt.*

1 Hen. VI.

(p. 60.) 1 Med' qđ Dñs Thes̃ libavit in Recept̃ Scacii viii° die Octobr̃ anno regni Regis *Henrici sexti* Acquietanc̃ *Barnardi de Lesparre.* *primo* unam acquietanc̃ fc̃am Dño Regi patri Dñi Regis nunc p *Barnardum de Lesparre* Dñm *de la Barda* cū una carta duobȝ sigill̃ sigillat̃ ⁊ signat̃ cū signeto uni⁹ molett̃ que quidem acquiet̃ ⁊ carta ponunt[r] in quad[a]m pixide ad tale signū

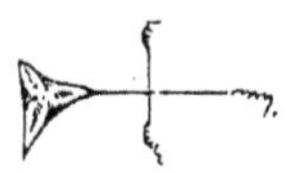

rem̃ in cista ad capud gradus domus computatoȝ.

‖Conclucio pacis int̃ Reges *Angl̃* *Henr̃ quintū* ⁊ *Karolū* *Francie.* 2 Md' " qđ Magist̃ *Jofies Stafford* Custos p[i]vati " sigilli libavit in Re[tā] Sc[a]cii *xvii°* die *Novēbr̃* anno " *primo* Reg̃ *Henrici sexti* tractatū ⁊ conclusionē " pacis [in Gallico] int̃ *Henricū quintū* Regē *Angl̃* " ⁊ *Karolū* Regē" *Francie* fact̃ Dat̃ *xxi°* die *Maii* anno Dñi *m*[l] *cccc° xx°* ⁊ regni Regis " *Franc̃*" *xl°* que rem̃ in una pixide ad tale signū

in magna cista cum tribȝ ‖ceruř sup[a] Consiliū Principat⁹ *Wallie.*

3 " Idem Magist̃ *Jofies* Cancellar̃ *Angl̃* libvit in " Re[tā] p̃dc̃am *xxi°* die *Maii* anno *x°* dc̃m tractatū "Conclusio "pacis int̃ "regna "p̃dc̃a." " pacis in Latinis cuj⁹ sigillū includit[r] in ‖quodam " ‖rotundo pixide existente in uno quadrato cofino " ad tale signū

" in cista sup[a] domū Consilii Principatus p̃dc̃i."

(p. 60 b.) 4 " Md' qđ Dux *Glouc̃* lib̃avit in Receptā Scacii " *xxi*° die *Novēbr̃* anno *primo* R *Henrici sexti* [p m " *Nic̃hi Dixoñ*] magnū sigillū aureū Cancellarie Dñi " Regis [" *H. quinti* "] quod quidem sigillū ponitur " p Camar̃ in una cista ferro ligata ubi moneta poni " solet infra Thesaurar̃ Dñi Reg̃ infra Abbiam *Westm̃* " in una baga de corr̃ sub sigillo dc̃i *Ducis* sigillat̃."

Sigillū aureū Cancellar̃.

5 " Dict̃ sigillū lib̃at̃ fuit Magr̃o *Joh̃i Staff*' Thes̃ " *Angl̃* p Camar̃ Scacii dc̃i Dñi Regis p p̃ceptū " ip̃ius Thes̃ *xxviii* die *Januarii* anno *qarto* Regis " p̃dc̃i sigillat̃ sub sigill̃ Ducis *Glouc̃* 't alioꝝ Dñoꝝ " de Consilio Reg̃ ad deferend̃ usq; *Seint Albones* 't " ibidē delib̃and̃ Duci *Bedford̃* 't aliis Dñis Magni " Consilii dc̃i Dñi Regis."

n[1]'

" Jocal̃ " lib̃at̃ " *Ric̃o* " *Rystoñ*."

6 Fait a rem̃br̃ q̃ *William Kynwolm̃ssh̃* Tresorer *dEngletre* lessa en la gaunde Tresory ||de Roy. c̃teyns joialx p luy rescieux de *Thomas Rokes* au temps q̃ la *Roigne* deptist ṽs le *Roy* en *Faunce* cest assavoir iii. salers d argent ennorrez l un coṽee i pair basyns d argent ennorez 't. ii. spiceplates d argent lez qeux joialx fuerent lyṽez le *xxii* jor de *Janver* l an *pimer* le Roy *Henr̃ le sisme* p Maister *Joh̃n Stafford̃* Tresorer *dEngletre* a *Ric̃ Rystoñ*. Clerk assigne pr l ostell̃ dez Embassitors du Counsell̃ de *Fance*, les queles joalx suisdc̃ez fuerunt deliṽez p [le] dit *Richard̃* [a] *Thomas Rokes* [le] *xv.* jour de *Maii* pchein ensuaunt a le use le Roy.

" *Merstoñ*."

(p. 61.) 7 ✠ Memorand̃ qđ "*Joh̃* [Ep̃us *Bathoñ*]" Thesaur̃ 't Camarii receperunt in magnā Thes̃ Dñi Reg̃ *xxii* die *Aprilis* anno *primo* Regis *Henrici sexti* duos cophinos corrii 't unū ligni in quib; continentr certa jocalia nup *Walt̃o Hungerford̃* Militi "invadiata" 't p eundem *dc̃is die* ꝛ *anno* in dc̃am "Thesaur̃" restituta ꝛ remanent in magna cista int̃ alia jocalia Dñi Regis quoꝝ ꝑcelle ꝑut in quadam indẽtura int̃ *Ric̃m Courteney* Ep̃m *Norwicen̄* ꝛ "dc̃m *Walterū*" fact̃ continet[r] ꝑticularit̃ seq̃unt[r]. En p[i]mez un tablet d ore de *Nr̃e Dame* esmaillez d asuer pendant ꝑ un cheyne d ore ovec un anell̃ d ore ꝛ d argent ovec un dyamande flatte de iii corners ꝛ de iiii rubies ii safires xx perles poysant de troye lviii unc̃ dĩ ꝑc̃ de tout iiii[xx]xi. li vi. s̃. viii d̃. It̃ un haute tabernacle d argent enorres. ovec vi. aungels sur le pee ovec un ymage de *Nr̃e Dame* en my lieu ꝛ sur la dit ymage un ymage de *Seint John Bapt* ꝛ ꝑamont un crucifix *Mary* ꝛ *John* pois̃ xxx lb̃ de troye p[i]c̃ le lb̃ xlvi s̃ viii d̃ lxx li.

Jocalia nuꝑ invadiata *Walt̃o Hungerford.*

8 Itm un tabernacle d ore d un ‖pice a deu[a]nt ꝛ ✠ a derer ✠ ꝛ a derer de Seint *John Bapt* ꝛ ꝑamont d un crucifix *Mary* ꝛ *John* esteant sur un pee d ore ovec un vert tarege ꝛ de vi. cerfz blankz garniz de. ii. diamandez un baloys un esmeraude ii safirez ꝛ la croyse desuz de ii. baloys ii. safirez ꝛ a derer de iiii groz ꝑles ꝛ de pluso[r]z autrez petitz ꝑlez assavoir ent̃ment garniz pois vi lb̃ ii. unc̃ ꝑc̃ del unc̃ xxvi s̃ viii d̃ ꝑc̃ de tout iiii[xx]xviii li. xiii. s̃. iiii d̃ Itm iii holowe esqueles d argent enorrez ovec un saucer d argent enorrez poisant ensemble vii. lb̃ ꝑc̃ le lb̃ xlviii s̃ lx. li. xvi. s̃.

"Et me[d'] qd̃ dc̃a disci ꝛ salsariū rem̃ ext[a] dc̃os "cophinos ꝛ ponūt[r] in uno panno lineo in dc̃a cista "signato sub sigillo Subthesaur̃" ✠

(p. 61 b.)

Impator̃.

Rex *Romanoꝝ.*

9 M[d'] qd̃ om̃es alligancie ꝛ tractat[9] hit̃ ꝛ fact̃, int̃ Reges *Angl*, et diṽs Impatores *Aleman̄*, tem-

ꝑibȝ Regum *Henrici quarti quinti* ⁊ *sexti* ꜟ remañ
Impatoꝛ̃. insimul in uno coffro pictato in una magna cista sup^a
Re^tam ubi ponit^r ꝑgamenū.

10 M^d' qđ "*xxvii.*" die *Maii* anno *primo* Regis
Frater *Joħes* *Henrici sexti* Dñs Thes̃ liƀavit ext^a Theserauɼ̃ Dñi
Randolf. Regis *Roƀto Babthorp̃* Militi ex precepto Dñi Ducis
de prestito *Exoñ* de prestito unū ꝑvū missale cooꝑtū in panno
auri quod quondam fuit Fr̃is *Joħis Randolf.*

(p. 62.) 11 Me^d' qđ *xv^o*. die *Junii* anno *primo* Reg̃ *Hen-*
Acquitanc̃ *rici sexti* " *Wiłłs* [*Kynwolmersshe*] " Thesauɼ̃ *Angł*
Xp̃oforі *Prestoñ.* liƀavit in Receptam Sc^acii unā acquietanc̃ *Xp̃ofori*
Prestoñ Armigi fc̃am Dño Regi nūc ⁊ executoribȝ
testamenti Regis *Henrici quinti* ⁊ ponit^r in quadam
pixide rem̃ in viridi cista infra dc̃am Receptam ad
tale signū

12 Me^d' qđ " *Wiłłs* [*Kynwolmersshe*] " Thes̃
"Jocał liƀał [*Angł*] liƀavit in magnā Thesauɼ̃ Dñi Regis ꝑcio
"in The- die *Julii* anno *primo* Regis *Henrici sexti* unū ciphū
"sauɼ̃ Reg̃." cooꝑtū argenti ⁊ deauratū ext^a "⁊ infra" albū ⁊

unū añulū pontificał argenti ⁊ deaurał qui rem̃ in
magna cista infra dc̃am Thes̃ int̃ ał jocał Dñi Regis.

13 " M^d' qđ *Petrus Pole* liƀavit in Re^tam Sc^acii
" *p^imo* die *Maii* anno *ix^o* dicł Regis unū recordū de
Deliƀac̃o " deliƀac̃oe gaole apud *Derby* pro *Roƀto Eyre* de
gaole *Derƀ.* " *Padeley* ⁊ ponit^r int̃ alia recorđ infra magnā Thes̃
" Dñi Reg̃."

(p. 62 b.) 14 Me^d' qđ *xii* die *Julii* anno regni Regis *Hen-*
rici sexti primo "*Wiłłs* [*Kynwolmersshe*]" Thes̃ *Angł*

iiii ||diamaunt [ovesq̧] i nouche p̱amount lour testez garnisez d un rubie i graund diamaund poynted ⁊ iii graundez p̱les ⁊ de soubz les pees du ditz dames sont ||assez ii saphiers ✢ poiš de troie vi unc̃. ✢ d̃i qªrt̃ ✢ p̃c̃ en tout xxiiii li. que ||quedam jocalia ponuntʳ in qªdam cista cū iii seruris "infra ||Theser̃ "Regis cū al̃ jocalib₃."

✢ Postea vidl̃t *pⁱmo* die *Novembr̃* p̱x̃ seqñ dc̃m almesdych̃ lib̃atʳ de mandato dc̃i Dñi Theš *Joh̃i Marstoñ* Cl̃ico jocaliū Dñi Reg̃ ad deaurand̃ ✢

2 ✢ Postea restituitʳ v₃ *vi* die *Decembr̃* anno *vii* ejusd̃ R̷ ✢

"Et postea v₃ *xiii* die *Juñ* anno ||*vii*° dc̃i R̷ "[lib̃atur] *Joh̃i fitz Rob̃t* aurifabro ad facienđ unū "scutū cū armis Reg̃ in fundo ejusđ."

(p.70.) 3 "Postea videl̃t *xxi* jour *d Octobr̃* l an *viii*ᵉ "*Henr̃* le ✢*vi*ᵉ✢ Roy *vi*ᵉ. dez joalx susditz sont liṽez

Merstoñ. "a *Joh̃n Merstoñ* lez joalx ensuantz cest assavoir "i grªunde almoigne dissh̃ pee d argent p̱cell̃ en-"norres ovesq̧ les armes de *Sʳ de Lowell* It̃ i petit "paxbrede d or ii cuclers d or ⁊ i chaundeller d or "i braselet d or" "fait de deux dames."

"It̃m le dit almusdissh̃ fuist deliṽe p̱ le Sire "*Hungerfordˀ* Theš *dEnglet̃* a *Joh̃n Hotoft* Thresor̃ "del hostiel nr̃e Sʳ le Roy le *xx*ᵉ joʳ de *Jul̃* l an "*vii*ᵉ."

4 ✢ "Mᵈ' qđ "*Walt̃us*" *Hungrefordˀ* Theš *Angl̃* "delib̃avit in ||Thesauriam Regis ib̃m custodienđ

Le coler appel *Iklyngtoñ.* "*xxv* die *Novembr̃* anno regni Regis *Henr̃ sexti vi*ᵗᵒ "un graunde coler d or de *Iclyngtoñ* que fuist a "Roy le pere le Roy suisdt̃e quaunt il fuist Prince "le dit coler garniz de iiii rubes iiii grossez saphiers "xxxii graundez perles ⁊ liii auťs perles d autre

" sort meyns poisaunt xxxvi unc̃. ⁊ iii quarton̄ " nadgayrs livͤe p̱ le Erchesvesq̧ de *Canterbers*. ⁊ " *Joh̄n Wakerhyng̃* Gardein du prive seal p̱ autorite

" q̧ lib̄at^r " *Joh̄i Mers-* " *ton̄* p̱ in- " dentur̃."

" [poair] ⁊ maundem̄t du dit nadgayrs Roy a " *Thomas Peverelł* le Evesq̧ de *Wycestr̃* ||a " *Ric̃* " [*Crosby*]" Priour de *Coventre* ⁊ lez Maier ⁊ " Comunaltee de la Cite de *Coventr̃* ⁊ *Wilł Wal-* " *tam* Clerk p^r suertee de la repaiem̄t de cynk centz " livers de eux criansez al oeps du dit nadgairs " Roy." ♣

(p. 70 b.)

5 Memoranđ qđ " *Waltus* Dominus" *Hungerforđ* Thes̃ *Angł* lib̄avit in Re^tam Sc^acii *xxii*^do die *Octobr̃* anno *sexto* Regis *Henr̃ sexti* quatuor indentur̃ ib̄m custodienđ videłt unam fc̄am int *Jacobum* Comit̃

Hib̄nia.

d Ormon̄ locum tenentem Dn̄i Regis t̃re *Hib̄nie* ✻ ||*Euvegeniū Oneyłł Hib̄nic̃.*

It̃ aliam indent̃ fc̄am int eundem Comitem ⁊ *Bernardum M'maghon̄* ⁊c̃.

It̃ aliam indenturam fc̄am int eunđm Comit̃ ⁊ *Dermoin̄ O Tothiłł* ⁊c̃.

It̃ aliam indēt̃ fc̄am int eunđ Com̄ ⁊ *Donatū O Bryn̄* ⁊c̃. Que ||quedem indentur̃ posite sunt in quodam longo |||ligni cophano in quadam cista existen̄ ad capud g^adus Cam̄e computatoꝝ ad tale signū

{**Dormond.**}

6 Memoranđ qđ *Waltus* [Dn̄s] *Hungirforđ* Thes̃ *Angł* lib̄avit in Thesaur̃ Regis ib̄m custodienđ "*xxiii*" die "*Januar̃*" a^o r̃ ℞ *Henr̃ vi*^ti *vi*^to viłt ♣ i hanape

Ascowe.

d argent dorrez fait a la m̄ de "i ||notte" poissant de troye iii lb̄ iiii unz q^at le lb̄ xlviii. s̃ ♣ viii li ♣ It̃

" Lib̄ant^r " *Joh̄i Ho-* " *toft.*"

i esquel ⁊ iiii sausers d argent poisant ensemble iiii lb̄ i unz p̄c̃ le lb̄ xxx s̃ ♣ vi li ii. s̃ vi đ que quedam jocalia delibaẗ fuerunt p *Ricm* nup Epm *Norwic* p indent *Johi Aske* Armigo p vad suis pfectur cu Dno Reg vsus ptes *Franc*.

" Quia libantr *Johi Hotoft* Thes Hospit Reg p " m *Johis Merston* ad inde faciend unu chaufyng- " dyssh p Dno Rege."

(p. 71.) 7 ||Soit a remembre q *Walter* Sr de *Hungyrford* ||Treserer d *Engletre* ad delivere en le Tresorye du Roy en mesme le Tresory a garder le *ix* jour de *Februar* l an du reigne de nre tssovaigne Sr le Roy *Henr vi*e aps le conquest *vi*e. i esqueller d argent dorrez poissant ii lb viii unc. pc le lb xlviii s. la sma vi. li viii s. " nadgairs en gages a *Thom Corbet* " Esquier p le * *Ric Courteney* lEsvesq de *Norwic*."

Corbet.

8 ¶ Fait a remembrer q *Walter* Sr de *Hungirford* Tresorer *dEngletr* ad delive en le Tresory nre Sr le Roy le *xii* jour de *Maye* l an *sisme* le Roy *Henr* le *sisme* ✠ ii crowettes & i petit sonet d or ✠ poissant ||emsemble xxiiii unz & di p'c le unz [xxvi s viii d. Sma xxxii li xiii s iiii d] queux fuerent livez p *Richard* nadgares Esvesq de *Norwic* a *Reynald Lental* Chr sur cez gages de guerre vs les pties de *Fraunce*.

Roulandus Lentall.

" q libantr " *Johi Merston* p in- " dent & bre " de priv " sigillo."

" q libantr " *Johi Merston*."

---

7 & 8 Hen. VI.

1 Md' qd *Waltus* Dns *Hungreford* Thes *Angl* libavit in Thesaur Dni Regis "*tcio*" die "*Decembr*" anno regni Reg *Henr sexti* [*viii*o] unu magnu florem voc *Floure de lys* cujusdam Corone garnizatu de una magna baleia & una tminora baleia uno rube trib; magnis saphirs decem magnis perlis et duodeci minorib; perlis nup vadiatu *Thome* nup Duci *Clarencie*

Flos. ꝛ p̱ ꝉidem nup̱ Ducem *Joħi Colvyłł* Militi liƀatū sup̱ vadiis guerre Et ponitur in quadam " baga de

Colvyłł. " canabo cū uno alio p̱vo flore ejusdem corone ut " sequitʳ."

" Istud pinaclm ponitʳ in quođ hanap̱io voc̃ ‖cop- " cas in magna cista infra Thesaur̃ R̷ *Westm̃.*"

2 Itm idem Dñs Thes̃ liƀavit in eandem Thesaur̃ *vi*ᵗᵒ die *Julii* dc̃o anno *viii*ᵒ unū "pinaclm" dc̃e corone ‖garniztū cū duobȝ saphiris ꝛ uno sqware baleys ꝛ

Pudsey. vi p̱les nup̱ vadiatū dc̃o Duci ꝛ p̱ ꝉidem Ducem liƀatū *Joħi Pudsey* Armig̃o p̱ vađ suis guerre ꝛ ponitʳ in quađ pixide cū dc̃o magno flore in quađ baga de canabo resident̃ in quađ magna cista infᵃ Thesaur̃ Reg̃.

" Istud pinaclm mittitʳ in p̃dc̃o hanap̱io ut supᵃ."

(p. 71 b.) 3 ✠ Mᵈ' qđ *Walt̃us* Dñs *Hungerforđ* liƀavit in Thesaurar̃ Dñi Regis p̱ m⁹ *Joħis Wodehous xxiii* die *Aprilis* anno *vii*ᵒ Regis *Henr̃ sexti* unū *Magnū* "*Circulū*" de auro garnisat̃ de quinquaginta ꝛ quatuor balys quadraginta saphuris octo dyamanđ ꝛ

Magnū Circlm. quadraginta ꝛ septem magnis ‖perls ponderis de troye iiii lƀ ✠ except̃ ✠ app̃ciat̃ ad viiiᶜ li nup̱ invadiat̃ p̱ reṽendᵐ in Xp̃o p̃rem *Henr̃ Cantuar̃* Archiep̃m ꝛ *Joħem Wakeryng̃* Custođ pⁱvati sigilli Majoribȝ ꝛ Cōitatibȝ Civitatū *Norwici* ꝛ *Lenne* ac aliis diṽs p̱sonis [p̱ mˡ mᵃr̃ un̄ remiserūt Regi l mᵃr̃] p̱ut in quadam indentura plenius continetʳ remanent̃ in hanap̱io de t̃mīo [*Pasche*] dc̃o anno *vii*ᵒ. ✠

[" qȝ liƀatʳ *Joħ Merstoñ* p̱ indentur̃ ‖vertute bris " de pⁱvat̃ sigillo int̃ manđ de t̃mīo *Mich* anno *viii*ᵒ " R̷. *H. sexti.*"]

4 Mᵈ' qđ Dñs Cancellar̃ *Angl* liƀavit t̃cio die

Junii anno *vii*° Reḡ *Henr̃ sexti* in Receptam Scªcii unam indenturam ibm custodienđ sigillatam sub sigillo secreto *Jacobi* Regis *Scotoꝝ* suꝑ treugis genl-alibʒ ꝑ terram ⁊ ꝑ mare duratur̃ ꝑ septenniū concordat̃ int ipm Regem *Scotoꝝ* ⁊ Cōmissarios Reḡ *Angl* ⁊c̃. ⁊ ponitʳ in †quođ pixide in quađ cista supª " Receptam Principatus *Wall*" ad tale signū

{**Scocia.**}

" Postea vʒ *xvii* die *Jun̄* ꝑx̃ seqñ libatʳ Dño " Cancellar̃ *Angl* [" in qªdam pixide "] in domo " Dñi Ducis *Glouc̃* ad delibanđ Magr̃o *Joħi Stokes.*"

" Postea viʒ *xiiii*° die *Decembr̃* anno *viii*° dc̃i " Reḡ idem Magr̃ *Joħ Stokes* restituit dc̃am in-" denturam cū duabʒ indentur̃ Cōmiss̃ Reḡ que " quiđ ||pixidis ponitʳ in alia magna pixide cū al " evidenc̃ tanḡ Reḡ *Angl* ⁊ *Scocie.*"

---

8 Hen. VI.

(p. 72.) 1 Fait a ||remenbr̃ q̃ *Reynalđ Kentewode* Dene de *Seint Poule* de *Londres*. executour des testemtz de *Joħn Chitterne* ⁊ *Walter Cook* clerkys ad delive le "*sc̃de*" jour de *Novembr̃* l an. ||oepisme ‚ le Roy *Henry* le *vi*ᵉ. a *Walt* Sʳ de *Hungſford* ⁊ Tresorer *dEnglet* ⁊ as Chamerleins des Cheker. i pair basoūs d or chasez al maner de une rose ⁊ ||ponsez ovesq, bosselettꝭ en les foūsez garnesez des [divs̃] ✝ armes ✝ armes assavoir en my lieu de *Saint George* ⁊ assuz de *Sainte Edward* ⁊ *Saint Edmūde* et en l un cost del ||*Empour* ⁊ l autre cost de *Englet* ⁊ *France* depties. et de soulz les [armes] del Princi-paltee de *Gales* ⁊ del Duchy de *Guyen̄* pois̃ en-

Decano *Sc̃i Pauli London̄.*

Pelves de auro.

semble del poise de troy xxviii lƀ viii unc̃. nadgairs mys en gage ꝑ *Thom̃ Chitt̃ne* Gardein des joualx le Roy *Henry* " pere a Roy qu or est as ♣ dite ♣ ditz " *Jon̄n* ꝛ *Walter* p^r^ repaiem̃t de vi^c^ m^a^rz a dit " nadgaire Roy [ꝑ eux] aprestez pur son passage " oultre le meer le quell̃ basous̃ sont mys en un " gr^a^unde cofer dedeins le graund Tresory."

" Postea delibant^r^ ‖dc̃i pelṽ Dño *Walt̃o Hungir-* " *ford̃* ex^a^ magnam Thes̃ ꝑ m^9^ *Jon̄is* ‖*Pouterell̃ xxii* " die *Decembr̃* anno *viii*^o^ ℞ *Henr̃ sext.*"

" Postea ‖dc̃i pelves ‖restituũt^r^ in dc̃am Thes̃ ꝑ " m^9^ *Jon̄is* ‖*Pouterell̃ xix*^o^ die *Januar̃* ꝑx̃ seqñ."

" rest." " Postea videl̃t *scd̃o* die *Maii* anno *x*^o^ dc̃e pelves " libant^r^ *Jon̄i Merstoñ* de mandato Dñi Thes̃ ꝑ " indentur̃."

" Et postea videl̃t *xvi*^o^ die *Maii* ꝑx̃ seqñ p̃dc̃us " *Jon̄es Merstoñ* delibavit [dc̃is] Thes̃ ꝛ Cam̃ar̃ " dc̃as pelves in Thesaurar̃ Reg̃ salvo custodiend̃."

" Postea sȝ *iiii* die *Febr̃* a^o^ *xi*^o^ ‖p̃dc̃i pelves ‖libati " fuerũt *Jon̄i Merstoñ* Armig̃o ꝑ bř̃e de p^i^vato " sigillo quarto folio sequẽti ꝭconsuetũ."

" Postea vȝ t̃cio die *Junii* anno *xii*^o^ dc̃i Regis rest^r^. " idem *Jon̄es Merstoñ* delibavit Thes̃ ꝛ Cam̃ar̃ de " Sc^a^cio p̃dc̃as pelves de auro in dc̃a Thes̃ Regis " salvo custodiend̃."

" Et postea *quarto* die *Junii* [" tũc ꝑx̃ sequẽte"] " ‖p̃dc̃i pelves cũ al̃ jocal̃ lib fuer̃ *Jon̄i Rus* auri- ex^a^. " fabro *Londoñ* ad invadiand̃ Dño Cardinali."

(p. 72 b.) 2 M^d^ ∗ *Rolandus Lentale* Miles libavit *Walt̃o* Dño *Lentale* *Hungerford̃* Thes̃ *Angl̃* ꝛ Cam̃ar̃ Sc^a^cii Dñi Regis " Libat^r^ Dño *viii*^o^ die *Novembr̃* anno *viii*^o^ Reg̃ *Henrici sexti* un " Cardinali tabelet d or del salutac̃on de *nr̃e Dame* garnez dez

“ *xxx* die “ *Marc̃* a^{o} “ *xvii*^{o}.” v bales v saphers ⁊ de xxv gros ꝑles ♣ dount i remaint en les mains ‖du dit *Rouland̃* ♣ pois̃ ensemble ii lb̃ . xi. unc̃ i. q^{a}rt̃.

“ Postea vȝ *xiii* die *Decembr̃* ꝓx̃ seqñ idem *Ro-* “ *landus* restit̃ ‖dc̃m ‖perle ad Re^{tam} Sc^{a}cii.”

3 M$^{d'}$ qđ *Wiłłs Meryng* Miles restituit “ *ix*^{o}. die “ *Decembr̃* ” anno *viii*^{o} Reg̃ *Henr̃ sexti Walt̃o* Dño *Hungerford̃* Thes̃ *Angł* ⁊ Camar̃ Sc^{a}cii ‖unū calicem

Meryng̃. cū pateno de argento deaurat̃ ponderant̃ ꝑ pondus de troy ii lb̃ iiii unc̃ ⁊ quatuoꝛ discos de argento insimul pond̃ ꝑ pondus ꝓdc̃m v lb̃ xi unc̃ nuꝑ

lib̃at̃ dc̃o *Wiłło* ꝓ vad̃ suis guerre ꝯsus ꝑtes *Francie* ꝑ *Ric̃m* nuꝑ Ep̃m *Norwic̃* ⁊ lib̃ant^{r} in magnam Thesaur̃ Reg̃ infra *Westm̃* ib̃m custodiend̃.

4 M$^{d'}$ qđ *Wiłłs* † “ ex^{a}.”

M$^{d'}$

5 M$^{d'}$ qđ *Wiłłs Porter* Ch̃r restituit *Walt̃o* Dño *Hungerford̃* [Thes̃ *Angł*] ⁊ Cam̃iis ‖Sc^{a}ci Dñi Regis *xxvi*^{o} die *Febr̃* anno *viii*^{o} Regis *Henr̃ vi*^{ti} unū ciphū auri ponder̃ ꝑ pond̃ de troy xxxi uncz . ⁊ . dĩ ꝓc̃ “ cujꝯlib̃ ” unc̃ xxvi s̃ viii. đ. temꝑe [nuꝑ] Reg̃ *Henr̃*

Porter. *v*^{ti} dc̃o *Wiłło* una cū ał jocalibȝ suꝑ vad̃ guerre [lib̃at̃] ⁊ ponit^{r} in quad̃ cista exist̃ in magna Thes̃ Reg̃ infra *Westm̃*.

“ Postea *iiii*^{to} die *Febr̃* a^{o} *xi*^{o} ℞ *Henrici sexti* lib̃at^{r} “ *Joh̃i Merstoñ* Armig̃o ‖vertute b̃ris de p^{i}vato si- “ gillo iiii^{to} folio seqñ consuti.”

(p. 73.) 6 Memorand̃ qđ *Walt̃us* Dñs *Hungerford̃* Thes̃ *Angł* posuit in custodiam Ab̃bis *Westm̃* *xxi* die *Aprilis* anno *viii*^{o} Reg̃ *Henr̃ sexti* unū circłum auri ad modum unius corone ⁊ tabulā cū tunica inconsutili ꝓ securit̃ uniꝯ Corone que nuꝑ fuit *Ric̃i*

nuꝑ Reğ *Angł sc̃di* eid̃m Dño Thes̃ ꝑ dc̃m Ab̃bem lib̃at̃.

7 M^d^ de una pixide [" in qua "] continet^r^ una carta ꝑ quam Rex *Franc̃* concessit ducatū *Aquitañ* p^i^mogenito Regis *Angł* ⁊ ponit^r^ in una sista " sup^a^ " Receptam Principatus *Wałł* ad tale signū "

8 M^d^ qđ *Moricius Brune* lib̃avit in Receptam Sc^a^cii Dñi Regis *xii°* die *Novembr̃* anno *ix°* Reğ *Henr̃ sexti Walt̃o* Dño *Hungˀford̃* [" Thes̃ *Angł*"] ⁊ Cam̃ar̃ unū pinacłm cujusd^a^m corone vocate *Crown Harry* ||carnizat̃ cū ii sapheris uno baleys ⁊ sex ꝑlis ponderant̃ unam unc̃ ⁊ dimiđ ⁊ unū denar̃ de pondere [troy] ⁊ ponit^r^ in quad^a^m baga de canabo cū aliis floris ⁊ pinacłis ejusđm corone residente in quad^a^m cista infra Thesaurar̃ Regis *Westm̃.*

Pinnacła Corone. " Istud pinacłm ponit^r^ cū ii aliis pinac̃lis in quođ " hanaꝑio voc̃ ||cupcas infra magnā cistam in The- " saur̃ ℞ *Westm̃.*"

It̃m *Joh̃es Caundysh̃* lib̃avit [" *xvi°* die *Nov' eođ* " *a°* "] in dc̃am Recept̃ dc̃is Thes̃ ⁊ Cam̃ar̃ †*dc̃is die* ⁊ *anno*‡ unū pinacłm dc̃e corone garnizat̃ cū ii sapheris una baleis ⁊ vi ꝑlis ponderant̃ unā unc̃ iii q^a^rtr̃ min⁹ i. đ. q^a^ de pondere.

(p. 73 b.) 9 Be yt had in mynde þat *Herry* [Byschop̃ of *Wynchestre* and] Cardynal of *Yngeland* hath restored [by þe handes of Sr *Joh̃n Burtoñ* Clerk̃] to *Walter* Lorđ *Hungurford̃* Tresorer of *Yngeland* and to þe Chamerleins of þe Cheker þe *xvii* day of *May* þe zere of Kyng *Herry* þe *vi*^te^ after þe conquest þe *viii.* þat ys to sayne . i pesane [other-

þe gret pesane y^t ye Cardenall hade.

vise cleped a coler] of gold enchased besaunde wytħ viii antilopes garnised wyth xx gret perles and garnysed in þe myddes of þe puisane wyth v. bales wherof iiii bien of entaille ‖sware . and i bales of vi ‖sware. It̃ ii gret ꝑles standyng ‖abowen̄ þe floures be twix þe saide bales also viii crownes of gold̄ in yche of þe saide crownes . wreten ⁏ *un sanz plus.* And in i of þe saide crownes ys set ii grete dyamaundes poynted̄ It̃ x nouches garnised w^t x gret "bales" of whicħ bien vii bales þat bien of entaille ‖sware and iii bien ronde ragged and yche of þe nouches is garnised wytħ vi gret ꝑles of di̵ses sortes. It̃ i litille nouche garnised wytħ i bales of viii suare of entaille and v ꝑles of smaller sort It̃ litel bagge of canvas in which is i gret longe ꝑle ⁊ ix other ꝑles rounde It̃ xiiii smale floures of gold.

10 ‖Soit a remembr̃ que le *xxix* jour de *Maii* [l an *oeptisme* le Roy *Henr̃* le *sisme*] Sire *Joħn fil̃ Jacobi* de *Radcliff*. ad deli̵e a *Walt̃ Hungirford̄* Sr *Hungirford̄* ♣ en le g^aunde Tresory ♣ ["⁊ as Chamƀleins d Escheker"] i tabelet d or ovecq̧. i. pece de ‖tunuca inconsutil̃ garniz de vi bales vi saphiers xii groos ꝑles ⁏ ⁊ xii autres meins pois̃ de troie ii lƀ v unc̃ p^is de tout xlvii ƚi pur la suerte de iiii^xx i ƚi xvi s̃. vii d̄ oƀ . le quele tabellet est mise le mesme jour en le g^aunde Tresory a *Westm̃.*

Tabula cū tunica inconsutili.

Radclyf. "Liƀ Cardinali *xxx*^o "die *Marcii* "a^o *xvii*^o."

---

9 & 10 Hen. VI.

1 M^d' qd̄ Dn̄i de Consilio liƀaverunt *quinto* die *Octobr̃* anno *ix*^o Regis *Henr̃ sexti* Thes̃ ⁊ Cam̃ar̃ unam lr̃am alligancie fc̃e int̃ Dn̄m *Henr̃* nuꝑ Regem

" Alligancia " Reḡ *Ro-* " *manoꝝ.*" *Angl̄ quintū* ⁊ *Sigismūdum* Regem *Romaor'* *semꝑ August̄* que ponitʳ in ||quod̄ quadrant̄ pixide residente int̄ alia memoranda in quad̄ sista supᵃ Receptam Principatus *Wallie* ad tale signū

(p. 74.) 2 Mᵈ' qd̄ "*Petrus* ||*Mavañ*" ⁊ "*Joh̄ Landoñ*" exec̄ [" testi "] *Edwardi* nuꝑ Ducis *Eboꝝ* restitueṝ in [" magnam "] Thesauṝ Dñi Reḡ *Wallo* Dño *Hungerford̄* Theš *Angl̄* ⁊ Camaṝ *xvii* die *Octobṝ* anno *ix°* Regis *Henṝ sexti* unū discū elemosinaṝ de

Le tygre. auro ad modū uniꝰ navis voc̄ *le Tygre* situat̄ suꝑ unū ursum ponderṝ xxii lb̄ i unce ⁊ d̄ ⁊ caret uno baleis i grosso ꝑle ⁊ duobꝫ ꝑvis ꝑles ⁊ ponitʳ in cista cū aliis jocalibꝫ infra Thesauṝ Reḡ *Westm̄.*

" Postea videl̄t *xvi* die *Maii* a° *decimo* dc̄i Reḡ " dc̄us disc̄ lib̄atʳ *Joh̄i Merstoñ* Custodi jocaliū dc̄i " Reḡ virtute bṝis de pⁱvato sigillo remanent̄ int̄ " bṝia de t̄io *Pasche* dc̄o anno *decimo.*"

" Itm̄ idem *Johes* restituit *eisdem die* ⁊ *anno* dc̄is " Theš ⁊ Camar duo turribula de auro insimul pon- " derant̄ ix lb̄ vii unc̄ ⁊ iii qᵃ et ponūtʳ cū dc̄a nave " in cista ꝑdc̄a " " ovesqꝫ xii homes d armes com- " bataunt3."

3 Meᵈ' q̄ *Richard Alred* Esquyer un de les Exec̄ *Thomᵃs* nadgairs Count de *Saresb̄riš* ad restituit as ditz Threš ⁊ Chaumb̄leyns le *prim̄* jorʳ de *May* l an *ixᵉ* le Roy *Henṝ* le *sisme* le gᵃunt nyef d argent ennorrez ovesqꝫ xii homes d armes combatauntz en toures ⁊ a chescun fyne du dit nyef un chastell saunz fanes poisᵃunt tout la nyef ove

le pee le jour du lyvere du dit nyef au dit nadgaire *Count* lxv lƀ iii unces pis le lƀ xlviii s̃ la sume clxvi ƚi xii s̃ de quel nyef le pee poise ꝑ soy xx lƀ vi unces de troy Et le dite nyef ꝑ soy ove les homes d armes ⁊ les deux chastels saunz le pee poise ore ovesqȝ ii lƀ vii unces d encres fait ꝑ le dit nadgairs *Count* xlvii lƀ iiii unces pris del unce iiii s̃ Sma tol del poys de tout l entier nyef ove l encres suisdit lxvii lƀ x unces dount la sume tol en ‖valoire clxii ƚi xvi s̃.

Itm deux chaundelours d ore chescun poisant ꝑ soy xiiii lƀ vii unces i qartr̃ pris del unce xxvi s̃ viii đ sma cccc lxvii ƚi vi s̃ viii đ pr un gaund chaundelour ovesqȝ un pee d une autre chaundelor d ore faitz de corious overage poisantz ensemble xix lƀ x unces pris del unce xxvi s̃. viii đ la sume ccc xvii ƚi vi s̃ viii đ jadys lyvez au dit nadgairs *Count* ovesqȝ autres joalx en temps le Roy *Henry le quynt* q̃ Dieu assoille sur ses gages de guerre.

" Et ponūtr in quađ magna cista cū aliis jocalibȝ " infra magnā Thesaur̃ Regis."

" ¶ Postea liƀātr *Joħi Merstoñ* ꝑ indētur̃ *sc̃do* die " *Maii* ao *xo* ℞ nunc."

" Postea videƚt *xvio* die *Maii* dc̃o *ao* *xo* ꝑdc̃us " *Joħes* restituit dc̃m discū eisđ Thes̃ ⁊ Camar̃ " in Thesaurar̃ Reg̃ custodienđ " † " ⁊ " postea *xviiio* die *Apiƚ* anno *xiio* liƀ *Joħi Mertoñ* " Custodi jocaƚ ꝑ indenturā simƚ cū divs̃ discis de " argento deauratis."

(p. 74 b.) 4 Md' qđ *Joħes Skeltoñ* liƀavit exta Retam Scc̃ii ‖*xvii* die *Febr̃* anno *ixo* ℞ *H. viti* de mandato *Walƚi* Dñi *Hungerford* Thes̃ *Angƚ* *Makeney* *Walweyñ*

‖scutifere Dñi *Typtot* unū colare de argento deauratˀ ⁊ duo alia colaria de argento et unū remañ in cista cū moneta computatoꝝ supª Re^tam^ p̄dc̄am.

5 M^d^' qđ *p^i^mo* die *Maii* anno *ix*° Rˀ *Henrici sexti Johes* ‖*Bayous* executor tesˀi *Thome Hauley* Chr restituit *Walˀo* Dño de *Hungerford* ‖Teŝ *Anglie* ⁊ Camariis de Scªcio ꝑ xii li viii ŝ ob ꝑ vađ suis guerre dicto *Thome* debiˀ unū par calcariū de auro cū rubiis ‖tysseus. ponđ p pondus troge vii. unc̄ ⁊ dĩ ⁊ i qªrˀ deducˀ inde ꝑ dicˀ ‖tusseus dĩ unc̄ p̄c̄ unc̄ xxvi ŝ viii đ. Smª ix li xiii ŝ iiii đ Itm unu aquariū de byrell garnizatˀ cū argenˀ deauratˀ ponđ p ponđ troye xxix unc̄ p̄c̄ unc̄ xx đ Smª xlviii ŝ iiii đ. Itm unū gladiū garnizatˀ cū plumis de ostrige de auro quonđ gladiū Dñi *E.* nup Principis *Wallie* [" p̄cii "] xxii li Smª to^l^ vaĺ xxxiiii^li^ xx^d^ de quibȝ quiđ xii li viii ŝ ob iđ *Johes* p mediacōem dc̄i ‖Teŝ remisit Regi xlviii ŝ ob ꝑ soluc̄ henđ de sūma seqñ x li. *Hawley.*

" Et ponūt^r^ intˀ alia jocalia in magna Theŝ Reg̃."

6 M^d^' qđ *Johes Pilkyngtoñ* ⁊ *Wills Bradshawe* restituerunt p m⁹ *Oliveri Chorley* ˀcio die *Decembr̃* anno *x*° dc̄i Reg̃ *Henr̃ sexti* dc̄is Dño Theŝ ⁊ Camar̃ unū ꝑvū tabelettū de auro cum armis *Angl* ⁊ *Franc̄* ⁊ cum una catena de auro fc̄a de lr̃is † ⁊ coronis ac unū bracelet cum una ꝑva serura de auro insimul ponderancia p pondus troge viii unc̄ ⁊ dĩ ⁊ i qª auri p̄cii unc̄ xxviii ŝ. Smª ɕ xi li xix ŝ viii đ dc̄is *Johi* ⁊ *Willo* p *Ric̄m Courtenay* nup clicum jocaliū Dñi *Henr̃* nup Reg̃ *Angl quinti* ⁊ pr̃is dc̄i dñi Reg̃ nunc libata ꝑ securitate vadioꝝ suoꝝ guerre Et ponunt^r^ in " quađ pixide re-" manente" in magna cista intˀ alia jocalia infra

magnam Thesaurar̃ Reg̃ *Westm̃* in claustro ad tale signū

7 "Itm *Waltus* Dñs *Hungreford* Thes̃ *Angl* "libavit in Thesaur̃ R *xxv*^to^ die *Febr̃* anno *x*° R "*Henr̃ vi* duos calices cū duabȝ patenis de arg̃ "deaur̃ ibm custod de bonis *Normannoꝝ* Regi foꝝ."

8 M^d^' qd *Johes Longevile* libavit Dño *Johi le Scrop* Thes̃ *Angl* ⁊ Camar̃ de Sc^a^cio *xii die Julii* anno *x*° Reg̃ *Henr̃ sexti* unā ꝑvā campanā de auro ponder̃ xx uncias ꝑc unc̃ xxvi s̃ viii d ⁊ unū cocliare de auro ponder̃ i unc̃ dĩ ⁊ dĩ q^a^rt̃ ⁊ ponūt^r^ in una baga de canabo int alia jocalia infra magnā Thes̃ Dñi Reg̃ infra *Westm̃.*

9 M^d^' quod *Johes Carpenter* libavit in Receptam Sc^a^cii *decimo* ⁎ *Decembr̃* anno *xi*° R *Henrici sexti*

Flescetes. duas obbas vocatas flascetez de argento deaurat̃ fact̃ ad modū scaloppes insimul pond ꝑ pondus ‖trge lxv lb iiii unc̃.

Postea vidlt *iiii*^to^ die *Febr̃* ꝑx̃ seqñ libant^r^ *Johi Merstoñ* clico jocal Regis ꝑ br̃e de p^i^vato sigillo ꝑx̃ folio seqñ consut̃.

(p. 75 b.) 10 "M^d^' *Joh Darrell* r̃ ex^a^ Re^tam^ Reg̃ sup g^a^dus "[dc̃e] Re^te^ ii olla de gyngebo i. iiii lb ⁊ ii lb *xviii* "die ♣ *octo* ♣ *Novembr̃* a° *viii*° R nunc."

11 M^d^' qd *Johes Skeltoñ* libavit ext^a^ cistam nuꝑ existent̃ in garderob Dñi *Henr̃* nuꝑ Regis *Angl*

Franc̃. *quinti xxviii*° die *Febr̃* anno *x*° R *Henr̃ sexti* Magr̃o *Willo Haytoñ* clico de mandato Dñi *le Scrop* Thes̃ *Angl* i pee de gre in papiro de "‖Regibȝ *Francie.*"

(In sched p. 75.) 12 *Henri* par la grace de Dieu Roy d *Engleterre* ꝛ de *Fraunce* ꝛ Seignur d *Irlande* As Tresorer ꝛ Chamberleins de nr̃e Eschequier saluz. Nous volons de l avis ꝛ assent de nr̃e counsail ꝛ vous mandons q̃ au tresreṽent Pier en Dieu nr̃e tresch̃ ꝛ tresame Cousin *Henri* Cardinal d *Engleterre* Evesq͡ʒ de *Wyncestr̃* facez deliverer hors de nr̃e Tresore les "joyalx" especifiez en une cedule quelle nous vous envoions closee dedeinz ycest̃ pur remaindr̃ ꝛ demorrer en sa garde pur sa seuretee jusques a ce qil soit plainement paiez ꝛ contentez de nous, de la sõme de dys mill̃ ꝛ troys mill̃ marcs nadgaires ꝑ luy a nous en ceste nr̃e graunde necessitee apꝓstez et aussi de la sõme de sys mill̃ livres nadgairs ꝑ luy, a nous ꝛ a nr̃e oeps, sur certaine intenc̃on condic̃on ou covenant deliṽez ꝛ bailliez pur la deliṽance a luy de c̃taines ses joialx nadgairs par noz ministres arrestuz a *Sandewich̃* de q̃ exꝓsse menc̃on est fait [en] noz autres lr̃es dessouz nr̃e prive seal a vous adressees de la date le *quinszisme* jo^r de *Juyn darrein passez*, pur deliṽer a mesme nr̃e Cousin les ditz joialx en gage pur la sõme de quatr̃ mill̃ noef' centz vynt ꝛ quatr̃ livres sys sould3 ꝛ oyt deniers ꝑcell̃ de la dc̃e sõme de dys mill̃ marcs ꝛ d icelle sõme de faire assignement a mesme nr̃e Cousin, et q aꝓs ce q il soit plainement paiez ꝛ agreez d icelle sõme de quatre mill̃ noef centz vynt ꝛ quatr̃ livres sys souldz ꝛ oyt deniers dessṡditz q il face plainement ꝛ entierement redeliṽer ꝛ bailler a vous mesmes noz joyalx nient countreesteantz. Doñ souz nr̃e prive seal a *Westm̃* le *xx.* jo^r de *Juyn* l an de nr̃e regne *douszisme.*

Benet.

13 Here ensuen þe juelx þat þe Tresorer and

Chambleins of þ Eschequier shal delive unto þe *Cardinal* for money borowed of him.

14 First a pusan of gold called *þe rich coler* conteynyng xvi. culpons or peces upon þe which are viii. antelops garnised with xx^ti^. greet peerles. And upon þe same coler are v. baleys whereof iiii. are of entaille square and þe v^the^. is vi. quartred. and upon þe same coler are ii. greet peerles joynyng untoo þe baleys. Also upon þe same coler are viii corones of gold ech of hem anameled wyth a resou of *une sanz pluis* and upon oon of þe same corones are ii. grete diamandes square and poynted. Also upon þe same coler are x. owches eche of hem wyth double floures of gold garnysed and on eche of þe same owches is a grete baleys and vi greete peerles of whych baleys vii are of entaille square and iii of hem are rounde and ragged. Also upon þe same coler is an oother litel owche wythe double floures of gold garnysed with a balays of entaille square. and v. peerles Also þ^r^ is yn a litel bagge of canwas wyth þe same coler a grete longe peerle and ix oþ^r^ peerles rounde. Also þere are in þe same bagge xiiii litil fioures of gold weying in alle lx unces and a half. and a half quarteron of troy þe prys. m^l^ m^l^ m^l^ m^l^. cc mark yn money.

15 Also þe said Tresorer and Chamberleins shal delive unto þe same *Cardynal* a greete owch of *Seynt George* armes yn þe whiche owche are sette viii balays vi saphurs. xiiii. diamandes and ii conterfait diamandes. iiii^xx^. xi. peerles. And upon þe same owche are viii troches vii. of hem conteynyng xxviii. peerles and þe viii^th^ troche conteynyng iii peerles And in þe same owche is a crosse of *Seynt George*

conteynyng̃ xiii baleys smale weyng̃ in alle xxx. unces of troy þe prys cc li in money.

16 Also þe said Tresorer and Chamberleins shal deliu̇e to þe said *Cardynal* a sweerd of goold called þe *Sweerd of Spayne* garnysed wyth v greet balays vi greet saphurs . iiii^xx. xix greete ples , upon þe skaberd and þe hilt is garnysed with iii. balays ii. saphurs * xvi. greete peerles , And þe pomel of þe same sweerd is garnysed with a balays a saphur and x peerles weyng̃ yn alle x. mark and an half and an half unce of troy þe prys D marc yn money.

17 Also þe said Tresorer and Chamberleins shal deliu̇e unto þe said *Cardynal* a tablet of goold of þe passion of *Cryst* mad in þe maner of a booke garnysed withe xliii diamandes xx. balays xx saphurs . wythynne which tablet are xl troches ech troch conteynyng iiii peerles . and withoute þe same tablet are xviii troches ech troche conteynyng̃ iiii. peerles . and yn þe same tabulet is a rubye and xxxv garnerdes which tablet weyth lx unces of troy þe pris cxx li. yn money.

18 Also þe said Tresorer & Chamberleins shal deliu̇e unto þe said *Cardynal* a tabernacle of gold . wythynne þe whyche is an ymage of *Oure Lady* . sette upon a grene tarage wyth þe figurs of *Adam* and *Eve* and iiii aungell at þe iiii corners of þe same tabnacle and a crucifixe of gold white enameld upon þe same tabnacle and upon þe same tabnacle is a chirche þe whiche tabnacle is garnysed withe ii rubyes iii dyamandes iiii balays iii saphurs lxxvii greet peerles . and xliii litil peerles which tabnacle weythe xlii. unces of troye þe pris lx. li. yn money.

19 Also þe saiđ Tresorer and Chamƀleyns shal deliũe unto þe saiđ Cardynal ii grete chaundlers of golđ garnysed wiŧħ iiii. saphurs . iiii balays . and iiii emeraudes and xxv ꝑles , whicħ chaundlers weyeñ to gedres xliiii marꝁ troy save ii unces prys of þe unce xxvi. s̃. viii. đ þe pis of þe same chaundlers cccc lxvi ŀi. xiii s̃ iiii. đ yñ money.

20 Also þe saiđ Trèsorer and Chamƀleins shal deliũe unto þe saiđ Cardynal a paire basyns of golđ chaceđ of þe mañe of roses , pounseđ wiŧħ grete boselettꝭ garnyseđ wiŧħ diũse scocheons þat is to saie in þe myddes of þe saiđ basyns þ armes of *Seynt George* . and aboute þeim þ armes of *Seynt Edwarđ Seynt Edmonđ* þ armes of þe *Empo*r þ armes of *Englonđ* and *Fraunce* deꝑtyđ þ armes of þe Principaltee and þ armes of þe Duchee of *Guyeñ* Whicħ basyns weye togedres . xliii marꝁ of troy pis þe unce xxvi. s̃. viii đ þe pis of þe saiđ basyns cccc . lviii. ŀi xiii. s̃. iiii. đ.

21 Also þe saiđ Tresorer and Chamƀleins shal deliũe unto þe saiđ Cardynal a grete shiꝑ calleđ þe *Tygre* garnyseđ with xix baleys xii grete ꝑles and xiiii oþ̃ smale ꝑles þe whicħ weythe xxxiii. marꝁ iii unces of troy pis þe unce xxvi. s̃. viii. đ. þe pis of þe said shippe ccc xxxii. ŀi yñ money.

22 Also þe said Tresorer and Chamƀleins shal deliũe unto þe said *Cardynal* a peire of sensures of golde þe whicħ weyeñ xiii. marꝁ . iii unces . i. quartern of troy þe pis of þe unce xxvi. s̃. viii. đ. þe pis of þe saiđ senseurs . cliii. ŀi. xiii. s̃. iiii đ yñ money.

(p.75 b.) 23 Memoranđ qđ jocalia specificata in quadam cedula huic folio consut̃ liƀat̃ ||fuit *Henrico* Dño

Cardinali ꝛ Epo *Wynt* virtute cujusdam pivati sigilli ||Tesaur ꝛ Camar direct cujus dat est *xx°* die *Jun* anno r Rx *Henr viti xii°.* que quidā jocalia sūt hec subsequencia

24 In pimis a pusan vocat *the Riche Coler of Gold* ||contenēt xvi pec garnis cū antelopis ꝛ perles ꝛ aliis lapidibȝ pciosis ꝑut in dca cedula expssantr.

Itm unū broche de armis *Sci Georgii* garnis cū baleys ꝛ al lapidibȝ pcios ꝑut in dca cedul.

Itm unū ensem *Espanie* garnis cū lapidibȝ pcios ꝑut in dca cedula ꝛc.

Itm unā tabulā auri de passione *Jhu X*i garnis cū lapidibȝ pcios ꝑut in dca cedul ꝛc.

Itm unū tabnaclm auri cū ymagine de *Sca Maria* ||infa cū figur de *Adam* ꝛ *Eva* ꝑut ꝛc.

Itm duo candelabra aurea garnis cū sapheres ꝛ emeradis ꝛ aliis lapidibȝ pcios ꝑut ꝛc.

Itm ||duo pelves de auro chaceat ꝛ garnezat cū armis *Sci Georgii* in medio ꝛ al ꝑut ꝛc.

Itm i. magnū discū elemosinar vocat *a Tygur* de auro garnizat ꝑut in dca cedul ꝛc.

Itm ii turribilia de auro pond xiiii mark iii unc i qart de troy pc unc xxvi s viii ꝑut * .

(In sched consut p. 75.) Furst a pusan of gold called þe *Riche Coler* conteynyng xvi culpons or peces upon þe which are viii antelops garnysed (*&c. as in* pp. 142—145, *Nos.* 14 *to* 22.)

(p. 76.) 25 Md' qd *Johes Stafford* Cancellar *Angl* libavit in Receptam Scacii *xxi°* die *Julii* anno *x°* Regis *Henr sexti* unam rotundam pixidem cū cartis litter ꝛ articulis tangentibȝ Regnū *Scocie* " ꝛ ponitr in qua-

"dam cista supª domū Consilii Principatus *Wallie* "ad tale signū"

Memorand' tangencia Regnu' Scocie.

11, 12, 13, 14, 15 Hen. VI. &c.

1 Mᵈ' qđ *ixº* die *Octobȓ* anno *xiiiiº* R̹ *Henȓ viᵗⁱ* *Rađus* Dñs de *Cromwelľ* Thes̃ *Anglˀ* ⁊ Camaȓ Recepte Dñi R̹ recepeȓ de *Davidˀ Breknoke* custođ garderob̄ excellentiss̃i Pⁱncipis *Joħis* nuꝑ Ducis *Bedforđ* ꝑ indentʳam unam cistam de mearemeo in qua sunt diꝟsi libri facienť mēciones de diꝟs̃ ‖appūctumētis fc̃is inť Reges *Anglˀ* ⁊ *Fªnc̃* ⁊ eciam sacr̃m ⁊ juramētū fc̃m ꝑ Ducē *Burgundie* ad ꝑimplenđ ⁊ obs̃vanđ concorđ fc̃am inť *Carolū* Regē *Fªnc̃* ⁊ *Henȓ quītū* nuꝑ Regem *Anglˀ* que quiđ cista ponitʳ in magna cista supª Receptam ad tale signū

Franc̃.

Sacr'm Duc' Burgundie.

"Et dc̃a indentª ponitʳ in eađ cista."

2 "Postea *xxvº* die *Febȓ* aº ȓ R̹ *Henȓ sexti* "*xvº* ‖lib̄atʳ Archiep̄o *Eboꝝ* ꝑ mꝰ *Joħis Stopyndoñ* "in quadam pixide ‖lr̃as pateñ Duc̃ *Burgunđ* de "juramenť [suo] ⁊ al̃ appunctuamenť inť Dñm *H* "*vᵗᵘ*. ⁊ dc̃m Ducem . ⁊ postea *xxvi.* die *Febȓ* ꝓx̃ "seqñ idem Archiep̄us restituit in Reᵗᵃᵐ Scªcii "ꝑdc̃as lr̃as pateñ ejusđ *Ducis* ⁊c̃."

"Lib̄ Dño "Thes̃ *xiiiº*

"Postea *xviº*. die *Januaȓ* anno *xxxº* ȓ *Henȓ viᵗⁱ*

"die *Junii* " [dc̃m juramētū] lib̃atʳ Arch̃o *Eboꝝ* Cardinal̃ Can-
"aº *xxxi*º." " cellar̃ *Angl̃* mandato Consilii ℞." " et postea
" restit̃."

3 " Mᵈ' qd̃ *ix*º die *Novēbr̃* aº *xxxiii*º ℞ *H. vi*ᵗⁱ
" dc̃m juramentū restituebatʳ in Thes̃ Dñi ℞ ꝑ mꝰ
" Ep̃i *London̄* exec̃ dc̃i *Cardinal̃* in *Cam̃ᵃ Stellat̃*
" coꝝ *Consil̃* Dñi ℞ ib̃m."

(p. 76 b.) 4 ✤ Mᵈ' qd̃ *Thomᵃs Sholden̄* Armig̃ Dñi Ep̃i

‖*Denolm̄* ✤ ⁊ *Joh̃es Carpenter* ✤ lib̃ in Recept̃ Scᵃcii *octavo* die *Decembr̃* anno *xi* ℞ *Henrici sexti* unā crucē " cū passione " Dñi de argento deaurat̃ ponderant̃ de pondere troge xii l̃i. xi unc̃ iii qᵃrt̃ ⁊ dĩ.

It̃m unū magnū siphum ‖dergent̃ deaurat̃ ⁊ ennamilat̃ de assur̃ ponderant̃ viii l̃i. ix unc̃ It̃m iii magnas ollas uniꝰ secte cū uno leone suꝑ coopertorio cujusl̃t olle simul ponderant̃ ponderis troge xl. lib̃ ix unc̃ Et postea *quarto* die *Febr̃* ꝑx̃ sequēte dc̃a jocalia lib̃ *Joh̃i Merston̄* Armig̃ꝰo ꝑ br̃e de privato sigillo huic folio consut̃. ✤

(Sched̃ p. 76.) 5 *Henri* par la grace de Dieu Roy *d Engleterre* ⁊ de *France* ⁊ Seignur *d Irlande*. As Tresorer ⁊ Chamberleins de nr̃e Eschequier saluz. Nous volons de l avis ⁊ assent de nr̃e conseil ⁊ vous mandons q̃ a nr̃e ame Esquier *Johan Merston̄* Gardein de noz joialx facez deliverer les parcelles dessouz escriptes cestassavoir deux grandes flaskettes d argent dorrez faitz al man̄e de scalopes poisantz du troie. lxv lb̃. iiii. unc̃. It̃m trois grandes pottes d une sort d argent dorrez ⁊ chacez ⁊ ch̃un ovec un lyon̄ sur les covercles ⁊ les ‖hancers faitz al man̄e de wrethes poisantz ensemble du troye. xl. lb̃. ix. unc̃ It̃m une croys d argent dorrez esteaunt sur un bas pee amaillez de la passion̄ nr̃e Sʳ

Jħu Crist poisant du troye . xii. lƀ. xi. unc̃ iii quart̃ . dĩ. Itm̃ un grand̃ coupe d argent enorrez ꝛ amaillez d asure poisant viii lƀ ix. unc̃. Itm̃ une coupe d or martillez jadys del doun del *Conte de Marche* poisant xxxi unc̃ dĩ ꝛ un paire basines d or chacez pounsonez ꝛ amaillez en les founces de div̓ses armes poisantz xxviii lƀ ꝛ viii. unc̃. Doun̄ souz nr̃e prive seal a *Westm̄* le *quart* jour de *Fevr̓er* l an du nr̃e regne *unzisme.*

(p. 76 b.) 6 M^d^' qđ *xv°* die *April* a° r̃ R̷ *Henr̃ vi^ti^ xii°* [Thes̃ *Angl* ꝛ Cam̓ar̃ de Sc^a^cio] receperunt unam acquietanciam Dn̄o nr̄o Regi fact̃ ꝑ *Thomam Bredon̄*

Flemyng̃. administratorem bonoꝝ *Ric̃i Flemyng̃* nuꝑ *Lincoln̄* Ep̄i de sūma DCXIX li xix s̃ viii. đ. rem̄ in viridi cista infra Receptam.

7 M^d^' qđ *xv°* die *Febr̃* anno *xiii°* R̷ *H vi^ti^* quidam Armig̃ vocat̃ † *Brydde* libavit in Receptam Sc^a^cii quandam c^u^cem ennamilat̃ cum

Bryd crux viridis cū *Maria* ꝛ *Johe.* ||viredi ħent̃ suꝑ xxxii ꝑles cū pede de auro que quedā crux nuꝑ invadiat̃ fuit eidm̄ † *Bryt* ꝛ cuidā alio Armig̓o vocat̃ *Witt Braunsepath* cū uno cipho ꝛ ciphus nōdū restituit^r^ ꝛ ponit^r^ in cista sup^a^ Recept̃ in ||quodam pixide cū tali signo

(p.77.) 8 "M^d^' qđ quidam *Magnus liber* vocat̃ *Registrum* "*Ducatus Lancastr̃* libat̃ [fuit] *Johi Leventhorp̃*" Armig̓o [Sen̄] in Cam̓a voc̃ *Sterre Chamƀ* coram *Consilio* Dn̄i Regis *die Sabbi px' ante festum Nat̃ Sc̃i Johis Bapte* anno r̃ R̷ *Henr̃ sexti xii°* virtute br̃is de p^i^vato sigillo huic folio consut̃ cujꝰ dat̃ est *xxvi°* die *April* a° *sup^a^dc̃o.*

(Sched p. 77.) 9 *Henr̃* par la grace de Dieu Roy *dEngleterre* ⁊ de *Fraunce* ⁊ Seignur *dIrlande*. As Tresourer ⁊ Chamberleins de nr̃e Eschequier saluz. Nous volons de l avis ⁊ assent de nr̃e counseil ⁊ vous mandons q̃ a nr̃e bñ ame Esquier, *Joħan Leventhorp̃* Gardein des Recordes ⁊ immunitees de nr̃e Duchie de *Lancastre*. facez liverer *ung registre* garde en nr̃e Tresourie touchant les immunitees ⁊ privileges de mesme nr̃e *Duchie*. pur yceł registre saufement ⁊ seurement garder a nr̃e oeps Douñ soubz nr̃e prive seal a *Westmonstier* le *xxvi*ᵉ jour d *Av̾ill* l an de nr̃e regne *douszisme*.

(p. 77 b.) 10 Mᵈ' qđ Dñi de *Consilio* Dñi Regis *xxvii*ᵒ die *Januar̃* anno r̃ ℞ *Henrici sexti duodecimo* delibaverunt Thes̃ ⁊ Camar̃ infra Receptam Scᵃcii dc̃i Dñi ℞ quandam pixidem continentẽ sigiłł †
Ducis de *Burboyñ* que quiđ pixis sigillat̃ est cũ ‖duobȝ sigiłł dc̃oꝝ Dñoꝝ de Consilio que remanet in quađ cista supᵃ Recept̃ Scᵃcii dc̃i Reg̃ ad tale signũ

B

11 Mᵈ' qđ *v* die *Februar̃* anno r̃ ℞ *Henr̃ sexti duodecimo* Executores *Joħis Clyff* nuꝑ uniꝰ mynstrał Dñi ℞ *Henr̃ quinti* delibaverunt Thes̃ ⁊ Camar̃ infra Receptam dc̃i Dñi Regis div̾s jocalia ✠ sibi invadiat̃ ✠ ꝑ eundem Dñm *H quintũ* ꝑ vađ suis guerr̃ in ꝑtibȝ Franc̃ anno ‖r̃ ‖℞ regni dc̃i ℞ *H v* ťcio eiđ *Joħi Clyff* invadiat̃ ut pat̃ ꝑ quanđ indenturam †   videłt unam lectrinã de argento deaurat̃ cũ uno pede ad modũ·tabnac̃li ‖stantẽ suꝑ quatuor pedes, duo aquaria de argento deaurat̃
Clyff. unũ ✠ cũ ✠ enamulat̃ cũ arm̃ *Angł* ⁊ *Franc̃* ⁊ aliud cũ ‖cervis argent̃ Itm unã tabnł cũ div̾s reliquis in

eađ conteñt stantē suꝑ duos leones, simił ponderant ꝑ pondus troge xxvi lƀ vi. uñc pⁱš liƀ xl š Itm unā magnā craterā cū tribȝ candelabris cū tribȝ pykes unū cocliar̃ magnū de argento ⁊ unū scumar̃ ⁊ unā peciam ‖dune ‖byde liƀat̃ Comit̃ ✠ *Marcħ* ✠ *Marescałł* ⁊ unū spiceplate de argento simił ponderant̃ xix lĩ p'c̃ libr̃ xxx š. Itm une cofre petit de argento deaurat̃ ⁊ unū chauffr̃ de argento deaurat̃ fact̃ ad modū pile simił ponđ ii lƀ ii uñc. " ⁊ " liƀantʳ in magnā Teš *xiiº* die *Febr̃ ꝑx' seq'ñ* ⁊ " defec̃ in ponder̃ ii uñc iii qᵃrt̃ uñc."

12 " Mᵈ' qđ *xiº* die *Febr̃* aº r̃ ℞ *H viᵗⁱ xvº* liƀat̃ " fuer̃ extᵃ Theš ℞ *Rađo Cromwełł* Theš *Angł* unā

" Extᵃ." " crateram de argento unū magnū cocliar̃ de argento " ⁊ unū scumar̃ de argento de jocał supᵃdc̃is."

13 [" Que quiđ cratera de argento magnū coc- " liar de argento ⁊ unū scumar de argento de " jocalibȝ supᵃdc̃is, idem Theš *Angł* ꝑ mᵒ *Ric̃i* " *Alred* deliƀavit *Joħi Penycok'* valect̃ robaꝝ ℞ " videłt *xvº* die *Febr̃*, anno *xvº* ℞ *Henr̃ sexti*."]

14 Mᵈ' qđ *decimo* die *Maii* anno r̃ ℞ *Henr̃ sexti duodecimo* Dñs *Rađus Cromwełł* Theš *Angł* deliƀavit in Thesaur̃ ℞ unam acquiet̃ Dño Reg̃ ꝑ *Thom̃ Bredoñ* administrat̃ bonoꝝ *Ric̃i Flemyng̃* nuꝑ Epi *Lincolñ* fact̃ de sūma DCXIX lĩ xix š. viii đ que rem̃ in [quađ cista] supᵃ Receptam Scᵃcii ad tale signū

15 Mᵈ' qđ *xviii* die *Apⁱł* anno *xiiº* Regis *Henr̃*

Merstoñ. *sexti Joħes M'stoñ* Cłicus jocaliū Regis deliƀavit in magnā Theš Regis unū almusdyssħ de auro voc̃ le

Tygre stanť suṕ unū ursum de auro garnisať cū xix baleis ⁊ xxvi ṕles ponderanť xxii lƀ i unč dĩ.

(p. 78.) "Indentra."

Md' ⁎ ||quidam pixis in quo ⁎ una indentra anno *xii°* R̷ *H viti* facta int̃ *Rad̃m* Dñm de *Cromwell* Thes̃ *Angl* ⁊ *Joh̃em Leventhorp̃* juñ Gen̄alem Receptorem dñioꝝ Ducať *Lancastrie* fact̃ de solucõe m[l] li ṕ m[9] *Joh̃is Chirch̃* ponitr in quadam cista supa Recepť ad tale signū

D

D

16 Md' qđ ||quidam pixis ||cooṕtus cū nigro corio ⁊ ferro |||ligatus in quo sūt xx sigilla aurea Dñi *Edmūdi* Regis *Sicilie* filii Dñi *Henrici* Regis *Angl* [quibusdam confirmacõib3 annexa] ponitr in magna cista supa Recetam ♣ Scacii ad caput gradus supa dictam †Rece videlt *xviii°* die *Junii* anno *xii°* R̷ *H viti* ♣ [Duc̃ *Lanc̃* in una baga de canabo ad tale signū]

Sigilla aurea R̷ *Sicilie.*

[de "quib3 ii. sigill abstrahuntr ṕ Eṕm *Karliol* Thes̃ "*Angl.*"]

17 Md' qđ ||quid pixis in qua ⁎ una indentra de m[l] m[l] mar3 fact̃ int̃ *Rad̃m* Dñm de *Cromwell* Thes̃ *Angl* ⁊ *Joh̃em* Ducem *Bed* ad delibanđ Cancell *Franc̃* ponitr in viridi cista.

Indentra Ducis *Bedeford.*

18 Md' qđ *xi°* die *Julii* anno *xii°* ejusđ Regis Thes̃ *Angl* ⁊ Camar̃ de Scacio delibaverūt *Willo Toly* Secretario Dñi Cardinal *Angl*, duos libros videlt ||unus |||liber vocať *Egesippus* incipienť scđo fol, *suis nactus*, ⁊ "||alt̃ |||liber" voc̃ *Lib de obs̃vanc̃ Pape*, incip̃ scđo fõ *Cardinalis qui s̃vit*

‖qui quiđ ‖libr, p̄dc̄us *Witts* tenet^r restituer̃ *xxi*° die *Octobr̃ px' seq'ñ*,

" Qui quidem libri restituunt^r p p̄dc̄m *Witm* " *Toly xxv*° die *Januar̃* anno *xiii*° ejusdem Regis, " et remañ sup^a Ret^am cum al libr̃."

ʃʃ " Et postea *xvii*° die *Febr̃* a° *xiii*° ejusđ Regis " iidem libri delibat fuer̃ eidem *Witto Toly* p m⁹ " *Johis Patesle* ad custodienđ p unū annū integrū " ꝛ dimiđ " de " mandato Thes̃ *Angl*."

" q in al " loco."

☩ M^d' qđ *xvi*° die *Febr̃* anno r̃ R *H vi*^ti *xiii*° lit̃a pcur̃ [Ducis] *Bauar̃* ac acquietanc̃ dc̄i Duc̃ de m^l m^arc̃ ac acquietanc̃ *Phi* Duc̃ *Burgunđ* de viginti quiq millib3 nobil ponūt^r simul in q^adam pixide talit̃ signat

{**Burgoyn Bayr**}

ꝛ ‖dc̄us ‖pixiđ ponit^r in ‖viredi cista.☩

---

13 Hen. VI.

(p. 78 b.)

1 M^d' qđ *xx*° die *Februar̃* anno r̃ R *Henr̃ sexti t̃ciodecimo Ric̃us Sellyng̃* Armig̃ excec̃ test̃i *Johanne* nup ux̃is ac executricis test̃i *Witti Bardolf* Militis. delibavit Thes̃ ꝛ Camar̃ Re^te Sc^acii unā acquietanc̃ sūmam ccc li continent in plenam soluc̃ DCC xlvi li vii. đ ob q^a eidem *Witto* de vađ suis apud *Cales̃* p Dn̄m Regē ☩rem̄☩ debit ut p ii billas de debent *Ric̃o Buklanđ* libat apparet ꝛc̃ que remañ in quađ pixide ad tale signū

R S

in quadam cista sup^a Receptā Sc^acii.

2 Md' qđ *xxi°* die *Febr̃* anno r̃ R̷ *Henr̃ viti tercio-decimo* delibat̃ fuit Thes̃ ⁊ Cam̃iis de Scacio p̱ m⁹ *Witti Alređ* ‖unā ‖pixidem cū una acquiet̃ *Benedc̃i* ‖*Bouremei* ꝑ Cancell̃ *Franc̃* ⁊ lr̃a ꝑcur̃ ꝑ dc̃o *Benedicto* p̱ *Joh̃em Sak'* ⁊ lr̃a Cancell̃ *Franc̃* missa Dñο Thes̃ *Angł* ꝑ.viiic xxxiii łi. vi s̃ viii đ. It̃ lr̃a ꝑcur̃ Ducis *Bavarr̃* ⁊ acquiet̃ ꝑcur̃ dicti Ducis de ml' marʒ It̃ unam acquiet̃ Ducis *Burgunđ* que quiđ pixis remañ in quadam cista supa Reta Scacii ad tale signū

{Burgūd' D' Bavar'.}

3 Md' qđ *quarto* die *Junii* anno r̃ R̷ *Henr̃ sexti xiii°* delibat̃ fuer̃ Thes̃ ⁊ Cam̃ar̃ de Scacio "quinqȝ" ‖acquietancias Ep̃i de *Tyrwyñ* Cancellar̃ *Franc̃* de div⁹sis solucõibʒ eidem Cancellar̃ fact̃ . que quidem acquietanc̃ remañ in una pixide in viridi cista infra Receptam Scacii ad tale signū

K

Itm in eadem pixide continetr una alia acquietancia *Joh̃is Lusshingbourñ* de clxvi łi xiii s̃ iiii đ.

Cardinał. 4 Mđ. qđ acquiet̃ Dñi *Henrici* Cardinał *Angł* ⁊ *Wyntoñ* Ep̃i cuj⁹ dat̃ *xxix°* die *Novembr̃* a° *xiii°* R̷ *Henrici sexti* que quiđ acquiet̃ est de sma ml' ml' ml' ⁊ quingent̃ marc̃ ⁊ ponitr in qadam pixide in ‖veridi cista cū acquiet̃ Ep̃i de *Tirwyñ* ⁊ ał acquiet̃ ad tale signū

K

5 Md' qđ *iii°* die *Julii* anno r̃ R̷ *Henr̃ sexti xiii°*. *Rađus* Dñs de *Cromwell* Thes̃ *Angł* cepit exta Thesaur̃ Regis *duos libros cronicoꝝ* qui nup̱ fuer̃ Dñi *H.* nup̱ Regis *Angł quinti* post conq̃m . p̱ m⁹ *Witti*

Cronycles.

Constable. " Postea libant^r *Rico Caudrey* p dcm " Thes *Angl.*"

(p. 79.) 6 M^d qd *xv* die *Julii* , anno r R *Henr sexti xiii^o Radus* Dns de *Cromwell* Thes *Angl* & Camar de Sc^acio de consensu & assensu Dnoz de Consilio dci Dni Regis deliberaverunt *Rico Caudrey* Magro *Collegii* pdci *Dni Regis* in Univsitate sua *Cantebr* divsos libros juris civilis & alioz libroz custodiend in eodem *Collegio* , q^amdiu dco *Dno Regi* placuit , ut pat3 p indentur de delibacoe dcoz libroz fact int dcos Thes & Camar , & dcm *Ricm* , que quidem indentur reman in hanapio de tmio *Pasche* anno *xiii^o* pdco.

Caudrey.

" Qui quid libri virtute bris de p^ivato sigillo " eisdem Thes & Camar direct de dat *scdo* die " *Julii* a^o *xviii^o* libant^r eidem *Collegio* , ibm imppm " remansur ut pat3 p idem bre de privato sigillo " reman in hanapio de tmio *Sci Michis* a^o *xix* " dci R."

7 Itm in eodem hanapio continet^r una alia indentura ex antiquo fca de pdcis libris " et eciam " de divsis jocalib3 dci Dni Regis capt apud *Meux* " p Dnm *H* nup Regem *Angl* prem Regis nuc , " cuj^9 quidem indentur dat est *vi^to* die *Octobr* , " anno r R *Henr* ||*sexti* pdci , *sexto.*"

---

14 Hen. VI.

1 M^d qd *xxi^o* die *Novembr* , anno r R *Henr sexti* post conqm *xiiii^o*. *Willms* Comes *Suff'* delibavit Thes & Camar de Sc^acio illud *Magnu Sigillu* ar-

Sigiłł de argento *H quinti.* genti quod Dñs *Henr̃* nuꝑ Rex *Angł* pat̃. dc̃i Dñi Regis nūc delib̃avit *Joħi* nuꝑ Duci *Bedeford̃* in ꝑtibȝ *Franc̃* custodiend̃ ꝛ exc̃cend̃ ib̃m noĩe ejusdem Dñi Regis, quod quid̃ sigillū ponitʳ in una bursa de corio in magna cista infra Ab̃biam *B'i Petri Westm̃,* salvo custodiend̃.

" Et postea *ultimo* die *Januar̃* aᵒ *xxviii*ᵒ ejusd̃ ℞ " *Henr̃ vi*ᵗⁱ idem Magnū Sigillū lib̃atʳ ad manꝰ dc̃i " Dñi ℞ in ꝑliamento suo apud *Westm̃* tent̃ exis- " tent̃ ꝑ mꝰ Dñi de *Say* Thes̃ *Angł* ꝛ Camar̃ de " Scᵃcio, virtute cujusd̃ acti in eod̃ ꝑliamento ex " mandato ℞ ꝛ d̃ assensu Dñoꝝ sp̃ualiū ꝛ temꝑaliū " ib̃m existent̃ editi."

2 Mᵈ' qd̃ *xxv*ᵒ die *Novembr̃* anno *xiiii*ᵒ ꝑdc̃o Dñs Cancellar̃ *Angł* delib̃avit Thes̃ ꝛ Camar̃ de Scᵃcio lr̃as Dñi Regis patentes sub magno sigillo

Burgond̃. facient̃ mencõem de lr̃is Dñi Regis missis *Sc̃issimo Pr̃i Pape,* et de ejus responsione tangent̃ absolucõem juramēti Ducis *Burgund̃* et ponitʳ in ‖quodam pixide ‖rotundo in una cista supᵃ Reᵗᵃᵐ Ducatꝰ *Lancastr̃* ad tale signū

" It̃ rem̃ in ‖eod̃ pixide unā bullā *Pᵃpe* tang̃ " Ducē *Burgundie.*"

It̃m *eodem die* delib̃at̃ fuer̃ eisdem Thes̃ ꝛ Camar̃ vii. ‖lr̃as ꝛ bułł tangent̃ composicões ꝛ tractat̃ in ꝑtibȝ *Franc̃.* ꝛ ponūtʳ in ‖quodā pixide ‖rotundo in cista ꝑdc̃a.

(p. 79. b.) 3 Mᵈ' qd̃ *xxviii*ᵒ die *Novembr̃* anno r̃ ℞ *Henr̃ vi*ᵗⁱ *xiiii*ᵒ *Rob̃tus Darcy* delib̃avit Thes̃ ꝛ Camar̃ de

Scᵃcio tres pixides in quibȝ conť divs̃ scripť ⁊ muniment̃ tangent̃ maner̃ de *Chirk'* ⁊ *Chirklandes* in *Chyrk'.* *Wall* ⁊ ponūtʳ in cista supᵃ Receptam Ducat⁹ *Lancastr̃.*

" Et postea *xii°* die *Junii* a. *xvii°* libantʳ *Dño* " *Cardinali* virtute bris de pⁱvato sigillo ut pȝ in " fine istius libri."

4 Mᵈ' qđ *xix°* die *Januar̃* anno r̃ R̷ *Henr̃ sexti xiiii°* Thes̃ ⁊ Camar̃ de Scᵃcio in p̃sencia Dñi Regis ⁊ ‖alioꝝ Dñoꝝ de Consilio delibaverunt *Custodi pⁱvati sigilli* dc̃i Dñi Regis duos libros ligno ligat̃ ⁊ corio rubio coopt̃, vocat̃ *Libros de Remembrances* tangent̃ divs̃ bull pap̃ ⁊ lr̃as ac cart̃ divs̃ dñioꝝ terr̃ ⁊ ten̄ tam in ꝑtibȝ *Angl Franc̃* ⁊ *Scoc̃*, qᵃm alibi, ꝑut in eisdem libris continetʳ. Itm *eodem die* ⁊ *anno* [⁊ in eadem p̃sencia] delibaverunt eidem *Custodi* pⁱvati sigilli unū aliū *Librum de Remembrance* coopt̃ cum uno albo suppello conť tractat̃ pⁱvileg̃ ⁊ al muniment̃ Ducat̃ *Aquitañ.*

" Qui quidem libri restituuntʳ ꝑ eundem *Custo-* " *dem pⁱvati sigilli xxi°* die *Januar̃* ꝑx̃ seqñ."

5 Mᵈ' qđ *xi°* die *Febr̃* anno r̃ R̷ *Henr̃ viᵗⁱ xiiii°*, *Henricus Wylughby* tenens tᵉraꝝ ⁊ ten̄ que fuerunt *Thome Mapurley* delibavit Thes̃ ⁊ Camar̃ de Scᵃcio unam zonam tinisat̃ cum auro cuj⁹ corpus de nigro satyñ embroudat̃ ponder̃ in toto v. unc̃ p̃c̃ in toto lxxiii s̃ iiii đ et rem̃ in magna cista cum aliis jocalibȝ in Thesaur̃ Regis.

(p. 80.) 6 Mᵈ' qđ *xx°* die *Marcii* anno r̃ R̷ *Henr̃ viᵗⁱ xiiii° Robtus Audemer* nuꝑ Scrutator Regis in portu ville *Sandewici* ⁊ in singlis locis ⁊ portubȝ eidem portui adjacent̃ libavit Thes̃ ⁊ Camar̃ de Scᵃcio xx ꝑvos ꝑles iiii berell̄ ⁊ xxiiii lapides de diṽsis sortibȝ ꝑ ip̃m *Robtum* arestat̃ ⁊ Regi forisfact̃ qui quidem ꝑles ⁊ lapides rem̃ in una ꝑva pixide in Thesaur̃ Regis cum aliis jocalibȝ, ad tale signū

7 Md' qđ *xxvii*° die *Marcii* anno *xiiii*° ꝑdc̃o Thes̃ *Angl* ⁊ Camar̃ de Scᵃcio receperunt quandam indentur̃ fact̃ int̃ *Johem Throkmarton̄* Clicum Thes̃ ⁊ *Willm Baron̄* ex una ꝑte, et *Johem Roos* Armig̃ū de *Chirburgh* ex ꝑte alt̃a, in qua quiđ indentur̃ specificantʳ diṽs estuffament̃ miss̃ ṽsus villam ⁊ castrū de *Chirburgh* ꝑdict̃ ꝑ salva custođ eoꝝdem, que quiđ indentur̃ rem̃ in hanapio de t̃mīo *Sc̃i Michis* anno *xiiii*° ejusdem Regis.

8 Md' qđ *ix*° die *Julii* anno r̃ R̃ *Henr̃ sexti xiiii*° Thes̃ *Angl* ⁊ Camar̃ de Scᵃcio receperunt quanđ relaxac̃oem dc̃o Dño Regi ꝑ *Willm de la Pole* nūc Comitem *Suff'* fact̃, de diṽsis pecuniaꝝ sūmis eidem Dño Regi relaxat̃, et rem̃ in una pixiđ in magna cista supᵃ Reᵗᵃᵐ Scᵃcii ad tale signū

T

(p. 80 b.) 9 Md' de una lr̃a *Majoris Stapule* ville *Cales* de xᵐˡ li de pʳma vendic̃oe lanaꝝ ⁊ pelliū lanutaꝝ ibm, que quidem lr̃a rem̃ in una ꝑva pixide in viridi cista ad tale signū 

15 Hen. VI.

1 Md' qđ *xxix*°. die *Octobr̃* anno r̃ R̷ *Henr̃ sexti xv*° delib̃at̃ fuit Thes̃ ⁊ Camar̃ de Scacio ||unam ||acquietanciam Ep̃i de *Tirwyñ* Cancellar̃ *Franc̃* cont̃ xix ml iiic xvi nobles v s̃ iiii đ p ip̃m Ep̃m recept̃ de *Rad̃o* Dño *Cromwell* Thes̃ *Angl̃* p solucõe facienđ cc hoĩm ad arma ⁊ vi c sagitt̃ cũ dc̃o Dño Rege retent̃ in ptib3 *Franc̃* videlt p t̃mĩs *Sc̃i Joh̃is Bapt̃e* ⁊ *Sc̃i Mich̃is* anno Dñi *mill̃o cccc xxxv*to, que quidem acquietanc̃ recitat duas alias acquietancias de div̄sis sũmis eidem Dño Thes̃, p ip̃m Ep̃m fact̃ sigillat̃ ⁊ delib̃at̃, que quidem acquietancia de xix ml iii c xvi nobles v s̃ iiii đ reman̄ in uno coffino in viridi cista infra eandem Receptam cum aliis acquietanc̃ ejusdem Ep̃i de *Tirwyñ* ad tale signũ

𝕿

2 Fait * remembrer q̃ le *iiii*e jour de *Novemb̃*, l an du regne le Roy *Henry sisme* puis le conquest̃ *xv*e, *Thomas Carrewe* Ch̃r ad deliv̄e as Tresourer ⁊ Chamberleyns del Escheqner une ewer d argent enorrez fait al maner d un coundyt ovec un fonell̃ d arg̃ blanc̃ pois̃ de troie xv lb̃ x. unc̃ pris de la lb̃ xlviii s̃ la some ꝯ xxxviii li, le quele ewer fuist mys en gage a dit *Thomas Carrewe* l an *tierce* du Roy *Henr̃ quinte*, ⁊ le dit ewer remaigne en le gaunde Tresoury du dit Roy deyns *Westmynstre*.

Thomas Carewe Chivaler.

(p. 81.) 3 Md' qđ *ix*° die *Novembr̃*, anno r̃ R̷ *Henr̃ sexti xv*° delib̃at̃ fuit quedam lr̃a patens *Edwardi* Regis *Portugal̃* sigillo plumbio sigillat̃ de armis ejusdem Regis, recitans pacem ⁊ concordiam int̄ p̄dc̃m Dñm nr̃m Regem ⁊ ip̃m Regem *Portugal̃* cuj9 dat̃ est

Portugal̃.

apud villam de *Sintre viii°* die mensis *Augusti* anno Dñi *millmo ccccxxxvi*^to^, et ponit^r^ in quadam pixide rotund existent infra cistam sup^a^ Re^tam^ Ducat⁹ *Lancastr̃*, ad tale signū

4 M^d'^ qđ *p^i^mo* die mensis *Marcii*, anno r̃ R̃ *Henr̃ sexti xv°*, *Robtus Rodes* delibavit Thes̃ ꝛ Camar̃

Dux Lancastr̃. de Sc^a^cio divs̃ munimenta tangenc̃ Ducem *Lancastr̃* ꝛ Ducatū ejusđ que quidem munimenta remañ in uno coffino in una cista sup^a^ Receptam Ducatus *Lancastr̃* p̃dict̃ ad tale signū

5 " M^d'^ qđ libat̃ in Thes̃ R̃ quedam sp̃alis assĩa " int̃ *Willm Flete Johem Hotoft Willm Alyngtoñ*

" *Flete.* " *Nichm Dixoñ* ꝛ *Johem Cokayñ* ꝛ alios de a° *vi*^to^ R̃

" Assĩa " sp̃alis." " *Henr̃ vi*^ti^ vȝ de teñ in *Watford* in Com̃ *Hert* ꝛ " ponit^r^ in quađ baga int̃ alias assĩas de tempore " p̃dc̃i Regis *H. vi*^ti^."

(p. 81 b.) 6 M^d'^ qđ *xiii°* die *Novembr̃* anno r̃ R̃ *Henr̃ sexti xv° Willm̃s Cheyne* Capitlis Justic̃ dc̃i Dñi Regis de Banco un⁹ execut̃ testi *Johis Hals* nup uni⁹ Justic̃ ejusdem Dñi Regis de eodem Banco delibavit Thes̃

Sp̃alis assĩa. ꝛ Camar̃ de Sc^a^cio in una baga de corio unam sp̃alem assĩam capt̃ apud *Exoñ*, coram dc̃o *Johe Hals* ꝛ al anno r̃ R̃ *Henr̃ sexti* p̃dc̃i *xii*, int̃ *Robtum Burtoñ* ꝛ *Elizabeth* uxem ejus quer̃ ꝛ *Margar̃ Bykebury Thomā Arundell* militem ꝛ alios de teñ in *Bykebury*, que quidbaga rem̃ in magna cista in una alia baga de canabo cum aliis spalibȝ assis de tempe Regis *Henr sexti.*

7 Itm *eodem die Johes Wydeslade* delibavit dcis Thes ⁊ Camar unam aliam spalem assiam capt apud *Chepyngtoryton* coram *Willo* ‖*Hankeford* ⁊ aliis, a° r R *Henr quinti p'mo*, int *Gilbtm Bysshop* quer ⁊ *Waltum Suthcote* de ten in ‖*Bouelegh*, que quid assia rem in eadem magna cista in "una alia" baga de canabo cum aliis spalibȝ assis, de tempe Regis *Henr* "*quinti.*"

Spalis assia.

(p. 82.) 8 Md' qd *viii°* die *Febr* anno r R *Henr sexti xv°* Thes *Angl* ⁊ Camar de Scacio receperunt unam acquietanciam Dni Cardinalis *Angl* de ml viiic lxix li xii s iiii d ob, fact eidem Dno Regi, et p manus custumar de *Suthl* eidem Dno Cardinali solut in ptem soluc ixml marȝ eidem Dno Cardinal debit p denar ab eo mutuat p recussu ville *Cales*, que quid acquietanc reman in hanapio de tmio *Sci Michis* * dco anno *xv°*.

9 Md' qd *xx°* die *Febr* anno r R *Henr vi^ti xv°*. *Robtus Rodes* delibavit Thes ⁊ Camar de Scacio dirsa appunctuamenta Ducis *Orlien* fact pdco Dno Regi *H.* ‖*sexti.*

Dux *Orlien.*

10 Itm unu foliu papiri cont divs articul de juramento ipius Ducis *Orlien.*

["Istud foliu rem in man Ducis *Glouc* vȝ in *Qua-*"*dragesima* a° *xv. H. vi^ti.*"]

11 Itm lras patentes Regis. *H. quinti* cont jurament int ipm Regem ⁊ *Sigismundu Romanoȝ* Regem, a° *iiii^to* pdci Regis *Henr quinti* fact, rem

Rex *Romanoȝ.*

Impator. in uno coffino supª Re^tam Ducatus *Lancastr̃* ad tal̃ sign̄

{**Rex Romanor'.**}

(p. 82 b.)

12 M^d' qđ *iiii^to* die mensis *Marcii* ⹁ anno r̃ R̸ *Henr̃ sexti xv^o* ⹁ *Ric̃us Dewe* un⁹ hostiar̃ de Scªcio dc̃i Dñi Regis delib̃avit Thes̃ ⁊ Camar̃ de Scªcio quinq̧ pecias panni linei ⹁ que nup̧ fuer̄t *Barth̃i* ||*Lumlyne* ⹁ ⁊ p̧ *Joh̃em Haukesworth̃* contªr̃ scrutinii Regis in portu *London̄* eidem Dño Regi forisfact̃ ⹁ ⁊ in Scªcio dc̃i Dñi Regis delib̃at̃ ⹁ videl̃t unam peciam de meliori sorte cont̃ xliii ulnas ⹁ aliam peciam de eadem sorte cont̃ xlii ulnas ⹁ ⁊ aliā peciam cont̃ xli ulnas ⹁ app̄ciat̃ ad xii l̃i xii s̃ videl̃t quel̃t ulna inde ad ii s̃. et unā peciam de sc̃da sorte cont̃ xliiii ulnas ⁊ dimiđ app̄ciat̃ ad xl s̃. iiii^d' ob̃ videl̃t quel̃t ulna ad xi đ ⁊ aliam peciam de eadem sorte cont̃ xxii ulnas app̄ciat̃ ad xviii. s̃. iiii. đ ⹁ videl̃t ["quel̃t"] ulna inde ad x đ app̄ciat̃ ad lviii s̃. viii. đ Smª to^l v^e pec̃ app̄ciat̃ xv l̃i xi. s̃ i. đ ob̃ que quiđ v^e pecie reman̄ in magna cista supª Re^tam Sc̃cii.

Pannū lineū.

Et postea *quinto* die *Marcii* p̄x seqñ ⹁ iidem Thes̃ ⁊ Camar̃ delib̃averunt *Rob̃to Rollestoñ* Cl̃ico magne garderobe dc̃i Dñi Regis in p̄cio x l̃i x s̃. iiii đ ob̃ ⹁ tres pecias de p̄dc̃is quinq̧ peciis ⹁ videl̃t uni⁹ pecie de meliori sorte cont̃ xliii ulnas ⁊ alt̃ius pecie de eadem sorte cont̃ xlii ulnas ⁊ t̃cie pecie de sc̃da sorte cont̃ xliiii. ulñ ⁊ dimiđ. Smª x l̃i x s̃ ix đ ob̃.

Lib̃at̃ eiđ *Rob̃to* de p̄stito sup̧ offic̃ suo.

13 It̃m *eodem die* idem Thes̃ *Angl̃* ex lib̃ac̃oe dc̃oꝝ Camar̃ h̃uit duas pecias residuas de p̄dc̃is quinq̧ peciis videl̃t uni⁹ pecie de meliori sorte cont̃ xli ulnas ⹁ videl̃t quel̃t ulna inde app̄ciat̃ ad ii s̃. ⁊ alt̃ius pecie

Lib̃at̃ *Rađo* Dño de *Cromwell̃* Thes̃ *Angl̃*

de p̄stito sup̄ officio suo. de sc̄da sorte cont̄ xxii ulnas, app̄ciat̄ queƚt ulna inde ad x d̄, p man⁹ *Georgii Swalclyve* s̄vient̄ dc̄i Thes̄, in precio — c s̄ iiii d̄.

(p. 83.) 14 M^d' qd̄ *xx°* die *Aprilis*, anno r̄ R. *Henr̄ sexti xv°* *Henr̄* Cardinalis *Angl̄* delib̄avit Thes̄ & Cam̄ar̄ de Sc^a cio unū p̄vū librū papiri in quatuor quat̄nis cont̄ div̄s̄ visus tam de revencōib3 & cōmoditatib3 eidem Dn̄o Regi infra Ducatum suū *Norman̄* spectantib3, q^a m div̄s̄ vis̄ de solucōib3 fact̄ div̄s̄ Consiliar̄ de Consilio ip̄ius Dn̄i Regis in p̄tib3 *Franc̄* & *Norman̄* ac de solucōib3 fc̄is div̄sis hoīb3 ad arma & sagittar̄ in p̄tib3 *Franc̄* & *Norman̄* p̄dict̄ existen̄ qui quidem liber reman̄ in magna cista sup^a Re^tam Ducatus *Lancastr̄*.

Franc̄ & Norman̄.

{**Liber.**}

15 M^d' qd̄ ∗ quedam relaxacio gen̄alis *Rob̄ti Wylughby* Militis fc̄a Dn̄o Regi cuj⁹ dat̄ est *decimo* die *Maii* anno *xv°* Regis *Henrici sexti*, et ponit^r in ‖quodam pixide in magna cista sup^a Re^tam Ducatus *Lancastr̄* ad tale signū

{**Wylughby R.**}

16 M^d' qd̄ ∗ quedam acquietancia *Henrici Borrat* nūcii Dn̄i *Pauli Rusderf* Ordinis *B'e Marie Teuthonico*ꝝ Magr̄i gen̄alis de *Prucia* de quingentis marcis p ip̄m *Henr̄* recept̄, anno *xv°* Regis *Henr̄ sexti*, et ponit^r in pixide cum acquietancia *Rob̄ti Wylughby* ut sup^a.

D m^a r3.

{**Prucia.**}

" infra."

(p. 83 b.) 17 Fait remembrance q̄ le p^i mer jour de *Juyll*, l an du regne le Roy *Henry vi*^me^ puis le conquest *xv*^e^ ◟ q̃ le ꝑsreꝰent pier en Dieu *Henry* Cardynall d *Engletre* ad deliꝰe as Tresourer ꝛ Chamberleyns del Eschequer ꝯteyñ jeweƚƚ ensuantz cestassavoir.

18 En p^i^mez une tabulet de *Seint George* d or garniz d un rub viii diamanđ ꝛ a une coste une "angeƚƚ" ten^a^nt son healme garniz d un rub ꝛ petitz ꝑles ꝛ a l autre coste une pucelle genulant ovec une brebis garniz d un rubie ◟ Et la tabulet tout entier garniz de xxv. bal ["xxv"] ✠ xxiiii ✠ saph ◟ iii esmeraudes lv. grose ꝑles iiii^xx^ ix ꝑles d autre sort ꝛ beaucoupe d autres ꝑles del doune du la reigne *Katine* poisant — lxxix unc̃ dĩ.

"Libant^r "*Dño Car-* "*dinali* p "inde it "*xxx*^o^ die "‖ *Merc̃* a^o^ "*xvii*."

19 Itm une tabulet d or ovec i pece de *Tunica inconsutili* garniz de xxv gros ꝑles poĩs — lxi unc̃.

20 Itm ii salers d or dount une hōme ꝛ l autre fēme ten^a^ntz les salers entre leur maines ꝛ le hōme garniz de vii rub vii troch chescun de iii ꝑles ꝛ sur le topet i. saph ꝛ le pee du dit hōme est garniz de vi rub vi saph ꝛ xlviii ꝑles poĩs xlv unc̃ dĩ i. quartñ ꝛ la fēme ten^a^nt une autre saler garniz de vii rub vii troches chun de iii. ꝑles ꝛ sur le topet i. saph — iiii^xx^ xiiii unc̃ dĩ.

"Libant^r "*Dño Car-* "*dinali xxx* "die *Marc̃* "a^o^ *xvii*^o^."

	⁊ le pee est garniz de vi rub̃ vi saph̃ ⁊ xlviii ꝑles poiŝ xlviii unĉ dĩ i. ferl̃ d or del doune de Duc de *Gloucestr̃* poiŝ ensemble	
	21 Itm̃ i. peitrell̃ d or q̃ fuist fait d un coler apelle *Iklyngtoñ Coler* garniz de iiii. rub̃ iiii gros saph̃ xxxii graundes ꝑles ⁊ liii autres ꝑles de meindre sort poiŝ	xxxvi unĉ i quartñ.
	22 Itm̃ une cercle d or [" w[t] x pynacles"] garniz de [" c viii"] garnades saph̃ [" ⁊ "] esmeraudes ⁊ " clxvi " ꝑles poisant	xvii unĉ i. q[a]rtr̃.
	23 Itm̃ une chalis d or ⁊ ii cruettes d or del doune du l Erchevesq̧ de *Caunterbury* poiŝ	xxix unĉ.
	24 Itm̃ ii cruettes d or ⁊ i. petit sonet d or poiŝ ensemble	xxiiii unĉ i. q[a]rtr̃.
" Lib̃ant[r] " *Dño Car-* " *dinali* ꝑ " indentur̃ " *xxx* die " *Marcii* a[o] " *xvii*[o]."	25 Itm̃ ii. petitz pottes d or del doune de Duchesse de *Clarence* poiŝ ensemble	xxxiii unĉ dĩ.
	26 Itm̃ i. haute coupe d or garniz de ꝑles ⁊ faut i. ⁊ sur le topet i. saph̃. Et une eger̃ d or de mesme la suyte donne au Roy ꝑ la Roigne *Johan* poiŝ ensemble	lxvi unĉ iii q[a]rtr̃.
(p. 84.)	27 Itm̃ une graunde almes-dissh̃ d arg̃ dorrez fait a la maner d un nief plein des hõmes darmez combatantz entour les costes poisantz ensemble ovec la pee	lxvii li ix unĉ.

28 It̃m vi chargeours ⁊ xii. saucers d arg̃ dorrez ⁊ dehors les bordures markes ovec lez armes du Roy poiš ensemble — xl lƀ xi unc̃.

29 It̃m ii gᵃundes chargeours d arg̃ dorrez poisantz — x lƀ ix. unc̃.

30 It̃m xiii esquelx d argent dorrez ovec i. saucer poiš ensemble — xxx lƀ viii unc̃.

31 It̃m xv holowe disshes ovec i saucer d arg̃ dorrez poiš — xxix lƀ xi unc̃.

"Liƀantʳ "*Dño Car*- "*dinali* p̲ "indent̃ "*xxx°* die "*Marc̃* a° "*xviii°*."

32 It̃m xii esquels ovec trois saucers d arg̃ dorrez poiš — xxxiiii lƀ iiii unc̃.

33 It̃m vi. saucers d argent dorrez poiš ensemble — vi lƀ vi unc̃.

34 It̃m i peire basyns d arg̃ dorrez chacez ⁊ pounsonez en lez founcez faitz de kermery de doune du Roigne *Johan* poiš — xx lƀ viii unc̃.

"‖P̶ ‖Duce "*Eboꝫ*."

35 It̃m une tabuler d arg̃ dorrez enameille bloy ⁊ vermeille "pʳ" jewer as tables poiš — xvii lƀ vi unc̃ đi.

36 It̃m une autre tabuler d arg̃ dorrez enameille bloy ⁊ vermeille pʳ jewer as eschees poiš — xix lƀ viii unc̃.

37 It̃m lez table meigne d arg̃ dorrez ⁊ enameillez bloy ⁊ vermeille poisant — ix unc̃ đi.

38 Itm xxxii chessh meigne d arḡ dorrez poiš ensemble	iii lƀ iiii unc̃.
39 Itm ii. ‖haignez ꝛ xlvi ‖scheynes p[r] jewer as mereillez poisantz	viii unc̃ i quart̃.
40 Itm i croise d arḡ dorrez enameillez ovec ‖de diꝰs ymages esteant sur une pee jadys resceux del *S[r] de Scrop̃* Tresourer *d Englet̃re* poiš	xii lƀ xi unc̃ di̇.
41 Itm i. g[a]unde coupe d arḡ dorrez ꝛ enameillez ꝛ sur le topet i. lyoū poisant	viii lƀ viii unc̃.

42 Les queux jewelx remayn[a]ūt ‖in la g[a]unde Tresory nr̃e ꝰs Soꝰayne S[r] le Roy deins *Westmynstre.*

" infra."

(p. 84 b.) 43 This makeþ mynde þ[t] þe *xiiii[e]* day of þe moneth̃ of *Juyll̃* þe yeer of þ[e] regne of Kyng *Herry* þe *sext* þe *xv[e]*, Wytnesseth̃ þat my *Lord Cardynall̃* by the handes of *William Port* hath deliꝰed to þe Tresourer of *Inglond* and to þe Chamberleyns of þe Eschequer ‖ꝰteyns jewelx, as yt aperith̃ her after in writyng.

"Lib *Dño* "*Cardinali* "p indent̃ "*xxx°* die "*Marcii* "a° *xvii°*."

44 ¶ Furst a swerd of gold callyd þe *Swerd of Spayne* garnysed w[t] v grete balays vi grete saphurs iiii[xx] xix grete peerles up on þe skaberd, *&c.* (*see p.* 144, *No.* 22.) þe pris . D. mark in money.

45 Also ii grete chaundlers of gold garnysed w[t] iiii saphurs *&c.* (*see p.* 145, *No.* 19.) þe pris of

þe same chaundlers cccc lxvi li xiii s iiii d in money.

46 Also a grete shipp called þe *Tygre* garnysed wt xix. balays *&c.* *(see p.* 145, *No.* 21.) þe pris of þe seid shipp ccc xxxii li.

47 Also a peir basyns of gold chaced of þe maner of roses pounsed wt grete boselettꝭ *&c.* (*see p.* 145, *No.* 20.) pris of þe seyd basyns cccc lviii li xiii s iiii d.

48 All þe whiche jewelx above seid, except þe seid basins, remayne in þe Kynges Tresory wt in *Westmynstre.*

49 [♣ " The which peir basins of gold remayne
" in þe handes of þe Tresorer of *Inglond* to hym
" deliv'ed by þe handes of þe seid *Willam Port*,
" now beyng in þe handes of *Will Estfeld.*" ♣

" And þe whiche ii basyns wer restored ageyn
" in to þe Kynges Tresory by þe handes of þe
" seide *Willam Estfeld* þe *xix* day of *Juyll* þe *xviie*
" yeer of Kyng *Herry* þe *sext.*"]

[" Exa."

50 " oon of þe seide basyns to þe seide *Will*
" and *Robt Large* by endentur for cc li by hem
" lent to þe Kyng þe *xxv* day of *August* þe *yere*
" *aforesayd* by þe hondes of *Pounde.*"]

51 " And þe whiche basyn þe seid *Th Pounde*
" restored in to þe Kynges Tresory þe *xxviii* day of
" *Octob* next aft'."

16 Hen. VI.

(p. 85.) 1 Md' qđ *xxx*° die *Novembr̃* anno r̃ R̷ *Henr̃ vi*ti *xvi*° *Gervasius de* ‖*Vulre* Secretarius ✝ꝛ Procurator ✝ dc̃i Dñi nr̃i Regis infra *Angliam* delibavit Thes̃ ꝛ Cam̃ar̃ de Scacio unam acquietanciam Ep̃i de *Tirwyn* Cancellar̃ *Franc̃* de ᴅ li recept̃ de eisdem Thes̃ ꝛ Cam̃ar̃ de exit̃ ꝓficuis ꝛ revenc̃oibȝ Ep̃atus *Elieñ* que quidem acquietanc̃ rem̃ in uno coffino in viridi cista infra eandem Retam cum aliis acquietanciis ejusdem Ep̃i de *Tirwyn* ad tale signū

2 Md' qđ *vii*° die *Decembr̃* anno r̃ R̷ *Henr̃ sexti xvi*°, *Johes Stepyngdoñ* delibavit Thes̃ ꝛ Cam̃ar̃ de Scacio " unā cartam " fact̃ p *Willm Eystoñ* de *Istelworth*, illustrissimo Principi ꝛ Dño nr̃o Dño *Edwardo* Dei gr̃a Regi *Angl* ꝛ *Franc̃*, anno regni sui *xlix*°, que quiđ carta rem̃ in ‖uno pixide in cista supa Retam juxta gradus computat̃ ad tale signū

{ Carta de Istelworth'. }

(p. 85 b.) 3 This maketh mynde þt þe *xvi*e day of *Fevʒer* the yeer of þe regne of Kyng *Herry* þe *sext* þe *xvi*e Wytnesseth þat *my Lorde Cardynall* by the handes of *Willam Port* hath delyvered to the Tresourer of *Inglond* and to þe Chamberleins of the Eschequer this jewell undir write.

" Libantr " Duci " *Eboȝ*." A peire of sensures of gold the whiche weyen xiiii. mark iii unces i quarteroñ of troye pris þe unce xxvi. s̃ viii đ, the pris̃ of þe seiđ sensures cliii li xiii. s̃ iiii đ.

4 Md' qđ *xx*° die *Marcii*, anno r̃ R̸ *Henr̃ sexti xvi*°, Mag̃r *Willm̃s Lynwode* Custos pivati sigilli Regis delibavit in Thesaurar̃ Regis, unam indentur̃ sigillat̃ diṽsis sigillis cont̃ treugas int̃ p̃dc̃m Dñm nr̃m Regem *Angl* et ptes *Prucie*, capt̃ p *Willm* Ep̃m *Lincolñ* Dñm de *Tiptot* ⁊ al̃ ex pte p̃dc̃i *Dñi Regis*, cuj⁹ dat̃ est *Londoñ xxii*° die *Marcii*, a°. r̃ R̸ *Henr̃ sexti xv*°.

5 It̃m *eodem die*, idem Mag̃r *Wills Lynwode* delibavit eisdem Thes̃ ⁊ Camar̃ unū instrumentū cont̃ treugas int̃ ptes p̃dc̃as, sigillat̃ sigillo Civitatis *Lubiceñ*, cuj⁹ dat̃ est in eadem civitate *Lubiceñ* anno a Nativitate Dñi *millmo cccc xxxvii*°, die *vicesima* mensis *Augusti*. Et ponūtr in quadam quadrante pixide rem̃ in cista supa Receptam Ducatus *Lancastr̃* ad tale signū

{ **Prucia & Hans.** }

(p. 86.) " exta."

6 This maketh mynde þt þe *xiiii*e day of *Marche* the yeer of þe regne of Kyng *Herry* þe *vi*e. the *xvi*e. Witnesseth þt the Tresourer of *Ingelond*, and the Chambleyns of þe Eschequer have delyṽed by endentre unto þe hygh and myghty Prynce *Richard* Duk of *York*, by þe handes of Maister *Robt Beamond* Clerk, and *John Wygmore* by vertu of a pryve seal of our seid *Sovlain Lorde* late directe to þe seid Tresourer ⁊ Chambleyns c̃teynes juelx of our seyde *Sovlain Lorde* to plegge for þe sōme of ml cl. markɇ by þe seid *Duke* lente to oure seid *Sovlain Lord*, the whiche juelx apperen herafter in writyng.

	7 First a shippe of golde called þe *Tygre* garnysed wᵗ xix baleys xii grete ples ⁊ xiiii small perles þe which weyeth xxxiii marke iii unces of troy pris þe unce xxx s̃ smᵃ	cccc li x s̃.
	8 Also ii. sensures of golde þᵗ weyth to gydres xiiii mark iii. unces of troy pris þe unce xxx s̃. smᵃ	clxxii li x. s̃.
	9 Also ii. crewettes [" of gold "] on of whiche hath a gret perle in þᵉ topet and i. litil belle of golde þᵗ weyeth xxiiii unces ⁊ i quarť troy pris þe unc̃ xxvi s̃ viii ď smᵃ	xxxii li vi. s̃ viii ď.
Ric̃us Dux *Ebor̃.*	10 Also a sercle of golde wᵗ x. pynacles garnysed wᵗ c viii. saphirs garnades ⁊ emerawdes and clxvi. perles þᵗ weyeth xvii unces troy pris þᵉ unc̃ xxv s̃.	xxi li v. s̃.
	11 Also a crosse of silver ov̾-gilt and enamaled þᵗ weyeth xii lb xi unc̃ ⁊ dĩ unc̃ troy pris þe unce xl ď	xxv li xviii s̃ iiii ď.
	12 Also a chalys of sylver and ov̾gylt þᵗ weyeth xxviii unc̃ troy pris þe unc̃ xl ď.	iiii li xiii s̃ iiii ď.
	13 Also a tabler of silver and ov̾gilt enameled blewe ⁊ rede to pley wᵗ atte þᵉ tables þᵗ weyeth xvii lb vi unc̃	

14 Also xxxii table meyne of silver ovegilt enameled blewe and rede þt weyeth to gyder ix unc̃ ⁊ dĩ unc̃

15 Also a tabler of silver ⁊ ovegilt enameled blewe ⁊ rede to play wt at þe chesse þat weyeth xix lb viii unc̃ troye

16 Also xxxii chessemayny of silver ⁊ overgilt þt weyeth togydres iii lb iiii unc̃ troye

17 Also ii foxes ⁊ xlvi houndes of silver ovegilt to play atte þe marelles þt weyeth to gidres viii unc̃ i quart troye

The which weieth in all xlii lb ⁊ a quart troye pryce of þe lb liii s̃. iiii d̃ Sma cxii li xiiii d̃.

(p. 86 b.) 18 Md' qđ *xx*o die *Junii* anno r̃ R *Henr̃ sexti xvi*o, *Radus* Dñs de *Cromwell* Thesaur̃ *Angl* libavit in Thesaur̃ Regis treugas captas p *Henricū Percy* Comitē *Northumbr̃ Johem* Dñm de *Tiptot* ⁊ al, int pdc̃m *Dñm nr̃m Regem*, et *Jacobum* Regem *Scottoꝝ*, unacum cōmissione ejusdem *Jacobi*. Que quidem treuge remañ in ‖uno pixide in cista supa Retam Ducatus *Lancastr̃* ad tale signū

{ **Angl' Scocia.** }

19 ☩ This maketh mynde þt the *xv*e day of the moneth of *Juyll* þe yeer of þe regne of Kyng *Herry* þe *sext* after þe conquest the *xvi*e, Wytnesseth þt *Constantyñ Wylughby* hath delived by þe handes of *Will*a*m Milrede* of *Londoñ*, in to þe Kynges Tresory cteyns jewelx and godes, whiche wer̃ long-

yng̃ to *Owen̄ app̄ Meredutħ* as they apere herafter in writyng.

	20 First a douszein gilt cuppes chased writhen weyng xvi lb̄ i unc̄ of troy pris þe lb̄ xl s̄ Smª	xxxii l̄i iii s iiii d.
" q̄ ven- " duntʳ."	21 Also an olde lowe gilt cuppe coṽed weyng xxi unc̄ ꝛ dĩ pris þe unc̄ ii s̄ viii d̄ Sª	lvii s̄ iiii d̄.
	22 Also a gilt chalice weyng xxi unc̄ ꝛ dĩ pris the unce iii s̄ Smª	lxiiii. s̄ vi. d̄.
	23 Also vi salt salers of silṽe grene enameled ꝛ brokyn wᵗ oon coṽcle ꝛ wᵗ a peerle theron, the cuppes of cokyle weyng iii lb̄ iiii unc̄ ꝛ dĩ pris þe lb̄ xxiiii s̄ Sª	iiii. l̄i. xii d̄.
	24 Also a paxbrede of silṽe ꝛ gilt wᵗ an ymage of *Seynt Cristofre* weyng v. unc̄ ꝛ dĩ pris þe unc̄ xl d̄ Sª	xviii s̄. iiii d̄.
(p. 87.)	25 Also an ewer of silṽe p̱cell gilt chased ꝛ writhen weyng xiii unc̄ i quarter pris þe unce ii s̄ viii d̄ Sª	xxxv s̄ iiii d̄.
	26 Also vi. course cuppes of silṽe Parys werk̄ þe bordures gilt weyng v lb̄ xi unc̄ ꝛ dĩ pris þe lb̄ xxxi s̄ Sª	ix l̄i iiii s̄ viii d̄.

27 Also a standyng cuppe of silver coṽeđ ꝑceƚƚ gilt lakkyng þe vyce weyng xv unc̃ ⁊ dĩ pris þe unc̃ ii. s̃ x. đ S^{a}

xliii s̃ xi đ.

28 Also a peir flacoũs of silṽe writhen wᵗ cheynes of silṽe weyng xi lƀ ii. unc̃ pris þe lƀ xxxii s̃ S^{a}

xvii ƚi xvii s̃ iiii đ.

29 Also another peir of flacoũs of silṽe pleyñ weyng x lƀ v unc̃ pris þe lƀ xxxi s̃ S^{a}

xvi. ƚi ii. s̃ xi đ.

30 Also a peir of candilstikkes of silṽe double wᵗ vices ⁊ ꝑceƚƚ gilt weyng iiii lƀ iiii unc̃ iii q^{a}rṽ pris þe lƀ xxxvi s̃ S^{a}

vii ƚi xviii s̃ iii đ.

31 ♣ Also a peir̃ of basyns wᵗ ii. ewers of silṽe writhen ꝑceƚƚ gilt weyng x lƀ viii unc̃ ⁊ dĩ pris þe lƀ xxxiiii s̃ Sm^{a}

xviii ƚi iiii s̃ i. đ.

32 Also another peir̃ of basyns pleyñ coṽed wᵗ a rose in þe ‖botme and armes ⸝ þe rose ⁊ þe bordures gilt weyng vii lƀ v. unc̃ ⁊ dĩ pris þe lƀ xxxii s̃ S^{a}

xi ƚi xviii s̃ viii đ.

33 Also ii spiceplates of silṽe writhen ⁊ ꝑceƚƚ gilt weyng v. lƀ. v. unc̃ ⁊ iii quartr̃ pris þe lƀ xxxii s̃ S^{a}

viii ƚi xv. s̃ iiii đ.

34 Also an hond kandilstikke of silṽe weyng iiii unc̃ pris þe unc̃ ii. s̃ vii. đ S^{a}

x s̃ iiii đ.

35 Also a brokyn flour̃ gilt weyng i quartr̃ ꝛ dĩ ꝛ a peny weyght pris } xii đ. ✝

"Sª cxxxvii li. x s. iiii d."

36 All þe whiche jewelx above rehersed þe *xxi.* day of *Juyll* next aft̃, the seyd Chamƀleyns have delyṽed by comaundement of þe Tresourer of *Inglond* to "*Willªm Estfeld*" of *London* "————————" for money borwed of hym þt ys to sey cxxxvii li x s̃ iiii đ and so nowe þe seyd jewelx remaygne in þe handes of þe seid *Willªm Estfeld*, as yt ys aforeseyd.

"q, vend." 37 ¶ "And nowe all þe seide jewelx by vertu "of a pryve seal directed to þe seid Tresorer ꝛ "Chamƀleyns be sold to þe seyd *Willªm Estfeld* "for þe seid sōme of cxxxvii li x s iiii d þe whiche "pryve seal remayneth in þe filace of *Mighellmes* "*ter̃me* the *xvii*e yeer of þe seid Kyng."

16, 17, 18, 19 Hen. VI.

(p. 88.) 1 This maketh mynde þt the *xv*e day of the moneth of *Juyll*, the yeer of þe regne of Kyng *Herry* the *Sext* the *xvi*e, Witnesseth þat *my Lord Cardynall* by the handes of *Willªm Port* hath deliṽed to the Tresorer of *Englond* and to þe Chamberleyns of þe Eschequer thise jewelx undir write.

"Libantr "*Dño Car-* "*dinali* p "indent "*xxx*o die "*Marcii* ao "*xvii*o R. "*H vi*ti."

2 Furst a pusañ of gold called the *riche Coler* conteynyng xvi culpons or peces up on þe whiche are viii antelops garnysed &c. (*see p.* 143, *No.* 14.) þe pris ml ml ml ml cc markꝭ in money.

"Libatr "Archiepo "Cantuar "p indent."

3 Also a gret ouche of *Seynt George* armes in þe which ouche are sette viii balays &c. (*see p.* 143, *No.* 15.) þe pris cc li in money.

4 "þe which is deliv͛ed to þe Archebysshop of "*Caunt͛bury* by endenture for cc li by hym lent to "þe Kyng þe *xxv day* of *August* þe *xvii*the yere of "þe Kyng þt nowe ys by þe hondes of *Pounde*."

5 "And þe *ix* day of *Novemb* next aft͛ þe seid "ouche was restored in to þe Kynges Tresory by þe "handes of *Thomas Pounde*."

(p. 88 b.) "Libantr "*Dño Car-* "*dinali* "*xxx*o die "*Marcii* ao "*xvii*o."

6 Also a tablet of gold of þe passion of *Crist* made in þe maner of a booke garnysed wt xliii diamand͛ &c. (*see p.*144, *No.*17.) whiche tablet weyeth lx unces of troy þe pris cxx li.

7 And as touching to þe tabernacle of gold, wt yn the whiche ys a ymage of *Our Lady* sette up on a grene tarage wt þe figurs of *Adam* & *Eve*, and iiii aungell atte þe iiii corners of þe same tabernacle and a crucifixe of gold white enameled up on þe same tab͛nacle, And up on þe same tab͛nacle ys a chirche, the whiche tab͛nacle ys garnysed wt iii. rubies iii dyamand iiii balays iii saphirs lxxvii grete peerles and xliii litil peerles, whiche tab͛nacle weyeth xlii unces of Troy the pris lx li, the seid *Lord Cardynall* ys discharged ayens þe *Kyng* of þe reliv͛e þerof, and þe said Tresourer and Chaumberleyns of þe Resseyt be discharged of the tab͛nacle above seyd by þe vertue of a pryve seal remaynyng of record in þe Resseyt, beryng date, þe *xv*e day of *Juyll* above seid.

8 All þe whiche jewelx above seyd, except þe

seid tab̄nacle ⸝ remayne in þe *Kynges Tresory* wᵗ yn *Westmynster.*

(p. 89.) "extᵃ."

9 This maketħ mynde þᵗ þe *xxiiii* day of þe monetħ of *Novemb̄* the yeer of þe regne of Kyng *Herry* þe *Sext* after þe conquest þe *xviiᵉ*⸝ wytnessetħ þᵗ my *Lorde Cardynall̄* by þe handes of *Willᵃm Port* hath resseyved by endenture of þe Tresorer of *Inglond̄* and of þe Chamb̄leyns of the Eschequer þise jewelx undirwryte.

10 Furst a grete ouche of *Seynt George* armes in þe whiche ouche are sette viii balays *&c.* (*see p.* 143, *No.* 15.) weyng in all xxx unces of troy.

11 Also ii. grete chaundlers of gold̄ garnysed wᵗ iiii saphurs iiii balays and iiii emeraudes & xxv peerles whiche chaundlers weyen to gydres xliiii mark̄ of troy ⸝ save ii. unces.

12 The whiche . ii. jewelx wer restored by þe handes of þe seid *Will̄ᵃm Port* in to þe Kynges Tresory þe *xiᵉ* day of *Maii* þe *xviiᵉ* yeer aboveseid ⸝ by endenture.

13 Mᵈ' qd̄ *xx* die *Marcii* anno *xviiº* p̄dc̄i R̄ *Joh̄es* Dux *Norff'* lib̄avit Thes̄ ꝛ Cam̄ar de Scᵃcio unam l̄ram attorn̄ ac unā aliam l̄ram *ejusd̄ Ducis* ꝑ *Joh̄e*

Dux *Norff.'* *Middelton̄* Armig̃o ⸝ ad recipiend̄ de dc̄is Thes̄ ꝛ Cam̄ar noīe ejusdem Ducis cclxxi. l̄i viii d̄ qᵃ⸝ que quidem l̄re rem̄ in ‖uno pixide in hanapio de t̃mīo *Sc̄i Mich̄is* dc̄o anno *xviiº*.

(p. 89 b.) 14 Mᵈ' qd̄ *xxviiiº* die *Januar̃* anno r̃ R̄ *Henr̃ sexti xviiº Will̄s Westbury* unus Justic̄ de Banco Regis delib̄avit Thes̄ ꝛ Cam̄ar̃ de Scᵃcio unam sp̄ealem assīam capt̄ apud *Welles* in Com̄ *Som̃s̃* coram *Will̄o*

Spēalis assīa.

Cheyne ꝛ al̄ anno regni ejusdem Regis *xvi*°, int̉ *Will̄m Paulet* Militem *Will̄m Halswell̄* ꝛ al̄ quer̄ ꝛ *Walt̄um Hungerford̄* Militem ꝛ al̄ de ten̄ * *Gotehurst Briggewat̉ Munketon̄ Abb̄is* ꝛ *Stoke Cursy*, que quid̄ assīa rem̄ in una baga de canabo in una magna cista infra Re^tam^ cum aliis spēalibȝ assis̄ de tempe Regis *Henr̄ sexti* p̄dc̄i.

15 M^d'^ qd̄ *iiii*^to^ die *Februar̄* a° r̄ R̄ *Henr̄ sexti xvii*° *Joh̄es Cottesmere* unus Justic̄ Dn̄i R̄ de Cōi Banco delib̄avit Thes̄ ꝛ Camar̄ suis de Sc^a^cio unam sp̄alem assīam capt̄ apud *Coventr̄* in Com̄ *Warr̄* corā p̄fato *Joh̄e* ||*Cottesmore* anno p̄dc̄o int̉ *Will̄m Byrmyngeh*^a^*m* Armig̉um ꝛ *Ph̄m Chetewynd̄* Militē ꝛ *Elenam* ux̉em ejus de ten̄ in *Byrmyngeh*^a^*m* que quid̄ assīa rem̄ in una baga de ||coreo int̉ alias spēales assīas de tempe R̄ p̄dc̄i in magna cista.

Spālis assīa.

16 M^d'^ qd̄ *xiii*° die *Febr̄*, anno *xvii*° dc̄i Regis. Magr̄ *Walt̄us Colles* Constabular̄ *Burdegal̄* delib̄avit Thes̄ ꝛ Camar̄ de Sc^a^cio unū certificatoriū sigillat̄ sigillo Senescalsie *Burdegal̄*, ꝛ sigillo Judicis *Vascon̄*, continens p̄cellas ꝛ noīa eoꝝ quibȝ *B. Angevyn̄* delib̄avit p̄ avisamētū consilii dc̄i Dn̄i R̄ *Burdegal̄* exist̄ p̄cillatim m^l^ ti quas ||dc̄us *B.* ꝛ *Walt̄us Colles* recep̄unt t̉cio die *Febr̄* a° *xvi*° dc̄i R̄ ad distribuend̄ in Ducatu *Aquitan̄* scd̄m vim formā ꝛ eff̄c̄m quaꝝdam lr̄aꝝ paten̄ dc̄o c̉tificator̄ annex̄, et rem̄ in "magna cista" sup^a^ Re^tam^ jux^a^ gradus computat̄ ad tale signū

{Walt'us Colles Burdegal'.}

(p. 90.)

17 Me^d'^ qd̄ *xxvii*° die *Maii* anno *xviii*° R̄ *Henr̄ sexti* lib̄ant^r^ ext^a^ Thesaur̄ R̄ v lr̄e de delib̄ac̄oe

Joħis nuꝑ Ɍ *Franc̃*, Magr̃o *Ade Molineux* Cl̃ico de Consilio Ɍ ad portanđ Archiep̃o *Eboꝝ* in Com̃ *Kanc̃.*

ꝭ Que quiđ vᵉ lr̃e postea *xi°* die *Junii* ꝓx̃ seqñ reportantʳ ⁊ liƀantʳ p ꝑdc̃m Magr̃m *Adam Molyns* in Thesaur̃ Ɍ et rem̃ in cista supᵃ Reᵗᵃᵐ Ducatus *Lancastr̃.*

18 Mᵈ' qđ *xiii°* die *Marcii* a° *xx°* Regis *Henr̃ sexti* Ep̃us *Lincolñ* liƀavit in Reᵗᵃᵐ Scᵃcii dc̃i Dñi Ɍ p mᵒ *Henr̃ Benet* duas lr̃as de tractatu ⁊ concordia fac̃t inᵗ Dñm *H.* nuꝑ Regem *Angl̃ quintũ*, et *Karolũ* Dñm de *la Brytte* de dat̃ *xvi°* die *Januar̃* anno Dñi *millmo iiiiᶜ xx°*, que quiđ lr̃e remañ in una pixide supᵃ Reᵗᵃᵐ Ducatus *Lancastr̃* ad tale signũ {D'n's de la Brytte.}

Brytte.

19 " Mᵈ' qđ *vii°* die *Julii* a° *xxi°* Ɍ *Henr̃ sext* " *Rađus* Dñs *Cromwell* Thes̃ *Angl̃* liƀavit in Thesaurar̃ Ɍ salvo custodienđ, unam sentenc̃ danđ " sup om̃es illos murdrat̃ ⁊ culpabiles de morte " *Joħis* nuꝑ Ducis *Burgunđ*, et rem̃ in cista supᵃ " Reᵗᵃᵐ Ducatus *Lancastr̃.*"

"*Joħes* nuꝑ "Dux *Burgunđ.*"

(p. 90 b.)

20 Mᵈ' qđ *xxviii°* die *April̃* anno r̃ Ɍ *Henr̃ sexti xviii°*, Dñi de Consilio Regis liƀaverunt Thes̃ ⁊ Camar̃ de Scᵃcio unã lr̃am alligancie fc̃e inᵗ Dñm *Henr̃* nuꝑ Regem *Angl̃ quintũ* et *Sigismũdũ* Regem *Romanoꝝ semp August̃* sigillat̃ cũ vii sigillis, de dat̃ *anno Dñi millo iiiiᶜ xvii°.*

21 Itm aliam lr̃am alligancie fact̃ inᵗ ꝑdc̃m Dñm *Henr̃* nuꝑ Regem *Angl̃*, et ꝑdc̃m *Sigismũdum*, sigillat̃ cum sigillo dc̃i Regis *Henr̃ quinti*, de dat̃ anno Dñi *millmo iiiiᶜ xvi°.*

Sigismundus Rex *Romanoꝝ.*

22 Itm ‖quedam ‖cōmissio dci Regis *Henr quinti* fact venabilib3 prib3 *Nicho Bathon* ⁊ *Wellen* Epo *Robto Saz Johi* Dño de *Tiptot* ‖*Hertauk' Van Clux* ⁊ al, ad tractand cum Principib3 eccliastic ⁊ secularib3 Ducib3 Marchionib3 eciam *Sacri Romani impii* Electorib3, cuj⁹ quidem cōmissionis, dat est *scdo* die *Decembr*, anno r R *Henr quinti quarto*, que reman in uno cofino signat.

"nūc ponūt[r] "in uno coffro pictato "in cista "ubi ponit[r] "pgamenū "‖iō ⁊c."

{Sigismu'dus Rex Romanor'.}

Et ponūt[r] in quadam cista sup[a] Receptam Principatus *Wallie*.

23 ✠ "M[d'] qd iste iii lre libant[r] Magro *Ade* "*Moleneux* *xi°*. die *Maii* a° *xviii°* ✱ psencia Dñi "Thes in Cam̃a Re[ne] *Westm*."

"ex[a]."

"Postea *p[i]mo* die *Junii* px seqn ‖iidem tres lre "libant[r] in Thesaur R p m⁹ dci Magri *Ade*."✠

"It iii script unū de appunctuament ligaz ⁊ "‖confiderat int oratores Regū *Romanoz* ⁊ [*Ricm* "Regem] *Anglie*. aliud de confirmacōe appunctua-"ment ligaz ⁊c tēpe dci R *Rici* ⁊ terciū scriptū de "confirmacōe *Sygysmundi* Impatoris fca cū Rege "*H. v*[to]. ⁊c. ⁊ ponūt[r] cū script supius specificat in "cofino pdco reman ut sup[a]."

(p. 91.) 24 This maketh mynde þ[t] þe *ferst* day of *Septemb* þe *xix*[e] yeer of Kyng *Herry* þe *sext* ther wer takyn oute of þe Kynges Tresory. by þe comaundement of þe Kyng and certeyn Lordes of hys Counseill, certeyn jewelx for to borwe upon hem a m[l] li, þ[t] ys to sey a peir basyns of gold and ii grete chaundlers of gold, the whiche jewelx wer leyde to plegge, by *Thomas Pounde* and *John* ‖*Poutrell*, un[to] *George Luke* and hys felawes, as yt aperith by endenture made by twene þe seid *Thomas Pounde* and *John* ||*Poutrell*, and þe seid *George* ꝛc.

25 "Et postea *xxx*° die *Januar̃* anno *xix*° p̃dc̃i "R̃ p̃dc̃us *Georgius* restituit in Thesaur̃ Regis, "salvo custodiend̃, om̃ia p̃dc̃a jocalia."

26 This makeþ mynde þ^t^ þe *xxiiii* day of *Janev̄e* þe *xix* yeer of þe seid *Kyng* by comaundement of all þe Lordes of þe Kynges Counseill *Waut̃ Stokker* delyv̄ed to Maister *Adam Molyns* v. lr̃es of þe ||Dukes of *Orliaunce* enselyd w^t^ hys owne seal, of div̄s appoyntement̃ made bytwene our seyd *Sov̄ayn̄ Lord* and þe seyd *Duke*, the whiche v. lr̃es þe seid Maist^r^ *Adam* shall restore ageyn̄ in to þe Kynges Tresory in all hast possible.

"The whiche v. lr̃es aft̃ þe *iii* day of *Fev̄er* next "aft̃ wer̃ deliv̄ed ageyne in to þe seyd Tresory."

27 M^d'^ qd̃ *vii*° die *Novembr̃* anno *xix*° dc̃i R̃ *Radus* Dñs de *Cromwell* Thesaur̃ *Angl* libavit in Thesaur̃ R̃ salvo custodiend̃ quandam indenturam int̃ p̃dc̃m *Dñm* nr̃m *Regem*, et Avūclm suū *Humfr̃m* Ducem *Gloucestr̃* de div̄sis castris ꝛ dñiis in ꝑtibꝫ *Aquitañ* que nuꝑ fuerūt Dñi *Bernardi de la Sparre*, que quid̃ indent^r^a remañ in una pixide, remañ sup^a^ Re^tam^ Ducat⁹ *Lancastr̃*, ad tale signū.

{**Dux Gloucestr' Guyen.**}

(p. 91 b.) 28 M^d'^ qd̃ *iiii*^to^ die *Julii* anno r̃ R̃ *Henr̃ sexti xviii*°, *Radus* Dñs *Cromwell* Thes̃ *Angl* libavit in Thesaur̃ R̃ duas lr̃as alliganc̃, de data *ultimo die* mensis *Febr̃*, anno Dñi *millmo iiii*^c^ *xxxvi*°, capt̃ ꝑ reverendū in Xp̃o pr̃em Dñm *Willm* nuꝑ Ep̃m *Norwiceñ* nūc Ep̃m *Lincolñ*, necnon *Johem Lescrop̃* ꝛ *Johem Tiptot*

Militès ⹁ ac Magr̃m *Johem* ||*Storthwayt* utriusqꝫ juris bacular̃ ꝓcurat̃ ⁊ ||amicos ex ꝑte Xp̃ianissimi Principis et Dñi ||Dñi *Henr̃* Dei gr̃a *Anglie* ⁊ *Franc̃* Regis ⹁ et
Gerardus de Clyvis Comes de *Marcka.* *Johem* ||*Upme* ||*Graue* ꝑ̄positū eccl̃ie *Sc̃i Andree Coloñ Arnoldū de* ||*Breympt* Armig̃ꝰū ⁊ *Johem de* ||*Ooeffeldia* decretoꝝ doctorem ꝓcuratores ⁊ ||amicos ėx ꝑte *Gerardi de Clivis* Comitis de *Marka* de ꝑtibꝫ *Alemañ.*

29 Itm̃ duas lr̃as indentatas de data *xii*° die mensis *Decembr̃* anno Dñi *millmo cccc° xxxix°* ⹁ capt̃ ꝑ *Johem* Dñm *Lescrop̃* Militem *Willm Lyndewode* utriusqꝫ juris doctorem Custodē p^i^vati sigilli Regis ⁊ *Johem* ||*Strothwayt* in utroqꝫ jure bacallariū ⹁ ꝓcuratores ⁊ nūcios ex ꝑte dc̃i Dñi nr̃i ℞ ⹁ et *Isbrandū de Merwyck'* Can^cū^ collegiate eccl̃ie *Sc̃i Ludgeri Monasterieñ* ⁎ Illustris Domicelli *Gerardi de Clivis* Comitis de *Marcka* ⹁ ex alt̃a ꝑte ꝑ ligis ⁊ amiciciis int̃ ip̃os Dñm Regem ⹁ et Domicellū Comitē tractand̃ paciscend̃ ⁊ concordand̃ ⁊ aliis negociis factū amiciciaꝝ huj⁹ conc̃nentibꝫ ⹁ ac de homagio ⁊ juramento ip̃ius Comitis ⹁ et que quid̃ lr̃e rem̃ in uno coffino remañ in cista sup^a^ Re^tam^ Ducatus *Lancastr̃* ⹁ ad tale signū

30 This makeþ mynde þ^t^ þe *xxx* day of *Marche*
(p. 92.) the yeer of þe regne of Kyng *Herry* the *sext* the *xvii*^e^ ⹁ Witnesseth þ^t^ *Rauf* Lord *Cromwell* Tresorer of *Inglond* and þe Chamb̃leyns of þe Eschequer by vertu of a pryve seal directed unto þe seyd̃ Tresorer ⁊ Chamb̃leyns remaynyng̃ in þe filace amonge oþer warantes in *Mighelmesse* t̃me þe *xvii*^e^ yeer aforeseid ⹁ in p̃sence of *Robt Rolleston̄* Warderober ⹁ and *John Merston̄* Keper of þe jewelx ⹁ have deliṽed to þe

right wurshipfull and reve̾rent Fader in God *Herry* Cardynall of *Inglond* and Bisshop̃ of *Wynchestre* for vii ^{ml} marke of money borwed of hym thise jewelx next folwyng after þe fourme ⁊ tenur of the Kynges lr̃es patentz ther upon made beryng date þe *xxx* day of *Marche* þe *xvii*^{e} yeer aboveseid ⸗ the whiche vii^{ml} mark̃ shal wel ⁊ truly be repayed unto þ^{e} seid Cardynal hys executo^{rs} or assignez at þe feste of *Estre* þ^{t} shall be in þ^{e} *m*^{l} *iiii*^{c} *xl* yere of our Lord ⸗ and in faute of repaiement of þ^{e} seid vii^{ml} mark̃ hyt shalbe lawfull to þ^{e} seid Cardynal hys executo^{rs} ⁊ assignes to have to hys owne use or selle þe said jewelx as hym best semeth and lyketh.

31 First a Pusan of gold called þe *riche coler* conteynyng xvi culpons or peces upon̄ þe whiche beth viii antelopes garnysshed w^{t} xx grete ples *&c.* (*see p.* 143. *No.* 14.) weyng in all lx unces ⁊ di quartr̃ of troy þe pris — m^{l}m^{l}DCCC li

32 ¶ Also a swerd of gold called þe *Swerd of Spayne* garnysshed
(p. 92 b.) w^{t} v. grete balys *&c.* (*see p.* 143. *No.* 16.) weyng in all x mark̃ and an half and half an unce of troye þe prys — cccxxxiii li vi. s viii d

33 ¶ Also a tablet of gold of þe *Passion̄ of Crist* made in þe maner of a boke garnysshed *&c.* (*see p.* 143. *No.* 17.) ⸗ whiche tablet weyeth lx unces of troye the prys — ||cx li.

34 ¶ Also a tablet of *Seynt George* of gold garnysshed w^{t} a

rubee viii. dyamandes and in þ^{t} oon ꝑtie ys an aungeƚƚ holdyng an helme garnysshed w^{t} a rubee and litil ꝑles ⸝ and in þat oþer ꝑtie ys a puseƚƚ knelyng w^{t} a lambe garnysshed w^{t}a rubee⸝ and þe tablet al aboute ys garnysshed w^{t} xxv balys xxv. saphurs iii. emeraudes lv grete ꝑles ⁊ iiii^{xx} ix ꝑles of anoþer sorte⸝ and a grete company of oþer ꝑles weyng lxxix unces ⁊ đi þe pris — ciiii^{xx} iiii ƚi.

35 ¶ Also a pusañ of golđ called *Iklyngtoñ Coler* garnysshed w^{t} iiii rubees iiii grete saphurs xxxii grete ꝑles ⁊ liii other ꝑles⸝ the pris — ccc ƚi

36 ¶ Also ii. salers of golđ wherof þ^{t} oon ys a mañ⸝ and þ^{t} oþer a womañ⸝ holdyng þe salers in her hondes⸝ and þe mañ ys garnysshed w^{t} vii rubees⸝ and vii troches ev̾y troche of iii ꝑles⸝ and upon þe topet ys a saphur⸝ and þe fote of þ^{e} same mañ ys garnysshed w^{t} vi. rubees vi. saphurs ⁊ xlviii ꝑles⸝ and þe womañ holdyng an oþer saler garnysshed w^{t} vii rubees⸝ and vii troches ev̾y troche w^{t} iii ꝑles⸝ and upon þe topet ys a saphur⸝ and þe fote ys garnysshed w^{t} vi rubees vi saphers ⁊ xlviii ꝑles weyng aƚƚ to gider iiii^{xx} xiiii unces the prys of aƚƚ — cxl ƚi.

37 ꟗ Also ii pottes of golđ weyng xxxiii unces ⁊ đi þe pris of ev͛y unce xxiii s̄ iiii đ sm^{a}	xxxix li̇ xx^{d}
38 ꟗ Also a chalys ⁊ ii cruettes of golđ weyng to gider xxix unc̄ the pris of ev͛y unce xxiii s̄ iiii đ sm^{a}	xxxiii li̇ xvi. s̄ viii đ
(p. 93.) 39 ꟗ Also a tablet of golđ of þe *Salutacioñ of Our̃ Lady* garnyssed w^{t} v. balys v. saphers ⁊ xxv grete ꝑles weyng xxxv unc̄ þe p^{i}s	lx li̇
40 ꟗ Also an image of *Seynt George* beyng upoñ a grene tarage w^{t} a damaselł knelyng garnysshed w^{t} xiiii balys viii saphers xvi troches ev͛y troche conteynyng iii ꝑles weyng li unces ⁊ đi the pris	lxviii li̇ xiii s̄ iiii đ
41 ꟗ Also a pair basyns of silv͛e ⁊ ov͛gilt chaced w^{t} double roses and pounsed þe burselł of keremery weyng xx lb̄ viii unc̄ 42 ꟗ Also a grete almes disshe of silv͛e ⁊ ov͛gilt made in mañe of a shippe fułł of meñ of armes feyghtyng upon þ^{e} shippe syde weyng in ałł lxvii lb̄ ix unc̄ of troye 43 ꟗ Also ii. grete chargeo^{rs} vi. lasse chargeo^{rs} xl disshes of dyv͛s sortes and xxiii sausers gilt pois̄ cliii lb̄ i unce	The sōme totałł of þe weyzt of þe seiđ basyns almes disshe and vesselł cometh̄ to ccxli lb̄ vi unces the prys of ev͛y lb̄ xxxiii s̄ iiii đ Sm^{a} ccccii li̇ x s̄

44 Also a standyng tablet of gold̄ wt a pece of *Tunica inconsutil̄* , garnysshed wt vi. balys vi. saphers xii grete ꝑles ⁊ xii. other lasse ꝑles , wt an image of *Oure Lady* whyte enameld̄ in þe toppe , and on eṽy syde an aungell̄ weyng xxviii unc̄ iii quartr̄ pris eṽy unce xxiii s̄ iiii d̄ sma	xxxiii li x s̄ x d̄
45 ¶ Also a standyng cuppe of gold̄ garnysshed wt xlv. ꝑles and upoñ þe topet ys a sapher , and an ewer of gold garnysshed wt xxix ꝑles weyng all to gider lxvi unces of troye pris of eṽy unc̄ xxiii. s̄ iiii d̄ sa	lxxvii li.
46 ¶ Also a flat tablet of gold wt a pece of *Tunica inconsutil̄* , garnysshed wt xxv grete ꝑles weyng lxi. unce pris of eṽy unce xxiii s̄ iiii d̄ sma lxxi li iii s̄ iiii d̄ and þe pris of þe perrey xiii li x s̄ x d̄ , the hole sōme of the tablet comeþ to	iiiixxiiii li xiiii s̄ ii d̄

47 All þe whiche jewelx above rehersed whiche wer̄ in þe keping of þe seyd *Cardynal* , þe *xxx* day of *Janever* the *xix*e yeer of þe seyd Kyng by þe handes of *Willam Port* were delyvered ageyne unto þe seyd̄ Tresorer ⁊ Chamb̄leyns , and bothe endentures of þe delyṽaunce oute of the Kynges jewelx aforeseyd cancellyd.

(p. 93 b.) 48 ¶ Hec indentra fc̄a *xii*o die mensis *Junii* anno r̄ R̄ *Henr̄ sexti* post conq̄m *xvii*o int̃ reverendissimū in Xp̃o p̃rem *Henricū* Cardinalem *Angł* ⁊ Ep̃m *Wyntoñ* ex ꝑte una, et *Radm̃* Dñm *Cromwełł* Thes̃ *Angł* ⁊ Camar̃ de Scᵃcio ex ꝑte alt̃a testatʳ qđ ꝑdc̃i Thes̃ ⁊ Camar̃ virtute cujusdam br̃is de pⁱvato sigillo cujꝰ data est *x*ᵒ die *Junii*, anno regni ejusdem Regis *xvii*ᵒ, remañ in ƚilac̃ de t̃mīo *Pasche* dc̃o anno *xvii*ᵒ, liƀaverūt eidem Dño Cardinali ⁊ ad ꝓpriū usum ejusdem ꝑ manꝰ *Wiłłi Port* diṽs cartas ⁊ evidenc̃ tangenc̃ castrū mañia t̃ras ⁊ teñ de *Chyrk* ⁊ *Chirkeslonđ* cum suis ptiñ ꝓut patēt inferius, transcriptū cujꝰ quiđ br̃is de pⁱvato sigillo sequitʳ in hec verba.

49 ¶ *Henricus* Dei gr̃a Rex *Angł* ⁊ *Franc̃* ⁊ Dñs *Hiƀnie* Thes̃ ⁊ Camar̃ de Scᵃcio nr̃o salutem, De avisamento ⁊ assensu Consilii nr̃i vobis mandamꝰ qđ om̃ia munimenta ⁊ evidencias in custodia vr̃a remanencia de t̃ris ⁊ teñ cū ptiñ, que quidem t̃re vulgarit̃ dici solent *Chyrkeslanđ* deliberetis ⁊ tradatis seu deliberari ⁊ tradi faciatis reṽendissimo in Xp̃o pr̃i *Henrico* Cardinali *Angł* avunclo nr̃o carissimo, ut ip̃e de ꝑdc̃is munimentis ⁊ evidenciis disponat ꝓut sibi melius videbitʳ expedire. Dat̃ sub pⁱvato sigillo nr̃o apud *Prioratū Sc̃e Marie de Ov̄ey* *x*ᵒ die *Junii*, anno r̃ ñ *xvii*ᵒ.

50 ¶ In pⁱmis unam cartam cujꝰ data est *pⁱmo* die *Julii* anno regni Regis *Henr̃ quinti* post conq̃m *Angł sexto*, ꝑ quā *Thomas fitz Nichołł* Miles *Roƀtus Pobelewe* Cłicus *David Holbache* ⁊ *Thomas Harlyng* Cłicus dimiserunt tradiderunt ⁊ confirmaverunt castrum mañia t̃ras ⁊ teñ ꝑdc̃a cum ptiñ ven̄abilibȝ in Xp̃o pr̃ibȝ *Thome* Ep̃o *Dunolm̃* *Joħi* Ep̃o *Norwic̃* *Johanne de Bohun* Comitisse *Herefordđ* *Wiłłmo Kynwolm̃ssħ* Cłico *Gerardo Braybrok'*

Militi *Wiłło* ‖*Haukford̄* Militi *Ric̄o Norton̄ Simoni* ‖*Gauustede* Cłico *Joh̄i Wodehous Joh̄i Leventhorp̄ Rob̄to Darcy Rob̄to Rykedon̄* ⁊ *Wiłło Ryman̄* heredibȝ ⁊ assign̄ suis impp̄m ⁊c̄.

51 ¶ Itm unam lr̄am attorn̄ cuj⁹ data est *p^{i}mo* die *Julii* ⸗ anno regni ejusdem Regis *Henr̄ quinti sexto* ⸗ fc̄am p p̄fatos *Thomam fitz Nichołł* Militem ⁊ soc̄ suos ⁊c̄ *Joh̄i* ‖*Heen* Cłico *Wiłło Paynour Ric̄o Irlond̄* ⁊ *Edwardo ap David* ad delib̄and̄ seīam cō-junctim ⁊ divisim p̄fatis *Thome* Ep̄o *Dunolm̄ Joh̄i* Ep̄o *Norwic̄ Joh̄ne de Bohun* Comitisse *Herefor̄d* *Wiłło Kynwolm̄ssh̄* Cłico *Gerardo Braybrok* Militi ⁊ aliis ut patȝ in eadem lr̄a attorn̄ de castro man̄iis t̄ris ⁊ ten̄ p̄dc̄is.

(p. 94.) 52 ¶ Item unam lr̄am attorn̄ cuj⁹ data est *p^{i}mo* die *Augusti* anno *vi^{to}* p̄dc̄o fc̄am p *Thomā* Ep̄m *Dunolm̄ Joh̄em* Ep̄m *Norwic̄ Johannam de Bohun* Comitissam *Herefor̄d* *Wiłłm Kynwolm̄ssh̄* Cłicum *Gerardum Braybrok* Militem ⁊ alios ut patȝ in eadem lr̄a attorn̄ *Edwardo de Cherlton̄* Dn̄o de *Powys* ⁊ *Wiłłmo Ludlowe* conjunctim ⁊ divisim ad recipiend̄ seisinam de eisdem castro man̄iis t̄ris ⁊ ten̄ ⁊c̄. noīe suo.

53 ¶ Itm quoddam scriptū indentatū cuj⁹ dat̄ est *xxii^{o}* die *Octobr̄* ⸗ anno *vi^{to}* p̄dc̄o ⸗ fact̄ int̄ *Johannā de Bohun* Comitissam *Herefor̄d* *Joh̄em* Ep̄m *Norwic̄ Gerardū Braybrok'* Militem *Rob̄tum Darcy Rob̄tum Rykedon̄* ⁊ *Wiłłm Ryman* Armig̃os ex una p̄te ⁊ *Thomam* Ep̄m *Dunolm̄ Wiłłm Kynwolm̄ssh̄* Cłicum *Wiłłm* ‖*Haukeford̄* Militem *Ric̄m Norton̄ Simonē* ‖*Gauustede* Cłicum *Joh̄em Wodehous* ⁊ *Joh̄em Leventhorp̄* ex p̄te alt̄a ⸗ faciens menc̄oem de div̄sis

condicōib3 ꝛ convencōib3 int̃ ꝑtes ꝑdc̃as fact̃ ꝑut in eodem scripto plenius apparet.

54 ¶ Item quandam indentur̃ de dat̃ *xxii*° die *Novembr̃* anno *vi*^to^ ꝑdc̃o fc̃am int̃ *Willm Kynwolm̃ssh* Deputat̃ Thes̃ *Angl* ex una ꝑte ꝛ *Willm Ryman* attorñ *Robti Pobelewe* ꝛ *Thome Harlyng* Clicoꝝ ex alt̃a ꝑte facientem mencōem de diṽs condicōib3 ꝛ convenc̃ ꝑut patet ꝑ eandem indenturam.

55 ¶ Item unã acquietanciam de data *viii*° die *Decembr̃* anno *vi*^to^ ꝑdc̃o fc̃am ꝑ *Robtum Pobelewe* ꝛ *Thomã Harlyng* Clicos de D li de *Willo Kynwolm̃ssh* Deputat̃ Thes̃ *Angl* ꝑ manus *Willi Rymañ* Attorñ ꝑdc̃oꝝ *Robti* ꝛ *Thome* receptis.

56 ¶ Itm unã aliam acquietanciam de data *iii*°. die *Febr̃*, anno *vi*° ꝑdc̃o fc̃am ꝑ *Thomã Harlyng* Clicum de ccc iiii^xx^ xvii li ix s̃ ii d̃, de *Willo Kynwolm̃ssh* Clico Deputat̃ Thes̃ *Angl* ꝑ man⁹ *Willmi Rymañ*, attorñ ꝑdc̃i *Thome* recept̃.

57 Itm quandam ꝑvam cedulam facient̃ mencōem de attornacōib3 ꝛ fidelitatib3 capt̃ de tenentib3 ꝛ nōib3 eoꝝdem de castro mañiis t̃ris ꝛ teñ ꝑdc̃is.

58 ¶ Item iiii^or^ cartas de dat̃ *xxii*° die *Novembr̃* anno regni Regis *Henrici sexti* post conq̃m *Anglie xiiii*°, ꝑ quas *Thomas* Ep̃us *Dunolm̃* †*Robto Darcy* ꝛ *Willm̃s Ryman* Armig̃i seꝑatim tradiderunt dimise- (p. 94 b.) runt libaverunt feoffaverunt ꝛ confirmaverunt ꝑdc̃a castrum mañia t̃ras ꝛ teñ excellentissimo Principi ꝛ Dño suo, Dño *Henrico* Regi *Angl* post conq̃m *Angl sexto*, sibi heredib3 ꝛ successorib3 suis imꝑp̃m, " que quidem indentura remañ in hanaꝑio de t̃mīo " *Pasch* ꝑdc̃o anno *xvii*°."

19 Hen. VI.

Acquietanc̃ Ducis *Bavar̃r* "ꝛ "al̃ munī- "ment̃ ꝛc̃."

1 Md' qđ *xxv*° die *Januar̃* anno *xix*° regni Regis *Henr̃ sexti Rađus* Dñs de *Cromwell* Thes̃ *Angl* lib̃avit in Thesaur̃ dc̃i Dñi ℞ salvo custodienđ quinque acquietanc̃ † Ducis *Bavar̃r* ꝛ ꝑcurat̃ suoꝝ de m¹ m¹ m¹ m¹ viii ᶜ mᵃrȝ eidem Duci "ꝑ dc̃m "Dñm nr̃m" Regem ⸝ solut̃ ⸝ que quiđ acquietanc̃ reman̄ in una pixide in cista supᵃ Reᵗᵃᵐ ♣ ubi ponitʳ ꝑgamenū ♣ ["Ducat⁹ *Lanc̃*."]

Bavar̃r.

2 Md' qđ *xxvi*° die *Januar̃* eodem anno *xix*° ⸝ Mag̃r *Adam Molyns* Cl̃icus Consilii dc̃i Dñi Regis lib̃avit in Thesaur̃ Regis salvo custodienđ unam lr̃am *Theoderici Colonien̄* Archiep̄i [Sacri *Romani* Imperii ꝑ *Italiam* Archicancell̃ *Westfalie* ꝛ *Angarie* Ducis] cont̃ c̃tos punctus cujusdam tractat⁹ concordie ꝛ pacis init̃ ⸝ int̃ ꝑdc̃m Dñm nr̃m Regem *Henr̃ sextū* ⸝ et ꝑdc̃m Archiep̄m ⸝ capt̃ ꝑ Dñm *Joh̃em Tiptot* Militem *Joh̃em* ||*Stopyndon̄* ꝑdc̃m Magr̃m *Adam Molyns* ꝛ alios Cōmissarios ex ꝑte dc̃i Dñi nr̃i Regis ⸝ et ven̄abil *Tilmannū* de *Lynsz* decretoꝝ doctorem ꝑpositū eccl̃ie *Sc̃i Florini Confluen̄* Consiliar̃ dc̃i Archiep̄i ⸝ cuj⁹ quiđ lr̃e ⸝ dat̃ in Civitate *Colonien̄* anno Dñi *millmo iiii*ᶜ *xl*° ⸝ *ultima die* mensis *Septembr̃* ⸝ que quiđ lr̃a ponitʳ in uno hanap̄io cum aliis div̄s lr̃is homag̃ Archiep̄i *Colonien̄* ⸝ capt̃ tempe Regis *Ric̃i sc̃di* ⸝ supᵃ Reᵗᵃᵐ Ducat⁹ *Lanc̃* in una ꝑva baga de canabo.

Lr̃a Archiep̄i *Colonien̄.*

(p. 95.)

3 Md' qđ *xxvi*° die *Januar̃* ꝑdc̃o anno *xix*° ⸝ idem Mag̃r *Adam Molyns* lib̃avit Thes̃ ꝛ Cam̄ar̃ de Scᵃcio salvo custodienđ ||quendam lr̃am in Gallicum ⸝ de tractatu pacis int̃ dc̃m Dñm nr̃m Regē ⸝ et *Joh̃em* Ducem *Britann̄* ⸝ capt̃ ꝑ Comitem *Som̄s̃* tunc locumtenent̃

Lr̃a Ducis *Britann̄.*

dc̃i *Dñi Regis* in ꝑtibȝ *Franc̃* ⁊ *Normañ*, ꝯujꝰ quid̃ lr̃e, dat̃ *xiii*° die *Octobr̃*, anno Dñi *millmo iiii*ᶜ *xl*°, que quid̃ lr̃a ponitʳ in una baga de canabo cum aliis div̾sis evidenciis Ducis *Britanñ* capt̃ tempibȝ div̾soꝝ Regū, "et rem̃ in cista supᵃ Reᵗᵃᵐ Ducatꝰ "*Lanc̃*."

4 Mᵈ' qd̃ *xxvi*° die *Julii* a° *xix*° dc̃i ℞ *Rad̃us* Dñs *Cromwell* Thes̃ *Angl* lib̃avit in Reᵗᵃᵐ Scᵃcii dc̃i Dñi ℞ unū quat̾nū papiri, "⁊" unā bagā de canabo cum div̾s̃ rotul̃, que nuꝑ fuer̃ Mag̃ri *Rog̾i Bolyngbrok'* et remanent in una cista ferrea in magna Thesaur̃ ℞ infra Westm̃ ib̃m salvo custodiend̃.

"Et postea *x*° die *Octobr̃* anno *xx*° ꝑdc̃i ℞ iidem "quat̾nus ⁊ baga de canabo cū rotul̃ ꝑdc̃is lib̃antʳ "eidem *Rad̃o Cromwell* Thes̃ *Angl*."

"Et postea *xi*° die *Octobr̃* ꝑx̃ seqñ ꝑdc̃us Dñs "Thes̃ lib̃avit in Thesaur̃ ℞ ꝑ m̃ꝰ *Rob̃ti Burtoñ* "ꝑdc̃m quat̾nū."

---

20 & 21 Hen. VI.

1 Mᵈ' qd̃ *xiii*° die *Octobr̃* anno *xx*° ꝑdc̃i ℞ *Henr̃ sexti Petrus Bowmañ* lib̃avit in Thesaur̃ ℞ in ‖uno ‖longo pixide, unū rotulū continent̃ totam retinenc̃ illustris Principis *Ric̃i* Ducis *Eboꝝ* v̾sus ꝑtes *Normañ* anno *xix*° ꝑdc̃i ℞ *Henr̃ sexti* tᵃnsmiss̃, qui quid̃ pixis rem̃ in magna cista supᵃ Reᵗᵃᵐ [Duc̃ *Lanc̃*] ♣ ubi ponitʳ ꝑgamenū. ♣

(p. 95 b.) 2 Mᵈ' qd̃ *xxi*° die *Octobr̃*, anno r̃ ℞ *Henr̃ sexti xx*°, *Joh̃na* nuꝑ ux̃ *Ric̃i Bukland̃* nuꝑ Thes̃ ville *Cales̃* lib̃avit in Thesaur̃ ℞ salvo custodiend̃ quoddam

Joĥna nuꝑ ux̄ *Ric̄i Buklanđ.* scriptum relaxac̄ōis ꝑ eandem *Joĥnam* eidem Dño Regi fact̄ tam ꝓ soluc̄ōe facienđ eidem *Joĥne* de m^l^m^l^vii^c^ lx ŀi. iiii s̄ ix^d^ q̄ eidem *Joĥne* debit̄, q^a^m ꝓ mille marc̄ eidem *Joĥne* debit̄, et ꝑ eanđ *Joĥnam* eidem Dño R̷ remiss̄ ꝓ soluc̄ōe ĥenđ de dict̄ m^l^m^l^vii^c^ lx ŀi iiii s̄ ix đ q̄, quod quiđ scriptū remañ in hanaꝑio de t̃mīo *Sc̄i Micĥis* dc̄o a^o^. *xx*^o^.

3 M^d'^ qđ *vi*^to^ die *Maii* anno *xx*^o^ R̷ *Henr̄ sexti* deliƀant^r^ Dño Cardinali *Eboꝝ* tres ŀr̄e quaꝝ due ŀr̄e sigillant^r^ sigillo magno Dñi Regis ⁊ t̃cia cū div̄s sigiŀŀ ruƀ ⁊ viriđ tangenc̄ maritag̃ div̄s Reginaꝝ *Angŀ* vȝ *Isabeŀŀ* ⁊ *Margaretam.*

¶ "Et postea *ix*^o^ die *Maii* ꝓx̄ seqñ idem *Dñs* "*Cardynaŀ* restituit in Re^tam^ Sc^a^cii easdem tres ŀr̄as, "quaꝝ q^i^dem triū ŀr̄aꝝ una liƀat^r^ Dño R̷ *E iiii*^to^ "ꝑ m^9^ Mr̄i *Wiŀŀi Hatclyff xiii*^o^ die *Oct̄* a^o^ *xiii*^o^ dc̄i "R̷ nūc."

4 M^d'^ qđ *x* die *Marcii* anno *xxi*^o^ R̷ *Henr̄ vi*^ti^ *Rađus* Dñs de *Cromweŀŀ* Thes̄ *Angŀ* deliƀavit in Thesaurar̄ Dñi R̷ quandam treugam capt̄ int̃ regnū

Treuge *Flandr̄.* *Angŀ* ⁊ t̃ram *Flandr̄* ac ꝑt̄ *Picardie* ꝑ mediac̄ōem Ducisse *Burgonđ* Et ponit^r^ in quadam cista sup^a^ Re^tam^ ✠ Principat^9^ ✠ Ducat^9^ *Lancastr̄* ad tale signū

ff

"Liƀ *Tĥ* "*Kent.*" "Vac̄ hic qꝫ ponit^r^ in aŀ pixide int̃ alia script̄ ꝑ "Mr̄m *Tĥ Kente* hic liƀ ꝓut pȝ in iiii^to^ folio seq̄."

(p. 96.) 5 M^d'^ qđ *sc̄do* die *Marcii* anno *xxi*^o^. Regis *Henr̄ sexti Rog̃us Hunte* deliƀavit Thes̄ ⁊ Camar̄ Re^te^ Sc^a^cii duas cartas sigillo suo sigillat̄ fc̄as eidem Dño

Stoke under Hampdoñ. nr̄o R̷ de mañiis de *Stoke under Hampdoñ Cory Malet* ⁊ aliis mañiis div̄s in aliis coñ que *Joĥes* Dñs de *Tiptot* nuꝑ tenuit ad t̃mī vite sue Et poñ in ||quodam pixide infra cistam sup^a Receptā int̃ alias evidencias ꝛc̃.

6 Md' qđ *xiiii*° die *Marcii* a° *xxi*° R̴ *H sexti Rađus* Dñs de *Cromwelł* Thes̃ *Angł* delib̃avit Camar̃ Ret^e Sc^acii duas lr̃as de tractatu capt̃ int̃ Dñm nr̃m Regē ꝛ hoı̃es de *Prucia* voc̃ *Hance* Et ponit^r in quađ cista int̃ ał tractatus sup^a Re^am ♣ Principat⁹ *Wałł* ♣ "Ducat⁹ *Lancastr̃*."

Hanss̃.
Prucia.

(p. 96 b.)

7 Md' qđ *xxvii*° die *Novembr̃* anno *xx*° Regis *Henr̃ vi*^ti delib̃at̃ fuer̃ hic in Re^ta Sc^acii Dñi Regis *Ric̃o* Duci *Eboꝝ* v. m^l łi in ꝑtem solucõis xx^ml łi ꝑ scđo anno retinencie sue videłt ꝑ m⁹ *Petri Bowmañ* q^am quiđ sūmam v^ml łi ꝓfatus *Petrus* delib̃avit ꝓdc̃o *Dño Duci xxi*° die *Januar̃* ꝓdc̃o anno *xx*°, apud *Rothomagū* ꝑut patꝫ ꝑ acquietanc̃ ꝓfati *Dñi Ducis* sub sigillo suo sigillat̃ ꝛ signo suo manuali signat̃, recepc̃oem sūme ꝓdc̃e testificant̃ ꝛ hic in Re^tam ꝑ ꝓfatū *Petrū* lib̃at̃ videłt *xi*° die *Maii* dc̃o anno *xx*°, que quiđ acquietanc̃ remañ in hanapio de t̃mı̄o *Pasche* ꝓdc̃o anno *xx*°.

Dux *Eboꝝ.*

Petrus Bowman.

8 Itm *p^imo* die mensis *Junii* ꝓdc̃o anno *xx*° *Thomas Hoo* Miles ꝛ *Johes Stanlowe* Armiger Thes̃ *Normañ* deputat̃ *Ric̃i* Ducis *Eboꝝ* lib̃aver̃ in Re^tam Sc^acii unā aliam acquietanc̃ ꝓfati *Dñi Ducis* sub sigillo suo sigillat̃ cont̃ xv m^l łi, in plenā solucõem xx^ml łi. ꝑ sc̃do anno retinencie sue, rem̃ in hanapio de t̃mı̄o *Pasche* ꝓdc̃o anno *xx*°.

Dux *Eboꝝ.*

9 Md' qđ *xix*° die *Octobr̃*, anno r̃ R̴ *Henr̃ sexti xxi*° *Rađus* Dñs *Cromwelł* Thes̃ *Angł* lib̃avit in Thesaur̃ Regis salvo custodienđ duo instrumenta notaria ꝑ que Magr̃ *Adam Molyns* retinuit ex ꝑte dc̃i Dñi nr̃i Regis in Curia *Romana* c̃tos consiliar̃

Magr̃ *Adam Molyns.*

ꝛ ꝑcuratores ⁏ remañ in una pixide in magna cista supª Re^tam Ducatꝰ *Lancastr̃* ad tale signū

{De c'tis conciliariis ꝛ p'curat' p' Rege retent' in Cur' Romana.}

(p. 97.) 10 M^d' qđ *xxii°* die *Novembr̃* anno *xxi°* Regis *Henr̃ sexti Rađus* Dñs *Cromwełł* Thes̃ *Angł* ꝑ manꝰ *Joħis Lentoñ* liƀavit in Thesaur̃ Regis salvo custodienđ unā acquietanc̃ *Wiłłi Elmedeñ* Militis nuꝑ Genłał Recept̃ dc̃i Dñi Regis castri ꝛ dñii suoꝝ de *Bamburgħ* ⁏ de cc iiii^xx xvi łi ix s̃ i. đ eidem *Wiłło* debit̃ de quodam suppluſ̃ ꝛc̃ ꝛ eidem Dño nr̃o Regi relaxat̃ rem̃ in una ꝑva pixide in coffro supª Re^tam Ducatus *Lancastr̃.*

Wiłł̃ms Elmedeñ Miles.

22, 23 Hen. VI.

1 M^d' qđ *vii°* die mensis *Novembr̃* anno r̃ R̸ *Henr̃ sexti xxii°* div̓s̃ *Dñi de Consilio* Dñi R̸ ⁏ tunc existeñ in ||*Camłar̃ Stellata* apud *Westm̃* liƀaver̃ in Thesaurar̃ R̸ salvo custođ unū coffinū de maheremio in quo continent^r xviii script̃ seu munimenta tangenc̃ div̓s̃ appunctuamenta fact̃ int̓ *Henr̃* nuꝑ Regem *Angł quintū* ꝛ *Karolū* nuꝑ Regem *Franc̃* ⁏ ac Comitem de *Foitz* ⁏ quod quiđ coffinū rem̃ in magna cista supª Re^tam Ducatus *Lancastr̃* ⁏ ad tale signū

{Angl' Franc' Comes de Foitz.}

2 M^d' qđ *ťcio* die *Febr̃* anno r̃ R̸ *Henr̃ sexti xxii° Roƀtus Rollestoñ* Cłicus magne garderobe Dñi R̸ liƀavit in Thesaur̃ R̸ unā acquietanciam execut̃ testi̇ *Thome* nuꝑ Comitis *Saꝝ* fact̃ [" tā "] ꝓdc̃o

Acquietancia *Thome* nuꝑ Comit̃ *Saꝝ.*

" Dño " nro Regi nūc qam Dño *H* nup Regi *Angl quinto* et rem in uno pixide supa Retam Ducat9 *Lancastr.*

(p. 97 b.) 3 Md' qd *xxiiiito* die *Aprilis* anno *xxiiio* Reg *Henr sexti Radus* Dñs de *Sudeley* Thes *Angl* ꝛ Camar de Reta Scacii delibaver venabili pri *Johi* Cardinali *Eboꝝ* p m9 Magri *Rici* ||*Tone* Clici unā pixidem. cont duos tractatus int Reges *Angl* ꝛ *Franc* ꝛ instrm sup eisdem.

⸿ Itm unam aliam pixidem tangent conclus pacis tempe R *Henr quinti.*

⸿ Itm unam aliam pixidem cont iiiior scripta concnent treugas int Reg *Ang* ꝛ Ducē *Britan* ac int R *Angl* ꝛ *Castell.*

⸿ Itm aliam pixidem cont ♣ duo ♣ [tria] script concnenc treugas *Franc* tempe *Henr quarti.*

⸿ Itm aliam pixidem tangen tractatū pacis int *Ricm* nup Regē *Angl scdm* ꝛc ꝛ Ducem *Britan* cū † aliis ||scriptis in ead.

⸿ Itm aliam pixidem cont quemdam al tractatū pacis int nup Regē *Angl* ꝛ Ducem *Britann.*

" Et postea *xxxo* die *Marcii* ao *xxviiio* ♣ r ♣ pdci R " *Henr viti*, idem Dñs Cardinal *Eboꝝ* p man9 pdci " Magri [*Rici*] ||*Tone* restituit in Thesaur dci Dñi " R muniment pdict."

---

24 Hen. VI.

1 Md' qd *xvio* die *Nov'* anno r R *Henr sexti xxiiiio*, Dñi de Consilio Regis libaver in Thesaurar dci Dñi Regis tres lras de treug capt int pdcm

Dn̄m nr̄m Regem, et Regem *Franc̄*, et ponūt^r in ||quadam pixide rem̄ in cista sup^a Re^tam Ducatus *Lancastr̄* ad tale signū

{Angl' Franc'.}

(p. 98.) 2 M^d' qđ *xxiiii°* die *Januar̄* anno r̄ R̄ *Henr̄ sexti* post conq̄m *xxiiii^to* *Dn̄i de Consilio* dc̄i R̄ libaver̄ in Thesaur̄ ejusdem Dn̄i R̄ iiii^or script̄ de ꝓrogac̄ treugaꝝ capt̄ int̄ Cōmissarios Regis *Angl̄*, et Cōmissarios Regis *Franc̄*, a p'mo die *April* anno *xxii°* dc̄i R̄ *Angl̄* usq₃ p'mū diem *Novembr̄* anno *xxv^to*, et ponūt^r in quodam hanapio rem̄ in cista sup^a Re^tam Ducat⁹ *Lancastr̄* ad tale signū

{Angl' Franc'.}

---

25 Hen. VI.

1 M^d' qđ *xx°* die *Octobr̄* anno r̄ R̄ *Henr̄ sexti* *xxv°*, *Robtus Rollestoñ* Clicus libavit in Re^tam Sc^acii unam acquietanc̄ Dn̄i *Egidii* fr̄is Ducis *Britanñ* de ccl marc̄ eidem Dn̄o *Egidio* solut̄ ut pat₃ ꝑ eandem acquietanc̄ rem̄ in ||uno pixide in viridi cista.

Dn̄s *Egidius* frat̄ Duc̄ *Britanñ*.

2 M^d' qđ *ix°* die *Febr̄* anno r̄ R̄ *Henr̄ sexti xxv°*, *Robtus Manfelđ* Armig̃ libavit in Thesaurar̄ R̄ unam indent^ram int̄ ꝑdc̄m Dn̄m Regem ex una ꝑte, et dc̄m *Robtum Manfelđ* Magr̄m ꝛ Supvisorem monete infra Turr̄ *Londoñ* ꝛ alibi de supvisu auri ꝛ argenti cunanđ ibm, que quiđ indentura remañ in cista sup^a Re^tam Ducatus *Lancastr̄*, ad tale signū

{Indentura monete.}

(p. 98 b.) 3 M^d^' qđ *xx°* die *Maii* anno r̃ ℞ *Henr̃ sexti xxv°* Magr *Thomas Kent* Clicus Consilii dc̃i Dñi Regis libavit in Thesaurar̃ Regis munimenta subscript̃ videlt lr̃as progacionū treug̃ capt̃ *Turoñ*. Itm lr̃as pmissionis convencõi ⁊ passagio attendenc̃ Avūc̃li. Itm ||cōmissio ||originalis Cōmissarioꝝ *Francie*. Itm appunctu^ta^ f'c̃a *Londoñ* p Ambasshes *Francie* ⁊ Cōmissarios Regis sup libacõe fructuū bñficoꝝ script̃ in foliis papiri ⁊ signat̃ ⁊c̃. Itm quoddam appunctu^tā^ fc̃m *Turoñ* int̃ Ambasshes Regis ⁊ Bursariū *Hispañ* p navibꝫ ⁊ m̃candisis p subditos hincinde capt̃ restituenđ ⁊c̃ que quiđ munimenta remañ in uno coffino in quadam cista sup^a^ Re^tam^ [" ubi pgamenū poni consuevit "] ♣ Ducatus *Lancastr̃* ♣ ad tale signū

{ Angl' Franc' a° xxv°. }

Duo cornua p venanđ libata Dño *Sudeley*.

4 M^d^' qđ *xiii°* die *Julii* anno *xxv^to^* ℞ *Henr̃ sexti* Thes̃ *Angl* ⁊ Camar̃ de Sc^a^cio virtute bris Dñi Regis de p^i^vato sigillo suo rem̃ in filac̃ de t̃mīo *Sc̃i Michis* dc̃o anno *xxv^to^*, eisdem Thes̃ ⁊ Camar̃ direct̃, libaver̃ Dño de *Sudeley* nup Camario dc̃i Dñi ℞ duo cornua p venanđ videlt unū cornu nigrū ⁊ aliud magis nigrū.

---

26 Hen. VI.

Major Stapule *Cales̃*.

1 M^d^' qđ *xxvi°* die *Octobr̃* anno *xxvi°* ℞ *Henr̃ sexti* Major Stapule *Cales̃* delibavit Thes̃ ⁊ Camar̃ unam obligacõem de sm^a^ ♂ x^ml^ m^a^rꝫ solvenđ ⁊c̃ in *fo Oīm Sc̃oꝝ* extunc px̃ seqñ que ponit^r^ in cista ubi moneta infra Re^am^ custodit^r^ ibm salvo custodienđ.

" Et postea *xx*° die *Febr̃* p̃dc̃o anno *xxvi*to Thes̃
" *Angl̃* ꝛ Cam̃ar̃ de Scacio virtute br̃is de pivato
" D obligͥ " sigillo eisdem Thes̃ ꝛ Cam̃ar̃ direct̃ int̃ mand̃ de
" xml mar3 " t̃mĩo *Sc̃i Mich̃is* anno supadc̃o remanent̃ lib̃aver̃
" ꝛc." " p̃dc̃o Thes̃ *Angl̃* p m9 *Thome Broun̄* Cl̃ici ejusd̃
" Thes̃ p̃dc̃am obligac̃oem de xml mar3."

(p. 99.) 2 Md' qd̃ *x*° die *Decembr̃*, anno r̃ R̷ *Henr̃ sexti xxvi*to, *Thomas Broun̄* Cl̃icus Thes̃ lib̃avit in Thesaurar̃ R̷ salvo custodiend̃ iiiior muniment̃ de ꝓrogac̃oe treug̃ *Franc̃*, vidl̃et tria muniment̃ inde sigillat̃ cū iiiior sigillis div̄s Cōmissar̃ ex ꝑte Advūc̃li nr̃i Regis *Franc̃*, de data *xxvii*° die *Julii* anno *xxv*° Regis *Henr̃ sexti*, et quart̃ muniment̃ sigillat̃ cū sigillo p̃dc̃i Advūc̃li Regis *Franc̃* de data *xiiii*° die *April* anno Dñi *mill̃mo cccc xlvii*°, et ponūtr in quodam coffino rem̃ in cista supa Retam ✠ Ducatus *Lancastr̃* ✠ [" ubi ꝑgamenū poni consuevit "] ad tale signū

{Co'missar' Reg' Franc'.}

" Et postea *xxviii*° die *Januar̃* dc̃o a° *xxvi*°, lib̃antr
" in Retam Scacii ꝑ Custodem pivati sigilli ꝛ alios
" *Dños de Consilio* R̷ p m9 *Joh̃is Broun̄* uni9 Cam̃ar̃
" de Scacio due carte de confirmac̃oe treugaꝝ p̃dict̃
" int̃ Reg̃ *Angl̃* ꝛ *Franc̃* sigillat̃ * *Karol̃* de *Franc̃*
" Advūc̃li dc̃i Dñi nr̃i Regis * viridi cera sigillat̃,
" et rem̃ in coffino p̃dc̃o."

3 Md' qd̃ *xviii*° die *Febr̃* anno r̃ R̷ *Henr̃ vi*ti *xxvi*° [" Magr̃ "] *Thomas Kent* Cl̃icus Consilii dc̃i Dñi Regis lib̃avit in Thesaur̃ R̷ x indenturas factas int̃ *Joh̃em* Comitem *Salop̃* Dñm de *Talbot* ꝛc̃, nuꝑ Locumtenent̃ p̃dc̃i Dñi Regis in t̃ra Regis *Hib̃nie* ex una ꝑte, et *Onell̃ Macmurghe* ꝛ alios de *Hib̃nia*

ex alia pte, de essendo fidel ligeos dci Dñi nři Regis & de aliis appunctuament in eisdem indentur content, rem in una pixide sup^a Re^tam Ducatus *Lanc* ad tale signū

{Hib'nia.}

" Et ||lre pateñ Dñi R de exemplific de terr " *Gilbert de Clar* ī *Hibnia* Et ||alia ||lra de divs " petic ī *Hibern* Et ponūt^r in cista sup^adict ad " tle signū " †

4 M^d' qd *sexto* die *Junii* anno r R *H vi^ti* [" *xxvi^o* "] Magr *Tho^as Kent* Clicus Consilii dci Dñi R libavit in Thesaur R unam lram sigillat cū iiii sigill conc treug int pdcm Dñm nrm Regem *Angl* et Regē de *Denmark'* de dat a^o Dñi *millmo cccc xxxii^do* capt p *Robm Shotesbrok'* Militem & Magrm *Willm* ||*Spreber* nuncios & pcuratores ex pte dci Dñi nri Reg *Angl* et ponit^r in quod^am cofino rotundo cū uno al recordo de eodm Rege de *Denmark'* in cista sup^a Re^tam Ducatus *Lanc* " ad " tale signū "

{Denmark.}

" Lra pdca [cū recordo pdco] lib Epo *Cic* Cus-
" rstaurat^r." " todi p^ivat sigill R *xiiii^o* die *Marcii* a^o *xxvii^o* apd " *Westm* &c."

(p. 99 b.) 5 M^d' qd *xiiii^o* die *Junii* anno r R *Henr vi^ti xxvi^to*. venabilis in Xpo pat *Thomas Bathon* & *Wellen* Epus in *Camba Stellat* apud *Westm* in psencia Dñi Cancellar *Anglie* & Magri *Thome Kent* Clici Consilii dci Dñi Regis libavit in Thesaurar R salvo custodiend in ||uno pixide ||rotundo quand^am lram sigillat cū divsis sigill int Dñm *Edwardū* nup Regem

Angl̄ p^i^mū et *Florenciū* Coñi de *Holand̄* *Robtum de Brus* Dñm de *Vale dAnande* ⁊ al̄ de ptibȝ *Scocie* cū una lr̄a attorñ sigillat̄ sub sigillo regim̄s regni *Scocie* deputat̄ de dat̄ anno Dñi *millmo cc lxxxxi* rem̄ in · una baga cū al̄ evidenciis Reḡ *Scocie* in cista sup^a^ Re^tam^ Ducat⁹ *Lancastr̄* ad tale signū

{**Scocia E p^i^mi.**}

6 M^d^ qd̄ *viii^o^* die *Julii* anno r̄ ℞ *Henr̄ vi^ti^ xxvi^o^.* Magr̄ *Thomas Kent* Cl̄icus Consilii dc̄i Dñi Regis lib̄avit in Thesaur̄ ℞ x script̄ de treuḡ ac de ꝓrogac̄oe treuḡ capt̄ int̄ p̄dc̄m Dñm nr̄m Regem ex una pte, et *Ph̄m* Ducem *Burgund̄* ⁊ al̄, et ponūt^r^ in quadam pixide quadrat̄ rem̄ "in cista sup^a^" Receptam Ducatus *Lancastr̄* ad tale signū

⊕ {**Flandr' treug'.**}

["Lib̄ Consilio Dñi ℞ *p^i^mo* die *Sept̄* a^o^ *xxix^o^* et "postea relib̄ Thes̄ ⁊ Cam̄ar̄ *viii^o^* die dc̄i *mens̄.*"]

7 ✠ "M^d^' qd̄ *xvii^o^* die *Octobr̄* a^o^ *xxvii^o^* ℞ *Henr̄* "*vi^ti^* lib̄at̄ fuer̄ mandat̄ Dñoꝝ de Consil̄ ii. script̄ de "p̄dc̄is ix script̄ Magr̄o *Ric̄o* ‖*Wetton̄* [miss̄ in] am-"bassiat̄ ℞ v̄s⁹ *Cales̄*" ✠ "qꝫ restaur̄"

---

27 Hen. VI.

1 M^d^' qd̄ *xviii^o^* die *Octobr̄* anno *xxvii^o^* Reḡ *Henr̄ vi^ti^* Magist̄ *Thomas Kent* Cl̄ic⁹ Consilii ℞ lib̄avit in Thesaur̄ ℞ quinqꝫ lr̄as ⁊ munimenta subscripta scilicet lr̄as treuḡ capt̄ *Lavardyn xi^o^* die *Marcii* a^o^ *millo cccc^o^ xlvii^o^*, It̄ lr̄as potestat̄ Ambassiatoꝝ Avunc̄li s̄ ad

capiend illas treugas. It lras p recōpensacōe eoꝝ qui dimiserūt tras ꝛ hereditamēta p delibacōem *Mans.* It lras sup convencōe Ambassiat R ꝛ sui avuncli ad limitand passagiū R ꝛ attēdenc avuncli p convencōe ꝛc It lras de protestacōe fca tēpe delibacōis *Mans* ꝛc que quid ponūt' in ‖uno pixide in cista sup Reta Ducat9 *Lancastr* ad tale signū

{Angl' Franc' Lavardyn.}

(p. 100.) 2 Md' de ii script de treuge capt int Dnm nrm Regem ꝛ *Jacobū* Regem *Scottoꝝ* [apd *Wyntoñ*] de dat anno [regni] dci Dñi nri R *xxvii*o libat hic ad Receptā Scacii *xxv*o die *Julii* ao *supadco* ✠ p ✠ salvo custodiend in ‖uno pixide sub ✠ ad ✠ ‖tale signo in cista sup Reta Ducat9 *Lancastr*

{Angl' Scocia Winton'.}

3 Md' qd *xxiido* die *Augusti* anno *xxvii*o R *Henr vi*ti venabilis in Xpo pater *Marmaduc9 Karliol* Eps Thes *Angl* ꝛ Camarii de Scacio virtute bris dci Dñi R sub pivat sigillo s eisd nup direct receper de *Willo Porte* uno exec testi *Henr* nup Cardinalis *Angl* Epi *Wintoñ* noib3 oīm ctoꝝ exec ejusd testi certa jocalia subscripta eid nup *Cardinali* p denar ab eo mutuat in vita sua invadiat p quib3 quid jocal dcus Dñs Rex p bre suū pdcm libare mandavit eisd execut mlml xliii li viii s ix d in assignac sup coll pima med uni9 xe eid Regi a *Clero* in ultia Convocacōe concess fiend Et simit mandavit idem Dñs Rex eisd Thes ꝛ Camar tā p bre pdcm qam p aliud bre sub magno sigillo suo cuj9 dat est *xxi*o die *Augusti* ao *supadco* qd jocalia pdca libentr Abbi *Gloucestr Th Mauncell* ꝛ *Johi Chirche* aut uni eoꝝ ut ipi seu eoꝝ un9 ad opus

Jocal p exec *Henr* nup Epi *Wintoñ* Cardinalis *Angl* restit ꝛ postea videlt *eod die Th Mauncel* ꝛ *Johi Chirche* libat.

℞ eađ jocalia invadiant^r ꝑ tāta sūma pecunie ut ipī ꝑ illis jocal optinere ꞇ recipe poťint aut un⁹ eoꝝ recipe poťit Que quiđ jocal virtute bri̅ū ꝑdicť liƀant^r ꝑfať *Thome Mauncell* ꞇ *Joh̄i Chirche* put pȝ p indenturꝛ inť ꝑfať Thes̃ ꞇ Cam̃ar̃ ac ꝑdc̄os *Thomā* ꞇ *Joh̄em* ꝑdc̄o *xxii^do* die *Augusti a^o ꝑdc̄o* remanenť in uno [magno hanapio] ♣ pixide ♣ ad Re^ta Sc^acii in quađ cista voc̄ *le green cofer* ["inť alias indentur̃ de divsis "jocalibȝ Reg̃"] ♣ sub tali signo ♣

4 Furst . i tablet of gold called þe *tablet of Lancastre* garnisshed with . xvi. balaiz iii. rubiz . liiii. ples ꞇ ii saphirez . weying altogedere . lxii. m^arc̄ . iiii unc̄ of troye. Itm . ii. basins of gold weying . xliii. marc̄. Itm i cuppe of gold coveđ of kerimery werk with . iii scuchons of þe Kingez armez in þe toppe . weying . iiii. marc̄ . ii. unc̄ . dī. Itm i. tablet of gold called "*Henr̃* Eps "*Winton̄* "Cardinal "*Angl.*" þe *tablet of Burgoigne* garnisshed w^t . xxvi. balaiz . xxii . saphires cxlii. ples . weying in all . lxx. marc̄. Itm . i. ymage of *Seint George* garnisshed with viii baleis . clxxviii ples weiyng altogeder . viii. lb. x. unc̄. Itm . i. tablet of *Seint George* bought by þe Kinge of *Estfeld* for . m^l m^l m^arc̄ . garnisshed with . xxx. diamantꝭ . cxxxii. baleis . xxxii. saphirez . xxxvi. rubiz v^c . lxii. ples . ꞇ . iii. emeraudes . weiyng altogedres lii. m^arc̄ . iii. uncꝭ Itm . i. ymage of *Seint Michael* garnisshed . with . clii. ples . iiii. saphirez . xxiii. baleis . weiyng altogedres . xi. lb. v unc̄.

5 Me^d' qđ *xxix^o* die *Octobr̃* anno r̃ ℞ *Henr̃ sexti xxviii^o Rađus* Dn̄s *Cromwell* unus Cam̃ar̃ de Sc^acio liƀavit in Thesaurar̃ Regis iiii^or rotulos continenť divs̃ *acta fact p Consiliū* dc̄i Dn̄i ℞ videlť Unū rotul

de annis *ixº* ꝛ *xº* R̷ *Henr̃ quinti* ꞌ ꝛ *p'mo scd̃o t̃cio* ꝛ *quarto* Regis *Henr̃ sexti* ꞌ Scd̃m rotul̃ de annis *vto viº* ꝛ *viiº* R̷ *Henr̃ viti* T'ciū rotul̃ de annis *viiiº ixº. x* ꝛ *xiº* dc̄i R̷ ꝛ Quartū rotul̃ de ais *xiiº* ꝛ *xiiiº* dc̄i R̷ *Henr̃ viti* qui quid̃ rotul̃ reman̄ in quadam baga de canabo rem̄ in cista supa Retam Ducatus *Lancastr̃* ad tale signū

{Acta de Consilio.}

---

27 & 28 Hen. VI. &c.

1 Md' qd̃ *ultı̄o* die *Octobr̃* anno *xxviiiº* R̷ *Henr̃ viti* *Witt̃mꝰ Yelv̄ton̄* unꝰ Justic̄ de Banco R̷ delib̃avit Thes̄ ꝛ Cam̄ariis de Scacio unam assı̄am specialē apd *Hadlegh̃* [in Com̄ *Suff'*] corā p̄fat̃ *Witt̃o* ꝛ al̃

Spalis assı̄a. ✠ capt̃ ✠ die *Jovis* in septı̄a *Pentecost̃* aº dc̄i Dñi R̷ *xxvito* capt̃ int̃ *Witt̃m Pecche* Armig̃um ꝛ *Henricū Parke* de ten̄ in *Hyntylsham Hadlegh̃ Reydon̄ Chatesham Wasshbroke* ꝛ *Aldham* que quid̃ assı̄a reman̄ in una baga de canabo cū al̃ div̄s̄ special̃ assis̄ de tēpe R̷ p̄dc̄i in una magna cista infra Receptā.

(p. 101.) 2 Md' qd̃ *xxº* die *Maii* anno r̃ R̷ *Henr̃ sexti* *xxviiº* *Thom̄as Broun̄* Armiger Clicus Thes̄ *Angl̃* lib̃avit hic in cur̃ ad Retam Scacii quoddam scriptū *Isabelle* Ducisse *Burgund̃* ꞌ sigillo ip̄ius Ducisse sigillat̃ ꞌ script̃ apud *Bruges xixº* die *Januar̃* ꞌ anno Dñi *mitt̃mo cccc xlviiiº* ꞌ et ponitr in quad̃ pixide cū ix al̃ script̃ capt̃ de treug̃ *Flandr̃* p̄ut patȝ [antea] in sc̄do folio istius libri ad tale signū

{Flandr' treug'.}

3 " Me^d qđ *xxi*° die *Junii* a° *v*^to R̷ *Edwardi quarti*
" *Hugo Fenne* Sb̃teš lib̃avit hic in cur̃ ad Recep^tam
" Sc^acii quodđ scriptū *Philipp̃* Duc̃ *Burgund̃* sigill̃
" ip̃ius Duc̃ sigillat̃ script̃ ap^d *Lille* ŧle *xxviii* die
" menš *Octobr̃* a° Dñi *m*^l*cccc lxiiii*^to et ponit^r in quađ
" pixiđ rem̃ in cista sup^a Recept̃ Ducat̃ *Lanc̃* ad
" tl̃e signū "

{ Flandr' ent'cours. }

(p. 101 b.) 4 Hec indent^ra fc̃a *xxvii*° die *Novembr̃* anno r̃ R̷ *Henr̃ sexti xxviii*° int̃ *Jacobum* Dñm de *Say* Theš *Angl̃* ⁊ Camar̃ Sc^acii Regis *Westm̃* ex una p̱te et *Joh̃em Merstoñ* Armig̃ū Theš Cam̃e Regis ⁊ Cust̃ jocaliū suoꝝ ex alt̃a p̱te testat^r qđ dc̃us *Joh̃es Merstoñ* virtute lr̃aꝝ sub p^ivat̃ sigillo Regis sibi direct̃ delib̃avit p̃fat̃ Theš *Angl̃* ⁊ Camar̃ Sc^acii jocalia Regis subscript̃ ponder̃ ut patȝ inferius p̱ libros *Joh̃is Merstoñ* ut dicit

5 In p'mis unā tabulett̃ auri cū imagine *Sc̃i Georgii* garnizat̃ cū uno rubeo ⁊ viii. diamanđ, et ex [una] p̱te imag̃is est un⁹ Angl̃s tenens i helme garnizat̃ cū i rube ⁊ p̱vis p̱ulis, et ex al̃ p̱te una puella genuflect̃ cū uno agno garnizat̃ cū i rub̃, et dict̃ tabulett̃ ult^a imagiñ garñ cum xxii bal̃ xxv saph̃ iii esmerauđ lv grosš p̱ul̃ ⁊ iiii^xx ix p̱ul̃ de minori sorte et cū plur̃ al̃ p̱vis p̱ul̃ ponderant̃	lxxix unc̃ i q^art̃

6 Itm̃ i salar̃ auri coop̃t ⁊ op̱at̃ cū floribȝ de lic̃ garnizat̃ cū

D jocal.	xiiii bal xv saph xxiiii troch quelt de iii pul et cū plur al pul pvis, et in medio adinfra dict salar est una lingua ꝯpent ꝛ i pecia unicorñ ponder p pondus trojañ	iiii lb vii unc iii qªrt
Johes Merstoñ.	7 Itm i magnū ciph auri coopt ꝛ chaceat garnizat cū ix saph ix peretot xviii trochis quelt de iiii pul, Et sup topett una geñosa genulans, et in medio adinfra dict ciphū est una lingua ꝯpent ꝛ i pecia unicorñ ponder	iiii xx xiii unc
	8 Itm i aliū ciphū auri coopt ꝛ garñ cū l. rub xliiii pul et topett garnizat cū ii saph ꝛ viii pul ponder	xlix unc i qªrtꝰ
	9 Itm iii oll argent deaurat ex una sorte cū handel fact ad modū de wrethis ponder p pondus trojañ	xxxix lb xi unc dī.
	10 Itm ii al oll argenti deaurat chaceat plenitꝰ cū armis Dñi de *Audeley* sup coopcla ponder	xix lb iiii unc
	11 Itm iii chargeours argenti deaur ꝛ signat cū i quartꝰfoill ꝛ capite leopardi ponder	xi lb i unc iii. qªrt.
	12 It v charg argenti deaur signat cū armis de *Courtenay* ponder	xvi lb iii unc iii qªrt

13 Itm̃ iiii charg̃ argenti deaur̃ unde i signatʳ cum uno quatꝰfoill̃ ⁊ iii non signantʳ ponder̃ } xiiii lƀ vii unc̃ iii qªrtꝰ

14 Itm̃ viii charg̃ argent̃ deaur̃ ⁊ signat̃ cū armis ℞ pond̃ } xl lƀ xi unc̃ i qªrtꝰ

15 Itm̃ iii disc̃ argent̃ deaur̃ ⁊ non signat̃ pond̃ } vi lƀ viii unc̃

16 It̃ iiii disc̃ argent̃ deaur̃ ⁊ gravat̃ cū band̃ in i scochoñ pond̃ } v lƀ viii unc̃ i. qªrtꝰ

17 It̃ ii disc̃ argent̃ deaur̃ signat̃ cū i quatꝰfoill̃ pond̃ } iii. lƀ

18 It̃ ii disc̃ argent̃ deaur̃ unde i signat̃ cū capite leopardi ⁊ altꝰ cum i cressant̃ pond̃ } ii lƀ ix. unc̃

19 It̃ ii disc̃ argent̃ deaur̃ unde i signatʳ cū capite, leopardi ⁊ at̃ cum quatꝰfoill̃ ⁊ i lozeng̃ in fundo disci pond̃ } iii lƀ

(p. 102.) 20 Itm̃ xiii disc̃ argent̃ deaur̃ signat̃ cū armis ℞ ponder̃ } xxix lƀ v unc̃ iii. qªrt̃

21 Itm̃ vii holow disc̃ argent̃ deaur̃ ⁊ signat̃ cū armis ℞ pond̃ } xiii lƀ iii unc̃ iii. qªrt̃

22 Itm̃ viii disc̃ argent̃ deaur̃ de ead̃ sect̃ pond̃ } xv li viii unc̃ iii. qªrt̃

23 Itm̃ xvi disc̃ argent̃ deaur̃ ⁊ non signat̃ ponder̃ } xxviii lƀ x unc̃ iii qªrt̃

24 Itm vi disc argent deaur ponder } xviii m^a^rc i. unc

25 Itm xii disc argent deaur de minori sorte pond } xviii m^a^rc iiii unc

26 Itm xxiiii salc argent deaur ꝛ signat cū armis de *Hereford* ponder } xv lb iii unc iii. q^a^rt.

27 Itm unū ciph auri coopt ꝛ esmaelit cū divs imagin ꝛ garnizat cū ii bales iiii saph ꝛ lxxvi pul pond } lxxiii unc iii q^a^rt

Johes Merston. 28 In cujꝰ rei testiōiū uni parti hujꝰ indentur remanent cū dcis Thes ꝛ Camar pfatꝰ *Johes Merston* sigillū suū apposuit alii vo parti ejusdem indentur reman cū dco *Johe Merston* sigillū officii Recept pdict est appensū Dat *die* ꝛ *anno sup^a^dict.*

29 " Que quid indent^r^a *xvi*^o^ die *Decembr* a^o^
" *xxviii*^o^ Regis *Henr sexti* libat fuit Dño de *Say*
" Thes *Angl* p mꝰ *Stephi Slegge* ad pquirend lras
" patentes dci Dñi R ad eadem jocalia invadiend ꝛ
" reliband."

" Et postea *xix*^o^ die *Decembr* px seqn idem
" " Dñs " Thes *Angl* p mꝰ dci *Stephi Slegge* resti-
" tuit indenturam pdcam, et rem in hanapio cum
" al indentur ||divs jocal R."

(p. 102. b.) 30 M^d^' qd *xvii*^o^ die *Decembr* a^o^ *xxviii*^o^ Reg *Henrici sexti* certa jocalia subscripta fuer delibat ꝛ restitut Thes ꝛ Camar de Sc^a^cio p *Johem Wenlok'* Militē unū exec testi *Johis* nup Dñi *Fawnhop* put patet p indentur inde int ptes pdcas *die* ꝛ *anno* *pdict* fact cujus tenor sequit^r^ in hec verba.

31 This endenture made bitwene *James Fynes* Knyzt Lorde *Say* Tresourer of *England* and the Chamƀleins of þe Eschequyer on þe oon ꝑt . [" and "] *John Wenlok'* Knyzt Chamƀlein to þe *Quene* oure soveine *Lady* oon of þe executours of þe testament of *John* late Lorde *Faunhop̃* on þe oþ'e part Witnessith þt where þe Kynges jewelx under writen þat is to say

32 ii grete chaundelers of gold garnisshed wt. iiii. saphirs &c. (*see p.* 145, *No.* 19.) pris þe unce . xxvi s̃ viii d Sma	cccclxvi li xiii s̃ iiii d.
33 Itm a swerd of gold callid þe *Swerd of Spayne* garnysshed wt. v. greet baleys &c. (*see p.* 144, *No.* 16.) weiynge in all x marc̃ and an half and half an unc̃ of troy þe pris	cccxxxiii li. vi s̃ viii d.
34 Also a greet ouche of *Seynt George* armes &c. (*see p.* 143, *No.* 15.) In þe same ouche is a crosse of *Seint George* &c. þe pris	cc li.
35 Also ii. newe sensurs of sylver ⁊ overgilt weiynge to giders vii lb vi. unces ⁊ iii qartr̃ pis every lb xl s̃	xv. li ii. s̃ vi d
D jocal. *Johes Wenlok* Miles. — 36 Also a cuppe of sylver of þe olde makynge enamelid the covercle is garnysshed wt lyons and þe topet of þe same covercle is broke of and lieth in þe same	xiiii li ix s̃

cuppe weiyng viii lb̃ viii unc̃ pris every lb̃ xxxiii s̃ iiii d̃ Sm[a]	
37 Also a litel coffre of sylver ꝛ ov̾gylt and a ‖chaufer of silv̾e made in mañ of a rounde balle weiynge ii lb̃. ii unces p'is þe lb̃ xxxvi s̃ viii d̃ Sm[a]	lxxix s̃ vi [d].
38 Wytħ a pusan of gold calleđ *Ikelyngtoñ Coler̃* garnyssheđ w[t]. iiii. rubyes iiii greet saphires xxxii. greet ꝑles ꝛ liii. lesse ꝑles pris of	ccc. li

were late delyvered by *Rauf* Lord *Sudeley* late Tresourer of *England* and þe Chamberleyns of þ[e] Eschequyer thenne beynge unto þe most worshipfull Fadr̃ in Gođ *Joħn* Archiebisshop̃ of *Caunterbury* and *Rauf* Lorde *Cromwell* coexecutours w[t] þ[e] said *Joħn Wenlok'* of þ[e] testament abovesaid fore þe sōme of m[l] m[l]. marc̃ of þe goodes of þe said Lorde *Faunhop̃* borghed of hē to þe use of oure *Sov̾aigne Lorde* þe Kynge, the whiche pusan of gold was late delyvered ꝛ restored into þe Resceipt of þe said Eschequer by þe said *Archiebisshop̃* and Lorde *Cromwell* upoñ þe repaiement of ccc li ꝑcell of þe said m[l] m[l] marc̃. The said *Joħn Wenlok* fore asmoche as he haþ[e] resceyved of þe Kynge assignemēt by his lr̃es patentz undre his greet seal fore þe repaiement of þe sōme of m[l] xxxiii. li, vi [s], viii [d] residue of þe said m[l] m[l] marc̃ beynge behynde ‖due unpaid for þe said jewelx . the same *Joħn Wenlok* haþe delyvered and restored into þe said Resceyte to þe said nowe Tresourer and Chamb̃leyns the abovesaid jewelx not delyvered byfore as above is rehersed of þe which jewelx above rehercid þe said Tresourer ⁊ Chambleins the said *John Wenlok'* and all oþ͛e executours to þe said Lorde *Faunhop̃* fully acquyte ⁊ in þ^{t} in theym is utterly discharge In witnes. wherof to oon p̃t of þis endenture remaynyng toward þe said *John Wenlok'* the said Tresourer and Chamberleyns have put þe seall of þe office of þe said Resceyte and to þe oþ͛e pt of þis endentur̃ remaynynge toward þe said Tresourer ⁊ Chambleyns þ^{e} said *John Wenlok'* haþe sette his seall. Written at *Westm̃* þ^{e}. *xvii.* day of *Decembr̃* þ^{e} yere of þe reigne of þe Kynge oure Sov͛aigne Lorde þe . *xxviii*^{ti}.

(p.103.) 39 M$^{d'}$ qd *xxiii*^{o} die *Decembr̃* anno *xxviii*^{o} Regis *Henrici vi*^{ti} Thes̃ ⁊ Camar̃ de Sc^{a}cio virtute cujusdam br̃is sub privato sigillo dc̃i Dñi Regis eisdm Thes̃ ⁊ Camar̃ nup direct̃ cujus dat̃ est *xxii*^{o} die *Decembr̃ anno sup*^{a}*dc̃o* in filacio de t͛mīo *Michis* eodem anno infra Recept̃ Sc^{a}cii p͛dc̃i remanent̃. libaver̃ *Thome Maunsell* Armig͛o certa jocalia subscript̃ put p3 p indenturam int͛ p͛fat̃ Thes̃ ⁊ Camar̃ ex una pte ⁊ p͛dc̃m *Thomam Maunsell* ex alt͛a pte nup confect̃ cuj⁹ tenor sequit^{r} in hec verba.

40 This endenture made þe *xxiii* daie of *Decembr̃* þe yere of the regne of our Sov͛aigne Lorde Kinge *Herri* þe *sext* the *xxviii*. Witnessith that *Jamys Fenys* Knyght Lorde *Saye* Tresorer of *Englond* and þe Chaumbleyns of þe Escheker by vertu of a prive seal to hem direct bering date the *xxii* daie of *Decembr̃* þe said *xxviii* yere remainyng in þe Resceit in þe filace of *Michelmasse* terme þe same yere have deliv͛ed to *Thomas Maunsell* Squier " þe jewelx underwriten "

	41 First ii grete chaundelers *&c.* garnisshed with . iiii. saphires *&c.* (*see p.* 145, *No.* 19.) price *&c.* Sm^{a}	cccclxvi^{li}. xiii^{s}. iiii đ
" D jocal." ✠ *Johes Wenlok* Miles. ✠ *Thom^{a}s Maunsell.*	42 Also a swerde of golde called þe *Swerd of Spayne* *&c.* (*see p.* 144, *No.* 16.) the price	cccxxxiii^{li}. vi s̃ viii đ
	43 Also a grete ouche of *Seint Georgez* armes *&c.* (*see p.* 143, *No.* 15.) þe price	cc. li.
	44 Also ii newe sensours of silver *&c.* (*see p.* 208, *No.* 35.) Sm^{a}	xv. li. ii. s̃. vi đ
	45 Also a cupp̃ of silver of þe old making *&c.* (*see p.* 208, *No.* 36.) Sm^{a}	xiiii li. ix. s̃
(p. 103 b.) " *Thomas* " *Maunsell.*" ✠ " *Johes* " *Wenlok* " Miles." ✠	46 Also a litell coffre of silver and ov̕gilt *&c.* (*see p.* 209, *No.* 37.) price þe lb xxxvi s̃ viii đ Sm^{a}	lxxix^{s}. vi đ

47 In witnessing of þe which to þat oon part of þis endenture remaynyng with þe said *Thomas Maunsel* the seal of þe office of the Resceit is put to and to þ^{t} oþer pt of þis endenture remainyng w^{t} þe said Tresorer ⁊ Chamberleins þe forsaid *Thomas Maunsel* hath put to his seal þe *daie and* þe *yere abovesaid.*

48 " Que quiđ indentura ✠ ac bře p̃dcm ✠ re-
" manet in uno hanapio remanēt in viridi cista inf^{a}
" Receptā Sc^{a}cii p̃dci int̕ alias indenturas de div̕sis
" jocalibȝ in eođ hanapio existeñ."

D jocal. 49 Hec indentra fca *xix*° die *Januar* anno r R *Henr sexti* post conqm *xxviii*° testat^r qd Camar de Sc^a cio dci Dni Regis virtute bris Dni Regis sub p^ivato sigillo suo eisdem Camar direct libaverut ext^a Thesaurar Regis ad man^9 *Jacobi Fenys* Militis Dni de *Say* Thes *Angl* jocalia dci Dni Regis subscript cuj^9 quid bris pdict dat est apud *Westm* *xxii*° die *Decemb* *anno sup^a dco* et rem in Re^ta Sc^a cii pdci in quodam hanapio in viridi cista int divs indentur ||al jocaliu Regis.

Jacobus Fenys Miles Dns de *Say* Thes.

50 In p^imis una tabulett auri cu imagine *Sci Georgii* garnizat cu uno rubeo ʇ viii diamand et ex una pte imagis est unus anglus *&c.* (*see p.* 204—207, *Nos. 5 to* 27.)

(p. 104.) 51 In cuj^9 rei testioiu uni pti huj^9 indentur remanent cum dcis Camar pdcus Dns Thes sigillu suu apposuit ||alio vero pti ejusd indentur reman cum dco Dno Thes sigillu officii Recept pdict est appensum. Dat *die* ʇ *anno sup^a dict.*

Que quid indentura ac bre pdcm remanet in uno hanapio remanent in viridi cista infra Re^tam Sc^a cii pdci int alias indentur de divs jocalib3 in eodem hanapio existent.

(p. 104 b.) 52 M^d' qd *ultio* die *Januar* anno *xxviii* R *Henr vi*^ti illud magnu sigillu argenti quod *Willm*^9 Comes *Suff' xxi*° die *Novebr* a° ejusd R *xiiii*° libavit Thes ʇ Camar de Sc^a cio libatu fuit ad man^9 dci Dni Reg in Pliamento suo ap^d *Westm* tuc tent sedente put pleni^9 apparet in folio xxv^to huj^9 libri ||psedent.

"M^d' de sigillo ex^a "Thesaurar "R Dno "Regi in "Pliameto "s libat."

53 M^d' qd *xxiiii*^to die *Marcii* anno *xxviii*° R *Henr vi*^ti libatu fuit p Epm *Elien* ad Re^ta Sc^a cii Thes ʇ Camar ibm in Thesaurar R custodiend quodda

scriptū in Latinis verbis sub sigillo *Karol* nup R *Francoꝝ* sigillat de appūctuamēto ꝛ concluc pace int *Henr* nup Regē *Angl* [*v*ᵗᵘ] ꝛ pfat Regē *Francoꝝ* capt de dat *xxi*ᵒ diei mensis *Maii* aᵒ Dñi *m*ˡ *iiii*ᶜ *xx*ᵐᵒ et regni dci R *Karol* *xl*ᵐᵒ Et rem in qᵃdᵃm pixide cū uno al scripto in Gallic scripto sub eod sigillo sigillat de dat scripti supᵃdci sub tal signo

(p.105.) 54 Mᵈ' qd *xxvii*ᵒ die *Junii* anno *xxviii*ᵒ Regis *Henr* *vi*ᵗⁱ Magr *Thomas Kent* Clicus Consilii dci Dñi Regis delibavit Thes ꝛ Camar de Scᵃcio Regis salvo ꝛ secur custodiend lras confirmacois *Jacobi* R *Scottoꝝ* sup treug ‖inhit int *Dñm nrm Regem* ꝛ pfat Reg *Scottoꝝ* de dat apud *Strivelin* *ix*ᵒ die mensis *Junii* anno Dñi *millmo cccc l*ᵐᵒ et regni dci Reg *Scottoꝝ* *xiiii*ᵒ. et rem in quod hanapio in cista supᵃ Recept Ducat⁹ *Lancastr* ad tal signū

{Scocia Strivelin.}

55 Mᵈ' q *ultimo* ⁎ *Junii* anno *xxviii*ᵒ. Regis *Henrici sexti*. Dñs Cancell *Anglie* ceteriq Consiliarii Dñi nri Regis mandarunt Thes ꝛ Camar ad deliband Magro *Thome Kent* Clico Consilii ituro in ambassiat Regis in ptes *Prucie*. tria script tangent appunctuaᵗᵃ illaꝝ pciū cū *Anglic* ꝛc.

"Que quidm scripta pfat⁹ Magist *Thomas* recepit "de pfat Thes ꝛ Camar *die* ꝛ *anno* *sup*ᵃ*dcis*."

56 Mᵈ' qd *vi*ᵗᵒ die *Maii* anno *xxix*ᵒ R pdci

libatū fuit p̄fat̄ Thes̄ ⁊ Camar̄ p "*Ricm Langport*" quoddam transumptū p̄dict̄ triū script̄ sup appunctua[tis] p̄dc̄is fact̄ sub sigillo Archi *Cantuar̄*. " ⁊ sub " signo *Robti Kent* Notarii et rem̄ in uno hanapio " posit̄ in una cista sup[a] Receptā Ducat⁹ *Lancastr̄* " ad tale signū"

{Sprucia.}

(p.106.) 57 Hec indent[ra] fc̄a *xxiii°* die *Marcii* anno r̄ R Henr̄ sexti *xxviii°* int̄ *Jacobū* Dn̄m *Say* Thes̄ *Angl* et Camar̄ Recepte Sc[a]cii Regis *Westm̄* ex pte una, et *Johem Merston̄* Armig̃um Thes̄ Came Regis ⁊ Custod̄ jocal̄ suoꝝ ex pte alt̄a, testat[r] qd̄ p̄fatus *Johes Merston̄* virtute lr̄aꝝ sub p'vato sigillo ejusdem Dn̄i R sibi direct̄ delibavit p̄fat̄ Thes̄ *Angl* ⁊ Camar̄ jocalia Regis subscript̄

	58 In p'mis unū ciphum auri coopt̄ ⁊ esmaelit̄ ‖applit̄ ⁊ ‖topett̄ garnizat̄ de i bales ⁊ iii pul̄ dat̄ *Dn̄o Regi* p *Radm Butiller* Militem ponderant̄	xlvi unc̄
D jocal̄.	59 Itm unū ciphum auri ‖plan̄ coopt̄ dat̄ *Dn̄o Regi* p Cardinalem *Angl* pond̄	lxv unc̄
	60 Itm unū aliū ciphū auri coopt̄ chaceat̄ ⁊ garnizat̄ cū xv troch qual̄t de iii rub xv troch quel̄t de iii pul̄, et sup topett̄ una generosa cū i dd̄ plan̄ in fronte sua dat̄ Dn̄o R p Ducē *Glouc̄* pond̄	xlii unc̄ dī

61 Itm̃ unū [ciph̃] auri ⁊ de calcidoñ garnizat̃ cum xix rub̃ i p̄vo esmer̃ una gross̃ pul̃ xxv pul̃ de uno sorte ⁊ xxiiii minoribȝ pul̃ ⁊ cum iiii antilop̃ auri sup̄ coop̄clm ⸝ dat̃ Dño Reḡ p̄ dc̃m Ducem *Glouc̃* ponder̃ — xliii unc̃

Johẽs Merstoñ. 62 Itm̃ unū aquar̃ auri esmaelit̃ virid̃ ⁊ cum cervis ⁊ al̃ bestiis dat̃ Dño Regi p̄ dc̃m Cardinalem *Angl̃* pond̃ — xxix unc̃ iii qart̃

63 Itm̃ unū salar̃ auri coop̄t̃ esmaelit̃ cū armis Reḡ ⁊ floribȝ vocat̃ *Margaretez* ⁊ topett̃ garñ cum uno bal̃ ⸝ dat̃ Dño Regi p̄ *Margar̃* Reginam *Angl̃* ponder̃ — liiii unc̃ i qart̃

64 Itm̃ unū al̃ salar̃ auri coop̄t̃ ⁊ fact̃ ad silitudinem hoĩs garñ cū ix bal̃ ix saph̃ i rub̃ ⁊ xxxvii pul̃ de div̄s sort̃ ⸝ dat̃ Dño Regi p̄ Ducem *Eboȝ* ponder̃ — xxxi unc̃ dĩ

65 Itm̃ unū al̃ salar̃ auri fact̃ ad modū uniꝰ Moresse garñ cum iiii bal̃ i. saph̃ i rub̃ ⁊ xvii pul̃ ⸝ dat̃ Dño Reḡ p̄ dc̃m Duc̃ *Eboȝ* pond̃ — xix unc̃ iii qart̃

66 Itm̃ unā tabulett̃ auri cum una pecia de *Tunica inconsutili* inclus̃ garñ cū vi bal̃ vi saph̃ xii gross̃ pul̃ ⁊ xii pul̃ minoribȝ pond̃ — xxviii unc̃ iii qart̃

67 Itm unū ciphū auri plañ coopt̃ ꝛ garñ sup topett̃ cum uno saph̃ ꝛ vi pul dat̃ Dño Regi p Reginam *Margaretam* p̃dc̃am pond̃	xxxix unc̃
68 Itm unū al ciphū auri fract̃ coopt̃ esmaelit̃ applit̃ ꝛ garñ cum v bal iii dd̃ ꝛ xxv pul, dat̃ Dño Reg̃ p dc̃m Ducē *Eboꝝ* pond̃	xxxix unc̃
69 Itm unā crucem auri que fuit *Sc̃i Lodowici* de *Francia* garñ cum uno gross̃ bal ꝛ viii bal minor̃ viii saph̃ ꝛ xii esmer̃ unde i. fract̃ pond̃	xlv unc̃ i qªrt̃

70 In cujꝰ rei testiōiū uni pti hujꝰ indenture remanent̃ cū dict̃ Thes̃ ꝛ Camar̃ p̃dc̃us *Johes Merstoñ* sigillū suū apposuit, alt̃i vero pti ejusd̃ indentur̃ rem̃ penes dict̃ *Johem Merstoñ* sigillū officii Recepte p̃dict̃ est appensū dat̃ *die* ꝛ *anno supªdict.*

(p. 106 b.) 71 Hec indentura fc̃a *xxiiii*° die *Marcii* anno regni Regis *Henr̃ sexti xxviii*°, int̃ *Jacobū* Dñm *Say* Thes̃ *Angl* ꝛ Camar̃ de Scªcio ex una pte, et *Ric̃m Joynour* civem ꝛ grocerum *Londoñ* ex alt̃a pte, testatʳ qd̃ iidem Thes̃ ꝛ Camar̃ virtute bñis de pⁱvato sigillo eisdem Thes̃ ꝛ Camar̃ direct̃ de dat̃ *xxii*° die *Marcii* dc̃o anno *xxviii*° remanent̃ in filac̃ de t̃mīo *Sc̃i Michis* p̃dc̃o anno *xxviii*°. libaverūt eidem *Ric̃o* jocalia Regis subscript̃ p securitate D li ab eo mutuat̃, videlt

72 In p^i^mis unū ciphū auri coop̃t ꝛ esmaelit̃ applit̃ ꝛ topett̃ garñ de i. bał ꝛ iii puł dat̃ Dño Regi p *Radm Butiller* Militem ponderant̃ } xlvi unc̃

73 Itm unū ciphū auri plañ coop̃t dat̃ Dño Reg̃ p Cardinalē *Angł* ponđ *&c.* (*see p.* 214—216, *Nos.* 59 *to* 69.) } lxv unc̃.

(p. 107.) 74 In cuj⁹ rei testīoniū uni pti huj⁹ indenture remañ cum dc̃is Thes̃ ꝛ Camar̃ p̃dc̃us *Ric̃us Joynour* sigillum suū apposuit, alt̃i vero pti ejusdem indenture remañ penes dc̃m *Ric̃m* sigillum officii Recepte Sc^a^cii est appensum, Dat̃ *die* ꝛ *anno sup^a^dict.*

" *Ric̃* " *Joyno^r^.*"

75 " M^d^' qđ mandato Dñi Thes̃ *xvii*^o^ die *Octobris* " anno *xxxi*^o^ ℞ *Henr̃ vi*^ti^ indentura p̃dc̃a lib̃ *Wiłło* " *Essex*' †Rememorati Reg̃ in Sc^a^cio p psecuc̃oe " inde p Rege ib̃m fiēđ."

76 M^d^' qđ sc̃do die *Augusti* anno r̃ ℞ *Henr̃ vi*^ti^ post conq̃m *xxviii*^o^ *Thomas Rothewel* Cłic⁹ Thes̃ *Angł* lib̃avit ad Receptā Sc^a^cii in Thesaurar̃ ℞ custodiēđ quoddam scriptū tangens treugas capt̃ int̃ *Angł* ꝛ *Franciam* de dat̃ *ult̃* die *Ap^i^lis* anno g^a^cie *m^l^ iiii^c^ xlviii* et ponit^r^ in ‖quod^a^m pixide quadrante sup^a^ Receptam Ducat⁹ *Lancastr̃* ad tale signū

Charles.

{**Charles.**}

(p. 107 b.) 77 Hec indentura facta *vicesimo p^i^mo* die *Julii* anno regni Regis *Henrici sexti* post conq̃m *vicesimo octavo* int̃ Thes̃ *Angł* et Camar̃ Sc^a^cii Dñi Regis ex una pte et *Thomam* ‖*Tirełł* Militem ꝛ *Ric̃m Waller*

Armig͛um ex alt͛a pte testat^r q̄d cum idem Dn̄s Rex p lr̄as suas patent̄ dat̄ *duodecimo* die mens̄ p͛dc̄e *anno sup^a dc̄o* assignav͛it p͛dict̄ *Thomam Tirell Ric̄m Waller* ⁊ alios cōjunctim ⁊ divisim ad om̄ia ⁊ singula bona ⁊ catalla jocalia ⁊ pecuniaꝝ. sūmas que quidam se noīans *Joh̄em Mortymer* p se ⁊ sibi adherentes in Com̄ *Kanc̄* secum detulit ⁊ asportavit in quoꝝcumq; manib; adtunc extiterunt seu extūc invenir̄ possent tam infra lib̄tates q^a m ext^a p Rege ⁊ noīe suo arestand̄ ⁊ capiend̄ ⁊ ea om̄ia ⁊ singula sub salva ⁊ secura custodia ad opus Regis jux^a sanas discreciones p͛dc̄oꝝ *Thome* ⁊ *Ric̄i* ponend̄ et quo eis melius videret^r ducend̄ ⁊ t^a nsferend̄ ⁊ tales ⁊ tantas sūmas inde talib; psonis de quib; eis visum foret ad utilitatem Regis ⁊ Regni sui presertim circa capc̄oem p͛dc̄i *Joh̄is Mortymer* ⁊ sibi adherenciū exponend̄ put in lr̄is p͛dc̄is plenius continet^r. quibusdam tamen certis de causis specialit͛ ip̄m Dn̄m Regem moventib; idem Dn̄s Rex p br̄e suū sub magno sigillo suo p͛fat̄ *Thome* ⁊ *Ric̄o* directū cujus dat̄ est *decimo octavo* die mens̄ *Julii* ultimo p͛t͛ito mandavit eosdem *Thomam* ⁊ *Ric̄m* q̄d om̄ia hujusmodi bona ⁊ catalla jocalia ⁊ pecuniaꝝ sūmas p ip̄os ⁊ alios in lr̄is p͛dict̄ specificat̄ arrestat̄ Thes̄ ⁊ Cam͛ar̄ suis p͛dict̄ aut uni eoꝝ vel eoꝝ aut alicujus eoꝝ deputatis sive deputato p indenturas inde int͛ ip̄os *Thomam* ⁊ *Ric̄m* . necnon Thes̄ ⁊ Cam͛ar̄ p͛dc̄os aut eoꝝ deputatos vel alicuj⁹ eoꝝ deputatū debit̄ conficiend̄ q^a mcicius pot͛int delib̄arent put in p͛dc̄o br̄i plenius apparet virtute cuj⁹ quid̄m br̄is p͛fat̄ *Thomas Tirell* Miles ⁊ *Ric̄us Waller* Armig̃ tradiderunt ⁊ delib̄averūt p͛fat̄ Thes̄ ⁊ Cam͛ar̄ p͛dict̄ ad Receptā Sc^a cii *die confecc̄ōis p͛senc̄* certa bona jocalia ⁊ pecuniaꝝ sūmas subscript̄ que p͛dc̄us *Joh̄es Mor-*

D bonis *Joh̄is Cade* al̄ dicti *Mortymer* pditoris.

tymer p se ⁊ sibi adherentes in Com̃ *Kanc̃* secū detulit ⁊ asportavit p p̃fat̃ *Thomam Tirelł* ⁊ *Ric̃m* arrestat̃ ⁊ capt̃ put p bre p̃dict̃ eis p̃cipit[r] videłt

78 In primis in pecunia num̃ata cv łi xv s̃

79 Itm in a round boxe of lether . vi. parysh cuppes of sylv̾ . ix spones of sylv̾ . i. purs̃ wroght̃ in the stole with xlvii count̾s of sylv̾ i. stone of birelł i. gerdilł of purple not harneysid a ||bitores clee harneysed i muske bałł . i. stone of berałł harneysid ii. laces of sylke.

80 Itm in two trussyng cofers ⁊ in two gardeuyances i. salt saler of silv̾e ⁊ gilt castelł wyse w[t] iii smale salt salers in iii corners and the iiii lakkith i. chalyce of golde garnyshed w[t] peerls and i. pateñ therto . ii. chargeours ⁊ xii. litelł disshes of silv̾e . ii. bolles of silv̾ i. nutte cov̾yd . iii. chaced cuppes . i. cov̾cle of a salt saler viii sponys of silv̾ iii. knoppes of cuppes a coler of sylv̾ i paire of knyves . ii. purses a diałł of silv̾ . iii. salers of silver w[t] a cov̾cle of a (p. 108.) cuppe i chalys of gold w[t] a pateñ i horñ harneysed w[t] silver ⁊ gilt . i. saler of gold cov̾yd garnysshed w[t] saphires ⁊ perlys i ewer of silver . ii potełł pott̾ gilt i spice plate of silver ⁊ gilt . ii stondyng cuppes of oñ sute . cov̾yd swaged ⁊ pounced i stondyng̃ bolle ||pote cov̾yd gilt w[t]out i peyre tabełł knyves . iii. in a shethe w[t] gilt haftes . i ewer of silver withoute knoppe i pece i crewet i paxbrede of silver ⁊ gilt i nose of añ kandelstyk of silver i. girdiłł of the olde faccyoñ harneysid w[t] silver . i scalop̃ of sylver i litełł pece of reed tarteroñ i pawkener wrought in the stole i potte of silver of a galoñ withoute a lidde i potte contenyng a potełł gilt . i quart potte of sylver i. gobelet of the olde faccioñ i ymage of silver

ꝛ gilt i cuppe coṽyd̛ stondyng gilt withoute pomell̛ i flatte cuppe coṽyd̛ gilt i salt saler coṽyd̛ of silver i litell̛ gobelet of sylṽ coṽyd̛ . i. chafure of silver . i blak remen^a^nt of velewet fugury i olde vestement i p^i^mer with̄ clapses of silver i peire of shetys . v. smale pecys of ‖vre . ix peces and remen^a^ntꝭ of baudekyñ cloth̄ of golde i stondyng cuppe coṽyd̛ ꝛ gilt i flatte cuppe of silver coṽyd̛.

81 In cujus rei testiõiū p̃dicti Thes̃ ꝛ Cam̃arii sigillum officii sui uni pti huj⁹ indentur̃ penes p̃fat̃ *Thomā* ꝛ *Ric̃m* remanenti apposuerūt Et p̃fati *Thomas* ꝛ *Ric̃us* alt̃i vero pti huj⁹ indentur̃ penes p̃fat̃ Thes̃ ꝛ Cam̃ar̃ remanenti sigilla sua apposuerūt Dat̃ *die* ꝛ *anno sup^a^dc̃is.*

82 Que quid̛ jocal̄ ꝛ pcell̛ sup^a^dc̃a virtute b̃ris Dñi Regis sub magno sigillo suo Thes̃ ꝛ Cam̃ar̃ de Sc^a^cio direct̃ int̃ mandata de t̃mio *Pasch̄* anno *xxviii*^o^ dc̃i Dñi Regis remañ p *Thomam Rothewell̛* Cl̄icum Thes̃ *Angl̛* vice ꝛ noĩbȝ dict̃ Thes̃ ꝛ Cam̃ar̃ vendebant^r^ divs̃ psonis p ‖sm^a^

83 D quibȝ responsum est Regi in pell̛ Re^te^ de t̃mīo *Pasch̄* eodem anno *xxviii*^o^ " vȝ " *xxix*^o^ die *Augusti* ut plenius ib̄m apparet in forma seqñ vȝ D *Pħo Malpas* de bonis dc̃i *Joħis Cade* cxiiii ł̄i ix s̃ iiii d̛ D *Ric̃o Joyno*^r^ de bonis dc̃i *Joħis Cade* xx ł̄i D *Thoma Rothewell̛* de bonis dc̃i *Joħis Cade* cxxxi ł̄i ix s̃ iii d̛ D *Thoma Stokdale* de bonis dc̃i *Joħis Cade* viii ł̄i ix s̃ x d̛.

Et rem̃ in ‖quod^a^m pixide ‖ligneo in virid̛ cista sub tali signo

{ **Cade alias d'ct' Mortem'.** }

29 Hen. VI.

(p. 110.) Anno *xxix*^{o} Reg̃ *Henr̃ vi*^{ti}.

(p. 109 b.) 1 M^{d'} qđ *sexto* die *Maii* anno *xxix*^{o} Regis *Henr̃ sexti Ric̃us Lampórt* Cłicus in officio p'vati sigilli dc̃i Dñi Regis liƀavit in Thesaurar̃ Regis salvo custodienđ, transumptũ sup appunctuament̃ int' Dñm ["*Henr̃* nup"] Regem *Angł quartũ*, et ptes *Prucie* quoꝝ originał Mag̃r *Thomas Kent* ⁊ *Johes Stokker* nup missi in Ambassiata Regis ad ptes *Prucie*, detulerũt secũ versus easdẽ ptes de mandato Dñi Regis in suo Consilio, cuj⁹ quiđ ‖transumptũ data est anno Dñi *milło cccc l*^{o}. Et rem̃ in uno hanapio in cista sup^{a} Re^{tam} Ducatus *Lancastr̃* ad tale signũ

{ **Transumptu' Prucie.** }

(p. 110.) 2 M^{d'} qđ *ix*^{o} die *Octobr̃*, anno *xxix*^{o} ℞ *Henr̃ sexti*, Mag̃r *Ric̃us Andrewe* Secretarius dc̃i Dñi Regis liƀavit Thes̃ ⁊ Camar̃ de Sc^{a}cio unam pixidem quadrantem continent̃ quinq; script̃ evidenc̃ concernenc̃ treugas fact̃ int' p̃fat̃ Dñm Regem ⁊ consanguineũ suũ Regem *Scottoꝝ*, p Dñm Epm *Dunelm̃ Johem* Vic̃ de *Beaumont* ⁊ ał Cõmissionar̃ ejusdem Dñi Regis quoꝝ quiđ scriptoꝝ unũ sigillat^{r} cum iiii^{or} sigillis de cera ruƀ de dat̃ *xv*^{o} die *Novembr̃* anno Dñi *milłmo iiii*^{c} *xlix*^{o}, et aliud scriptũ sigillat^{r} cum viii^{o} sigillis de cera ruƀ de dat̃ *xxviii*^{o} die *Augusti* anno Dñi *milłmo iiii*^{c} *xlix*^{o}, et ał duo script̃ sunt instrumenta sup eisdem fact̃ videłt unũ de liber̃ usu t'raꝝ ppe villam de *Berewyk'* ⁊ castrum de *Rokesburgh* vocat̃ vulgarit' *Batable lonđ*, ⁊ aliud instrumentũ ptestac̃ois ⁊c̃, una cum lr̃is patent̃ Regis *Scottoꝝ* continent̃ potestatem dat̃ Ambassiat̃ suis ⁊c̃, que quið pixis rem̃ in cista supª Retam Ducatus *Lancastr̃* ad tal̃ signū

{Scocia Berewyk'.}

3 Be yt remembred þt þe *vi* day of *Octob̃* þe *xxix* yeer of þe regne of Kyng *Henry* þe *sext* ⸝ the Lorde *Beauchamp̃* Tresorer of *Englond* delyv̓ed in to þe Resseyt of the Eschequer an obligacioñ in þe whiche *Philipp̃ fitz Lowes* of *Essex'* Squyer ⸝ and *John Aps* of *Essex'* Gentilmañ ar bounde to oure seyd Sov̓ayne Lorde and to þe seyd Tresorer in cc mªrz st̓linges to be payd in þe fest of *Cristmasse* next comyng ⸝ þe seyd obligacioñ beryng date þe *iii* day of þe seid moneth in þe yeer aforseid ⸝ þer to be kept in þe Kynge Tresory ⸝ to suche entent ⁊ condicioñ as folweth ⸝ þt if þe seid *Philip* ⁊ *John* at þe fest of *Alhalwes* next comyng bringe un to þe seid Tresorer ⁊ Chambleyns an obligacioñ in þe whiche they ⁊ oþer iiii sufficeant ꝑsones shall be bounde un to our seyd Sov̓ayne Lord þe Kyng̃ ⁊ to hys Tresorer in þe same sōme of cc mªrz to be payd at þe seid feest of *Cristemesse* [or elles] restore un to prysoñ in to þe *Tour of Londoñ* nowe beyng þer in prisoñ þe ꝑsone of oon *John Lowes* þt þan þe seid first obligacioñ be delyv̓ed ageyñ un to þe forseid *Philip fitz Lowes* ⁊ *John Aps* or to oon of theym ⸝ the which obligacioñ ys in a box remaynyng in þe grene coffer in þe Resseyt.

Obligacio *Phi fitz Lowes* de cc mªrz.

(p. 110. b.) 4 Hec indentura facť *xxiii*° die *Julii* anno regni Rege *Henrici sexti vicesimo nono* int̓ *Johem* Dñm de *Beauchamp̃* Thes̃ *Angl* ⁊ Camar̃ Scªcii Reg̃ ex ꝑte una et *Johem Merstoñ* Armigerū Cusť jocaliū Reg̃ ex ꝑte ‖altra testatur qd idem *Johes Merstoñ* virtute lr̃az sub pivat̃ sigillo Reḡ sibi direct̃ quaz dat̃ est *xxii*do. die *Julii* anno p̃dict̃ delib̃avt p̃fat̃ Thes̃ ⁊ Camariis jocale Regis subscript̃ viȝ

5 Unũ magñ spiceplat̃ auri coopt̃ et sup topett̃ coopc̃li est una aquila *&c.* (*see below, No.* 8.) Et infra in medio ejusdm spiceplat̃ exist̃ una aquila garñ cũ bales̃ ⁊ iiii pul̃ ⁊ i saph̃. *Merstoñ.*

6 Postea lib̃ *Joyno*r ut ✠inf✠ sequitr p indentur̃ cuj9 tenor sequitr in hec verba

7 Hec indentura fc̃a *xxiiii*to die *Julii* anno regni Reḡ *Henr̃ vi*ti post conq̃m *xxix*o int̃ *Joh̃em* Dñm [de] *Beauchamp* Thes̃ *Anglie* ⁊ Camar̃ de Scacio Dñi R ex una pte ⁊ *Ric̃m Joynour* de *Londoñ* grocer ex pte alt̃a testatr qd̃ iidem Thes̃ ⁊ Camar̃ virtute lr̃az sub privato sigillo Reḡ eisd̃ Thes̃ ⁊ Camar̃ direct̃ [de dat̃] *xxii*do die *Julii* eod̃ ao rem̃ in filacio de t̃mĩo *Pasche* dc̃o anno *xxix*o lib̃aver̃ eid̃ *Ric̃o* jocale Reḡ subscriptũ videl̃t *Ric̃us Joyno*r.

8 Unũ magnũ spyceplate auri coopt̃ et sup topett̃ coopc̃li est una aquila cũ una balec̃ pendent̃ in suo beek ⁊ circa dc̃m topett̃ sunt x ball̃ ⁊ saphir̃ ⁊ vi pul̃ ac eciam formantr quatuor aquile sup dc̃m coopcl̃m ⁊ in quol̃t beek eazd̃ aquil̃ exist̃ unũ pul̃ ⁊ ulta hoc circa id̃m coopcl̃m sunt ccxx pul̃ xxi bal̃ ⁊ saphir̃ ⁊ xxiiii troch̃ quel̃t de iiii pul̃ ⁊ in quol̃t troch̃ ✠est✠ i dyamond̃ Et infra in medio ejusd̃ spiceplate existit una aquila garñ cũ iiiior bales ⁊ } xx lb̃ dĩ unc̃.

iiii^or^ pul ꝛ i saphir pendent in le beek de ead aquila Et pes ejusd spiceplate garn cū iiii bal iii saph ꝛ cxii. pul pond ||pit p pondus trojan

9 In cujꝰ rei testiōiū uni pti hujꝰ indenture rem penes pdcm *Ricm* sigillū officii Re^te^ Sc^a^cii est appensum alti vero pti ejusd indentur rem penes ✝ dcm ✝ dict Thes ꝛ Camar dcus *Ricus* sigillū suū apposuit *die* ꝛ *anno sup^a^dcis.*

10 M^d'^ qd mandato Dñi Thes *xvii^o^* die [" *Oc-* " *tobr* "] ✝ *Novēbr* ✝ a^o^ *xxxi^o^*. R *H vi^ti^* indentura pdca lib *Willo Essex'* Rememoratori R in Sc^a^cio p psecucōe inde p Regē ibm fied.

(p. 111.) 11 M^d'^ qd *xxv^to^* die *Julii* anno *xxix^o^* Reg *Henr vi^ti^* Thes ꝛ Camar de Sccio R libaver *Henrico Redford* Militi unam obligacionem *Witti de Harecourt* Comit de *Tankerville* de vi ^ml^ saluȝ . de financia Duc *Orleaaunse.* ||*Orealensis* virtute cujꝰd^a^m bris sub p'vat sigillo ✝ eid ✝ eisd Thes ꝛ Camar *xxiiii^to^* die *mens* p'dci *a^o^ sup^a^dicto* direct put pȝ p indentur inde int pfat Thes ꝛ Camar ac pfat *Henr* confect re- *Redford.* manēt in q^o^d^a^m cofino depict int alias obligacōes divs Dnoꝝ ac appūctuamenta dci Duc.

" Quod quid bre de p'vato sigillo rem in filac de " tmio *Pasche* a^o^ *xxix^o^* dci R."

---

30 Hen. VI.

(p. 111 b.) Anno *xxx^o^* regni Reg *Henrici sexti.*

1 M^d'^ qd *xiii^o^* die *Novembr* anno *xxx^o^* R. *H vi^ti^* libat^r^ Thes ꝛ Camar de Sc^a^cio p venabilem in Xpo

Quedam lr̃a *Sigismondi* R̷ *Romanoꝝ.*

P̃rem *Joħem Cantuar̃* Archiep̃m quodđ script̃ ad modū uni⁹ lr̃e in papiro in Latinis verbis incipient̃ *Sigismūdus Dei gr̃a Romanoꝝ Rex* ꝫ ꝉ ꝑminans ꝫ *octavo* ꝫ et ponitʳ in quođ cofro depict̃ int̃ al̃ evidenc̃ dc̃i *Sigismūdi* ꝉc̃.

Scocia.

Due pixiđ rotunđ. *Blake.*

"D relax- "acõe regni "*Scocie.*"

2 Mᵈ' qđ *xix*° die *Novembr̃* anno *xxx*° dc̃i R̷ *Joħes Blake* un⁹ Cl̃icoꝝ Signeti dc̃i Dñi Regis mandat̃ ejusđ Dñi Regis lib̃avit ad Reᵗᵃᵐ Scᵃcii Thes̃ ꝉ Camar̃ ib̃m duas pixides rotunđ de ligno sub sigillo Dñi *Cromwell* Camerar̃ R̷ sepatim sigillat̃ ꝫ div̉s scripta secreta eisdem Thes̃ ꝉ Camar̃ ignota continentes in magna Thesauraria Regis custodienđ que quiđ pixides remanēt in eadem Thesaurar̃ in quadam cista ubi magna Corona R̷ existit.

3 " Mᵈ' qđ *xxiiii*ᵗᵒ die *Maii* a° *xxx*° dc̃i Dñi R̷ " p̃dicte due pixides ut supᵃ sigillat̃ ꝉ infra se " cōtinēt̃ scripta supᵃdc̃a mandato *Consilii* R̷ apᵈ " *Westm̃* existen̄ exᵃ dictā magnā Thesaurar̃ R̷ Dño " Thes̃ Comiti *Wigorñ* lib̃at̃ fuer̃ ‖differēđ Dño Regi " usqꝫ *Shene.*"

" Et postea iđ Dñs Thes̃ restituit pixides p̃dict̃ " sub sigillo suo sigillat̃ Et rem̃ ✠ ut supᵃ ✠ in " cista ubi pargamenū ponitʳ supᵃ Receptam cū al̃ " ii pixiđ postea hic lib̃at̃ p † *Hardyng̃* put " pꝫ in vᵗᵒ fol̃ seqñ in una baga."

Angl̃ } Scocia }

4 Mᵈ' qđ *xix*° die *Novembr̃* anno *xxx*° p̃dc̃i Dñi R̷ lib̃at̃ fuer̃ in *Cam̃a Stellat̃* R̷ Thes̃ ꝉ Camar̃ Scᵃcii coram *Dñis de Consilio* Regis p Magr̃m *Ric̃ Andrewe* Secretar̃ R̷ ꝉ *Walt̃um Lucy* Militē nup Ambassiat̃ Dñi Regis ad ptes *Scocie* miss̃ lr̃e ꝉ munimenť subscript̃ videl̃t.

Una lr̃a treug̃ int̃ *Dñm nr̃m Regem* ; et consanguineū suū *Regem Scocie* sigill̃ Cōmissionar̃ R̷ *Scocie* sigillat̃.

Itm̃ instrument̃ ꝑtestacōis fact̃ p dc̄os Ambassiat̃ ꝑ homagio *Scocie* Dño nr̃o Regi debit̃.

It̃ instrument̃ sup terr̃ ||contensiosis voc̃ *Batable Landes* ||ꝑ *Rokesburgh* ⁊ *Berwyk*.

Itm̃ due cōmissiones sub magno sigillo Regis *Scocie* virtute quaꝝ dc̄e treug̃ p Ambassiat̃ suos ꝑ ꝑte sua concluse fuer̃.

" It̃ in ead̃ pixide ꝯtinēt^{r} lr̃e confirmator̃ R̷
" *Scottoꝝ* de treugꝭ ꝑdc̄is in Thes̃ R̷ p *Johē Wode*
" lib̃at̃ ut pꝫ pleniꝰ in [dors̃] fol̃ ꝑx̃ seq̃."

" It̃ ||lr̃as R̷ *Scottoꝝ* pateñ de ꝑrogac̃ treugaꝝ dat̃
" aº Dñi *m^{l} iiii^{c} lvii*º p *Johem Brouñ* lib̃at̃ in p^{i}ma
" ꝑte dorsi sexti folii seqñ."

[✠ " Lib̃ Comiti *Wygorñ* Thes̃ *Angl̃ xxiiii*^{to} die
" *Maii* aº *xxx*º."   " Postea rest̃."✠]

[✠ " Lib̃ ista vii scripta Custodi p^{i}vati sigilli p
" Thes̃ *Angl̃ iii* die *Jul̃* aº *sc̄do* R̷ *E. iiii*^{ti}." ✠]

[" Postea rest̃ *ix*º *Jul̃ eod̃ a*º."]

Aº *xxx*º.

(p. 112.) 5 M$^{d'}$ qd̃ *xvi*º die *Marcii* anno *xxx*^{mo} R̷ *Henr̃ vi*^{ti} Dñs Rex lib̃avit ad manus *Thome Rothewell* Armigi Clici Thesaurarii *Angl̃* ad salvū ⁊ secur̃ custodiēd̃ in Thesauraria ejusd̃ Dñi R̷ tria scripta de forma juramenti eid̃ Dño Regi p *Ric̄m* Ducē *Eboꝝ Thomā* Comitē *Devoñ* ⁊ *Edwardū* Dñm *Cobham* nup ꝑstit̃ ; manubꝫ eoꝝd̃ Ducꝭ Comitis ⁊ Dñi subscript̃ ⁊ suis sigillis sepatim sigillat̃ ; quequid̃ scripta ponūt^{r} in ||uno pixide ||ligneo ||rotundo in magna cista sup^a Receptā ubi pargamenū ponit^r remañ ad tale signū

{ **Jurame'tu' Duc' Ebor' Com' Devon' & D'ni Cobham.** }

sub custodia Thes̃ & Camar̃ &c̃.

(p. 112 b.) Anno *xxx*°.

6 M^d qđ *x*° die *Maii* anno *xxx*° R̃ *Henr̃ vi*^ti. *Johes Wode* Cłicus Thes̃ *Angł* lib̃avit ad Receptā Sc^acii lr̃as pateñ confirmatorias Reg̃ *Scottoꝝ* de treug̃ int̃ regna *Angł* & *Scocie* ult̃ capt̃ eiđ *Johi* ꝑ Dñm *Cancellar̃* & ał de Consilio R̃ in *Cam̃a Stellata* salvo & secur̃ ✝ cust̃ ✝ in Thesaurar̃ R̃ ꝑ Thes̃ & Camar̃ custodienđ lib̃at. & ||ponit^r in quađ pixide int̃ alias evidenc̃ easđ treugas conc̃nēt sub tali signo

{ **Angl' Scocia.** }

---

31 Hen. VI.

(p. 113.) Anno *xxxi*°.

1 M^d qđ *xxviii*° die *Junii* a° *xxxi*° R̃ *H vi*^ti *Johes* Comes *Wygorñ* Thes̃ *Angł* lib̃avit in Thesaur̃ R̃ ib̃m custodienđ bullam Sc̃issimi Patris Dñi *Eugenii* Pape in Sinodo geñal̃ apud *Florenciam* de reduccõe *Grecoꝝ* sigillat̃ cū plumbo & cum sigillo aureo *Grecoꝝ*, et rem̃ in una pixide quadrante, in una cista sup^a Receptam Ducat^9 *Lancastr̃* ad tale signū

Bulla Dñi *Eugenii* Pape.

2 Md' qđ t̃cio die *Julii* aº *xxxi*º R̷ *H vi*ti Mag̃r *Ric̃us Andrewe* Secretarius dc̃i Dñi R̷ lib̃avit in Thesaur̃ Dñi nr̃i Regis iii, script̃ de ꝓgacõe treugaꝝ capt̃ int̃ Cōmissarios Regis *Scottoꝝ* et Cōmissarios ꝑdc̃i Dñi nr̃i Regis *Angl̃* ꝑ tribus annis duratur̃ videl̃t unū script̃ sigillat̃ cum sigillo *Jacobi* Comitis de *Douglas* ⁊ *Rob̃ti Liddale* Armig̃i ⁊ unā lr̃am patent̃ de potestate Cōmissar̃ dc̃i R̷ *Scocie* sigillat̃ cū magno sigillo dc̃i R̷ *Scocie*, ac unū instrument̃ de confirmacõe treug̃ ꝑdc̃aꝝ, et rem̃ in una pixide quadrant̃ in cista sup^a Receptam Ducat^9 *Lancastr̃* ad tale signū

{Scocia Dowglas.}

3 " It̃ *xv*º die *Octobr̃* ꝑx̃ seqñ Thes̃ *Angl̃* lib̃avit " in Thesaur̃ R̷ unā aliā lr̃am patent̃ sub magno " sigillo Regis *Scottoꝝ* de ꝓgacõe treugaꝝ capt̃ int̃ " ꝑdc̃m Dñm nr̃m Regem *Angl̃* ⁊ dc̃m Regem *Scottoꝝ* et remañ in pixide ut sup^a."

" Et postea *vii*º die *Julii* aº *sc̃do* R̷ *E quarti* ꝑdict̃ " iiii^or script̃ lib̃at̃ fuerunt Mag̃ro *Thome Kent* Cl̃ico " Consilii dc̃i Dñi R̷."

32, 33 Hen. VI. &c.

(p. 114.) Anno *xxxii*do. Reg̃ *Henr̃ vi*ti.

1 Md' qđ *x*º die *Septembr̃* anno *xxxii* R̷ *H vi*ti *Jõhes* Comes *Wigorñ* Thes̃ *Angl̃* lib̃ Cam̃ar̃ Sc^acii dc̃i Dñi Reg̃ in Thesauraria sua salvo custodienđ unā pixidem ligneam ꝑ ip̃m Thes̃ ||sigillatū ⁊ ||supscriptū ṽbis sequētibꝫ.

2 ¶ The p'myse made by Rychard' Duke of Yorke under hys signet ⁊ signe manuel in ratifycacyon' of hys othe sealed with hys seal of hys armys.

¶ Que quid̄ pixis ponitur in quad^{a}m magna cista lignea cū iii ceruī̄ cerata supra Receptam ubi pgamenū ponit^{r} ad tale signum

{Yorke.}

3 M^{d,} qđ *viii*° die *Februaŕ* anno ||*xxxii*^{do} Reḡ *Henŕ sexti Johes Markham* unus Justic̄ R̄ de Banco delibavit Thes̄ ⁊ Camaŕ Sc^{a}cii dc̄i Dn̄i R̄ p indentuŕ quinq̄ recorda de gaolis delibanđ coram ip̄o ⁊ aliis nup capt̄ in div̄s Com̄ *Angl* ⸝ v3 unū in Com̄ *Bed* anno *xxv*^{to} capt̄ ⸝ unū in Com̄ *Norff'* a° *xxix*° capt̄ ⸝ duo in Com̄ *Cant* a° *xxix*° capt̄ ⸝ ⁊ unū in Com̄ *Lincoln̄* anno *xxv*^{to} R̄ nūc capt̄ que quidem quinq̄ recorda ponunt^{r} in quadam baga de canabo infra Thesaur̄ R̄ sub custodia eoꝝdem Thes̄ ⁊ Camaŕ exist̄.

Recorda gaol libat̄ p *Johem Markham.*

4 M^{d,} qđ *xii*° die *Februaŕ* anno ||*xxxiii*° R̄ *Henŕ sexti Thom̄ Litteltoñ* unus s̄vientū ad leges delibavit Thes̄ ⁊ Camaŕ Sc̄cii Dn̄i R̄ unū recordū de gaola libanđ apud *Coventŕ* coram ip̄o *Thoma* ⁊ aliis nup capt̄ v3 de anno *vicesimo nono.*

Recordū gaole p *Littelton̄.*

(p. 114 b.)

Anno ||*xxx*°.

5 M^{d,} q^{d,} *xxii*° die *Marcii* anno regni Regis *Henrici sexti* ||*xxxii*^{do} ||venābile in Xp̄o Patre *Johe* pmissione divina titulo *Sc̄e Balbine* Ep̄o Cardinali Archiep̄o *Cantuaŕ* tocius *Anglie* ||P^{i}mato ⁊ ||Appostolice Sedis Legato Cancellario *Anglie* defuncto sigillū dc̄i Dn̄i Regis de Cancellaria sua nup in custodia ip̄ius nup Cancellarii dum vix̄it existens unacū duob3

aliis sigillis videłt unū de auro ꝛ ał de argento ejusđm Dñi Regis in quadᵃm ꝑva cista lignea positū ꝛ incluš sub sigillis *Riči* Ducꝭ *Eboꝝ*. instantꝭ ꝑliamenti ꝓsidentꝭ ꝛ alioꝝ divˢs *Dñoꝝ de Consilio* Regis sigillat̃
Sigillū Cancellarie. ꝑ *Johem* Comitē *Wigorñ Angł* Theš *Ričm* Comitem *Warr̃* ꝛ *Rađm Cromwełł* Camarios de Scᵃcio dči Dñi Regis ac *Johem* Dñm ||*Stoʳton* unū de Consilio Regis ex avisamento ꝛ assensu Dñoꝝ tam sp̃ualiū qᵃm temꝑaliū in ꝓsenti ꝑliamento existeñ in magnā Thesaurariā Dñi ꝶ apᵈ. *Westm̃ die* ꝛ *anno ꝓdčis* ibm salvo ꝛ secur̃ custodienđ libatū fuit.

Et postea videłt *pᵢmo* die *Aprilis anno supᵃdčo* sigillū ꝓdčm in cista ꝓdča unacū sigillis ꝓdčis in eađm cista incluš ut supᵃ sigillat̃ avisamento et assensu Consilii ꝓdči ꝑ ꝓfatos Theš ꝛ Camar̃ in Camªa ꝑliamenti Dñis sp̃uał et tempał ibm existeñ exᵃ dčam Thesaurariā libatū fuit *Ričo* Comiti *Saꝝ* ꝑ Regem et suū Consiliū Cancellar̃ *Anglie* constituto ibm libanđ.

---

33 Hen. VI.

(p. 115.) Anno *xxxiii*° ꝶ *H. viᵗⁱ*.

1 Mᵈ' qđ *xvii*° die *Julii* , anno r̃ ꝶ *Henr̃ sexti xxxiii*° venabił in Xp̃o Pat̃ † *London̄* Ep̃us unus executoꝝ *Johis* nuꝑ Arch *Cantuar̃* ꝓsbiti Cardinał defuncti , libavit Theš ꝛ Camar̃ Scᵃcii dči Dñi Regis in Thesauraria ꝶ custodienđ quoddam script̃ modo cujusdam instrumenti in ꝑgameno in Latinis ꝛ Gallič vbis script̃ et cum duobꝫ sigillis cera viriđ sigillat̃ de dat̃ anno Dñi *milłmo cccc xxxiiii*° menš *Novembr̃* die *vicesima nona* , continens sacramenta fča de pace finali ꝑ Ducem *Britanñ* fr̃es suos ꝛ Ep̃os

⁊ Barones de patria s̃ et ponitʳ in quadam pixide de ligno rem̃ in cista supᵃ Reᵗᵃᵐ Ducatus *Lancastr̃* ad tale signū

{Sacr'm Ducis Britann'.}

2 Mᵈ' qđ *xxix°* die *Julii* anno *xxxiii°* R̷ *Henrici sexti* ✻ fuit p̱ Vic̃ ‖*Bouzer* Thes̃ *Angł* ⁊ *Rađm* Dñm *Cromwel* unū Camar̃ Scᵃcii Dñi R̷ in Thesaurariā R̷ custodienđ quoddam scriptum acquietancie Dño Regi fact̃ p̱ *Oliverū Perret* M'catorē patrie de *Normandy* ⁊ cera rubea sigillat̃ et rem̃ in quadᵃm p̱va pixide ‖ligneo in viridi cista sub tribȝ ceruris in dc̃a Reᵗᵃ sub tali signo

{Acquietanc' Oliveri P'ret.}

---

34 Hen. VI.

(p. 115 b.) Anno *xxxiiii*ᵗᵒ.

1 Mᵈ' qđ *xix*ⁿᵒ die *Marcii* anno r̃ R̷ *Henr̃ sexti xxxiiii*ᵗᵒ Vicecomes *Bourchier* Thes̃ *Angł* lib̃avit in Thesaurar̃ dc̃i Dñi Reg̃ p̱ m⁹ *Thome Pounde* unā lr̃am patent̃ sub sigillo Burgimag̃ri ⁊ Consuł Civitat̃ *Lubicen̄* [de treug̃ h̃it int̃ p̃dc̃m Dñm nr̃m Regem ex una p̱te et ‖p̃dc̃i ‖Burgimag̃ri] ex alt̃a p̱te p̱ octo annos ‖duraturos, sub sigillo Civitatis *Lubicen̄* Dat̃ *vii°* die mensis *Januar̃* anno ⁊c̃ ‖*l sexto*, Rem̃ in ‖uno pixide in quadam cista supᵃ Reᵗᵃᵐ Ducat⁹ *Lancastr̃* ad tale signū

{Lubicen' Hanza.}

2 Mᵈ' qđ *eisđm die* ⁊ *anno* lib̃atū fuit ad Recep-

Creditores *Jo͞his* [D͞ni] *Stourto͞n* Militis nuꝑ The͠s Hospi͠c R͞.

tam Scᵃcii quoddam warrantū Dn̄i Regis sub privato sigillo s̃ The͠s ꝛ Ca͞mar͠ Scᵃcii direct͠ ꝑ solu͠c fiend͠ creditorib3 R͞ de tempe *Jo͞his* Dn̄i *Stourto͞n* Milit͠ nuꝑ The͠s Hospi͠c d͠ci Dn̄i R͞ cū xxxix rotulis ꝑga-meni no͞ia d͠coȝ creditoȝ ac sūmas eisd͠m ꝑticularit͛ debit͠ continent͠ Et rem͠ in fila͠c int͛ mandat͠ de t͛mīo *Mic͞h* anno *xxxiiii*ᵗᵒ R͞ nūc.

---

35 Hen. VI.

(p. 116.) *xxxv. H. vi*ᵗⁱ.

1 Mᵈ' qd͠ *die Lune xxx*ᵒ die *Nov'* anno *xxxv*ᵗᵒ R͞ *H. sexti* li͞bantʳ in Scᵃcio Dn̄i Reg͠ in plena cur͠ The͠s ꝛ Ca͞mar͠ i͞bm salvo ꝛ secur͠ in ‖Thesauria R͞ custo-diend͠ jocal͠ subscripta que nuꝑ fuer͠ in custodia *Simonis Eyre* Civis ꝛ Aldermañ *London͞* v3

Jocal͠ R͞ nuꝑ in custod͠ *Simonis Eyer* Aldermañ *London͞*.

2 Unū ciphū chaceat͠ de auro ✤ sine cooꝑtorio ✤ ["i braunche of golde i serpētyñ set in golde"] pon-derans ꝑ pond⁹ de troy † unū ciphū de auro cooꝑtum garnizat͠ cū lapidib3 ꝑ̄ciosis ꝛ ꝑut͠ ponder-ant͠ ꝑ pond͠ ꝑ̄d͠cm xxxix. unc͠ ꝛ unam dimidiā unc͠ ⹁ unū ciphū de jaspide cooꝑtū garnizat͠ cum lapidib3 ꝑ̄siosis ꝛ ꝑut͠ ponder͠ ꝑ pond⁹ ꝑ̄d͠cm ✤ xiii mᵃr3 ✤ [xxv. unc͠] unū spiceplate ꝛ unū pedem uni⁹ crucis de argento deaurat͠ ponder͠ ꝑ pond⁹ ꝑ̄d͠cm xiii mᵃrc͠ ꝛ vi unc͠ unū layer de argento deaurat͠ ꝛ unū stan-dardū uni⁹ crucis de argento ponder͠ ꝑ pond⁹ ꝑ̄d͠cm quatuor marc͠ ꝛ quatuor unc͠ duas pelves de argento deaurat͠ ponder͠ ꝑ pondus ꝑ̄d͠cm xx mᵃr3. que quedᵃm jocal͠ ponūtʳ in quadam cista supᵃ Receptā.

Et postea v3 *xv*ᵒ die *Decembr͠ eod͠ anno* ead͠m jocal͠ virtute b͞ris de pⁱvat͠ sigillo dat͠ *vii*ᵒ die [*Decembr͠*] eod͠ anno eisđ Theš ꝛ Camar̃ direct̃ rem̃ in filac̃ de t̃mīo *Mich̃is* a° supᵃdc̄o lib̃at̃ fuer̃ Dño Regi p m⁹ *Ric̃i Davy* Cleric̃ jocal̃ Reg̃ put patet p indenturā dc̄i *Ric̃i* in hanapio ejusđ t̃mini rem̃.

---

36 Hen. VI.

(p. 116 b.) *xxxvi. H. viᵗⁱ.*

P̃sentacio cuj⁹dᵃm cantarie fact̃ p Camar̃ Scᵃcii ex pte Reg̃.

1 Uniṽsis ꝛ singl̃is Xp̃i fidelib3 ad quos presentes lr̃e pven̄int *Thomas Nevill* Miles ꝛ *Humfridus Bourgchier* pleno jure habentes ꝛ occupantes officiū unius Camar̃ Scᵃcii Dñi nr̃i Regis ac ‖successoris *Johannis Wodehous* defuncti in eodem officio salt̃m in Dño sempit̃nam. Cum donac̄o ꝛ collac̄o ppetue Cantarie in Capella inferiori vocat̃ *le Charnell* in honore *Sancti Joh̃is Evᵃngeliste* infra p̃cinctum Eccl̃ie Cath̃ *Sc̄e Tⁱnitatis* Civitat̃ *Norwic̃* dedicata de uno capell̃o ppetuo fundat̃ quandocūq3 Cantaria illa p mortem cessionem resignac̄oem privac̄oem vel alio modo quocūq3 vacaṽit ad nos rac̄oe officii predc̄i juxᵃ ordinac̄oes ꝛ statuta dicte fundac̄ois ip̃ius Cantarie pleno jure spectet ꝛ ptineat put in eisdem statut̃ ꝛ ordinac̄oib3 plenius liquet. Noṽitis nos prefatos *Thomam* ꝛ *Humfridum* ‖dedisse ꝛ contulisse p pn̄tes dilecto nobis in Xp̄o *Johanni* ‖*Boffett* Cl̃ico Cantariam predc̄am jam p mortē Dñi *Joh̃is Sparham* vacantē ꝛ ut p̃mittitʳ ad nr̃am donac̄oem ꝛ collac̄oem spectant̃, habenđ cum jurib3 ꝛ ptinen̄ suis quibuscumq3 eundemq3 *Joh̃nem* [*Buffet*] sup sacr̃o suo coram nobis in Recepta Scᵃcii predc̄i p̃stit̃ ad ordinac̄oes ꝛ statuta predict̃ p ip̃m fidelit̃ obs̃vanđ in corpalem possessionem Cantarie predict̃ p lib̃ac̄oem sibi presenciū imposuisse juxta vim formā ꝛ effectum ordinac̄onū

ꝛ statutoꝝ p̃dictoꝝ In cujus rei testimonium sigillū officii Recepte Scacii p̃dict̃ p̃ntibȝ fecimus apponi Dat̃ in Recepta Scacii predict̃ *octavo* die mens̃ *Febr̃* anno regni Regis *Henrici sexti* post conquestum *tricesimo sexto*.

2 ¶ Memod' qđ †

3 Med' qđ *xv*o die *Novembr̃* anno *xxxvi*to Ꝝ *H vi*ti. *Joĥes Hardyng̃ de Kyme* delib̃avit Dño *Joĥi Talbot* Comiti *Salop̃* Thes̃ [*Angl̃*] ꝛ Camar̃ Scacii quinq, lr̃as
Scocia. patentes tangentes regnū *Scocie* ꝛ unam indentur̃ de treug̃ put patet in quadam indentura int̃ eos fact̃ de data supadc̃a vȝ unam lr̃am patent̃ p quam *David*
Hardyng. Rex *Scocie* recogñ se tenẽe regnū *Scocie* de *Edwardo* t̃cio Rege *Angl̃* p homagiū ligeū ꝛ fidelitatem. Item al̃ lr̃am patent̃ p quam *Rob̃tus* Rex *Scocie* recogñ se tenẽe regnū *Scocie* de *Edwardo* Rege *Angl̃* t̃cio ꝛ her̃ suis p homagiū ligeū ꝛ fidel̃ Item al̃ lr̃am patent̃ p quam om̃es Comites Barones ꝛ Magnat̃ regni *Scocie* fecer̃ homag̃ sua Regi *Scocie* salvis semp homag̃ supiori Dño *Edwardo* Regi *Angl̃* ꝛ her̃ suis supior̃
(p. 117.) Dñis regni *Scocie* Item unam al̃ lr̃am patent̃ p quam *David Strabolgy* Comes de *Athell̃* indc̃atus de pdic̃oe compuit in pliamento *Scocie* ||alligans se non esse culpabil̃ de pdic̃oe sibi imposit̃ p hoc qđ devenẽat ligeus homo Reg̃ *E.* t̃cii eo qđ Reges *Angl̃* semp ab antiquo fuer̃ supiores Dñi regni *Scocie* ꝛ p hanc alligac̃oem approbat̃ p recorda pliamentoꝝ *Scoc̃* ꝛ coram Justic̃ in itinẽibȝ suis *Scoc̃* fuit inde quiet̃ It̃m unam al̃ lr̃am patent̃ p quam *Joĥes Grame* Comes de *Menteth̃* indc̃atus vȝ de pdic̃oe ex causa p̃dc̃a ||alligavit in pleno pliamento qđ non fuit inde culpabilis p hoc qđ devenẽat ligeus homo Ꝝ *E.* t̃cii ut supa ꝛ p recorda coram Camar̃ ꝛ Justic̃ *Scocie* in itinẽibȝ suis

fuit inde quiet̃ Item unam indentur̃ de treugis ꝛ abstinenc̃ guerr̃ capt̃ int᷒ *Edwardū t̃ciū* ex ꝑte una ꝛ *David* Regem *Scocie* ex alt᷒a ꝑte ꝑ quam *David* Rex recognovit ꝓdc̃m Regem *Edwardū* esse Dñm supiorem *Scocie* postqªm dc̃us *Edwardus* fec᷒it dc̃am relaxac̃oem.

4 " Que quid̃ v lr̃e pateñ et indentura ponūtʳ in " ‖ii pixid̃ ‖ligneū quadrant̃ et ponūtʳ in magna cista " ubi ꝑgamenū ponitʳ supª Receptā ad tale signū"

{Scocia Hardyng.}

5 Mdʼ þᵗ þᵉ *xxi* day of *August* in þᵉ *xxxvi* yere of King *Harry* þᵉ *sext* þe Chaunceller of *England* delyv᷒ed unto *John Brouñ* Undertresorer to be kept in þe Tresorye a lyv᷒ee of þᵉ crowne of sylvyr ꝛ gilt with̃ ii estryche fethers enamelyd blew ⸗ þᵉ whiche is put in þᵉ ꝑchemyn cofre.

---

37 Hen. VI.

(p. 117 b.) *Anno xxxvii°*.

1 Mdʼ qd̃ *xviii°* die *Octobr̃* anno *xxxvii°* ℞ *Henr̃ vi*ᵗⁱ *Johes Brouñ* Cl̃ic᷒ Thes̃ *Angl̃* recepit de Dño Cancellar̃ *Angl̃* quasdªm lr̃as pateñ *Jacobi* ℞ *Scottoꝝ* de dat̃ *ult̃ diei Decēbr̃* a° Dñi *mill̃o iiii*ᶜ *lvii°* ꝛ regni sui ‖*xxvii°* de ꝓrogac̃oe treugaꝝ int᷒ regna *Anglie* ꝛ *Scocie* ꝑ iiiiᵒʳ annis et ponitʳ in quodªm cofino ligneo [cū al̃ evidenc̃ *Scocie*] †ad tale signū⊥ remañ infra c̄istam ubi pargamenū poni consuevit sub tali signo

{Angl'. Scocia.}

(p.118.) *xxxvii H vi*ti.

{ Sar'. }

2 This endenture made þe *xxi* day of *Octob̄* the yeer of þe regne of King *Harry* þe *sext xxxvii* bitwene þe Tresorer of *Englanđ* and þe Chamb̄leyns of þe Eschequer on þt * part and þe right wurshipfull ꝛ reṽent Fader in God *Richarđ Beauchamp̄* Bisshop̄ of *Salisbury* on þt other part. Witnesseth þt þe seiđ Tresorer ꝛ Chamb̄leyns by vertu of a pryve seal beryng date þe *xx* day of *Octob̄* þe *xxxvii* yeer of þe regne of oure seiđ Soṽayne Lorde þe Kyng remaynyng in þe filas of *Michelmesse* ṫme in þe *xxxvii* yeer of our seiđ Soṽayne Lorđ amonges oþer warrant̄ direct to þe seiđ Tresorer ꝛ Chamb̄leyns. have delyṽed to þe seiđ Bisshop̄ certeyñ evydences. ꝛ ||munnymentꝭ concernyng convencions cōmynycacions tretys legues ꝛ trewes bytwis þis Reawme ꝛ oþer lanđ ꝛ countrees þt ys to sey.

3 First i boke coṽed wt rede lether named a *Register* which begynneth in þe seconđ foyle after þe calender of þe same boke *trois mois.*

[" Et postea *vi*o die *Nov'* ||p̄x seqñ idem Ep̄us " restituit dc̄m librū."]

4 Also anoþer boke coṽed wt rede lether named a *Register* whiche begynneth in þe seconde foyle after þe calender of þe same boke *qđ illi.*

[" Et postea *vi*o die *Nov'* p̄x seqñ idem Ep̄us " restituit dc̄m librū."]

5 In witnesse wherof þe seal of thoffice of þe Resseyt of thEschequer to þt oon part of þis endenture remaynyng wt þe seiđ reṽent Fader ys put

to ⸗ and þe seal of þe foresaid revent Fader to þt oþer part of þis endenture remaynyng to þe seid Tresorer ⁊ Chambleyns ys put to ‖in þe *day* ⁊ *yeer* aforeseyd.

" Que indentur continet^r in ‖q^o d pixide rem in " virid cist ad tle sig^m ut in capite."

(p. 118 b.) 6 Omib3 Xpi fidelib3 ad quos presens scriptū pvenit *Jacobus* Comes *Wiltes* Thes *Angl* saltm Cum nup Dns. *H.* Rex *Angl* pat metuendissimi Dni Regis nūc quand^a m Cantariam ppetuam de uno capellano ⁎ divina singlis dieb3 in quad^a m cappella inferiori vocat *le Charnell* in honore *Sci Johis Ev^a ngeliste* ⁎ pcinctū ecclie cathedral *Sce T^i nitatis* civitat *Norwicen* dedicat celebratur fundavit et cantariam illam *Johi Sparh^a m* capello dedit ⁊ ipm *Johem Sparh^a m* in corporalem possessionem ejusdem cantar cū suis jurib3 ⁊ ptin posuit ac eidem *Johi* ⁊ successorib3 suis in dotacoem ⁊ sustentacoem suam ecclie de *Geyton* ac rectoriam ejusdem dedit insupq3 idem Dns Rex pat Dni Reg nūc ordinavit qd *Johes Wodehous* tunc unus Camar ipius nup Reg durant vita sua ⁊ post mortem suam omes ⁊ singli dcm officiū Camar hentes deceto herent collacoem ejusdem Cantarie in singlis vacacoib3 suis ita qd quocienscunq3 eandē Cantariam p mortē cessionem resignacoem aut alicuj^9 beneficii acceptacoem seu alias qualitcumq3 vacare contigit pfat^9 *Johes Wodehous* durante vita sua ⁊ post mortē suam successores sui officii pdci Cantar pdcam alio capello idoneo sigillo officii Camar pdcoz in custod eozdem existent infra unū mensem a tēpe vacacois Cantarie illius conferrent ⁊ ipm in corporalē possessionē ejusdē ponent vel

" De Can-
" taria ad
" collacoem
" Camar le
" Sc^a cio
" ptinens de
" fundacoe
" *Johis*
" *Wodehous*
" nup Camar
" ibm ⁊c."

poni facent Et si dict⁹ *Johes Wodehous* seu successores sui p̄dc̄i hujusmodi collac̄oē p unū mensem necgligentes fuerint vel remisi tunc collac̄o Cantarie illius ad Thes̄ *Anglie* qui p tēpe fuit illa vice devolvat^r Quiquidē *Johes Wodhous* ꝛ *Johes Sparkam* mortui sunt ꝛ Cantaria p̄dc̄a p q^amplures menses elaps̄ vacavit ꝛ vacua existit divinaq; in capella predc̄a jux^a ordinac̄ ꝛ fundac̄ Cantarie illius p magnū tempus incelebrat̄ ꝛ infecta fuerunt ꝛ adhuc existunt sicut p inq^isic̄oem corā nup esc̄ *Norff'* capt̄ ꝛ in Sc^acm Dñi Reḡ ret^rnat̄ liquet manifeste Sciatis me Cantariā p̄dc̄am dilco michi *Robto Martham* capello qui coram me ꝛ Cam̄iis Sc^acii Dñi Reḡ tactis sacrosc̄is Dei Ev^angeliis sacrm p̄stitit corporale qd ip̄e om̄ia ꝛ singla ordinac̄oes declarac̄oes ꝛ statuta p dc̄m nup Regē in fundac̄oe Cantarie p̄dc̄e ordinat̄ ꝛ declarat̄ quant̄ ad eū attinet seu attinere poterit
(p. 119.) firmit̄ tenebit ꝛ inviolabilit̄ observabit, dedisse ꝛ contulisse p p̄sentes, ac dilc̄m nob *Edmundū Moore* Gentilman attorñ nrm ad eundē *Robtū* in plena ꝛ ||corporale possessione cantarie illius ꝛ rc̄orie p̄dc̄e cū om̄ibȝ juribȝ ꝛ ptiñ suis ponend constituisse ꝛ assignasse similit̄ p presentes In cuj⁹ rei testiōiū huic p̄sent̄ scripto sigillū meū apposui Dat̄ apud *Westm̄ sextodecimo* die mensis *Febr̄* anno regni Regis *Henr̄ sexti* post conquestū *tricesimo septimo*.

---

38 Hen. VI.

(p. 119 b.) *xxxviii^o H. vi^ti*.

1 Memo^d' qd *xv^o* die *Febr̄* anno *xxxviii^o* Regis *Henr̄ sexti Willm̄s Grymesby* Armig̃ Subthes̄ *Angl*

lib̃avit in Thesaur̃ Regis itm̃ custodiend̃ iiii^or obligac̃oes sequentes v3

2 In p^i mis unam obligac̃oem in qua *Jok̃es Mylewater* Armig̃ tenet^r p̃dc̃o Dño Regi in cc m^a r3 solvend̃ sub c̃tis forma 't condic̃oe in eadem obligac̃oe specificat̃.

3 Itm̃ unam obligac̃oem in qua *Henr̃ ap Griffytk̃* Armig̃ tenet^r dc̃o Dño Regi in c li solvend̃ sub c̃tis forma 't condic̃oib3 in eadem obligac̃oe specificat̃.

4 Itm̃ unam obligac̃oem in qua *Rog̃us Bodenh^a m* tenet^r dc̃o Dño Regi in c m^a r3 solvend̃ sub c̃tis

Oblig̃. forma 't condic̃oib3 in eadem obligac̃oe specificat̃.

5 Itm̃ unam obligac̃oem in qua *Thomas fitz Harry* Armig̃ tenet^r dc̃o Dño Regi in c li solvend̃ sub c̃tis forma 't condic̃oe in eadem obligac̃oe specificat̃.

6 Queq^i dem obligac̃oes ponunt^r in una pixide ||ligneo remañ in magna cista ubi pgamenũ poni ||consuet^r sup^a Receptam sub tali signo

{ **Oblig'.** }

7 M^d' qd̃ *xv*^o die *Maii* anno r̃ R̃ *Henr̃ sexti xxxviii*^o *Jacobus* Comes *Wiltes̃* Thes̃ *Angl̃* lib̃avit in Thesaur̃ dc̃i Dñi R̃ p man^9 *Jok̃is Whytyngtoñ* s̃vient̃ ejusd̃ Thes̃ duas lr̃as concernent̃ treug̃ int̃ p̃dc̃m Dñm nr̃m Regem et *Ludovicũ de Valle* ||Reg̃m in *Janua* Locumtenentẽ 't Gub̃natorem 't Consiliũ Antianorum inclite cõmunitat̃ *Janue* p quatuor annos duratur̃ que quidem due lr̃e sigillant^r cum rubia cera inclus̃ in duab3 pvis pixid̃ de ligno rotund̃, de dat̃

Janue die *xiii Febr̃* ‚ anno Dñi *millmo cccc lx*° ‚ que quid̄ lr̃e ponūt^r in una pixide rem̃ in cista sup^a Receptā ubi ponit^r pgamanū ad tale signū

{Treug' Janue.}

" Et libat̃ fuit ista treuga *Johi Say* Sbtes̃ *xviii* " die *Julii* a° *p*^io ℞ *Edwardi quarti.* Et restituit^r " *xxi* ‖*p*^io die *Julii eod̄ a*°."

INVENTORY

OF THE

REGALIA, JEWELS, &c. OF HEN. VI.

DEPOSITED IN THE TREASURY.

(A. I. 3. p. 15.) 1 First the Kynges *grete Crowne of gold̃* whyche ys closed with yn a lityl coffyn of lether and bounde w^{t} yroñ and lokyñ w^{t} dyṽs lokes and keyes and also a seled w^{t}oute with̃ dyṽs Lordes seles whiche ys w^{t} yn *Westmynstre* in þ^{e} Kinges *Grete Tresoury.*

2 " M$^{d'}$ þ^{t} the *xiii* day of *Marche* in þ^{e} *seconde* " yere of Kyng *Edward* þ^{e} *iiii*th the seyd *Crowne* " was delyṽed ꝛtc. unto *Wylliam Porte* Tresorer of " þe Kyngꝭ Chamber" *&c.* (*see vol. iii. p. 2, No.* 7.)

(p. 16.) 3 Also a Pusan of gold̃ called þe *riche coler* conteyning xvi. culpons or peces upon þe whiche beth̃ viii. antelopes *&c.* (*see p.* 143, *No.* 14.) þé prys	m^{l} m^{l} DCCC ^{li}
(p. 16 b.) 4 Also a swerd̃ of gold̃ called þ^{e} *Swerd̃ of Spayne &c.* (*see p.* 144, *No.* 16.) þ^{e} prys	cccxxxiii^{li}. vi^{s}. viii^{d}.
5 Also a tablet of gold̃ of þe *Passioñ of Crist* made in þ^{e} maner of a boke garnysshed w^{t} xl dyamandꝭ *&c.* (*see p.* 144, *No.* 17.) þe prys	‖cx. li.

(p. 17.)	6 Also a tablet of *Seynt George* of gold̃ garnysshed w^{t} a rubee viii dyamandes *&c.* (*see p.* 184, *No.* 34.) þe prys	ciiii^{xx} iiii l̄i
	7 Also a Pusan of gold̃ called̃ *Iklyngtoñ coler &c.* (*see p.* 184, *No.* 35.) þe pris	ccc ^{li}
(p. 17 b.)	8 Also ii. salers of gold̃ wher-of þ^{t} oon ys a mañ and þ^{t} other a woman *&c.* (*see p.* 184, *No.* 35.) þe prys of all	cxl. l̄i.
	9 Also ii. pottes of gold *&c.* (*see p.* 185, *No.* 37.) Sm^{a}	xxxix^{li} xx^{d}
	10 Also a chalys and ii. cruettꝭ of gold *&c.* (*see p.* 185, *No.* 38.) Sm^{a}	xxxiii^{li}. xvi^{s}. viii^{d}
(p. 18.)	11 Also a tablet of gold̃ of þe *Salutacion* (*see p.* 185, *No.* 39.) þe prys	lx. l̄i
	12 Also an Image of *Seynt George* of gold̃ beyng upon a grene tarage *&c.* (*see p.* 185, *No.* 40.) þe pris	lxviii^{li}. xiii^{s}. iiii^{d}
	13 Also a standyng tablet of gold̃ w^{t} a pece of *Tunica Inconsutil̃ &c.* (*see p.* 186, *No.* 44.) Sm^{a}	xxxiii^{li}. x^{s}. x^{d}
(p. 18 b.)	14 Also a standyng cuppe of gold garnysshed w^{t} xlv ꝑles *&c.* (*see p.* 186, *No.* 45.) Sm^{a}	lxxvii^{li}

	15 Also a flat tablet of gold̄ w^{t} a pece of *Tunica Inconsutil̄ &c.* (*see p.*186, *No.*46.) the hole sōme of the tablet cometh to	iiii^{xx}iiii^{li}. xiiii^{s}. ii^{d}
(p. 19.)	16 Also a pair basyns of sylver and ov̄gilt *&c.* (*see p.* 185, *No.* 41.) weyng xx lb̄ ꝛ viii unces 17 Also a grete almes disshe of silver and ov̄gilt made in maner of a shippe *&c.* (*see p.* 185. *No.* 42.) The sōme totall̄ of þ^{e} weyzt of þe seyd basyns almes dissh and vessell̄ cometh to ccxli. lb̄. vi unces þe pris of ev̄y lb̄ xxxiii^{s} iiii^{d} Sm^{a} 18 Also ii grete chargeours vi lasse *&c.* (*see p.* 185. *No.* 43.) weyng cliii lb̄ ꝛ i. unce	iiii^{c} ii^{li}. x^{s}.
(p. 20.)	19 Also a shippe of gold̄ called the *Tygre &c.* (*see p.* 171, *No.* 1.) Sm^{a}	cccc^{li}. x^{s}.
	20 Also ii. sensures of gold̄ *&c.* (*see p.* 171, *No.* 8.) Sm^{a}	clxxii^{li}. x^{s}.
	21 Also ii crewettes of gold̄ *&c.* (*see p.* 171, *No.* 9.) Sm^{a}	xxxii^{li}. vi^{s}. viii^{d}
(p. 20 b.)	22 Also a sercle of golde *&c.* (*see p.* 171, *No.* 10.) Sm^{a}	xxi^{li}. v^{s}.
	23 Also a crosse of silv̄e *&c.* (*see p.* 171, *No.* 11.) Sm^{a}	xxv^{li} xviii^{s} iiii^{d}

	24 Also a chalys of silṽe *&c.* (*see p.* 171, *No.* 12.) Sm^{a}	iiii^{li}. xiii^{s}. iiii^{d}.
(p. 21.)	25 Also a tabler of silṽe and oṽegilt enameled blewe and rede *&c.* (*see p.* 171, *No.* 13.) þ^{t} weyetħ xvii lƀ ⁊ vi. unces of troye	The whiche weyen in alł xlii^{lb}. ⁊ . i. quartr̃ of troye pris of eṽy lƀ. liij^{s} iiii^{d} Sm^{a} cxii^{li}. xiiii^{d}.
	26 Also xxxii. tables meyne of silṽe *&c.* (*see p.* 172, *No.* 14.) þ^{t} weyetħ *&c.* ix unces ⁊ dĩ of troye	
	27 Also a tabler of silṽe ⁊ oṽgilt *&c.* (*see p.* 172, *No.* 15.) þ^{t} weyeth xix lƀ ⁊ viii. unces of troye	
	28 Also xxxii. chesse mayne of silṽe *&c.* (*see p.* 172, *No.* 16.)	
	29 Also . ii. foxes and xlvi. houndes of silṽe *&c.* (*see p.* 172, *No.* 17.)	
(p. 21 b.)	30 Also a grete ouche of *Seynt George* armes *&c.* (*see p.* 143, *No.* 15.) the pris	cc ^{li}
(p. 22.)	31 Also ii. grete chaundlers of golđ *&c.* (*see p.* 145, *No.* 19.) Sm^{a}	ccccclxvi^{li} xiii^{s}. iiii^{d}
	32 Also a palet called þe *Palet of Spaygne* garnysshed̄ w^{t} golđ and w^{t} xxxv baleys ⁊ rubees bastarđ iiii sapħ xv grete emeraudes ciii litil emeraudes ⁊ ccc	‖c. łi

	litil ples the weyght of þe same palet viii lb ꝛ vi unces þe pris of þe same palet	
(p. 22 b.)	33 Also ii. basyns of gold chased in þe maner of roses *&c.* (*see p.* 145, *No.* 20.) the prys of þe seyd basyns	ccccl viii[li] xiii s. iiii. d
	34 Also a litel flaket of berell garnysshed w[t] gold and w[t] vi. dyamandes ix. baleys ꝛ xxiii ples the prys of þe same flaket	xv [li].
(p. 23.)	35 Also a grete flour [of gold] called *Flour de lys* of a Crowne garnysshed w[t] a grete baleys and anoþer lasse baleys a rubee . iii. grete saph x grete ples ꝛ xii lasse ples also anoþer litil flour of gold of þe same Crowne þe pris of bothe floures	lxx [li].
	36 Also a pynacle of gold of þe same Crowne garnysshed w[t] ii. saphers and a square baleys and vi. ples þe pris of the same pynacle	x [li].
	37 Also a litil belle of gold weyng xx unces pris evy unce xxiii s. iiii. d Sm[a]	xxiii[li]. vi[s]. viii[d].
	38 Also a spone of gold weyng i unce di ꝛ di quartr pris þe unce xxiii s iiii d Sm[a]	xxxvii[s]. vi d.

(p. 23 b.)	39 Also a litil tablet of gold with tharmes of *Englond* ꝛ *F^a^unce* w^t^ a cheyne of gold made of lres and crownes and a bracelet w^t^ a litil bokk weyng all to gydres viii unces di ꝛ i. q^a^ auri p^i^s evy unce xxiii s iiii^d^ S^a^	x. li.
	40 Also anoþer litil tablet of gold garnysshed w^t^ iiii baleys ꝛ xi ples and an ymage weyng iii. unc ꝛ di quarter þe pris of all	c. s

41 " M^d'^ þ^t^ þ^e^ *xx* day of *Febr* in þe *fyrst* yere of " Kyng *Edward* þ^e^ *iiii* the seyd tablet was delyved " to þ^e^ Kynge."

42 " Et postea restituit^r^ *p^i^mo* die *Julii* a^o^ *iii*^o^ *E.* " *iiii*^ti^ p *Th Colt.*"

43 Also a purs of gold garnysshed w^t^ iiii ples a baleys ꝛ a sapher and a broche of gold wiþ ii. armes ꝛ w^t^ xxi ples and an emeraude weyng to gydre i. unce ꝛ iii q^a^rtr pris all	iiii li.

44 " M^d'^ þ^t^ þ^e^ *xx* day of *Fever* þe *first* yeer of " Kyng *Edward* þ^e^ *iiii*^e^ þe seid ii. pcell wer delyved " to þe *Kyng.*"

45 " Et postea *p^i^mo* die *Julii* a^o^ *iii*^o^. *E. iiii*^ti^ restit " in Thesaur ℞ p *Thomā Colt* Camar."

46 Also a litil Crosse of gold enameld w^t^ grene havyng ther upon xxxii. ples, w^t^ a fote of gold weyng vii unces ꝛ di pris of evy unce xxvi s viii d S^a^	x li

(p. 24.) 47 Also a peyre spores of gold w^t^ rede tisseux weyng vii. unces di ⁊ . i. q^a^rtr abate therof for þe seyd tisseux . d. unce þe pris of evy unce of gold xxiii. s. iiii. d Sm^a^ — viii^li^. iii^s^. iiii^d^

48 "M^d'^ þ^t^ þe *xx* day of *Febr* in þe *fyrst* yere of "Kyng *Edward* þ^e^ *iiii*^th^ þ^e^ seyd spores were delyved "to þ^e^ Kyng."

49 "Et postea *p*^i^*mo* die *Julii* anno *scio E. iiii*^ti^ "restituit^r^ in Thesaurar R p *Thomā Colt* Camar."

50 Also a swerd garnysshed w^t^ estriche fetherys of gold som tyme beyng þe *Prynces* of *Wales* the pris of the same swerd — xiii^li^ vi^s^ viii^d^

51 "M^d'^ þ^t^ þ^e^ *xx* day of *Febr* in þe *fyrst* yere of "Kynge *Edward* þ^e^ *iiii*^th^ þ^e^ *seyd swerd* was delyved "to þ^e^ Kyng."

52 "Et postea *p*^i^*mo* die *Julii* a^o^. *iii*^o^. *E. iiii*^ti^ "restituit^r^ in Thesaurar R p *Thomā Colt* Camar."

53 Also in a litill box ys contenyd xx litil ples iiii berell and xxiiii stonys of dyvs sortys.

54 "Libat *Regi xx*^o^ die *Febr* a^o^ *p*^i^*mo E. iiii*^ti^."

55 "Et postea *p*^i^*mo* die *Julii* a^o^. *iii*^o^ *E iiii*^ti^ resti- "tuit^r^ in Thesaur R p *Thom Colt*."

(p. 24 b.) 56 Also a standyng Tabernacle of silve and ovgilt w^t^ iiii berell standyng [upon iiii corners] for þe sacrement w^t^ iii. aungell standyng upon iii. corners upon þe fote , and — xx^li^. viii^s^. iiii^d^

the wynges of þat oon aungell hangeñ by weyng x. lb̄ ii. unc̃ ꝛ dĩ pris of ev̾y lb̄ xl s̃. Sa

57 ¶ "Quod quid̄ jocale *xviii°* die *Febr̃* anno "*xviii°* R̷ *Henr̃ sexti* Thes̃ *Angl̄* ꝛ Camar̃ de Sc^a cio "libaver̃ Magro *Stepħo Wyltoñ* Clico misso in am- "bassiata R̷ v̾sus *Cales̃* ꝛ alibi in ꝑtibꝫ *Flandr̃* ꝑ "plegio xx. li. ut patꝫ ꝑ indentur̃ rem̃ cū aliis "indentur̃ in viridi cista."

Stepħus Wyltoñ.

58 ¶ "Et postea *xviii°* die *Augusti* a°. *xxii°* dc̃i "R̷ idem *Stepħus* restituit in Thesaur̃ R̷ jocale "p̾dict̃."

59 Also anoþer standyng tab̄-nacle of silv̾e and ov̾gilt w^t a berell w^t ynne in þe myddes and w^t a crucifixe in þ^e topet of þe same weyng v lb̄ . ꝛ dĩ . p^is ev̾y lb̄ xl s̃ Sm^a — xi li

60 Also . ii. newe sensures of silv̾e and ov̾gilt &c. (*see p.* 208, *No.* 35.) Sm^a — xv^li. ii^s vi^d

61 Also ii chaundlers of silv̾e and ꝑcell gilt wherof þ^t oon lakkeþ a pyke and a bolle and þ^t oþer chaundler lakkeþ a pyke weyng to gydre xiii lb̄ ꝛ ix unc̃ p^is ev̾y lb̄ xxxii. s̃. S^a — xxii li

(p. 25.)

62 Also ii Hertes of silver and ov̾gilt weyng to gydre iiii. lb̄ . i. unce ꝛ i quartr̃ pris ev̾y lb̄. xxxiii s̃. iiii. d̄ Sm^a — vi^li xvi^s x^d

63 Also a coupe of silv̓e and ov̓gilt cov̓ed ⁊ broke and wᵗ a berell̄ in þe myddes and an aungell̄ above wᵗ a cheyne &c. Smᵃ	x. l̄i xiii s̄. iiiiᵈ
64 Also a cuppe of silver and ov̓gilt made in maner of a note weyng iii. lb̄. iiii. unces pⁱs ev̓y lb̄. xl. s̄. Smᵃ	viˡⁱ. xiiiˢ. iiiiᵈ.
65 Also a cuppe of silver of þe olde makyn̄g enameld̄ the cov̓cle garnysshed wᵗ lyons [" and þe " topet of þe same cov̓cle ys broke " of ⁊ lyth in þᵉ same cuppe"] weyng viii. lb̄ viii. unces pris ev̓y lb̄ xxxiii s̄. iiii. d̄. Smᵃ	xiiiiˡⁱ. ixˢ.
66 Also a disshe of silver and ov̓gilt weyng ii. lb̄ ix unces pris ev̓y lb̄ xl s̄ Smᵃ	cx. s̄
(p. 25 b.) 67 Also iiii. disshes of silver weyng to gydres v lb̄ xi unces pris ev̓y lb̄ xxxii. s̄. Smᵃ	ix l̄i ixˢ. iiiiᵈ.
68 Also an ewer of berell̄ garnyshed wᵗ silver and ov̓gilt weyng xxix unces pⁱs þe unce iii s̄ iiii d̄ Smᵃ	iiiiˡⁱ. xviˢ. viiiᵈ
69 Also a berell̄ to putte yn relykes, þe fote ys garnysshed wiþ silver and ov̓gilt weyng xix unces pris ev̓y unce ii. s̄. viii. d̄. Smᵃ	l s̄. viii. d̄

	70 Also ii chalys w^t ii patyns of silver and ov̄gilt weyng to gydre ii. lb̄ vi. unces pris þe lb̄. xxxiii s̃. iiii. d̄ S^a	iiii^li. iii^s. iiii^d
(p. 26.)	71 Also an ewer of silver and ov̄gilt made in maner of a condyte wiþ a fonell of whyte silver weyng xv lb̄ vi unces pris of ev̄y lb̄. liii. s̃ iiii. d̄ Sm^a	xli^li vi^s viii^d
	72 Also a lectrou̅ of silver and ov̄gilt w^t a fote in maner of a tabernacle standyng upon iiii fete. And ii. ewers of silver and ov̄gilt þat oon enameled w^t tharmes of *Inglond* and *F^aunce* and þat oþer w^t hertes. Also a tabulet w^t dyv̄s relykes conteyned w^t yn þe same standyng upon ii. lyons weyng all to gydre xxvi. lb̄ vi. unces pris ev̄y lb̄. xxxvi. s̃. viii d̄ Sm^a	xlix^li xi^s viii^d
(p. 26 b.)	73 Also a lytil cofre of silver *&c.* (*see p.* 209, *No.* 37.) pris þe lb̄. xxxvi. s̃. viii. d̄ Sm^a	lxxix s̃ vi d̄
	74 Also a pece of a ‖Bye of þe lyverey of þe *Erle Marchal* and a spyceplate of silver. And iii chaundlers of silver oon lakkyng a pyke weyng all to gydre vii. lb̄ pris þe lb̄. xxxi. s̃. Sm^a	x^li. xvii s̃

75 Also a basyn and an ewer of silver and ꝑcell gilt weyng v lb̄ xi unces ⁊ dĩ pris þe lb̄ xxxii s̃. S^{a} — viii^{li} vi^{s}. viii^{d}

(p. 27.) 76 Also a litil cuppe of silver cov̄ed gilt w^{t}oute and whyte w^{t}ynne, w^{t} a ryng and a candil-stykke of silver weyng to gydre xxii unces p^{i}s þe unce ii. s̃. viii. đ. Sm^{a} — lviii s̃. viii đ

77 Also a standyng maser of silver and gilt uncov̄ed w^{t} þarmes of *Englond* and *F^{a}unce* and w^{t} a poyse write *Good Edward* weyng xxi unces . p^{i}s þe unce . iii s̃ iiii đ Sm^{a} — lxx. s̃

78 Also anoþer standyng maser upon a light fote ꝑcheryd weyng xv unces ⁊ iii q^{a}rtr̃ pris ye unce ii s̃. vi đ. Sm^{a} — xxxix s̃ iiii đ

(p. 27 b.) 79 Also iii Gripes eyes cov̄ed garnysshed w^{t} silver and gilt weyng vi. lb̄. v. unces p^{i}s þe unce . ii. s̃. vi. đ S^{a} — ix^{li} xii^{s} vi^{d}

80 Also ii notes cov̄ed garnysshed w^{t} silver ⁊ gilt weyng xxiii unces p^{i}s þe unce ii. s̃ vi đ Sm^{a} — lvii. s̃ vi đ

81 Also ii litil masers called *Godardes* cov̄ed and anoþer litil maser uncov̄ed weyng to gydre — lxiii^{s}. ix^{d}.

ii. lb̄. i. unce ⁊ dĩ p^is þe unce ii. s̃. vi. d̄ Sm^a

82 Also a coler w^t esses of silver and ov͛gilt weyng iii. unces i. q^artr̃ pris þe unce iii s̃. iiii. d̄ Sm^a — x s̃ x d̄

(p. 28.) 83 Also a Coronall of silver and ov͛gilt beyng in dyv͛s pcell w^t doublette and w^t a pontifical ryng w^t a doublet weyng all vi. lb̄ p^is þe lb̄ xxxii. s̃. Sm^a — ix^li. xii s̃

84 " The seyd Coronall was deliv͛red to þe " *Kynge* þ^e *xx* day of *Febr̃* þ^e *fyrst* yere of his " regne."

85 " Et postea p^imo die *Julii* a^o. *iii^o*. ℞ *E iiii^ti*. " restituit^r in Thesaur̃ ℞ p *Thomā Colt* Camar̃."

86 Also a moose of silver and ov͛gilt garnysshed w^t litil ples and w^t vii doublette weyng iiii unces i q^artr̃ p^is þe unce v. s̃ Sm^a — xxi. s̃ iii d̄

87 Also a kombe of ivery garnysshed w^t silver ⁊ ov͛gilt and enameld̄ and a litil cov͛cle of silver ⁊ ov͛gilt weyng to gydre xv unces ⁊ dĩ p^is þe unce ii. s̃. vi d̄ Sm^a — xxxviii^s. ix^d.

88 Also ii. grehond̄ colers of silk enbrouded w^t lr̃es of gold and garnysshed w^t silver ⁊ ov͛gilt pris all — xl. s̃

89 “ M^{d}’ þ^{t} þ^{e} *xx* day of *Febr̃* in þ^{e} *fyrst* yer̃ of
“ Kynge *Edward* þ^{e} *iiii*th þ^{e} seyd colers were deliu̇ed
“ to þ^{e} *Kynge.*”

(p. 28 b.) 90 “ M^{d}’ qđ *xxvii*^{o} die *Januar̃*
“ anno *xix*^{o} Regis *Henr̃ sexti*
“ *Nic̄hus Yoo* Civis ⁊ Pannarius
“ *London̄* ꝑ mꝰ *Ric̄i Dewe* uniꝰ
“ Hostiar̃ Sc^{a}cii dc̄i Dn̄i Regis
“ lib̄avit Thes̄ ⁊ Cam̄ar̃ dc̄i Sc^{a}cii
“ salvo ⁊ secur̃ custodienđ, une
“ haut coupe d argent enorrez
“ appellez *l anap̄ de les pinacles*
“ pois de troie vii lb̄ pris la lb̄ xl s̄
“ S^{a} — xiii li

91 “ Qui quiđ ciphus nuꝑ invadiatus fuit *Rob̄to*
“ *Brut* Armigꝰo ⁊ *Witt̄o Braunspath̄* Armigꝰo ꝑ *Ric̄m*
“ *Courtenay* nuꝑ Ep̄m *Norwicen̄* nuꝑ Thes̄ Cam̄e
“ Regis *Henr̃ quinti* ꝑ securitate vadioꝝ ⁊ regardoꝝ
“ suoꝝ.”

(p. 29.) 92 Also a tabulet of gold w^{t}
an ymage of *Seynt George* hauyng
a crosse upon hys armure gar-
nysshed w^{t} xviii rub̄ i diamanđ
and ix ꝑles and hys helme gar-
nysshed w^{t} a rub̄ and uppon þe
ende of hys sper̃ i ꝑle and hys
shelde garnysshed with vii bal̄ and
xxvii ꝑles and þe seyd tabulet gar-
nysshed withinne w^{t} v bal̄ v. saph̄
and xvi. ꝑles [“ and a peler of þ^{e}
“ same is broke”] and w^{t}owte with
vi bal̄ xi. saph̄ and lxviii ꝑles and — ciiii^{xx}xix^{li}. vi^{s}. viii. đ

þe fote of þe seyd tabulet garnysshed w^t^. ii. esmeraud̃ ii bal̃ vi. sapħ ꝉ xxxii ꝑles and w^t^ xii lyons enamelyd whyte somtyme yevyñ un to y^e^ *Kyng* by Quene *Johane* weyng vi. lƀ i. unc̃ pris of eu͛y unce of þ^e^ gold xxvi s̃. viii. d̃ s^a^ iiii^xx^xvii^li^ vi^s^ viii^d^ the sōme of þe perrey cii. ľi. the hole sōme of the tabulet comeþ to

93 Also a saler of gold cou͛ed and made like a Carle garnysshed w^t^ vii bal̃ vii sapħ l ꝑles and þe cou͛cle garnysshed w^t^ iiii ꝑles [and þ^e^ fote of þ^e^ same ys ꝑcell̃ broke] somtyme yevyn un to þe *Kyng* by the Duke of *Gloucestr̃* weyng li. unce pris eu͛y unce xxvi^s^. viii^d^. s^a^ lxviii ľi. the pris of the perrey xxiii. ľi. the hole sōme of þ^e^ saler cometh to — iiii^xx^xi ľi

(p. 29 b.) 94 Also a tabulet of gold w^t^ an ymage of *Seynt George* garnysshed w^t^ xiii bal̃ xiii. sapħ cxii ꝑles and uppon þe sayde tabulet a Crucifix garnysshed w^t^ ii. bal̃ ii. sapħ ꝉ xxvii ꝑles and uppon þe breste of the said ymage a ruƀ yevyn unto þe *Kyng* of þe biquest of the right noble Pryncesse Quene *Kat͛ine* weyng viii lƀ viii unc̃ dĩ pris of eu͛y unce — ccvii ľi of þe gold xxvi s̃ viii đ sa cxxxix łi vi. s̃ viii đ the pris of þe perrey lxvii łi xiii. s̃. iiii đ the hole sōme of þe tabulet cometħ to

(p. 30.) 95 Md' qđ *xiiii°* die *Marcii* anno r̃ R̷ *Henr̃ sexti xxii°* *Jol̃es Merstoñ* Armig̃ Custos jocaliū Dñi Regis lib̃avit in Thesaurar̃ Regis jocalia subscripta videłt

96. ¶ First ii grete flagoūs of silver and gilt chaced and made in maner of scalopis weyng of troye weyght lxiiii. lƀ ix. unc̃ iii. qart̃.

97 ¶ Also a saler of gold cov̓ed and made in maner of a man wt a kendale hode upon hys hede and stonding upon a tarrage enamelid grene and whight and þe sayd saler in all ys garnysshed wt xii rubies xxiiii ꝑles and a saph̃ upoñ þe topet weyng xxi. unc̃ i qart̃.

98 ¶ Also an other saler of jaspis cov̓ed and garnysshed wt gold and wt xlvii rubies cxviii ꝑł and vi smale ꝑł hanging upon þe topet of þe cov̓cle of þe same saler weyng xxiii. unc̃.

(p. 30 b.) 99 ¶ Be yt remembred þt þe *xie* day of *Apprilł* the yeer of þe regne of our Sov̓ayne Lord Kyng *Herry* þe *sext* þe *xxiiie* Sir *Willam Estfeld* Knyght and *Thomas Broun* Squyer have delyv̓ed un to *Rauff* Lord *Sudeley* Tresorer of *England* þis jewelł underwrite whiche was bought of *John Rollyngswerd* Marchaunt of *Almayne* and servaunt to þe Erchebisshop̃ of *Coloigne* unto þe use of our seyd Sov̓ayne Lord þe Kyng for ml ml mark.

100 ¶ A peytrewe of gold garnysshed wᵗ x diamandꝭ lxx rubees cxl grete ꝑles and a nouche hangyng upon þe same peytrewe garnysshed wᵗ a grete diamanđ flat lozengwise iii feyre rubees and iii grete ꝑles weyng in all wᵗ ii. cheynes xiii. mᵃrƺ iii. unc̃ dĩ.

101 ¶ The whiche jeweƚƚ forth̄ wᵗ þe *same day* the seyd Tresorer of *England* bare yt un to þe *Kyng*.

(p. 31.) 102 ¶ Also a tab̄nacle wᵗ an ymage of *Seynt George* of gold garnysshed wᵗ dyv̾s stonys ⁊ ꝑles late bought of *Willᵃm Estfelđ* Knyght for mˡ mˡ markꝭ þe whiche tab̄nacle ys discryved in þis wyse. A tab̄nacle in þe maner of a casteƚƚ of silver ⁊ ov̾gilt wᵗ an ymage of gold of *Seynt George* garnysshed wᵗ stonys ⁊ ꝑles þᵗ ys to say upon þe hede and þe body of þe seyđ [*George*] garnysshed wᵗ xix balys xx diamantꝭ. ii. smale rubees vii. saphers cix ꝑles. Also a sheld of gold garnysshed wᵗ vii grete balies cxvi. ꝑles. Also a sper̃ [of gold] garnysshed wᵗ xi. balyes i saffre xxxi. ꝑles. Also a litil swerd [of gold] garnysshed wᵗ vii smale balyes i diamante xx ꝑles. Also a Dragon of gold under þe said *George* garnysshed wᵗ ii. rubies in þe yeñ xiii baleys iii safres iii esmerauđ iiiiˣˣ vi. ꝑles. Also above þe seyd casteƚƚ ys a Kyng ⁊ a Quene of gold garnysshed wᵗ ♣ stones ⁊ ꝑles þᵗ ys to seye ♣ xxi baleys xvii. saffres and ‖bye aboute þe Quenes nekke garnysshed wᵗ v. rubies v. diamantꝭ and upon þe templers beth ii. rubies ⁊ ii. diamantꝭ and upon þe ymages of þe Kyng and þe Quene be clv ꝑles. Also a damyseƚƚ of gold garnysshed w^t xxii smale rubies i. diamant iiii saffres lx ples and a lambe of gold white enameld. Also i aungell of gold w^t i. nouche garnysshed w^t iii. rubies iii ples i. diamant in þe myddes and upon þe same aungell be x. balys iii saffres xxxiii. ples and upon hys hande ys a rubee. Also ii. wenges of þe same aungell be garnysshed w^t xlii. balys clii ples pond. lii. m^a rc iii unc.

(p. 31 b.) 103 ¶ A nouche of gold garnysshed w^t iii grete baleys ⁊ a grete saphir and in þe myddes of þe same nouche ys a grete ple made in þe maner of a cocle w^t iii cheynes of gold hangyng atte þe ende of evy cheyne a grete ple.

104 ¶ Also anoþer nouche of gold garnysshed w^t iiii grete baleys and in þe myddes ys a grete ple made in þe maner of a cocle w^t iii cheynes of gold hangyng atte þe ende of evy cheyne a grete ple.

105 ¶ Whiche ii. nouches wer bought of þe executo^rs of þe Lorde *Fawnhope* for } DXL. li

(p. 32.) 106 ¶ Also a tablet of gold called *þe Tablet of Lancastre* garnysshed w^t xvi baleys iii rub liiii ples ⁊ ii saphers weyng al to gedere lxii m^a rȝ iiii unc of troye.

107 ¶ Also a tablet of gold called *þe Tablet of Burgoigne* garnysshed w^t xxvi baleys xxii saphers cxlii ples weyng in all lxx m^a rȝ.

(p. 32 b.) 108 ¶ Also an image of *Seynt George* garnysshed w^t. viii baleys clxxviii ples weyng all to geder viii lb x. unc.

109 ¶ Also a cuppe of gold coṽed of kermery werk̃ wᵗ iii scuchons of þᵉ *Kynges armes* in þe toppe weyng iiii markꝭ ii. unc̃ dĩ.

(p. 33.) 110 ¶ Also i. ymage of *Seynt Michael* garnysshed wᵗ clii. ꝑles iiii saphers xxiii. baleys weyng all̃ to geders xi lb̃. v. unc̃.

INVENTORY

OF THE

REGALIA AND GOLD PLATE

OF

HEN. VIII.

I.

(A. 6. 22.) Juellę of golde certeñ of them garnished w[t] stone and ple and certeñ ungarnisshed.
(p. 4 b.)

1 Furste the *Kingis Crowne* of golde the bordure garnysshed w[t] six balacis five saphures five poynted dyamontę twenti rubyes nyntene ples and iiii collettę w[t]-oute stones and one of the crosses of the same *Crowne* garnysshed w[t] a greate saphure an emerade ||crasid iiii balacis and nyne ples not all of a sorte.

Item opon the lefte side of the same crosse a *flower de luce* set w[t] an image of *Criste* w[t] a greate balace broken and a lesse balace a poyntyd dyamont twoo ples a collett w[t]oute a stone and a crampioñ w[t]oute a ple.

Item next that an other crosse w^{t} a course saphure foure course balacis a fayer litell emerade a lozengid dyamont like a harte a rubye eight ꝑles and a crampion w^{t}oute a ꝑle.

Item next that an other *flower de lnce* sett w^{t} a *Seynt George* a fayer balace a poyntyd dyamont three ꝑles a collett w^{t}oute a stone ⁊ a leeff w^{t}oute collett ⁊ stone.

iiii^{xx}. x. oz.

Itm̃ ||nex that an other crosse w^{t} a large rounde saphure foure balaces foure ꝑles a collett w^{t}oute a stone and five crampyones w^{t}oute ꝑles.

Itm̃ next that an other *flower de luce* sett w^{t} an image of *our Lady* ⁊ her childe a balace a poyntid dyamont three ꝑles and twoo collettꝭ w^{t}oute stones.

Item nex that an other crosse sett w^{t} ii saphures foure balaces eight ꝑles ⁊ a crampioñ w^{t}oute a ꝑle.

Itm̃ next that an other *flower de luce* sett w^{t} an image of *Criste* a balace a poyntyd dyamont three ꝑles and two collettꝭ w^{t}oute stones.

Item next that an other crosse sett w^{t} a course saphure foure balaces nynȩ ꝑles ⁊ a collett wt-oute a stone.

Item next that an other *flower de luce* sett wt an image of *Criste* wt a balace a small poyntid dyamont three ꝑles and twoo collettꝭ wtoute stones.

Itm̃ on the dyadyme above xii. poyntyd dyamontꝭ sōme better then the other iii triangle dyamontꝭ one table dyamont and twenty eight ꝑles twoo in a troche weyinge to giders

2 Item a *payer of brasselettꝭ* garnysshed wt six balaces not fyne six bigge course ꝑles moche of a sorte ⁊ v lesser ꝑles of a sorte weyinge to giders wt twoo blacke lase poyntes — vii. oz. dĩ.

3 Item a *Septo*r *of golde* wt a dove theropon weyinge — xii. oz.

4 Item a *Rodde of golde* weyinge — iii. oz dĩ. dĩ qarť.

5 Item a *Rounde Balle* wt a crosse of golde weyinge — xvii. oz dĩ

6 Item the *Quenes Crowne of golde* the bordure sett wt six saphures not alł of a fynes twoo lesse saphures six balaces not fyne foure smałł balaces of litełł

	value twenty and foure bigge ples not fyne and eight smałł ples Item six crosses of golde ev̛y crosse sett wᵗ a saphure a balace ꝛ iiii ples not greate Item six *flower de luces* of golde ev̛y flower de luce sett wᵗ a balace a saphure ꝛ v smałł ples the saphures ꝛ balaces not fyne wᵗ a dyadyme ꝛ a crosse of golde not garnysshed weyinge to giders	xlvii. oz
(p. 5.)	7 Item a *Septoʳ* of golde wᵗ a *dove* ‖one the knopp̃ for the *Quene* waying	vi. oz . qᵃrter
	8 Item a *Serclett* of golde for the *Quene* sett wᵗ a fayer emerade foure faire saphures foure roosys of dyamontꝭ foure balaces all sett in rooses and xiiii ples like of a sorte weyinge wᵗ the silke	xviii. oz . dĩ.
	9 Item a tablett of golde wᵗ reliques called the *Tablet of Burbone* garnyshed wᵗ the iiii Evangelistꝭ eight saphures not fyne and x course balasses the glasse of the leves broken in many placꝭ and dyv̛se of the reliques shaken oute lackyng one claspe weying to gidders	clxxvii. oz dĩ.

10 Ītm a *cheyne of golde* pte enaymyled white and redde wa-inge	x oz. dī.
11 Item twenty smalle *cheynes of golde* wayinge to gidders	xx. oz iii. quarts.
12 Item a *Coller of golde* conteynyng xxvi garters knytte to gidders wt xxvi. laces of golde for the *Kyngs* waryng wayinge	xxviii oz qrt. dī.
13 Item a *George* ‖one horssebake the forepte of the *George* of dyamonts the mayle of his curaces and rivett of the same of silver dī gilte wt a swerde in his hande of golde a lozengid dyamont like a shilde and a dragon of golde wayinge	iii oz dī. dī qart.
14 Item a *Coller of golde* wrought wt paunsis and roosis white and redde wayinge	xviii oz. qart.
15 Item a *Cheyne of golde* of a good fasshion the one half enamyled white and redde wayinge	xviii. oz qart.
16 Item a pece of an *unicornes horne* not garnysshed weyinge	iii qart. dī scant.
17 Ītm an other *cheyne of golde* of the same the one half enamyled white and blewe wayinge	xi. oz iii qarts dī.

18 Itm̃ a *braunche of golde* wt five serpent tonges weyinge	xv. oz . dĩ.
19 Itm̃ a *coller* of lyle pottꝭ wt a griffen golde the wyngꝭ and hooke sylver wayinge	xvii oz iii. q̃rtꝭs
20 Itm̃ a *devise of golde* of paunsis wayinge	vii . oz . iii qartꝭs dĩ.
21 Itm̃ a *horne of golde* enamyled wt redde and white columbynes wt a girdyƚƚ of silke enbrawdred wt redde and white roosis wayinge	vii . oz.
(p. 5 b.) 22 Item a *botell* for roosewater of golde blewe enamyled wt butterflyes golde garnysshed wt xii good ꝑles of ii. sortꝭ wayinge	xiii. oz iii. qartꝭs
23 Itm̃ an image of *Seynt George* on horssebake in a *camewe* sett in golde wt a litell cheyne weyinge	iii. oz qartꝭ.
24 Itm̃ an image of a *woman* in a *camewe* sett in golde wt a cheyne wayinge	ix. oz . qartꝭ.
25 Itm̃ a *yerde of Moyses* garnysshed wt golde wt the armys of *Englanđ* and *Casteƚƚ* wayinge	iiii. oz iii qartꝭs.
26 Itm̃ a *roose* of golde wt ix braunches of rosis of golde gar-	

nysshed w^t leves and buddes and a light saphure in the toppe stondyng opon a foote borne upe w^t iii oxen of golde wayinge } xxi. oz iii q^{a}rt̃s.

27 Itm̃ a *garter* wrought in the stole garnysshed w^t golde way-inge } iii. q^{a}rt̃s dĩ.

28 Itm̃ a *devyse of golde* sett w^t xxviii course rubyes and xxvii small hangyng ꝑles waying } viii oz . iii q^{a}rt̃s.

29 Itm̃ a *garter* wrought in the stole the bocle pendaunt lr̃es and barres of golde enamyled wayinge } ii. oz . dĩ scant.

30 Itm̃ a *devise* of golde w^t columbynes sett w^t iiii course rubyes a light triangle diamont and vi ꝑles wayinge } vi. oz . dĩ dĩ q^{a}rt̃.

31 Itm̃ a *cheyne* of golde enamyled white and redde con-teynyng xlviii lynkꝭ wayinge } xii. oz . dĩ q^{a}rter.

32 Itm̃ twoo *ꝑper bells* of golde for *hawkes* wayinge } dĩ oz dĩ q^{a}rt̃.

33 Itm̃ a lytyll tablett of golde *w^t our Lady* graven in a garnett and a lytyll ꝑle a cheyne and a hooke wayinge } ii oz . iii q^{a}rt̃s dĩ.

34 Itm̃ a *Fawcon* of a *camewe* the hede golde w^t a garland sett

wᵗ vi litell course emerades and six course balaces and his breste sett wᵗ iiii course broken emerades ꝛ seven other emerades twoo course balaces and viii ꝑles bordured aboute wᵗ lytyll small emerades and lxvi small garnysshyng ꝑles and opon the tayle iiii small emerades a course balace and xxxviii garnysshyng ꝑles and iii bigge ꝑles wayinge	xxvii. oz dĩ scant.
35 Itm a lytell *George* of golde to hange at a *coller of garters* wayinge	i. oz . qᵃrt dĩ.
(p. 6.) 36 Itm a *coller of garters* wᵗ a *George* of crowne gold wayinge	xxx oz dĩ dĩ qrt.
37 Itm a *roose* of golde wᵗ ix braunches stondyng opon iii. acornes ꝛ a course saphure in the toppe wayinge	xxi. oz.
38 Itm a *rose* of golde wᵗ ix braunches stondyng opon three lyones feete and a course saphure in the toppe wayinge	xix. oz dĩ.
39 Itm a *castyng botell* of golde wᵗ a lytell cheyne wᵗ a white roose and [a] redde in a bussell a both sides wayinge	ix oz . qᵃrt.
40 Itm a *goodly bawderyke* of golde and therin viii fayer	

balaces stondyng ‖betwne angellę wᵗ xxxvi ꝑles wayinge aƚƚ to gidders	iiii^xx xvii oz dĩ.
41 Itm̃ a *coller* of *Spaynisshe* worke wherin byn xvi fayer balacę vi great poyntyd dyamontę twoo great rockyd dyamontę twoo great table dyamontę square lozengid one other longe table dyamont square one other dyamont harte fasshioned one table dyamont six square a greate tryangle dyamont one longe lozengid dyamont and the great myrroʳ wayinge aƚƚ to gidders	iiii^xx viii oz scant.
42 Itm̃ a *cheyne* of golde gable fasshion wàyinge	vi^xx. iiii oz dı.
43 Itm̃ a *bezaunte* of golde weyinge	†

II.

(p. 6 b.) Crucifixis of golde certen of them garnisshed wᵗ stone ⁊ ꝑle ⁊ certen ungarnisshed.

1 Item a *crucifix* of golde wᵗ an image twoo angellę stonding ‖one ii pyllers sett ‖one a base of golde havyng in their hands twoo chalices the crosse fuƚƚ garnysshed wᵗ smaƚƚ ꝑles and vi. smaƚƚ balaces	xxii oz iii q̃rt̃s dĩ.

of no fynes ii borne wt twoo angellꝭ wayinge

2 Itm a crucifix of golde stondyng upon vi pillers wt iiii pynnacles and iiii ꝑles the base sett wt an emerade a saphure twoo dyamontꝭ sett in twoo troches wt iiii ꝑles in a troche and in the same base xii troches or tuftꝭ wherof vii byne sett wt counterfaite stones or glasses and xlvi garnysshing ꝑles vi white hartꝭ opon the bace wt crownes ii hole cheynes and ii. peces of cheynes [of golde] ||aboutꝭ their neckes and lxxvi small ꝑles upon the hartꝭ hede ⁊ amongs the hartꝭ v. busshes wt xxi. smalł ꝑles and an image of our *Lady of Pite* sett wt a light saphure viii stones or glasses of no value and xxxii smalł ꝑles and an image of *Seynt John Baptist* sett wt a light saphure ix glasses or stones ⁊ xxxii ꝑles wtin the pynnacles, and wtin and opon the pynnacles xxxii smalł ꝑles twoo angellꝭ holdyng a balasse garnysshed wt xvi. smalł ꝑles in ałł opon both sides and opon the foote of the crosse *Mary* and *John* sett wt xli smale ꝑles and opon the crosse a crucifix sett wt twoo balaces twoo saphures and iiii^{xx} xvii smale ꝑles wayinge — lxxiiii oz qart.

3 Item a *crosse of golde* broken wt one image stondyng opon a base of sylver and gilte the image nayled wt three poynted dyamontę in his side a balace and one his dyadyme twoo course saphures a course balace and vii bigge ꝑles the crosse garnysshed wt xli good garnysshing ꝑles the enameƚƚ of the image defased and the arme broken wayinge to gidders — xl. oz. scant.

4 Itm̃ a *ꝑper crosse* wt a crucifix weƚƚ wrought sett wt iiii. light balaces and iiii. ꝑles wayinge — xi oz iii quarts dĩ.

5 Itm̃ a *crucifix* of golde wt three poyntid dyamontę and an image havyng a ruby in his side wayinge — †

6 Itm̃ a crosse of the *Holly crosse* garnysshed wt golde wt iii light balaces ⁊ twoo light saphures wt a cheyne of golde wayinge to gidders — †

(p. 7.) 7 Item a *crosse of golde* stondyng opon a mountayne garnysshed one the one side wt vii dyamontę of dyvse sortes and eight lr̃es of dyamontę full garnysshed wt ꝑle and one the other side a fayre rubye a pyllor, a

sponge a spare a ladder all fully garnysshed savyng one staff of the ladder whiche ys lackyng and iii images also stondyñg opon the said mountayne either of them havyng a dyadyme fully garnysshed w^t smale ꝑle wey-inge	iiii^{xx} xi oz.

III.

(p. 7 b.) Chalacis cruettꝭ ⁊ holliwat͛stockꝭ of golde certeñ garnisshed w^t stone ⁊ ꝑle ⁊ certeñ ungarnisshed

1 Item a *chalice of golde* chasid w^t braunchis and iiii images [enamyled] w^t a patent graved w^t the *Trynite* wayinge	xxv oz q^{a}rt͛.
2 Itm̃ a *chalice of golde* w^t a patent enamyled w^t the *Trynyte* opon the patent and *Mari* and *John* wayinge	l oz . iii. q^{a}rt͛s.
3 Item two *cruettꝭ* of golde w^t xii roses white ⁊ redde ‖one their feete pois	xvi. oz iii q^{a}rt͛s.
4 Itm̃ a *holly waterstocke* of golde garnysshed w^t five smale dyamontꝭ xiii smale rubyes one course emerade xix ꝑles ℌ. and ‖ℜ. crownyd w^t a strincle and a smałł cheyne of golde wayinge	xxiiii. oz . q^{a}rt͛.

5 Itm a *holly waterstocke* of golde wt a light saphure in a roose white and redde the handell garnysshed wt iiii smale rubyes a smale poyntyd dyamont ⁊ twoo small dyamontę triangle wt xvi garnysshing ples a litell cheyne and a holliwaterstrincle garnysshed wt xii. garnysshing ples weyinge	xxv. oz qarť.
6 Itm a *chalice of golde* enamyled grene wt a patent havyng one the inside an image of the *Trynite* enamyled redde and one the other side the *Cardynallę armys* weyinge	lviii. oz. dĩ.
7 Item a *chalice of golde* sett wt stone and ple wantyng one stone weyinge xlvi oz. iii qarťs havyng a patent of sylver and gilte weyinge x oz. and weyinge all to giders	lvi oz iii qarťs.
8 Item a *payer of cruettę* of golde thone markyd wt A. and the other wt A. W. in the toppes weyinge	ix. oz iii qarťs.

IV.

(p. 8.) Images of golde certen of theme garnisshed wt stone and ple ⁊ certen ungarnisshed.

1 Item an image of *Seynt George* of golde stondyng one a

base of sylver and gilte w^{t} a mayden and a lambe w^{t} xi ꝑles one her hede and under Seynt *George* ys ffeete a dragon of sylver w^{t} iiii braunches of golde and opon the shilde a balace ⁊ viii good ꝑles and opon his sleves lii smale ꝑles and opon his girdyll v course balaces iiii ꝑles w^{t} iiii bellis opon his bawderike xviii bellis xiiii light rubyes and xvii smale ꝑles and opon his helmet a tufte w^{t} an estriche feder twoo balaces ⁊ xi good ꝑles w^{t} a swerd in his hande of silver the pomell a ꝑle wayinge — ci. oz q^{a}rt.

2 Itm̃ a hede of *Seynt Thom^{a}s* of *Canterbury* of golde stondyng opon a base w^{t} vi course stones or glasses and vi troches of small garnysshing ꝑles eũy troche conteynyng five ꝑles w^{t} a coller aboute his necke sett w^{t} five course stones or glasses and three troches eũy troche conteyning v ꝑles and one troche conteynyng iiii ꝑles and the bordure of his mito^{r} sett w^{t} viii course stones or glasses and vii troches conteynyng in all xxxiii smalle ꝑles and in the residue of the mito^{r} xviii course stones or glasses and iiii^{xx} iii smale ꝑles wayinge — vii. oz q^{a}rt.

3 Itm an image of *Seynt Xpo-fer* of golde stondyng opon iiii pillers the base sett w^t xiii saphures xi balaces and lxviii smale ples and thre trees sett w^t xliii smale ples the *Xpofer* w^t *our Lorde* ‖one his sholder and a staff w^t a saphure in his hand twoo men at his feete wherof one of them w^t a lanthorne wayinge	lxii. oz iii q^a rters.
4 Itm an image of *Seynt George* of ivery garnisshed w^t golde w^t a *joynte of Seynt George* enclosed wayinge	ix oz qrter.

V.

(p. 8 b.) Paxis tablettę tabernacles ꝛ corporas cases of golde certen garnisshed w^t stone and ple ꝛ certen ungarnisshed

1 Itm a paxe of golde of the Baptyme of *Criste* garnisshed w^t ten rubyes and xxiiii garnysshing ples and a saphure sett in the toppe wayinge	x oz. scant.
2 Itm a tablett or monstraunce of golde w^t an image of *Seynt John the Evangeliste* writyng garnisshed opon the base w^t iii course balaces v course sparkes of emerades xx^ti garnysshing ples havyng	xl. oz iii qrtrs.

opon all the rest seven saphures v. balaces xii smalƚ sparkes of emerades and lxi smale ꝑles wey-inge

3 Itm̃ a tablett of golde sett wt viii light garnisshing saphures ix good ꝑles *the Trinite* wt vi other imagꝭ golde ⁊ closed in the foote wt *costa Sc̃i Andree* wt a cheyne and a hooke sett wt a light saphure wayinge to gidders — xxv oz iii qartꝭs.

4 Item a tabernacle of golde wt *our Lady* techyng her sonne wt an angeƚƚ bering an owche sett wt a smale balace and five good garnisshing ꝑles wt iiii angellꝭ beryng iiii light garnysshing ba-laces ⁊ a light table saphure wt an ymage in the toppe ⁊ a litell ꝑle waying — xvi oz dĩ dĩ qart.

5 Itm̃ a tablet of golde of *the Salutacyon of our Lady* garnysshed wt margarettꝭ wayinge — xxv.oz dĩ. dĩ qart.

6 Item a tabernacle of golde wt byrraƚƚ and wtin the byrraƚƚ the *Trynite* and *our Lady* wt her childe in her armys garnysshed wt ꝑles and above the *Salutacyon of our Lady Seynt John Baptist Seynt Kateryñ* and an angeƚƚ weyinge — xxii oz dĩ.

7 Item a tabernacle of golde w^{t} *our Lady of Pyty* w^{t} her sonne in her lappe w^{t} ii angellẻ behynde garnysshed w^{t} a bigge light rubye and garnysshing ꝑles w^{t} a cheyne ꞇ a hooke wayinge	x. oz.
8 Item a *corporace case* of golde garnysshed w^{t} vi course saphures twoo course balaces ꞇ x course ꝑles weyinge	clxix oz dĩ.

VI.

(p. 9.) Cuppis bollys and cuppis of assaye of golde certen garnisshed w^{t} stone ꞇ ꝑle ꞇ certen ungarnisshed

1 Item a *cuppe of golde* garnissed w^{t} roosis [enamyled] white and redde the knoppe a crowne impiall w^{t} vi small hangyng ꝑles and one the bordure [of the] cover and foote xv light stones or glasses wayinge	lxxi. oz iii. q̃rt͛s.
2 Itm̃ a *cuppe of golde* w^{t} imageri the knoppe a crowne impiall and aboute the bordure [of the] cover and foote a crowne garnisshed w^{t} lxii garnysshing ꝑles weyinge	lxxix. oz.
3 Item a *cuppe of golde* pounsid w^{t} wrethes of roosis wayinge	lxi. oz . scant.

4 Itm a *cuppe of golde* chasid wt flower de lucis the knoppe a crowne impiall garnysshed wt ix small poyntyd dyamonte and xiiii smale garnysshinge ples wayinge } lii. oz scant.

5 Itm a *cuppe of golde* called the *Dreame of Parris* havyng opon the cover therof the images of *Parris Jupiter Venus Pallas* and *Juno* and *Parris* horsse opon the cover garnysshed wt xix dyamonte greate and smale and [in] the vth bordure of the same cover xxxi gret rubyes *Jupiter* garnysshed wt ten small rubyes and *Parris* helmett garnysshed wt ii smalle rubyes *Venus* and *Pallas* either of them havyng one small rubye opon their brest *Juno* lackyng her chaplett the horsse of *Parris* havyng vii smalle rubyes havyng also opon five bordures of the said coverynge xlti greate ples *Jupiter* havyng his garment garnysshed wt xxxi small ples *Parris* havyng one smale ple opon the toppe of his cappe *Venus* havyng twoo ples hanging downe from her chaplett *Pallas* havyng no ples and *Juno* havyng opon her chaplett hangyng downe ii smale ples and opon her buttocke other ii smalle ples and the horsse gar- } cxx. oz.

nysshed wᵗ xxvii ꝑles greate and smale wᵗ a small fane in the toppe of the cover the cuppe havyng opon the foote and shanke xxvi rubyes greate and smalle ix dyamonts of dyṽse sorts iiii saphures xxxiiiiᵗⁱ ꝑles great ꞇ smalł waying to gidders	
6 Item a *cuppe of golde* chasid wᵗ roosis flower de lucys and margarettꝭ lozengid wᵗ wrethis white and redde ꞇ grene enamyled wᵗ a lyon one the toppe in a baskett garnysshed wᵗ lxviii ꝑles wayinge	liiii. oz dĩ dĩ qᵃrt̃.
(p. 9 b.) 7 Item a *cuppe of golde* wᵗ margarettꝭ garnisshed aboute the bordure [of the] foote and cover wᵗ iii light saphures and nyne balacys and xxiii garnysshinge ꝑles wᵗ roosis enamyled white and redde and opon the knoppe a white roose wᵗ a greate course saphure wayinge	xlvii oz iii. qᵃrt̃s.
8 Itm̃ a *cuppe of gold* imbossid wᵗ redde and white margarettꝭ wᵗ a crowne above the cover and foote garnysshed wᵗ xxvi garnysshyng stones or glasses and xlvi garnysshyng ꝑles the knoppe a crowne impiałł weyinge	xlvii oz iii q̃rt̃s dĩ

9 It̃m a *cuppe or bole of golde* chasid and garnysshid w^{t} roosis white and redde crowned w^{t} a knoppe garnysshed w^{t} lxiii garnysshyng ꝑles and a balace weyinge	iiii^{xx} iiii oz dĩ.
10 It̃m a *cuppe of golde* welł wrought w^{t} lozengis . 𝔥. and . 𝔎. crownyd the knoppe crownyd w^{t} a dyadyme w^{t} v garnysshinge ꝑles wayinge	l. oz.
11 Item a *cuppe of golde* chasid w^{t} waterflowers the foote garnysshed w^{t} iiii light saphures iiii light balacis and xxiiii garnysshinge ꝑles and the shanke garnisshed w^{t} ii course saphures ii course balacys and xvi ꝑles the bordure of the cover garnysshed w^{t} viii light saphures viii light balacys and xlviii ꝑles the knoppe a crowne impiałł garnysshed w^{t} iiii course rubyes and xiiii smale ꝑles wayinge	xlii. oz iii. q^{a}rt̃s.
12 It̃m a *cuppe of golde* w^{t} a wreth̃ like a crowne aboute the cover and foote sett w^{t} clxxv garnisshinge ꝑles wayinge	xlii oz . q̃rt̃.
(p. 11.) 13 It̃m a *cuppe of golde* and *byrrałł* w^{t} viii imag̃e enamyled opon the cover and iiii images opon the foote wayinge	xvii oz dĩ.

	14 Itm̃ a *cuppe of jasper* garnysshed wᵗ golde wayinge	xxix. oz . dĩ.
	15 Item a *cuppe of golde* graven wᵗ roosis and poundegarnettę wᵗ a redde roose and a white one the cover wayinge	xiiii oz iii q̃rt̃s.
	16 Itm̃ a *stondyng cuppe of golde* wel̃l wrought wᵗ roosis white and redde one the cover body and foote wᵗ a crowne impial̃l garnysshid wᵗ xi course stones or glasses and xxxii garnysshinge ples weyinge	li. oz qᵃrt̃ scant.
	17 Itm̃ a *stondyng̃ bol̃l of golde* wel̃l wrough̃t garnisshed wᵗ white ꝛ redde roosis one the foote and cover garnysshed wᵗ iiii course stones or glasses ꝛ xi course garnysshinge ples wayinge	cxxviii oz scant.
(p. 10.)	18 Item a *stondyng bole of golde* pounsid wᵗ greate marteletteę the knoppe a crowne imperial̃l weyinge	lxxvii oz q̃rt̃.
	19 Itm̃ a *bolle of crowne gold* caret v. đ in evy unce the foote garnysshed wᵗ vi garnysshing balacis moche after a sorte ꝛ vi greate ples wᵗ vi smale ples after a sorte and one the cover xxiiii balacis moche after a sorte and xviii troches of good garnisshinge ples twoo in evy troche and vi	cxlii. oz.

ꝑles one in a troche moche of the same sorte and aboute the knoppe eight smale balacis after one sorte and xvi ꝑles after a sorte and opon the knoppe a table balace ⁊ a rockey balace w^t iiii fayer ꝑles and *Sampson̄* bestridyng a lyon̄ in the myddes wayinge aƚƚ to gidders	
20 Itm̃ a *bolle of golde* w^t a cover and the *Kynge͛ armys* in a garter w^t a crowne impiaƚƚ wayinge.	lxxvi oz q̃rt͛.
21 Item a *cuppe of golde* w^t a cover chasid rockey and a dĩ knoppe w^t the *Kynge͛ armys* weyinge	lx oz iii q̃rt͛s dĩ.
22 Itm̃ a *cuppe of golde* weƚƚ wrought w^t a pellicane opon the knoppe wayinge	lviii oz.
23 Itm̃ a *cuppe of golde* w^t a cover chasid bulliones w^t two bordures aboute the body and cover and opon the knoppe ii nakyd boyes holdyng the *Kynge͛ armys* w^t a crowne impiaƚƚ wayinge	lxii oz iii q^art͛s scant.
24 Item a *cuppe of golde* w^t a cover chasid rockey havyng thre bordures of leves enamyled aboute the body cover and knoppe and opon the knoppe iii angelle͛ beryng a crowne impiall wayinge	lxi. oz dĩ.

25 Itm a *cuppe of golde* w^t^ a cover the cover havyng dragones hedd*e* enamyled white and redde w^t^ braunches of roosis betwixt them and chasid w^t^ dropes underneth and the knoppe havyng a rose enamyled white and redde the body chasid w^t^ runnyng leves havyng two angell*e* of either side w^t^ the *Kyngs armys* and w^t^ dragons and greyhound*e* chasid beringe them the shanke of the cuppe havyng runnyng leves enamyled white and redde the foote pounsid w^t^ droopes and chasid w^t^ ronnyng leves wayinge	lviii oz q^a^rt.
(p. 10 b.) 26 Item a *cuppe of golde* w^t^ a cover the foote w^t^ a wreth of leves redde enamyled and aboute the body and cover twoo wrethes enamyled redde and grene ⁊ opon the knoppe a dragone ⁊ a greyhounde beryng the *Kyngis armys* w^t^ a crowne impiall weyinge	lxv. oz.
27 Itm a *cuppe of assaye* of *crowne golde* weyinge	vii oz dĩ q^a^rt scant.
28 Item a *cuppe of golde* w^t^ a cover and iii bordures aboute the foote cuppe ⁊ cover and under the knoppe three wormeshedes and opon the knoppe a white roose and a redde wayinge	lix oz iii q^a^rts.

29 Item a *cuppe of golde* garnysshed w^t roosis flower de lucis . 𝔥 . and . 𝕽 . w^t a crowne aboute the cover the knoppe a crowne impiall wayinge } xlviii oz dī.

30 Item a *cuppe of golde* w^t a cover and theropon an angell knelyng w^tin five pyllers holdyng a *Cardynallꝭ hatte* and w^tin the cover under the pomell the *Cardynallꝭ armys* and a *Cardynallꝭ hatte* enamyled weyinge } lviii oz dī.

31 Item a *cuppe of golde* w^t a cover and therõ an image of *Seynt Kateryne* enamyled white w^t a wreth of pomegarnettꝭ aboute it weyinge } xxxiiii oz dī.

32 Itm a *cuppe of golde* w^t a cover w^t the *Cardynalls armys* holdeñ w^t ii boyes of the knoppe of the cover weyinge } lix oz.

33 Itm a *cuppe of golde* w^t a cover and a crowne impiall havynge opon the bordure of the same cover v greate balaces v dyamontꝭ stondyng in v. troches evy troche conteynyng iiii greate ples and x troches conteynyng evy troche iii ples of a lesse sorte and over the said bordure vi dyamontꝭ sett in flowers and xi greate ples sett in crampyones betwene the

said flowers the said flowers garnysshed w^t lx smalł ples and opon the dyadyme xxxvi greate ples and aboute the knoppe under a longe balace xii smale ples the balace havyng sett opon the same a flower de luce of golde and under the dyadyme vi smale ples and aboute the bole of the said cuppe teñ poyntyd dyamontę sett in x troches evy troche conteynyng iiii greate ples and under the said x troches other x troches evy troche conteynyng iii smalł ples and aboutes the bordure of the foote of the same cuppe vi longe ples sett in crampyones w^t columbynes and six lr̃es of . JF . sett in the said foote in white roosis weyinge all to giders — cclxix. oz.

34 Item *three bollis* of golde pleyne w^t one cover w^t frers girdellę aboute the feete ⁊ cover and also aboute the knoppe of the cover a doble Romayne A. and w^tin the armys of *Fraunce* ⁊ a crowne above weyinge — cciiii^xx xviii oz.

35 Itm̃ *iii bollis* [*of golde*] w^t one cover of the same sorte weyinge — ccciii oz.

36 Itm̃ a *bole of golde* w^t a high foote chasid w^t the cover

and opon the cover a liberdes hede risynge oute of a crowne and in his mougth a greate rynge of golde and w^t^in the cover under the pomell the *Cardynallys armys* enamyled under a *Cardynallę hatte* weyinge } ciii oz.

VII.

Candelstickę of golde for the Chaundry.

(p. 11 b.) 1 Item *three candelstickes of golde* w^t^ prickes for a table garnysshed w^t^ lres . ℌ . and . ℜ . enamyled redde well wrought } iiii^xx^xi oz di.

2 Item *a candelsticke of golde* w^t^ a prickett for a table garnysshed w^t^ lres . ℌ . and . ℜ . enamyled redde well wrought weyinge } xxxv oz qrt scant.

3 Item *a candlesticke of golde* for a sise w^t^ a stele a chayne a payer of snoffers ꝛ graven one the bakeside w^t^ . ℌ . and . ℜ . a roose and pomegarenett wayinge } ix oz iii q^a^rts.

4 Item *twoo candlestickes of golde* Spanysshe worke well wrought and enamyled w^t^ imageri †an flowers w^t^ sheves of arrowes sett above the base wayinge } iiii^xx^vi oz q^a^rt.

VIII.

(p. 12.) Goblettes of golde wherof one garnisshed wt stone and ꝑle.

1 Item a ꝑper *goblett* wt a cover chasid like a roose weyinge	x. oz.
2 Item a *goblett of golde* well wrought wt braunches enbatelid one the coṽ lackyng six batilmentꝭ wt roosis white and redde wt paunceꝭ weyinge	xvii oz dĩ.
3 Itm̃ a *goblett of golde* chasid upright wt . 𝔥. and . 𝔎. knytte to gidders aboute the bordure wt a doble roose opon the cover weyinge	†
4 Itm̃ a *goblett of glasse* wt a foote [of golde] garnysshed wt roosis white and redde ꝛ a crowne impiall the *Kyngꝭ armys* opon the cover and the coṽ of the same goblett glasse wayinge to gidders wt the glasse	xii oz qart.
5 Item a *goblett of golde* wt a cover chasid rockey weyinge	xvi oz dĩ scant.
6 Item a *goblett of golde* wt a cover garnysshed wt course rubyes and ꝑles wantyng iii ꝑles the lower ꝑte of the cuppe a jasper and opon the knoppe of the cover a smale rubye weyinge	xii. oz dĩ.

IX.

(p. 12 b.) Saltis of golde certen garnisshed wt stone ꝛ ꝑle ꝛ certen ungarnisshed.

1 Item a *salte of golde* wt a cover borne up wt a *Moreañ* the *Moreañ* havyng aboutę his necke v. course rubyes and vi garnyssh-ing ꝑles wt one that he hath in his honde havyng aboutę the foote xii course rubyes ꝛ xii course garnysshing ꝑles the cover havyng in the toppe xviii course rubyes ꝛ one course dyamont ꝛ xii course garnysshinge ꝑles and aboutę the bordure of the cover vi course dyamontę vi course rubyes ꝛ xii course garnisshinge ꝑles weyinge } xlvi oz. dĩ scant.

2 Item a *salte of golde* called the *Moresdaunce* havyng the foote garnysshed wt vi greate saphures xv course dyamontę xxxviii course rubyes xli smalle garnisshinge ꝑles havyng opon the shanke iii greate course saphures and iii. greate course ꝑles havyng opon the bordure above the shanke xii course dyamontę xviii course rubyes ꝛ l garnysshing ꝑles and stondyng above that v. mores-dauncers ꝛ one tabrett [havyng emongę alł the said v mores-dauncers and tabrett] xi smalle

garnysshing ples ꝛ one rubye the lady holdyng the salte havyng opon her garmentꝭ from her foote to her face xxiii course garnysshyng ples and x course smale rubyes or glasses the foote of the said salte havynge iiii course rubyes or glasses ꝛ iiii course dyamontꝭ or glasses the bordure aboutꝭ the mydle of the said salte havynge v course dyamontꝭ or glasses and vii rubyes or glasses and vii ples and opon the knoppe of the said salte iiii dyamontꝭ iiii rubyes and iii greate ples havyng opon her attyre ꝛ her hedde xiiii course rubyes xii course dyamontꝭ and xxiii course garnysshing ples wayinge — cxlvii. oz.

3 Item a *salte of golde* wᵗ a cover like a braunche wᵗ a woman like a housewyff wᵗ a blacke hoode garnysshed on the foote wᵗ viii light rubyes ꝛ viii troches of ple and on the cover vii rubyes ꝛ xi ples weyinge — xxiii. oz.

4 Itm̃ a *salte of golde* wᵗ a cover like a tower wᵗ iiii porteculliceꝭ five vanys ix smale ples borne wᵗ ii lyones ꝛ ii smale dragones wayinge — xxii oz qᵃrt.

5 Item a *salte of golde* weƚƚ wrought wᵗ portecolicis crownyd the cover chasid and garnisshed wᵗ viii light rubyes ꝛ viii troches of smalle garnysshinge ꝑles and the knoppe iii portecolices wᵗ iii cheynes ꝛ a margarett opon the knoppe wayinge	xviii oz qªrt.
(p. 13.) 6 Item a *liteƚƚ ꝑper salte* of golde wᵗ a cover weƚƚ wrought wᵗ .𝔓. and .𝔎. ꝛ redde roosis enamyled wayinge	viii oz. qªrt dı.
7 Itm̃ a *salte of golde* wᵗ a lyon̄ a dragone ꝛ a greyhounde stondynge opon a foote wᵗ vi liteƚƚ turrettꝭ crownyd wayinge	l. oz. dī dī qªrt.
8 Itm̃ a *salte of golde* rockey fasshion wᵗ a roose ꝛ a pomegar-nett on the knoppe weyinge	ix oz dī qªrt.
9 Item a *salte of golde* vi square wᵗ starres enamyled white and redde wayinge	v. oz iii q̃rts.
10 Itm̃ a *salte of golde* wᵗ a cameƚƚ one the cover wᵗ a mother of ꝑle one his backe and a man enamyled his leggꝭ ‖crasid the cover garnysshed wᵗ ii course emerades ii corse dyamontꝭ ꝛ a course rubye weyinge	xxiiii oz dī scant.
11 Itm̃ a *rownde salte of golde* chasid lozengewyse wrethen "——"	v. oz iii qªrt dī.

12 Itm a pper *salte of golde* chasid wt roosis and pomegarnette the knoppe a portecolice " ——"	v. oz.
13 Itm a *salte of golde* [wt a cover] chasid fether fasshion wayinge	vi. oz. qart.
14 Itm a *pper salte* wt a cover chasid rockey of golde wt a braunche of roosis white ꝛ redde ꝛ a pomegarnett one the knoppe wayinge	†
15 Itm a *litell salte of golde* chasid wrethyn wt litell ples wayinge	iii oz. di.
16 Itm a *salte of golde* wt a casaden therin wt a cover garnysshed and a pale aboute the foote wantyng of the garnysshing ii rubyes and iii ples wayinge	†
17 Itm a *salte of golde* wt a cover wrought wt pomegarnette redde roosis ꝛ white wt a ple one the knoppe wayinge	xv oz. di scant.
18 Itm a *pper rounde salte of golde* wt a cover graven wrethen fether fasshion wayinge	v. oz. qart scant.
19 Itm a *salte of golde* fagott fasshion chasid wayinge	ix oz. di.

(p. 13 b.)

20 Item a *salte of golde* chasid rockey wt a wreth enamyled white and blacke aboute the knoppe wayinge	†
21 Itm a *salte of golde* chasid fether fasshion wayinge	v. oz. di.
22 Itm a *salte of byrrall* garnysshed wt golde redde ꝛ white roosis weyinge	x oz.
23 Itm a *salte of golde* ꝛ *jasp* wt a cov white ꝛ redde roosis wayinge	v oz. qart.
24 Itm a *salte of golde* wt a sythern wt a cov white ꝛ redde roosis wayinge	vi oz iii qarts scant.
25 Itm a *salte of byrrall* garnysshed wt xviii light rubyes or glasses and l smalle garnysshing ples weyinge	x oz iii qarts.
26 Itm a *salte of golde* wt a cover and in the cuppe a white jasper and in the cover a nother white jasper garnysshed wt xxxiii rubyes stondyng in collette xliiii ples stondyng in crampiones ꝛ xlii hangyng ples wantyng a * doble rose white ꝛ redde opon the knoppe wayinge	xviii. oz. qart.

27 Itm a *salte of golde* wrought w[t] braunches of strawburyes w[t] a tufte of strawburyes or hawse opon the cover wayinge	xxi. oz. di di q[a]rt.
28 Itm a *salte of golde* w[t] a cover chasid w[t] dropes havyng a doble rose graven ⁊ enamyled in the knoppe wayinge	x oz iii qrts di.
29 Itm a *salte of golde* w[t] a cover the foote ⁊ the bolle rounde the bole of jasper the shanke vi. square enamyled blew upon the knoppe of the cover a nakyd childe settyng the salte and the cover full garnysshed w[t] course stonys and ples weyinge	xix oz iii q[a]rts.
30 Itm a *salte of golde* w[t] a cover the shanke of the salte a man knelyng opon a grene mountayne holdynge in his hand a staff w[t] a ple at th ende the *Kyngs armys* in a shelde fastoned to the staff the foote beneth garnysshed w[t] course stonys and ples and in likewise the cover havyng opon the knoppe of the cover a redde rose and a white enamyled weyinge	xxxvi oz di.

X.

(p. 14.) Sponis of golde certeñ garnisshed wᵗ stone ⁊ ꝑle ⁊ certen ungarnisshed.

1 Item a *spone of golde* graven wᵗ an ℌ. and a rose wayinge	i oz qᵃrt̃ dĩ·
2 Itm̃ a *spone of golde* wᵗ a rubye at th ende wayinge	ii. oz dĩ q̃rt̃.
3 Itm̃ a *spone of golde* wᵗ ℌ and ℜ graven at th ende wayinge	ii oz scant.
4 Item iiii *sponys of golde* wᵗ rosis and pomegarnette buddes at th endes wayinge to gidders	v. oz dĩ dĩ qᵃrt̃.
5 Itm̃ a *spone of golde* wᵗ a flate stele wᵗ twoo redde rosis ii. portecolice and a margarett opon the stele wayinge	ii oz qᵃrt̃ scant.
6 Item *twoo sponys of golde* wᵗ roosis and pomegarnett buddes at th endꝭ waying to gidders	ii oz iii qᵃrt̃s.
7 Itm̃ a *goodly spone of golde* wᵗ a rose white ⁊ redde opon the knoppe wayinge	iii oz. qᵃrt̃ dĩ.
8 Itm̃ sixe *sponys of golde* wᵗ white ⁊ redde rosis at th endes wayinge	xi. oz qᵃrt̃.
9 Itm̃ a *spone of golde* wᵗ a crrowne impiall̃ wayinge	iii oz q̃rt̃.

10 Itm̃ a *spone of golde* w^t a rose white and redde at th ende wayinge	i. oz dĩ dĩ q^{a}rt.
11 Itm̃ a *spone of golde* w^t a goodly table dyamont at th ende wayinge	iii oz. iii q^{a}rt's.
12 Itm̃ a *spone of golde* w^t a redde rose at th ende wayinge	ii. oz dĩ q^{a}rt'.
13 Itm̃ a *spone of golde* w^t a dyamont at th ende wayinge	†
14 Itm̃ a nother *spone* w^t a wrethen stele and a doble roose white and redde at th ende way-inge	†
15 Item a *spone of golde* w^t a rose budde one the ende and one portolice pounsid wayinge	†
16 Item a *spone of golde* way-inge	iii oz q^{a}rt'.
17 Itm̃ a *spone of golde* w^t a wrethen stele and roosis redde and white at th ende wayinge	iii oz dĩ.
18 Itm̃ a *spone of golde* w^t a wrethen stele ⁊ playne at th ende wayinge	iii oz. dĩ scant.
19 Item a *spone of golde* w^t a wrethen stele ⁊ a brode knoppe ♣ at th ende ♣ w^t a playne plate wayinge	iii oz dĩ scant.

	20 Itm a *str^a^yner of golde* for orrenges waying	x oz dī q^a^rt.
	21 Itm a *spone of golde* the stele of hit made like chesse men wayinge	iii oz dī dī q^a^rt.
(p. 14 b.)	22 Itm xviii *sponys of byrrall* garnysshed w^t^ golde one of them lackyng his stele of byrrall & his knoppe of golde wayinge to gidders	xxi. oz.
	23 Item a *spone of golde* w^t^ an image of *Jhus* and a dyadyme sett w^t^ twoo litill emerades and a smale rubye wayinge	iiii oz. dī scant.
	24 Item a *spone of golde* w^t^ a flatte stele w^t^ a knoppe havynge one eyther side the knoppe a rubye and garnysshed w^t^ vii ples weyinge	iii. oz q^a^rt dī.
	25 Itm xiiii. *sponys of golde* of dyvse sortes weyinge to giders	l. oz. iii. q^a^rts. dī.

XI.

(p. 15.) Layers ewars & basones of golde certen garnisshed w^t^ stone & ple & certen ungarnisshed.

1 Item a *layer of golde* & byrrall enamyled w^t^ margeron potte havyng opon the toppe v	l. oz.

hangyng ples ꝛ holdis no water wayinge	
2 Itm̃ a *layer of golde* chasid chevernwyse w[t] a redde rose one the cover wayinge	ix oz dĩ dĩ q[a]rt̃.
3 Itm̃ a *ꝑper layer of golde* chasid rockeywyse w[t] a pomegar-garnett one the cover wayinge	x. oz . scant.
4 Itm̃ an other *ꝑper layer of golde* graven w[t] roosis and flower de lucis in lozengis w[t] a crowne impiall̃ wayinge	xi oz q[a]rt̃.
5 Itm̃ a *layer of golde* the foote garnysshed w[t] twoo light balacis twoo light saphures iiii troches of course ples iii in a troche and aboute the body one course balaice iii course saphures w[t] iiii troches of course ples iii in a troche and one the cover thre course balacys iii course saphures ꝛ vi troches of course ples iii in a troche and one the knoppe twoo course balacys ꝛ xii garnysshing ples w[t] a lyon holdyng the *Kyngs armys* wayinge	lxv oz dĩ q̃rt̃.
6 Itm̃ a *layer of golde* w[t] v white hartis one the body ꝛ cover garnysshed w[t] ples blew flowers ꝛ cheynes wayinge	xix oz scant.

7 Ĩtm a *basoñ of golde* the bordure garnysshed w^{t} redde ⁊ white roosis 𝕳. and. 𝕶. wayinge	cxxxii oz scant.
8 Ĩtm an *eware of golde* garnysshed w^{t} roosis redde ⁊ white and 𝕳 and 𝕶 wayinge	xlvii oz dĩ.
9 Ĩtm a *basọn of golde* w^{t} the bordure garnysshed w^{t} redde ⁊ white roosis ⁊ 𝕳 ⁊ 𝕶 wayinge	cxxxvii oz q^{a}rt' iiii peny weyte.
10 Item a *layer of byrraƚƚ* garnysshed w^{t} golde and ꝑle wantynge ii ꝑles weyinge w^{t} the byrraƚƚ	xix oz q^{a}rtꝰ scant.
11 Ĩtm one payer of coꝰvyd *basones of golde* w^{t} frers girdellꝭ aboute the edges and also aboute the bussellꝭ in the bothomes and w^{t}in the bussells in the bothomes the armys of *Fraunce* w^{t}in a shilde under a crowne weyinge	cccxxxiii oz dĩ.
12 Ĩtm a *layer of golde* w^{t} thes wordes *Loyaƚƚ* ||*in* ||*cure* opon the cover a white roose and a redde weyinge	xxiiii. oz dĩ.
13 Ĩtm ii. greate *ewers of golde* the spowtes serpentꝭ w^{t} frers girdells aboute the feete and opon the liddes the armys of *Fraunce* ⁊ a shilde under a crowne impiaƚƚ weyinge	cclv oz.

14 Itm̃ a *leyer of golde* the cover garnysshed wt course balaces and ples and opon the leyer and cover roosis and opon the knoppe of the cover a rose redde ⁊ white lackyng ii balaces weyinge — xxii oz dĩ lackyng half peny weight.

XII.

(p. 15 b.) Glasses garnisshed wt golde and crucis of golde.

1 Item a *glasse* wt a cover garnysshed wt golde wt iiii squytchynes wt the *Kyngis armys* wayinge — xii oz iii q̃rt̃s.

2 Itm̃ an other, *glasse* wt a cover the foote ⁊ cover garnysshed wt golde wt the *Kyngẽ armys* one the knoppe wayinge — ix oz . dĩ.

3 Itm̃ a *cruse of golde* wt a cover chasid wt hernes wt a crrowne impiall̃ and a redde roose one the cover wayinge — ix oz iii qarts dĩ.

4 Item a *cruce of golde* wt a cover chasid wt rosis and pomegarnettẽ wt ronnyng leves the cover havyng a crowne impiall̃ wt a white roose ⁊ a redde wayinge — xv oz.

5 Itm̃ an other *cruce of golde* of the same makyng wt a cover weyinge — xv. oz.

XIII.

Flagones ꝛ casting botellꝭ of golde.

1 Item one *payer of flagones* of golde wᵗ frers girdellꝭ aboute the feete and liddes opon the sydes dragones and opon the bellis of the said flagones rounde sercles compassid wᵗ frers girdells and therin plates of the armys of *France* weyinge	ccc iiii^{xx} xiiii. oz dĩ.
2 Itm̃ a *castynge botell* of golde wᵗ a deysy of eyther side weyinge	v. oz qᵃrtꝰ dĩ.
3 Itm̃ a *castynge botell* of golde pleyne and of either side a lepordes hede graven risinge oute of a crowne weyinge	iiii oz iii q̃rtꝰs.

INVENTORY

OF THE

REGALIA, &c. OF JAMES I.

I.

A Booke conteyninge the remayne of all suche jewells and other ꝑcellꝭ as are remayninge in the *Kinges Ma*^{te} secrete jewelhouse wth in the *Tower* of *London*, accordinge to a survey thereof taken by *th Erle* of *Dorsett* Lorde High Thr^{u}er of *Englande*, *Charles* Erle of *Nottingham* Lorde Admyrall of *Englande*, *Thomas* Erle of *Suffolke* Lorde Chamberleyne of the Kinges householde. *Edwarde* Erle of *Worcester* Master of the Horse, and *George* Lorde *Howme* of *Barwycke* Chauncello^{r} ꝛ Underthr̃er of thExchequier, by vertue of his Highnes warr^{a}unte under the privie seale dated the *xxii*th daye of *Marche* in the *seconde* yeare of his Ma^{te} raigne of *Englande Fraunce* and *Irelande* and of *Scottlande* the *xxxviii*th.

JAMES R.

Jewelles remayninge in an yron cheste in the secrete jewelhouse wth in the *Tower* of *London*.

1 Fyrste a *Crowne Imperyall* of golde sett about the nether border wth ix^{en} greate pointed dyamondes,

and betwene everye dyamonde a knott of perle sett by fyve perles in a knott, in the upper border eight rocke rubies and xx^{tie}. rounde perles / the fower arches beinge sett eche of them wth a table dyamonde / a table rubye / an emeralde / and uppon twoe of the arches xviii^{en} perles / and uppon the other twoe arches xvii^{en} perles / and betwene everye arche a greate ballace sett in a collett of golde ⁊ uppon the topp a verye greate ballace perced / and a lytle crosse of golde uppon the top enamelled blewe.

2 Itm̃ a *Coronett of Golde* sett about the nether border wth. iiii^{or} blewe saphyrs / iiii^{or} ballaces one emeralde / v roses of dyamondes ⁊ xiiii^{en}. rounde perles / and about the upper border sett wth three blewe saphyrs three ballaces / and vi quaters of perles / †ever quater havinge in the middest a small pointed dyamonde.

3 Itm̃ a *Circlett of Golde* sett wth a greate ballace rubye / viii table dyamondes / ix^{en} emeraldes / xxxvi rocke rubies / and lvi rounde perles.

4 Itm̃ one *Circlett* newe made for the *Quene* conteyninge in the myddest viii fayre dyamondes of dyverse fashions viii fayre rubies / viii emeraldes and viii saphyrs garnished wth xxxii small dyamondes / xxxii small rubies and lxiiii^{or} ꝑles fixed / and on eche border xxxii small dyamondes and xxxii small rubyes nowe remayninge wth the *Quene*.

5 Itm̃ a *Coller of Serpentes of Golde* enamelled conteyninge viii table dyamondes / wth a flower hanginge at it / wth a table rubye and a fayre dyamonde cutt lozengewise.

6 Itm̃ a *Coller of Gold* conteyninge xiii$^{e}{}_{n}$ greate ballaces ⸝ and xiii$^{e}{}_{n}$ peces of golde wth xiii$^{e}{}_{n}$ cinques of perles betwene them.

7 Itm̃ a *Coller of Golde* conteyninge xiiii^{en} greate table dyamondes ⸝ and twoe other much bigger beinge in nomber xvi^{en}⸝ and xiiii^{en} quaters of greate perles.

8 Itm̃ a *Coller of Golde* conteyninge fyve fayre table dyamondes ⸝ three greate rocke rubies ⸝ twoe table rubyes ⸝ lxiii litle rubyes ⸝ and xii quaters of perles wantinge twoe perles and xxxvi small dyamondes in the peces.

9 Itm̃ a *Coller of Golde* conteyninge viii fayre poynted dyamondes and one table dyamonde wth lr̃es of ℌ. and 𝔐. havinge to each of them a perle pendaunte.

10 Itm̃ a *Coller of Golde* wth viii greate rocke rubyes ⸝ and one greate pointed dyamonde in the myddest ⸝ and xx^{tie} greate perles sett in twoes wth one longe perle pendaunte.

11 Itm̃ a *Coller of Golde* conteyninge xiiii^{en} knottes of golde sett wth vii^{en}. fayre dyamondes ⸝ and xiiii^{en}. lytle rubyes wth xiii$^{e}{}_{n}$ perles pendaunte ⸝ whereof one dyamonde in the myddest is greate.

12 Itm̃ one *Coller of twoe joyntes* sett wth vi table dyamondes ⸝ vii^{en} rocke rubies ⸝ vii^{en}. emeraldes ⸝ and xviii^{en} knottꝭ of perles ⸝ twoe perles in a knott.

13 Itm̃ one *Coller of Golde* sett wth x^{en} blewe saphyres in collettꝭ of golde ⸝ and x^{en} knottꝭ of rounde perles ⸝ everye knott conteyninge xiiii^{en}. perles ⸝ one knott wantinge iiii^{or} perles.

14 Itm one *Coller of Golde* sett wth xiiii^{en} emeraldes in collettę of golde ˏ and xiiii^{en} knottę of rounde perles ˏ in every knott ix^{e}n perles.

15 Itm one *Coller of Golde* sett wth ix^{en} verye greate ballaces in collettę of golde ˏ and x^{en} knottes of perles everye knott conteyninge xvi^{en} rounde perles.

16 Itm one *Coller of Golde* wthout stone of the order of *St. Michaell* conteyninge xxiiii^{or} knottę of golde and xxiiii^{or} knottes of duble skalloppe shelles havinge at th ende of it *St. Michaell* hanginge by twoe lytle cheynes.

17 Itm one *Coller of Golde* devyded into twoe braunches ˏ conteyninge in the same x^{en} table dyamondes one bygger then the rest ˏ x^{en} rubies viii beinge rocke rubies and twoe table rubies and xxxvi rounde perles in twoes.

18 Itm one [ryche] *Coller of Golde* conteyninge x^{en} fayre table dyamondes ˏ one pointed dyamonde in the myddest ˏ xii peces of gold smythes woorke ˏ wrought lyke friers knottes ˏ and sett wth iiii^{xx} xii perles ˏ wth a flower of golde ˏ therein a fayre table dyamonde ˏ and three perles pendaunte ˏ twoe fayre and the thirde meane.

19 Itm a shorte *Coller of Golde* conteyninge iiii^{or} table dyamondes ˏ three rubyes ˏ and viii peces of golde in eche twoe perles ˏ one lytle dyamonde and one small rubie.

20 Itm one *Upper Habillamente* conteyninge xiiii^{en} peces of golde eche havinge one fayre table dyamonde.

21 Itm one *Upper Habillament* conteyninge x^en^ peces of golde eche havinge one table dyamonde, and vi peces of golde eche havinge one rubye.

22 Itm tenne *Buttons* sett wth tenne dyamondes for his Ma^te^ wearinge, remayninge in the chardge of the Lord *Barwycke.*

23 Itm one *Upper Habilliamente* conteyninge xiii^en^ peces of golde havinge in eache fower perles.

24 Itm twoe *Rynges of Golde*, th one sett wth a topas, and thother wth a white saphyr.

25 Itm one *Rynge of Golde* enamelled grene and white havinge a fayre rocke rubie sett in fower clawes.

26 Itm a *Ringe of Golde* enamelled blacke blewe white and grene, havinge a great rocke rubye in fower clawes enamelled grene.

27 Itm tenne *Buttons of Golde* sett wth tenne table dyamondes remayninge in the chardge of the Lorde *Barwycke.*

28 Itm *Parte of a Byllamente* conteyninge twoe peces of golde sett wth twoe dyamondes.

29 Itm one *Brouche of Golde* enamelled and sett wth a dyamonde.

30 Itm one *Button of Golde* sett wth a dyamonde and one greate ragged perle pendaunte.

31 Itm fyftene *Perles* pcell of one and fortie ragged perles pendaunte and eight pendaunte perles tyed unto a purple stringe.

32 Itm twentie *Buttons of Golde* sett wth fower perles a pece and truelove knotte.

33 It̃m one greate blewe *Saphyr* unsett.

34 It̃m one greate *Amatiste* sett in golde.

35 It̃m xxiiii^{or} *Buttons of Golde* eche havinge one fayre dyamonde of dyverse cuttes.

36 It̃m xix^{e}n rounde *Buttons of Golde*, eche havinge one dyamonde some fayrer then other, rem̃ in the chardge of the Lorde *Barwycke*.

37 It̃m eight longe *Peces of goldsmythes woorke* eche havinge one fayre dyamonde.

38 It̃m three longe *Peces of Golde* eche havinge one rocke rubye.

39 It̃m a parte of a *Flower of Golde*, beinge a rocke rubye wth a longe ꝑle pendaunte.

40 It̃m a *Flower* wth a verye greate table dyamonde sett in golde called *the Myrror*.

41 It̃m a fayre *Flower* wth three greate ballaces in the myddest a greate pointed dyamonde, and three greate perles fixed, wth a fayre greate ꝑle pẹndaunte called *the Brethren*.

42 It̃m a *Flower of Golde* wth a table dyamonde and a greate ꝑle pendaunte.

43 It̃m a fayre *Rubye Ballace* wthout foyle, hanginge in a case of golde enamelled.

44 It̃m a *Jewell* beinge a fayre rocke rubye ballace wthout foyle, and a fayre longe perle pendaunte at it.

45 It̃m a *Perle* pendaunte and a snayle on it.

46 It̃m one lardge *Agatt* graven wth the picture

of Kinge *Henrye* the *viii*th. and Kinge *Edwarde* the *vi*th.

47 Itm a pendaunte of fower *Perles* in a cluster.

48 Itm a *Flower of Golde* wth a rocke rubye and a perle pendaunte.

49 Itm a fayre greate blewe *Saphyr* wthout foyle and a longe perle pendaunte.

50 Itm one *Fanne of Feathers* of sondry coulors the handle of golde fullie furnished wth dyamondes and rubyes, wth a dyamonde lyke a nayle of th one syde, and an emeralde on the other beinge loose, wt a ringe on th ende of the handle wth a sharpe pointed dyamonde.

51 Itm a greate and ryche *Jewell of Golde* called the *Myrror of Great Brytaigne*, conteyninge one verye fayre table dyamonde, one verye fayre table rubye, twoe other lardge dyamondes cutt lozengewise th one of them called the *Stone of the lre* H. *of Scottlande*, garnished wth small dyamondes, twoe rounde perles fixed, and one fayre dyamonde cutt in fawcette bought of *Sauncey*.

52 Itm one fayre *Jewell* lyke a *feather of golde*, conteyninge one fayre table dyamonde in the middest, and xxv. diamondes of diverse formes. delivered by the Lo *Barwyck*.

53 Itm one *Jewell of Golde of the lre* J. havinge one fayre longe dyamonde in the myddest twoe greate ballace rubies. and one small tryangle dyamonde in the topp.

54 Itm dyverse *Antiquyties* in a purse of blacke velvett in all weyinge xv oz di di qarter.

55 Itm one lesser bagge wth sondrye *Sylver Mettallꝭ.*

56 Itm a purse of blacke velvett w^th *Medalias of Golde* some of them cheyned together.

57 Itm a purse wth sondrye *Mettallꝭ of Copper.*

58 Itm one longe pece estemed for an *Unicorns Horne.*

59 Itm three other peces estemed likewise to be *Unicornes Horne.*

60 Itm one greate *Twoe handed Sworde* garnyshed wth sylver and guylte , presented to King *Henry* the *viii*^th by the Pope.

JAMES ℞.

This booke is agreeable to a former booke made by me and doth conteyne the entrye of all the Kinges Ma^te jewellꝭ remayninge in the *Tower of London.*

Fra. Goston.

II.

JAMES ℞.

Jewelles of the saide secrete Jewelhouse in the Tower geven by the Kinges Ma^tt owne handes to the *Quene* at severall tymes.

1 Fyrste one *Jewell* wth a dyamonde and a spynell or rubye and fyve perles wth a longe ragged ꝑle pendaunte.

2 Itm a *Jewell* beinge an H. conteyninge seven dyamondes thereof fyve poynted and twoe tabled wth three perles pendaunte.

3 Itm a *Crosse* of golde wth fyve longe dyamondes and a fayre ple pendaunte.

4 Itm a *Flower* of golde wth a sharpe pointed dyamonde, a rubye, an emeralde, and a longe perle pendaunte.

5 Itm a *Flower* of golde wth a sharpe poynted dyamonde and a rubye wth a ple pendaunte.

6 Itm a *Flower* of golde wth a table dyamonde a table rubye and a small perle pendaunte.

7 Itm a *Flower* of golde wth a pointed dyamonde a table rubye and a perle pendaunte.

8 Itm eight and fortye perles pcell of one hundreth and xii rounde perles.

9 Itm one hundreth foure score nynetene perles.

10 Itm one greate longe perle pendaunte, taken from a flower of golde wth a verye greate table dyamonde.

11 Itm a *shorte Coller* of golde havinge three greate dyamondes, three fayre rubyes, and three greate emeraldes, wth. xxtie perles sett in twoes of gold smythes woorke.

12 Itm one *Carkanett* or *Billamente* of golde conteyninge seventene peces of golde sett wth seventene dyamondes.

13 Itm a *Crosse of golde* wthout a heade, havinge twoe poynted dyamondes, twoe fayre table dya-

mondes and one lozenge dyamonde wth a perle pendaunte.

14 Itm̃ a *Crosse* wth fower longe dyamondes ⸝ and three *Scottisshe* perles pendaunte.

15 Itm̃ a *fayre Tablett* wth a crosse of xxiii dyamondes on the one syde ⸝ and a worde conteyninge sixtene lr̃es of dyamondes ⸝ *Dieu et mon droyt* wth a lytle knobb pendaunte therein twoe litle table diamondes ⸝ and twoe rubyes wth a clocke in it.

16 Itm̃ one *lytle Bottle* of an agatt sett wth one rubye ⸝ and a small cheyne of golde.

17 Itm̃ a *Jewell* of golde wth a greate dyamonde a greate rubye and a longe perle pendaunte.

18 Itm̃ a *Jewell* of golde sett wth three dyamondes ⸝ and one rocke rubie ⸝ and one greate ragged ꝑle pendaunte.

19 Itm̃ a *Jewell* of golde sett wth a pointed dyamonde twoe rubies and one emeralde ⸝ and twoe ragged perles pendaunte beinge a whistle.

20 Itm̃ a *Jewell* of golde garnished wth fyve pendaunte perles ⸝ fyve rocke rubies ⸝ fower dyamondes ⸝ and twoe emeraldes and a ragged ꝑle in the myddest.

21 Itm̃ one *castinge bottle* of golde sett wth small dyamondes and sparkes of rubyes.

22 Itm̃ a *Flower* of golde conteyninge three dyamondes twoe tabled and one poynted wth a flatt perle pendaunte at it.

23 Itm a *Tablett* of golde like a sheilde wth a rose of dyamondes in the myddest uppon a spredd eagle, wth a table dyamonde, a poynted dyamonde, an emeralde and a rubie and three fayre perles pendaunte.

24 Itm a *Crosse* of golde wth xii dyamondes.

25 Itm a *Jewell* of golde wth one dyamonde cutt lyke a nayle, wth one rubye, one emeralde, and a longe perle pendaunte.

JAMES R.

This agreeth wth a former booke made by me wch was signed by the *Kinges Matie*, and doth conteyne an entrie of such jewells remayninge in the *Tower of London*, as have bene delivered by the Kinges owne handes to the *Quene*.

Fra. Goston.

THE COMPENDIUM

OF THE

RECORDS IN THE TREASURY,

COMPILED AND DIGESTED BY

ARTHUR AGARDE, Esq. 1610.

A distinginguishinge of the *Threasauries*.

1 The Recordes in the Kinge's Majesties *Threasury* at *Westm̃*, under the custodie of the *Lord Threasurer* and the two *Chamberlaines* there, may bee very conveniently distinguished for the better understandinge of them into two sortes; that is to say

- Recordes
  - Forreine
    - *Id est*, Leagues or treatyes betwixt Prince and Prince, or States of sundrie Nations. } Arcana Imperii.
  - Domesticall bee such
    - Such as concerne matters of estate and the *Crowne* only. } Arcana Imperii.
    - Pleadinges betwixt the Prince ⁊ Subject for the p̃servinge of the Kinge's prorogative.
    - Pleadings betwixt Subject and Subject.

Accoumpts of the Prince and concninge some of the Prince's landes and of the Subjectes also, &c.

Which recordes and monuments are layd up for their better pservacion in fower sevall *Threasauries*, (except some few kept in private officers handes, whereof I will hereafter make mencion,) under three sevall kayes, kept by three sondry officers distinct th one kay from an other, and uppon each dore three lockes, of which fower *Threasauries*, their places and what recordes they contaigne, hereafter shall be declared.

Threasauries of Recordes. 4.

- The first in the *Court of Receipt.*
- The seacond in y^e *Newe Pallace* at *Westm̃.*
- The third in the late dissolved Abbey of *Westm̃* in the old *Chapter House.*
- The fourth in the *Cloister* of the sayd *Abbey.*

And for the more readines in findinge of the same recordes when occasion shall bee, both for the Kinge's service, and for answeringe of the Subject that repayreth to search, I have thought good to sett downe in what *Threasauries* the records are to bee found, and what records are layd upp in each *Threasurie,* (soe farre forth as my memory shall serve me,) beeing a great multitude, and the diversitie and pticlers thereof I am not hable to recount at large hearin, beeseeching all them y^t shall succeed me in the name of God for the ꝯvice of the Prince, satisfyinge of the Subject, and dischargeinge of theire owne duty with a good conscience, to have a speciall regard to observe some instructions (I presume soe to call them, because by longe experience I have learned and noted them,) which I shall lay downe heareunder, both for the ꝑservacõn of the same recordes and for the ready findinge of them.

2 There is a fower fould hurte that by necligence may bringe wracke to recordes, that is to say	Fier, Water, Rates ꝛ mice, Misplacinge.

Which may bee ꝑvented, so farre foorth as man's witt may doe, (because all thinges are but vayne and ꝑish dailie,) by a fouerefould diligence and care to bee had about them.

Fier. First, for fier: to putt them in vawltes wherein sondry are now, and into the same vawltes might bee brought manie moe. Againe it is an awncient ordre to be observed, and hath bene kept in the said Threasauries, that noe candles should bee brought into ye Threasauries but in candlestickes set in lanthorns, for avoydinge daunger of fier.

Water. The seacond, for water: th officers are bound by an auncient order, after a great glut of raigne snow or tempest to resort into the sayd Threasauries and to viewe whether the same wett weather have pearced through the vawlts and buildings and annoyed the same recordes; and if any such hurte have befallen to give ordre for present redresse of reꝑacõns and to lay abroad the same recordes soe wett to th end they maye drie by aire especially, (or els before a fire, which is both dangerous and hurtfull;) for by defect of speedie reparacõns and removeinge and dryinge, many worthy recordes have beene blemished and decayed.

Rattes ⁊ Mice.

For the third remedy against rates, mice, weesels, ⁊c. the best way is to put the recordes in boxes chestꝭ and stronge presses: and surely I finde that many goodly and notable recordes have bene spoyled with that kind of vermin by gnawinge - - - - yea rates and mice will pearce through with gnawinge the presses of timber, if they bee not looked into sometimes to redresse the same.

Misplacinge.

For the fourth, *id est* misplacinge; it is an evill that riseth by th officer that produceth the record for the search or service, and it is an enemye to all good ordre, and the bringer in of all horror and inconvenience amonge records. For if theere bee not had regard for evy record to be placed in its right or knowne chest or presse ⁊ in its nature, but one thrust into an others bagge or misplaced in its Kinge's time ⁊c. (as I sayd before,) it is impossible to find any thinge certaine, yea and th officer shall bee discredited when it shall be pleaded against him, *Nul tiel record.*

Now havinge set downe these fower inconveniences procuringe hurt and losse to recordes, with theire redresses, soe farr fourth as in my simple opinion may bee applied; there followeth yet a last daunger woorse then some of the former, that is even plaine takinge of them away: and that aryseth twoe manner of wayes, the first when one Privie Counsellor or moe Justicꝭ or any of the Kinges learned Counsell direct a warrant to th officers to bringe to them leagues books or other records, and then the same must bee left wth them, * although th officers come for them ⁊ demaund them never soe oft, yet shall he seldome or never gett them out of their handes, as by experience I have found. The second, is the lendinge of bookes roles or records, to great officers or others, wherein it appeared to me that sundry have failed, for I have hard many things asked for w[ch] have beene sent in [y[e]] Threasaurie. But y[e] that bee officers and doe not respect the ꝑservinge of them, may be sayd to have but smalle regard to ther othes.

" Now called " Auditor of " the Receipts' " Office."

3 Before I begin to shew what recordes lie in every *Threasaury*, I thinke it convenient to shew what particler records lie in the handes of private officers. And first M[r] *John Bingley* ["Esq[r]"] keepeth all privie seales and inrolm[ts] of patents and warrants for the issueinge of treas[e] and th accoumpts thereof from the tellors, whereof he hath a great number in bagges and ꝑsses in an office close by the Court of Receipt, and in an other office which he hath below, neere his house.

" Pell Office."

M[r] *Gidiok Warder* keepeth the two Pelles, th one of *Redditus* called *Introit*ꝰ and the other of *Exitus*, whereof both sorts in a partičler office in a rome appoynted for that use nerre the Court of Receipt, a greatē number from Kinge *Edw. the First* untill nowe.

4 And soe farre forth as my memory will supplie, I will, with Gode's assistance shewe what recordes are arrayed and layd upp in every of the sayd fower *Threasauries*, and namely, first,

The *Threasaurie* of the Court of Receipt.

Two of the most auncyentest bookes of record in the Realme, made in *William* the Conquerers time (called *Domesdei,*) in the *xx*th-yeare of his raigne. Th one booke in quarto contayninge the description of *Essex Norff'* ⁊ *Suffolk*, and in th other in folio, the like for all the Shires in *England*, from *Cornwall* to the river of *Tyne*.

" *q're de hoc*, for *Durham* is not mentioned; " it should be the river " *Teyse* which parts " *Yorkshire* & *Durham*."

Item the *Black Book* made in *Henry the Seconds* time, *De necessariis Scacii observanciis*, and in the same are the othes and admittances of officers inrolled, and other notes of some consequence.

Item a Patent Role of *Edward the seacondę* time.

" These are removed " into the litle roome " nere the Courte & " are put together in a " bagge, all excepte the " Booke of Forests wch " is transferred into the " chest of other Records " of Forests there."

Item a booke in parchmt of the pambulacōns of all the Kinges Forrestes beyond *Trent*, and the Justice seate held in them by the deputies of the Lord *Crumwell* Justice there, made in *Henry the eighte's* time.

Item a bagg of canvas of speciall recordes, abbreviated in a sheete of paper in the bagge, " the abbreviation and bag wanting, the re- " cordes being put into their proper countys."

Item the auncyent Keys of the Treasaury of leagues in the Cloyster of *Westminster Abay*, in an inner chest or division thereof.

" These being rustie " & unserviceable are " made newe. Ao.D'ni " 1624."

Item sondry bagges of the foyles of Sherriffes and Bailliffs tallies, which by default of ordre in the Pipe, weare never joyned.

Item sondry bookes of remembrances and abbreviac̃ons of records.

Item the seale of the Court of Receipt in silver, very auncyent, with the Kings face, and written about, *Sigillum Officii Recepte Scc^{a}ii R in Anglia.*

5 There is a little rome adjoyninge to the same Court, wherin are three chestes in which are records placed, vizt

The first next to the dore, conteyneth pleadinges of *Quo Warranto coram Justic̃ itinerantibȝ* and *Pl̃ita Corone* and *Pl̃ita de Jur̃ et Assis̃*, in and thorough the most part of the Shires of *England* in Kinge *Ed. the firstes* time onely: put by me, some two shires in a bagge, and some one shire, for the more easy findinge and p̃servac̃on where before they lay confused togeither.

" These are put into " a p^{r}esses for y^{t} pur- " pose on the left hand " of ye dore. 1633— " And divided into y^{e} " p^{r}ope^{r} Countys."

6 The next chest beyond y^{t} hath iii devisions in it.

The first being on the right hand, hath in it a very faire booke of parchm^{t} in folio, conteyning an abbreviac̃on of the twoe former spoken of bookes of *Domesdei*, verbatim with that booke in the custodie of ye Kinges Remembranc^{r} [of] th Eschequer.

Item an other booke large in parchm^{t}, contayning the inrolem^{t} of Popes Bulles, deeds of landes conveyed to the Prince by sondry p̧sons, some leagues of Princes especially of *Wales* ⁊c. Inrolm^{ts} of Statutes of *Winchester*, *Glouc^{r}* ⁊c.

Twoe great bagges of Survey of sondry dissolved Abbayes, by Cardinall *Wollsey* and such like.

"This book never "seen by P. L."

Item a bagge of sondry Charters graunted to divers for landes and liberties in *England*, the contents whereof I have in a blacke booke in paper abbreviated, intituled *Carte tangeñ diverŝ libtates de diversis Monasteriis et al.*

"The bookes not to "be found nor ever by "m seene J.B."

Item a great bagg of Roles of Assis in *H.* 3. time: *E.* 1: *E.* 3: & . *H.* 4: all abbreviated by me into bookes, very redie to be found by the number rolle.

Item a booke of the Threasaurer's and Chamblaine's deputies deliverance of records and jewells, and receipt of leagues and delivery of them out from *E.* 3es time untill *H.* 8. time, and many good noates therein to be observed.

Item an ould catalogue of leagues betwixt Prince and Prince and Popes, intituled *Calendarium seu Repertoriū.*

"These put amongst "the rest of the Popes "Bulles."

Item a basket wherein are contaigned viii bulles of Popes, of ratificacōn of the libties of *England* graunted to ye Kinges, Clergie, and Nobilitie of England.

"Put into the presse "of *London*."

Item a role of landes given in mortmaine in *London* ab ao *viii*vo *E.* 1. usq; annum *xxx*mum p *tcambar et al telimoziñ* susteined.

"Put into the presse "of Rolles of Counter "Pelles."

Item some Chamblaines Counter Pelles of the times of *Phillip* and *Marie*, and of Queene *Elizabethes* raigne.

Item a bagge of bookes, intitled bookes of survey and others, *de quib; quere*, in wch bagg especially is a large booke entituled, *Extent manerii de Bradford Eboȝ.* "That survey of "*Bradford* is put into the *Yorkshire* press ꝛ the "other surveye into the proper countys where "the lands lay."

7 The middle devision.

Hath onely *Pl̃ita forestar̃* w[ch] are devided into three bagges: one bagg conteyneth small bagges wherein are menc̃oed y[e] ꝑticler shires or forrests and on the out side are menc̃oed y[e] shires.

The like is in another bagge.

"All these Fo[r]est "Rolls are put into a "presse togethe[r] by the "Cou[r]t ma[r]kt *Forest'*."

The third bagg containeth records of forrests in div̾s Shires.

There is alsoe a fourth bagge wherein are contayned Inquisic̃ons in sondry forrests, but in them you shall finde nothinge in effect for evidence, because they menc̃on specially *De malefactoribȝ de venac̃one et de viridi.*

In the bagg of *div̾si Comitatus* is a bagg of such Ꝑliam[t] Rolls as I could find in my time and collect togeither, beeinge especially in *E.* 1. time, which I have abbreviated into a booke, and they bee very worthy records, and some of them touch matters of forrests.

"This book never "seen by P. L."

Item the *Innovate* role is theire.

8 The third devision contayneth

Pl̃ita de quo warranto in *E.* 2. time —
- *London* in a bagge.
- *Jerses* ꝛ *Garnsey* — in a bagge.
- *Kanc̃* in a great roll.

" All put into their ꝑper presses of *London, Jer-*
" *sey, Guernsey, Kent.*"

Placita de quo Warr̃ in *E.* 3. time in { *Northt̃* ⁊ *Bedd̃* } in one bagge ⁊ therein are Inquisicions about the fennes.

" All put into their ꝑper presses of *Northt̃* ⁊
" *Bedf'.*"

9 The third chest contayneth

Accompts and Court-rolls of { *Southwales* ⁊ *Northwales* } in severall bagges in *E.*1. *E.*2. and *E.* 3. tyme.

" Put into a press intitled *Wales South* ⁊
" *North.*"

Chester the like in a bagge. " Put into the
" press intitled *Cestr̃.*"

" This book never " seen by *Peter Leneve.*"

Item two other great bagges of accompts, court rolles, and such like, of the King's and sondry other men's landes in *England*, abbreviated into a booke by me.

[" These accounts ⁊ court rolls, so many of
" them as contained lands in one county only,
" were after the making of this book put into
" respective bags of the ꝑper countys, ⁊ those
" which contained lands in more countys then
" one, into a bag of accounts of divers
" countys."]

Item a bagge of very auncyent recordes of accompts of sondry mannors intituled *Parcos.*

[" The like of this bag."]

Item a bagg of accompts of the landes called *Warwick* landes, and of the Earle and Countesse's of *Devonshire's* landes, wherein is an accompt of *Edw.* Duke of *Buck.* landes and a booke of survey of his landes made in *a° xiii°* of *H.* 8.

["Most of these are in the bagg of accounts "of divers countys, ⁊ the rest in the presses ⁊ "bags of their ꝑper countys."]

Item a bagg conteyninge auditors accompts in *H.* 7. and *H.* 8. time, *De terris perquisitis.*

["The like of these."]

Item, *Compta staple Caless.*

Item, *Compta forinseca* { *Hanapia facult* "*q^re^ de his.*" / *Jocal.* / *Weston juxta Baldok.* }

Item, *Windsor Barkhamsted et Hampton Court* compt.

10 Baggs hanginge on the wall there.

"Most of them put "into the respective "presses of the Countys "to which they be- "long."

Next the dore on the left hand, a bagg intitled †*Regemannorum*, in which are Inquisicõns made in divers shires thorough the hundredes touchinge libties ⁊c. withdrawen and witholden from the Kinge in *E.* 1. time ⁊c. *quere quid plus.*

"Put into the p'per "County."

Item, a bagg of like Inquisicõns in Com̃ *Salop̃* in *E.* 1. time.

"Put into the p'per "County."

Item, the like in Com̃ *Wiltes̃.*

"Put into the p'per "County."

Item, the like in Com̃ *Devoñ.*

"Most of them put "into the p'per Coun- "tys."

Item a bagg of tenures which are but few, *quere quid plus,* and therein a rolle of Com̃ *Lincolñ* a°. 3 *E.* 3. of scutaige: alsoe a coppie of the book called *Kirby quest, E.* 1. in *Yorkshire* and *Nomina Villaȝ, E.* 2.

Item ouer the third chest hange these bagges.

"Put into the *Essex* "& *Norff*' bags."

A bagge of ould evidences and courtrolles of *Wykes Abbay,* dissolved by Cardinal *Wolsey:* and a Priory called *Mountjoy.*

Item a bagg of Indentures made betwixt the Judgẽ and th Officers of the Threasury, for the receyvinge into the Threasury, recordes of sondry natures.

Item a bagg of matters concerning the Minte, and advauncinge or abasinge the Coyne.

"Put into the p'per "Countys."

Item a bagg of records which are abbreviated into a booke, by me remayninge in a chest in the Courte.

11 In the *Seacond Threasaurie* which is in the newe Pallace of *Westm̃* over the little Gatehouse there, locked with 3 lockes and keyes, are conteined these recordes followinge in presses which I will declare, in goinge round about the same.

On the left hand at the cominge in, the next presse marked wth chalke

E. 1. *E.* 2. *E.* 3. *Ric.* 2.	Pelles. 1. in one presse.	*H.*4. *H.*5. *H.*6.	in the seacound presse marked Pelles 2.

In the third presse beyond that marked with chalke

Pelles: 3.

E. 4.
H. 7.
Phus ꝛc *Maria*
Elizabeth

"Put into their p'per "Countys except where "lands in divers Coun- "tys in one deed, & "where the County was "not known then put "into 2 bags one there- "of, called a bag of di- "vers Countys ye other "*Quor' Comitatus igno-* "*ratur.*"

In the 4th presse beyond that marked with chalke B.

Sondry boxes of landes purchased and bought by sondry Princꝭ.

In the 5th presse marked with chalke ⓜ.

Bookes of mustars of sundry Shires of *England*, especially of *H.* 8. time.

Lienge in ye floore at th end of this rancke.

Sondry old stampes of Coynes, especially of *E.* 3. time as the *Rosenoble* and *Spurriall* ꝛc.

12 Now returninge backe with a rancke of dubble presses, beeinge in the middest of the rome.

In the furthermost presse marked thus . A : with chalke, are contayned divs records and remembrances, which are all bound up severally into bundells and uppon every bundle written ye

" This book never " seen by P. L." contents thereof and kalendred into a booke † contayninge six leaves, of which I will mencion some.

Some accompts of the *French territories* whiles *England* had them.

Accompts of the cheefe Buttler's office.

Bookes of accompts of fortificacõns at *Callayes*, and of the staple there.

Bagges of the Treasons of Sr *Thomas More*, Busshop *Fisher*, the Countisse of *Salisbury*, the Earle of *Devoñ*, *Cortney*, *Montague* ꝛc. and a bagg of Treasons of *Aske*, the Lord *Darcy*, and other rebbells in *Yorkshire* and *Lincolñ*, bookes of Busshop *Fisher's* found in his studie: *cum multis aliis que nunc ꝑscribere longū est.*

In the next presse to that outward marked wth chalk R.

" This book never " seen by P. L." Popes Bulles put into 4 severall bagges, every one marked with a lr̃e A: B: C: D: and kalendred into a booke, the number of every Popes time.

In the next presse to that outward marked with chalke T: H:

Are sondry recordes touchinge mens landes, and some of y[e] *Kinges* affayres which are calendred in a booke particularely. Memorandum that " This book never " seen by P. L." under these 3. presses at the bottome thereof, are bagges of lether, wherein are contayned the goale deliveries in all shires from *E.* 1. tyme to *H.* 6.

In the next outward, a presse marked with chalke V. are contayned.

Assise de tempibȝ { *H.* 4. / *H.* 5. / *H.* 6. } *Et de a*° 17. *H.* 8. *apud Eboȝ de querelis sed pauca determinata.*

In the presse next to that outward, still marked with chalke R are,

Assise de tempe Regis Edw. s̃cdi.

At th end of this middle rancke one presse, marked with chalke A are,

Assise de tempe Regis Richardi s̃cdi.

In the presse on the further side this rancke goinge forward, marked thus 𝕮.

"Md' these deeds & "rolls put into the re- "spective Countys of "*North'ton Warr'* &c. "where the lands lye, "except where divers "Countys or the County "not known & then in "the p'per bags of *di-* "*vers' Com'* & *Quor'* "*Com' ignoratur.*"

Robt Catesby the treator's evidence, selected out of twoe great hamps delivered in to me by my late Lord Threasaurer th Earle of *Dorset*, by the com̃aundment of Sr *Henry Hubbard* Attorney Generall, which cost me a quarter of a yeare's worke.

Item waightes of *Haverdupoiz.*

Item the measure of ealne and yard, and the mould thereof.

Itm a presse next m̃ked with chalke 𝔄, nothing now, because there weare leagues, wch are transferred into the *Threasaur̃ of Leagues* in the *Abbay.*

In a presse marked with R are,

Assise de tempe R E. 3.

In a presse next to R marked with D:

Assise de tempe R E. 1. in Com̃ *Eboȝ, Lin-*

colñ, Westm̃land, Cumbland, Northumbland, Lancastr̃, Norff', ⁊ Suff', cum aliis; et p̃lita Corone.

In a presse at th end next to D: marked thus E. lr̃es given to Cardinall *Wolsey* and *Thomas Cromwell.*

In other two presses next to E marked ⍙.

Diverse assise in diversis aliis Com̃ de tempe R E. 1. scilt in ptibȝ orientalibȝ occidentalibȝ austral et †meriditaneis.

In a little cupboord in the wall, next ye north window at the ||fudermost end m̃ked thus, *Collected:* 1610: are conteyned divers recordes of accompts ⁊c. bound up in bundles, and on every bundle the contents written, which are alsoe entred into a booke and conteyne twoe leaves.

"This book lost & "never seen by *P. L.*"

In one other cupboord in the sayd wall marked thus ⋈ are the like.

13 Then returninge backe by the wall is a presse marked thus ✱ wherein are conteined,

"Put all into the "p'per Countys except "as aforesaid."

Coffers and boxes of olde evidences touchinge the landes †one the *Spencers*, the father and the sonne.

Alsoe th olde evidence of the Priory of *Lewes* in *Com̃ Sussex* for their landes, aswell in *Norff' Suff'* ⁊c.

Olde evidence of the Priory of *Anglesey* in the Countie of *Cant* in a box by themselves.

Old evidence of S[t] *Trinities* of *London* in a old chest.

In the next presse m̃cked ⊕ are conteined

Divers baggs of evidences of sondry mens lands, but specially of *Bassets* of the *West Countrey*, and in a box therein evidencẽ and many ||others writinges touchinge th Earle of *Northmb̃l* S[r] *Edward Seymor* and divers others, w[ch] are entred into a booke N° 15 and contayne ii. leaves.

"This book never "seen by P. L."

14 At the cominge up into the *Threasaurie* on the right hand iii presses, in which are conteined records hereafter specified.

In the foremost from the dore marked, thus *Hibernia*, a bagge of *Irish* matters, begining in *H.* 4. time and menc̃oninge some matters of *H.* 8. time, entred into a book fol. 17 conteyninge one leafe.

"This book never "seen by P. L."
"The bag in letter "H."

In the next presse to that towards the dore marked thus ☧ with chalke, is contayned

A booke intitled *Compendiũ cõptoꝫ*, wch is a visytac̃ōn made by twoe Doctor[s], wherein is declarac̃ōn made of the * vycyous liffe of all the religious houses beyonde *Trente*, the Busshopriks of *Coveñ* ⁊ *Lich* and *Norw*[ch] wth their reliques.

An auncyent great booke of entries of Treaties of peace betwene *England* and *France*, and *England* and *Aragon* and *Spaine;* and much about *Aquitaine, Gascoine* ⁊c.

A box wherein are the Statutes of th Orders of *S*[t] *George* and *Michaell*, and therein a booke intituled *Advertisement p*[r] *un Roy ou Prince*

" And an Indenture between Q. *Eliz.* ꝛ the " Dean ꝛ Canons of *Windsor* dated 30th *Aug*t " *a*°. *regni primo*, concerning the lands given " for the maintenance of the 13 poor Knights."

Item; what a kinge what a tirant.

Itm̃ a box of Indentures of divers Lord Threasaurers, for deliṽy of jewells and receivinge of leagues.

Item a longe box touchinge the Divorce of *H*. 8.

Item a box supscribed thus, *Juramenta prestita sub manibꝫ propriis qđ Romanus Pontifex non h̃t aliquam majorem jurisdic̃oem a Deo sibi in hoc regno Anglie quam quivis alius Episcopus* ꝛc. ꝑ *cler̃ Anglie et Wallie.*

Item a box wherein is a deed of the Lordꝭ spirituall and temporall, under their handes and seales, signifyenge to the Pope *Clement* that if he will not condescend to Kinge *H*. 8. divorce, that then the themselves would take ordre ꝛc.

Item a cōmission made a°. 1. *R*ne *Eliz.* to take the oth of all the Judgs ꝛc. to the supremacy accordinge to the statute, put into a litle black box and layd in the box of the Oath of the Cleargie.

Item the stablishinge of the Minte 6 *Dec̃ a*° *regni R*ine *Eliz. iii*cio under the great seale, lapped with an other of *Calays* of auncyent tyme.

In the bottome of this presse.

xxtii long boxes wherein the Lr̃es Patents of *H*. 8. condescendinge to conferre the landes of the dissolved Monasteries, doone by Cardinall *Wolsey*, unto the sayd Cardi.

Item a booke of Statutes concerninge *Cardinall Colledg* in *Oxford.*

*Item examinačo sive confessio dči Cardinalis de div̄sis malefactę suis contra coronam practitatę, unde prius pdonabat*r, *et postea continuatę unde condempnatus extitit,* in a square box.

*Diversi libri predicator̃ et alioꝝ et eoꝝ racões cont*a *Papam* ; with div̄s others by me collected into a booke N° 19 contayninge † leaves.

" This book never " seen by P. L."

15 In the *Third Threasaury*, beinge in the *ould Chappter House* of the Abbay of *Westm*r under a dore with three lockes, are contayned these recordes; put very faire into chestę with locks and written uppon wth parchmt, as followeth

First turninge up in the left hand in the upper rank of chests, are conteyned in chests, noted with lr̃es in manner followinge

A.	The first chest	*Pedes finium* ⁊ *Pl̃ita tempib*ꝫ	*Ric.* 1. *Johis.*
B.	In the second chest	*Pedes finium* *Pl̃ita de Banco* *Pl̃ita corā Dño Rege* *Pl̃ita corā Justič itinerantib*ꝫ	Tempe R̸ *H.* 3.

put into order by me, in a summer spent onely therein.

C. In the third chest { *Plita coram Dño Rege temp̃ Regis* } *E.* 1.

which are abbreviated by me into a booke covered wth redd lether, written into pchm^t^ and since that time, xx^ti^ yeares after, reviewed and put into a booke entituled *Omissa E.* 1.

" These 2 books still " remain."

D. E. In the 4th ⁊ 5th chestę { *Plita de Banco* and the fift chest *Pedes finium* } *tempore R Edw'i primi*

F. In the 6 chest are { *Plita coram Dño Rege tempore Regis* } *E.* 1.

G. H. In the 7 ⁊ 8 chestę are { *Plita de Banco tempore R* } *E.* 2.

I. K. In the 9 ⁊ 10 chestę { *Plita * Dño Rege tempore R* } *E.* 3.

and for the more easie findinge thereof devided into two chests under foote over against them; looke with in the chest, and you shall finde uppon the liddes what yeares bee there.

L. M. N. O. P. Q. In the 11. 12. 13. 14. 15 ⁊ 16 chestę are { *Plita de Banco tempe Regis* } *E.* 3.

These of the Kings Bench are all pticlerlie abbreviated by me into divs books coved with velome, " ⁊ some of them still remain in the " office."

R. In the †7th chest are { *Plita coram Dño Rege tempe R* } *R.* 2.

" This book remains." abbreviated by me into a booke coved w^th^

velome, and devided into a chest underfoote for the more ready findinge.

S. T. V. W.	In the 18, 19, 20 ⁊ 21 chests	*Pl̃ita de Banco tempe R̸*	*R.* 2.
X.	In the 22th chest	*Pl̃ita coram Dño Rege tempe Regis*	*H.* 4.

"This book remains." abbreviated by me into a booke.

Y.	In the 23th chest	*Pl̃ita coram Dño Rege tempore Regis*	*H.* 5.

"This book remains." abbreviated by me 1607.

Z.	In the 24th chest	*Pedes finium tempe Regis*	*H.* 6.
	In the 25th chest are	*Pedes finium tempe R̸*	*H.* 7.
	In the 26 chest is	*Pedes finiū tempe R̸*	*E.* 2.
	In the 27 chest is	*Pedes finiū tempe R̸*	*E.* 3.
	In the 28 chest	*Pedes finiū de tempibȝ regū*	*R.* 2. *H.* 4. *H.* 5.

In the lower ranck.

One chest under the chestes of fines before menc̃oed, contayninge

Pedes finium in divers Kinges times, *de quibȝ quere, scil̃t de tempibȝ E.* 3. *R.* 1. *R.* 2. *E.*1. *E.*4. *R.* 3. ‖*H.* 3.

Item there are chests wherein are contained c̃taine writts of *H.* 4. 5. 6. both in the *King's Bench* and *Common Place.*

Item at the comeinge in of the same Threasaury, are sondry chests with writs of *E.* 2. and *E.* 3. time.

*In sm*a. The recordes there may bee mencõed more breefe in this manner.

Fines de tempibʒ	*R.* 1. *Jo.* *H.* 3. *E.* 1. *E.* 2.	*E.* 3. *R.* 2. *H.* 4. *H.* 5. *H.* 6.	*E.* 4. *E.* 5. *R.* 3. *H.* 7.

Pl̃ita corā Dño Rege	*R.* 1. *Jo.* *H.* 3. *E.* 1. *E.* 2.	*E.* 3. *R.* 2. *H.* 4. *H.* 5.	*et de Banco*	*R.* 1. *Jo.* *H.* 3. *E.* 1.	*E.* 2. *E.* 3. *R.* 2.

Pl̃ita coram Justic̃ itin̄antibʒ tempibʒ	*R.* 1. *Jo.* *H.* 3.

16 In the *Fourth Threasaurie*, beinge in the *Cloyster* of the said Abbay of *Westm̃* locked with 5 stronge keyes and within two stronge double dores, are kept †the recordꝭ wth others, which I cannot now name at large, because I tooke notes but on a suddaine, by reason I could not make any stay there, but as I remember in ꝑte.

Goulden leagues 3. in ye chest next the dore on the right hand.

The first betwixt *Henr̃ the* 8 and *Frauncis* Kinge of *France*, the seale beeinge worth an c^{li} at least.—" Not worth above a tenth part so " much, it being hollow ꝛ filled with wax."

Item another betwene the Kinge of *England* and the Kinge of *Castile*.

Item Pope *Clement's* Bull for the title of *Defensor fidei* geven to *H.* 8.

Item *Henry* 7 will.

Item *Henry* 8 will.

Item th exemplificacõn of it in a·box sealed, delivered in *July* 1602.

" 16. *July* 1696
" M^{d}' this bag of cord-
" ove^{r} being worne out,
" it was brought before
" the Privey Councell
" at the triall of the pix
" this 16th of *July*.1696
" & opene^{d} befo^{r}e them,
" who orde^{r}e^{d} what was
" in it to be put into a
" woo^{d}en box & seale^{d}
" with the seales of 2
" of the Privey Coun-
" cell videl't. the Right
" Hono^{r}able *Charles*
" *Montague* Esqr Chan-
" cele^{r} of the Excheq^{r}
" *John Smith* Esqre both
" Lord' Cõmissioners of
" his Majesties T^{r}ea-
" su^{r}y and of the Privey
" Councell, which [was]
" imme^{d}iatly ^{d}one ac-
" cordingly in thei^{r} pre-
" sence, and put up into
" the same chest by us
" *John Lowe* & *Peter Le*
" *Neve* Deputy Cham-
" berlains of the Excheque^{r}.

Item a bagg of cordover sealed with the seales of Privy Councello^{rs}, and is not to be opened but by the Prince and those of the P^{i}vy Counsell, wherein are matters of seacret.

Item assayes of gould and silver, and indentures of minte matters of Kinge *H.* 8. time Queene *Eliz.* and the Kings Mat^{y} that now is, Kinge *James*.

Item a very faire booke covered wth ||vellet, imbosed with silv^{er} gilt, touchinge the foundacõn of *Westm̃* Chappell by *H.* 7. put into a box lined with crimson silke quilted.

Item sondrie old seales of customs ꝛc.

" M^{d}' it contains some few essays of gol^{d} & silve^{r} in severall King's times, some we^{d}ges of " silve^{r}, severall old seales, some old stamps of coin, old weights, old ^{r}olls, of the t^{r}iall of the pix, " wa^{rr}ants and accounts the^{r}efo^{r}e, *ita testor Peter Le Neve.*"

In the next chest to that on the left hand.

Item sondry bookes therein covered with blew vellet very faire imbossed, touchinge an agreem[t] made betwene *H.* 7. and *Islip* then Abbot of *Westm*[r], concerninge masses, obsequies, dirgs and such like for priests, moncks, freres, both the universities, for the soule of *H.* 7. & annual pencons geiven to them for ever, for doinge thereof.

Item a box wherein are instrum[ts] of divers Bushops and the Univsitie of *Cambridge*, acknowledging *H.* 8. supremacy.

In twoe great wod chests on the left hand.

Leagues and treaties betwixt *England* and *Scotland* put into boxes, and kalendred into this booke.

In a ranck of presses next to the south-east side.

The bagg of matters touchinge the divorce of *H.* 8. from Qeene *Katherine* dowager.

Item a booke beeinge a lre from Cardinall *Poole* to Kinge *H.* 8. and an other to the Counsell, *Quo paras* ‖*Cæsar*.

In certaine drawinge boxes are contained

Sondry treaties of peace betwene *England* and *Fraunce*.

Item some matters touchinge *Ireland*.

Item sondry broad seales and privy seales cancelled for the lone of money.

In a chest there, and in sondry presses and drawers.

Sondry prive seales cancelled for the lone of money, conteined in a great canvas bagg.

In twoe chestes under the window there.

xv[tene] buckram bagges, wherein are contained the leagues betwixt the Kinges of *England* and sundry other nac̃ons, which are abbreviated and calendred by me into this booke.

INDEX.

INDEX.

A.

Abbatis Munketon', 178.
Adam and Eve, 144, 146, 176.
Adbrygton' Husee, 78.
Agnes uxor Willielmi de Arundell', 49.
Agyncourt, 96.
Albaniæ, Dux, 59, 80, 89.
Albones, Seint, 110.
Aldham, Tenementa in, 203.
Alemannia, 182.
Alemanniæ, Imperator, 111.
Alencon', Johannes Comes de, 84.
Alfonsus Rex Castellæ, 94.
Alfonsus Rex Ispanniæ, 94.
Alfonsus Rex Portugaliæ, 89.
Alicia uxor Willielmi fitz Wauter, 12.
Almadana, Johannes Valesci de, 88.
Almayne, 255.
Alnewyk, Johannes,—Custos Privati Sigilli, 121.
Alred, Richard, Ricardus, 138, 151.
Alred', Willielmus, 154.
Aluarus, Johannes, Decanus Visen', 88.
Alverniæ, Johannes, Dux Bituriæ et, 84.
Alyngton', Willielmus, 160.
Ampulla cum oleo benedicto, 116.
Anande, Dominus de Valle de, 200.
Andreæ, Costa Sancti, 275.
Andrewe, Ricardus, Secretarius Regis, 221, 225, 228.
Angevyn', B., 178.
Angle, Guychardus de, 40.
Anglesey, Priory of, 326.
(*Anglia*, *Angliæ*, *&c.*)
Anglia, 1, 2, 3, 4, 5, 7, 8, 9, 13, 27, 30, 31, 49, 50, 58, 60, 62, 67, 68, 71, 81, 82, 157, 172, 187, 192, 194, 196, 197, 201, 217, 225, 227, 235.
Angliæ, Ambassiatores, 65, 66, 67, 68, 80, 140.
Angliæ, Archiepiscopi et Episcopi, 81.
Angliæ, Arma, 104, 150.
Angliæ, Cancellarius, 34, 44, 61, 80, 132, 133, 156, 199, 213.
Angliæ, Cardinales, 161, 214, 215, 217.
Angliæ, Clerici, 328.
Angliæ, Domini, 46.
Angliæ, Ecclesia, *vel* Ecclesia Anglicana, 121.
Angliæ, Ecclesiæ Cathedrales, 2.
Angliæ, Magnates, 70.
Angliæ, Mercatores, 75.
Angliæ, Portus, 82.
Angliæ, Prelati, 81.
Anglia, Privilegia Regis in, 121.
Angliæ, Regnum, 77, 84, 89, 94.

Angliæ, Rex, 20, 36, 45, 46, 65, 71, 76, 77, 81, 83, 89, 91, 92, 99, 111, 120, 133, 169, 170, 195, 198, 199, 228.
Angliæ, Thesauraria et Thesaurarius, 42, 43, 52, 53, 54, 59, 60, 61, 62, 71, 72, 75, 79, 103, 104, 149, 153, 154, 155, 158, 161, 197, 198, 203, 204, 228, 238, 248.
Angliæ, Cancellarius, Archiepiscopus Ebor' Cardinalis, 148.
Angliæ, Cancellarius, Michael de la Pole, 17.
Angliæ, Cancellarius, Johannes Stafford, 109, 146.
Angliæ, Cardinalis, Henricus, — Henricus Episcopus Winton', 154, 163, 201, 202.
Angliæ, Thesaurarius, Thomas Comes Arundell', 84, 91.
Angliæ, Thesaurarius, Episcopus Bathon', Johannes Stafford, 110, 113, 114, 115, 117, 120, 122, 123, 124.
Angliæ, Thesaurarius, Johannes Dominus de Beauchamp, 223.
Angliæ, Thesaurarius, Vicecomes Bouzer, 231.
Angliæ, Thesaurarius, Radulphus Dominus de Cromwell', 89, 147, 151, 152, 154, 155, 159, 162, 172, 179, 181, 187, 190, 191, 192, 193, 194.
Angliæ, Thesaurarius, Episcopus Dunolm', Johannes, 19.
Angliæ, Thesaurarius, Henricus Fitzhugh, 97.
Angliæ, Thesaurarius, Walterus de Hungerford' *vel* Dominus Hungerford', 123, 124, 125, 127, 128, 129, 130, 134, 135, 136, 138, 139, 140, 141.
Angliæ, Thesaurarius, Episcopus Karliol', 152, 201.
Angliæ, Thesaurarius, Willielmus Kynwolmersshe, 101, 103, 112, 113, 189.
Angliæ, Thesaurarius, Dominus de Roos, 70.
Angliæ, Thesaurarius, Johannes Rotheuale, Miles, 101.
Angliæ, Thesaurarius, Comes Salop', Johannes Talbot, 234.
Angliæ, Thesaurarius, Jacobus Dominus Say, 204, 207, 212, 214, 216.
Angliæ, Thesaurarius, Johannes le Scrop', 141.
Angliæ, Thesaurarius, Radulphus Dominus de Sudeley, 195.
Angliæ, Thesaurarius, T. Tiptot, 78.
Angliæ, Thesaurarius, Jacobus Comes Wiltes', 237.
Angliæ, Thesaurarius, Johannes Comes Wygorn', 85, 226, 227, 228, 230.
Angliæ, Clericus Thesaurarii, Thomas Rothewell', 220.
Angliæ, Subthesaurarius, Willielmus Grymesby, Armiger, 238.
(*See also England, Engleterre, &c.*)
Anna Regina Angliæ, *vel* Anne la Roigne, 43, 46, 50, 51, 52.
Annesley, Hugo de, 48.
Aps, John, of Essex', 222.
Aquitanniæ, Ducatus *vel* Principatus, 14, 27, 35, 43, 45, 52, 84, 125, 136, 157, 178, 181, 327.
Arnaud, Colynet, 36.
Aron', Virga, 116, 123.
Arthurus de Britannia filius Ducis Britan', 97, 98.
Artoys, Carolus de, Comes de Augo, 98.

(*Arundell, Arondell.*)
Arundell', 56.
Arundell', Prioratus de, 14.
Arundell', Arondell', Conte de, 28, 40.
Arundell', Comes, Ricardus, 14, 57.
Arundell', Comes, Thomas, Thesaurarius Angliæ, 84, 91.
Arundell', Ricardus de, 27, 75.
Arundell', Thomas le, 160.
Arundell', Willielmus de, 57.
Arundell', Willielmus de, et Agnes uxor ejus, 49.
Ascowe, 130.
Aske, Johannes, 131.
Aske, treasons of, 324.
Assh', Jacobus, 53.
Asshton', Robertus de, 3, 45.
Aston', Thomas, 41.
Asty, Henricus, 22.
Athell', David Strabolgy Comes de, 234.
Atte More, Simon, 23.
Atte Roulles, Johannes, 24.
Attilbrigg, Johannes, 100.
Audeley, Arma de, 205.
Audemer, Robertus, nuper Scrutator Regis in Portu Villæ Sandewici, 157, 158.
Augo, Comes de, Carolus de Artoys, 98.
Augustini Cantuar', Abbas et Conventus Sancti, 51.
Auneys nadegaires la femme Adam Franceys, 25.
Aurelien', Karolus Dux, 84.
Aurilianens', Dux, 64.

B.

Babthorp', Robertus, 112.
Bacheley de Muscham, Willielmus de, 31.
Bacon', Johannes, 5, 15.
Bacun, Johannes, 8.
Baiou', 27.
Baldok, Weston juxta, 321.
Bamburgh', 194.
Bangoren', Decanus et Capitulum, 20.
Bangoren', Episcopus, 67.
Bangoren', Episcopus, Johannes, 20.
Baptist, Saint John, Images of, &c., 111, 118, 268.
Barbour, Thomas, 61.
Barda, Barnardus de Lesparre — Dominus de la, 109.
Barde, Bardes, Gauterus de, 16, 19.
Bardolf, Willielmus, 99.
Bardolf, Willielmus, et Johanna uxor ac executrix testamenti ejusdem Willielmi, 153.
Barges, Gauter de, 9.
Barkhampsted, 321.
Baron, Willielmus, 158.
Barselonia in Catelonia, Oliverus Petrus de, 74.
Barseloniæ, Carracha, 74.
Barstaple, Burgus de, 72.
Barton, Petrus de, 1.
Barton' super Humber, 44.
Barwycke, Lord, 303, 304, 305.
Barwycke, George Lorde Howme of, 299.
Basset, Johannes, 126.
Basset, Ricardus, 31.
Basset of the West Country, 327.
Batable Lond', Batable Landes, 221, 226.
Bathon',—Bathon' et Wellen', Episcopus, 55, 56, 60, 66, 69, 71, 108.
Bathon', Episcopus, Johannes, 110.
Bathon', Episcopus, Johannes Stafford, — Thesaurarius Angliæ, 122.
Bathon' et Wellen', Episcopus, Nicholaus, 180.

Bathon' et Wellen', Episcopus, Thomas, 199.
Bavaria, 59, 69.
Bavariæ, Bavarr', Dux, 69, 153, 154, 190.
Bavariæ, Dux, Rupertus Comes Palatinus, 59.
Bayous, Johannes, 140.
Beamond', Robert, 170.
Beatæ Mariæ, Liber de Concepcione, 97.
Beatæ Mariæ, Henricus de Plalvo Frater Ordinis, 81.
Beatæ Mariæ de Graciis, Abbas et Conventus, juxta Turrim London', 57.
Beatæ Mariæ Teuthonicorum, Dominus Paulus Rusderf Frater Ordinis, 163.
Beati Petri Westmonasterii, Abbacia, 156.
(*Beauchaump*, *Beauchamp'*.)
Beauchamp, Johannes Dominus de, Thesaurarius Angliæ, —Beauchamp, Tresorer of Englond', the Lorde, 222, 223.
Beauchaump, Johan, 25.
Beauchamp de Holt, J. de, 25.
Beauchamp', Richard,—Bisshop of Salisbury, 236.
Beauchamp, Walterus, 104.
Beauchamp, William, 18.
Beaumont, Johannes Vicecomes de, 221.
Bedford, 320.
Bedford', Comitatus, 229.
Bedford', Dux, 98, 110, 115, 116, 123.
Bedford, Bedeford, Dux, Johannes, 122, 147, 152, 156.
Bedumeny, Thomas, 60.
Bele, Patricius Dunbar de, 89.
Bello Campo, Rogerus de, 30.
Belman, Henricus, 90.
Benet, 142.
Benet, Henricus, 105, 179.
Berewic' super Twedam, Castrum de, 123.
Berewyk', Villa de, 221, 222, 226.
Berkamstede, 5.
Berners, Jacobus, 57.
Berry, Duc de, 27.
Beurley, Simond' de, 27.
Beverlacy, Villa, 13.
Bewemound', 108.
Bewemount, Henricus, 108.
Bilbau, Chastel et Lieu de, 39.
Bingley, Mr John, 315.
Birkes, Johannes del, 32, 33.
Biscaie, Terre de, 39.
Bituriæ, Dux, 64.
Bituriæ et Alverniæ, Dux, Johannes, 84.
Blakamore, Willielmus, 8.
Blake, Johannes, 225.
Blakenay, Johannes Frere de, 45.
Blanchia filia Regis Henrici, Domina, 69.
Blanchia Domina de Ponynges, 52.
Bloys, Johannes, 52.
Bodenham, Rogerus, 239.
Boffett, Johannes, 233.
Bohemiæ, Rex, 9.
Bohun, Johanna de,—Comitissa Hereford', 187, 188.
Bolton', Robertus, 30.
Bolyngbrok, Rogerus, 191.
Bonevile, Willielmus, 115.
Bordeux, Chastel de, 37.
Borrat, Henricus, 163.
Borthwyk, Willielmus de, 89.
Boteler, Johannes, 44.
Botreaux, Johannes, et Elizabeth uxor ejus, 90.
Bouelegh', Tenementa in, 161.
Bourgchier, Humfridus, 233.
Bouland, Johannes, 6, 16.
Bourboniæ, Dux, 64, 116.
Bouremeus, Benedictus, 154.
Bouzer, Vicecomes, Thesaurarius Angliæ, 231.
Bowes, Willielmus, 115.

Bowet, 71.
Bowman', Petrus, 191, 193.
Boys, Rogerus de, 47.
Bradford, 319.
Bradshawe, Willielmus, 140.
Branketre, Johannes, 30.
Braunсepeth', — Braunsepath', — Braunspath', — Willielmus, 48, 149, 253.
Bray, Johannes, 95.
Bray, Willielmus, 99, 100.
Braybrok, Gerardus de, 48, 187, 188.
Bredon', Thomas, 149, 151.
Breknoke, Davidus, Custos Garderobæ excellentissimi Principis Johannis nuper Ducis Bedford, 147.
Brember, Nicholaus, 25.
Brettigny, 98.
Breybrok, Reginaldus, 48.
Breympt, Arnoldus de, 182.
Brian, Guido de, 30.
Briggewater, Tenementa in, 178.
Bristoll', Villa, 60.
Bristuyt, Johannes de Lascels de, 22.
Britain, Brytaigne, Great, 305.
Britannia, Bretaigne, Dux, Duc, de, 2, 6, 24, 26, 43, 54, 76, 83, 91, 92, 190, 191, 195, 230, 231.
Britannia *vel* Bretaigne, Johan Duc de, 30.
Britannia, Arthurus de, filius Ducis Britanniæ, 97, 98.
Britanniæ, Dominus Egidius frater Ducis, 196.
Brocas, Arnaldus, 24, 25.
Brocas, Bernard', 5, 41.
Brokaz, Johannes, 14.
Broker, Nicholaus, 50.
Broune, Broun, Johannes, 104, 226.
Broun', Johannes, — Camerarius Scaccarii, 198.
Broun', John, Undertresorer, 235.
Broun', Thomas, 198, 203.
Broun, Thomas, Squyer, 255.
Browych, Johannes de, 48.
Bruges, 203.
Brune, Moricius, 136.
Brus, Robertus de, 200.
Brustwyk', Manerium et Dominium de, 115.
Brut, Robertus, Armiger, 253.
Brays de Scocia, David de, 15.
Brydde, 149.
Bryt, 149.
Brytte, Dominus Karolus de la, 169.
Bubbewith', Bubwith', Bubwyth', Nicholaus,—Custos Privati Sigilli, 67, 69, 73.
Buckingham, Edward Duke of, 321.
Bukland', Ricardus, Thesaurarius Cales', et Johanna uxor ejus, 122, 153, 191, 192.
Bukyngham, Richardus, 26.
Bukyngham, Thomas Comes de, 11, 12.
Burbon', Burboyn', Dux, 90, 156.
Burbon', Johannes Dux, 84, 115.
Burbon', Lodewicus de,—Comes de Vandom', 96.
Burbon', The Tablet of, 262.
Burdegal', 178.
Burdegal', Senescalcia, 178.
Burdegal', Constabularius, Walterus Colles, 178.
Burges, Cite de, 37.
Burges, Thomas, 115.
Burgh', J., 77.
Burgh', Johannes, Thesaurarius, 87, 89, 91, 92, 94.
Burgh', Simon de, 8.
Burgis, Cite de, 39.
Burgis, Esglise Cathedral de, 38.
Burgman de Congover, Nicholaus, 59.
Burgund', Burgoigne, The Tablet of, 202, 257.

Burgundiæ, Burgoyne, Dux, Duc de, 64, 95, 99, 117, 147, 154, 156.
Burgondiæ, Burgund', Ducissa, 192.
Burgundiæ, Ducissa, Isabella, 203.
Burgundiæ, Dux, Johannes, 179.
Burgundiæ, Dux, Philippus, 153, 200, 204.
Burguyllon', Robertus, 34.
Burle, Manerium de, 11.
Burley, Johannes de, 27, 75.
Burley, Simon de, 27, 57, 75.
Burnell', Hugo,—Dominus de Holgot, 95.
Burrewell', Johannes, 41.
Burstalle, Willielmus, 3.
Burton', Johan, Clerk to Walter Lord Hungurford, Tresorer of Yngeland, 136.
Burton', Philippus, 61, 62.
Burton', Robertus, 191.
Burton', Robertus, Camerarius de Scaccario, 125.
Burton', Robertus,—et Elizabetha uxor ejus, 160.
Burwell', Manerium de, 22.
Bussy, Johannes, 54.
But, Johannes, 60.
Butiller, Radulphus, 214, 217.
Butt, Robertus, 45.
Bykebury, 160.
Bykebury, Margareta de, 160.
Bykenore de Claveryng', Johannes, 47.
Bykenore de Derteford', Robertus de, 47.
Byllyngford', 49.
Byngham, Manerium de, 48, 49.
Byngham, Willielmus de, et Isabella uxor ejus, 49.
Byrmyngeham, 178.
Byrmyngeham, Willielmus, 178.
Bysshop', Gilbertus, 161.

C.

Caborne, Willielmus, 11.
Cade, Johannes, 218, 220.
Cadomo, Abbatissa de, 48.
Cales', Calais, Calays, Callayes, 30, 53, 95, 98, 99, 153, 161, 200, 248, 321, 324, 328.
Cales', Major Stapulæ Villæ, 158, 197.
Cales', Thesaurarius, Ricardus Bukland', 122, 191.
Cales', Thesaurarius Villæ, Ricardus Merlawe, 82.
Caluilegh', Hugo, 8.
Cambridge, Universitie of, 334.
Camera Stellata, 199, 225, 227.
Camera de Normanton', Robertus de, 32.
Cantebrig', 10.
Cantebrig', Comitatus, 229.
Cantebrig', Universitas, 155.
Cantebrig', Comes, Edmundus, 10.
(*Canterbury*, *Cantuar'*, *&c.*)
Canterbury, 272.
Cantuar', Archiepiscopus, — Canterbers, Erchesvesque de, —Caunterbury, l Erchevesque de, 70, 82, 121, 128, 130, 165, 176, 214.
Cantuar', Archiepiscopus, Henricus, 132.
Cantuar', Archiepiscopus, Johannes, 225, 230.
Caunterbury, Archiebisshop' of, John, 209.
Cantuar', Archiepiscopus, Johannes, Sanctæ Balbinæ Episcopus Cardinalis, Cancellarius Angliæ, 229.
Canterbury, Saint Thomas of, 272.
Cantuar', Prior et Conventus, 43.
Cantirbirz, Prior et Conventus de, 43.

Cantuar', Sancti Augustini, Abbas et Conventus, 51.
Cardikan, 40.
Cardinall Colledg in Oxford, 329.
Carolus Rex Franciæ, 99, 147. (*See Karolus.*)
Carpenter, Johannes, 141, 148.
Carrewe, Thomas, Chivaler, 159.
Castellæ, Rex, — Castile, Kinge of, 38, 333.
Castellæ, Regnum, 94.
Castellæ, Rex, Alfonsus, 94.
Castellæ, Rex, Petrus, 37, 93.
Castellæ et Legionis, &c., Rex, 19, 27, 46, 58, 88, 91, 92, 195.
Castellæ et Legionis, Rex, Dux Lancastriæ, Johannes, 1.
Castellæ et Legionis, Toleti, &c., Rex, Johannes, 20, 91.
Catalonia, 74.
Catesby, Johannes de, 34.
Catesby, Robertus, 325.
Catrik', Johannes, 77.
Caudrey, Ricardus, 155.
Caundysh', Johannes, 136.
Cawedre, Ricardus, 93.
Chaddesley, Johannes, 60.
Chapter House of the Abbay of Westminster, third Treasury in, 312, 329.
Charnell', Capella vocata le, 233, 237.
Chartres, 98.
Chaterton', Henricus, 97.
Chatesham, 203.
Chaundos, Johan, 40.
Chaungeour, Adam, 4.
Chaworth', Thomas, 128.
Chenduyt, Johannes, 124.
Cheny, Matheus, 19.
Chepyngtoryton', 161.
Cherlton', Capella de, 113.
Cherlton', Edwardus de,—Dominus de Powys, 188.
Chester, 320.
Chetewynd', Philippus, et Elena uxor ejus, 178.
Cheyne, Johannes, 48.
Cheyne, Matheus, 11.
Cheyne, Willielmus, 160, 177, 178.
Chippeham, 6.
Chirburgh', Castrum et Villa de, 11, 19, 20, 46, 158.
Chirche, Johannes, 152, 201, 202.
Chirk et Chirklandes, in Wallia, Maneria de, 157.
Chirkeslond', Chyrk, 187.
Chitterne, Johannes, 133.
Chitterne, Chyttern', Thomas, — Clericus jocalium, — Gardein des joualx le Roy Henry,—Clericus jocalium Regis Henrici Quinti, 101, 102, 125, 134.
Chorley, Oliverus, 140.
Cicestr', Episcopus, 199.
Clare, Gilbertus de, 199.
Clarence, Duchesse de, 165.
Clarenciæ, Thomas nuper Dux, 131.
Claryngdon', Parcus de, 113.
Claryngdon', Rogerus de, 7.
Claveryng, Johannes Bykenore de, 47.
Clay, Weston' in the, 33.
Clement, Pope, 333.
Clifford', Lodewycus de, 48.
Clifford', Rogerus Dominus de, 21.
Clipston' o'the Hill', Manerium de, 49.
Clivis, Gerardus de, Comes de Marka, 182.
Clux, Hertauk' Van, 180.
Clyff, Johannes, — Ministrallus Henrici Quinti, 150.
Clynton', Johannes de, 54.
Clyuelond', 72.
Cobeham, Manerium de, 89.
Cobham, Dominus de, 89, 227.
Cobham, Edwardus Dominus, 226.

Cock', Johannes, 32, 33.
Codegrave, 49.
Cokayn, Johannes, 160.
Coldham, Manerium de, in Comitatu Essex', 47.
Colepeper, Johannes, 90.
Colles, Walterus, Constabularius Burdegal', 178.
(*Cologne, Colonia, &c.*)
Colonien' Civitas, 190.
Coloniæ, Reges, 123.
Coloniæ, Ecclesia Sancti Andrææ, 182.
Colonien', Archiepiscopus, — Cologne, the Erchebisshop' of, 58, 255.
Colonien', Archiepiscopus, Sacri Romani Imperii per Italiam Archicancellarius, Westfaliæ et Angariæ Dux,—Theodericus, 190.
Colt, Thomas, Camerarius Scaccarii, 246, 247, 252.
Colvyle, Colvyll', Johannes, 94, 115, 132.
Common Place *or* Common Pleas, 332.
Compendium Theologicæ Veritatis, Liber vocatus, 97.
Conceptione Beatæ Mariæ, Liber de, 97.
Confluen', Ecclesia Sancti Florini, 190.
Congover, Nicholaus Burgman de, 59.
Consilio Regis, Domini de, 76, 176, 194, 196, 198, 230.
Consilium, Acta facta per, 203.
Constable, Willielmus, 154, 155.
Constantinople, 58.
Constantinopolitanis Imperator,—Constantinoble, Imperator de, 58, 63.
Cook, Walter, 133.
Corbet, Thomas, 131.
Cornwall, Cornubia, 72, 316.
Cornewaill', Countee de, 28.
Cornewayle, Johannes, 96.
Cory, Manerium de, 192.
Cottesmore, Johannes, 178.
Cotum, Robertus, 36.
Coucy, Dominus de, 1.
Courtenay, 83.
Courtenay, Arma de, 205.
Courtenay *or* Cortney, The Earle of, 324.
Courtenay, Ricardus, nuper Episcopus Norwicen' et Thesaurarius Cameræ Regis Henrici Quinti, — Courtenay, Ricardus, nuper Clericus jocalium Henrici V[ti] Regis Angliæ, — Courtnay, Richard, l'Evesque de Norwicz, 104, 106, 111, 127, 131, 140, 253.
Courteney, Philippus de, 17.
Courteney, Ricardus, 82.
Court of Receipt, 312.
Covelyng, Manerium de, 89.
Coventre, Villa de, 70, 178, 229.
Coventre, Maier et Comunaltee de la Cite de, 130.
Coventre, Richard' Crosby Priour de, 130.
Coventry and Lich', Bushoprik of, 327.
Craddok, Ricardus, 4.
Crane de Cranebrok', Johannes, 23.
Creon', Balliva de, 7.
Cressewell', Johannes, 29.
Cristofre, Seint, 173, 273.
Cromlyn, Manoir de, 17.
Cromwell', Dominus Radulphus de, Thesaurarius Angliæ, —Lord Rauf', Tresorer of Inglond', 89, 114, 115, 147, 151, 152, 154, 155, 159, 162, 172, 179, 181, 182, 187, 190, 191, 192, 193, 194, 202, 209, 225, 230, 231.
Cromwell *or* Crumwell, Lord, 316.

Cromwell', Thomas, 326.
Crumwell', Willielmus, 115.
Crosby, Richard', Priour de Coventre, 130.
Crull', Robertus, 8.
Cumberland', Comitatus, 24, 326.

D.

Dalburgh', Johannes Camerarius de, 59.
Dalthorndik', Campus de Normanton apud, 31.
Dalton', Johan de, 18.
Dalyngrege, Edwardus, 48.
Dame, Nostre,—Oure Ladye, 70, 111, 118, 119, 144, 146, 176, 261, 268, 275.
Darcy, The Lord, 324.
Darcy, Robertus, 156, 188, 189.
Darell', Johannes, 70, 141.
Darell, Willielmus, Subthesaurarius, 124, 125.
Dartasso, Janico, Jenicus, 26, 81.
Dautre, Johannes, 45.
David Dux Rothesaye, 56.
David Rex Scociæ, 234, 235.
David primogenitus Regis Scociæ, 59.
David, Edwardus ap, 188.
David, Evesque de Seint, 70.
David, Johan Evesque de Seint, 41.
Davy, Gerardus, Mercator Florenciæ, 96.
Davy, Ricardus, 233.
Dene, Comes de, 16.
Deneye, Manerium de, 6.
Denmark', 199.
Denmark', Rex, 199.
Deram, Ricardus, 9.
Derby, Gaola, 112.
Derteford', Robertus de Bykenore de, 47.
Dertem', Johannes Hawele de, 28.
Despenser, Anne le, 11.
Devon', Comitatus, 322.
Devon',Comes,—Devon',TheEarle of, 227, 324.
Devon', Comes, Thomas, 226.
Devonshire, The Earle and Countesse of, 321.
Devyses, Castrum de, 6.
Dewe, Ricardus, 162.
Dewe, Ricardus, unus Hostiariorum Scaccarii, 253.
Dionisia que fuit uxor Willielmi de Sutton', 5.
Dixon', Nicholaus, 110, 160.
Dodyngton', Johannes de Leyre Rector Ecclesiæ de, 11.
Domini de Consilio Regis, 76, 176, 194, 196, 198, 230.
Dorset, The Earle of, 325.
Dorset, The Erle of, Lorde High Tresorer of Englande, 299.
Douglas, Comes de, Jacobus, 228.
Drwe, Laurencius, 54, 56.
Duaco, Homines de, 113.
Dunbar' de Bele, Patricius de, 89.
Dunolm', Dominus, *vel* Episcopus, 73, 92, 148, 221.
Dunolm', Episcopus, Johannes, Thesaurarius Angliæ, 19.
Dunolm', Episcopus, Thomas, 61, 187, 188, 189.
Dunolm', Episcopus, Walterus, 64.
Durant, Thomas, 2.
Durwarde, Johannes, 125.
Duryngton', Robertus Seman de, 57.
Dutton', Thomas, 124.
Dyghton', Sr William de, 17, 24.

E.

Ebor', Archiepiscopus, 44, 147, 179.
Ebor', Archiepiscopus, Cardinalis, Cancellarius Angliæ, — Ebor', Dominus Cardinalis, 148, 192.
Ebor', Cardinalis, Johannes, 195.
Ebor', Civitas, 13.
Ebor', Comitatus, 319, 325.
Ebor', Dux, 42, 166, 169, 215, 216, 227.
Ebor', Dux, Edwardus, 88, 138.
Ebor', Dux, Ricardus, 171, 191, 193, 226, 230.
Ebor', Thesaurarius Ecclesiæ, 70.
Edenham, Ecclesia Parochialis de, 50.
Ederose, Prior Ecclesiæ, juxta Parcum de Clarendon', 113.
Edmond, Seynt, his Armes, 145.
Edmundus Comes Cantab', 10.
Edmundus Rex Siciliæ, filius Henrici Regis Angliæ, 152.
(*Edwardus*, *Edward.*)
Edward Duke of Buckingham, 321.
Edwardus Dux Ebor', 88, 138.
Edward Erle of Worcester, Master of the Horse, 299.
Edwardus Princeps Walliæ, — Edward Prince de Gales, 45, 125, 140.
Edwardus I., — Edwardus Primus, Rex Angliæ,—Edward fitz a Roy Henry, 86, 199, 200, 315, 317, 318, 320, 321, 322, 323, 324, 325, 326, 330, 331, 332.
Edwardus II. nuper Rex Angliæ, avus Regis, 1, 3, 316, 320, 325.
Edwardus III. Rex Angliæ, 18, 30, 32, 33, 34, 47, 53, 94, 98, 100, 234, 235, 305, 320.
Edwardus IV., Edwardus Quartus, 192, 204, 226, 228, 240, 241, 246, 247, 252, 253, 323.
Edwardus Rex Portugaliæ, 159.
Edward, Seynt, his Armes, 119, 145.
Edwardus ap David, 188.
Egesippus, Liber vocatus, 152.
Egidius, Dominus, frater Ducis Britanniæ, 196.
Elena uxor Philippi Chetewynd', 178.
Elien', Episcopatus, 169, 212.
Elizabetha uxor Roberti Burton', 160.
Elizabethe, Quene,—Elizabeth the Quene, 318, 323, 328, 333.
Elizabeth' uxor Johannis Botreaux, 90.
Elmeden', Willielmus, 194.
Eltham, 30.
Elvet, Johannes, 59, 79.
Ely, Johan Evesque de, 41.
Emendatione Vitæ, Liber vocatus Libellus de, 97.
Emma uxor et Johanna filia Nicholai Taillour de Yeuele, 90.
Emperour, the, his Armes, 145.
(*England*, *Engleterre*, *&c.*)
England, Engleterre, 256, 299, 318, 320, 324.
Englande, Lord Admyrall of, Charles Erle of Nottingham, 299.
England and Castile, Armes of, 264.
Engleterre et France, Armes de, 117, 120, 145.
Engleterre, Cardinal de, Evesque de Wynchestre, Henri, 142, 164.
England, Chaunceller of, 235.
England, Kinges of,—Engleterre, Roys de, 38, 43, 87, 333, 335.

England and Scotland, Leagues between, 234.
England, Shires of, 316, 317.
England and France, Treaties between, 327.
England', Engleterre, Tresorer of, 70, 106, 128, 236, 256.
Englond', Tresorer of, the Lorde Beauchamp, 222.
Englande, Lord High Tresorer of, the Erle of Dorsett, 299.
Englond', Tresorer of, Jamys Fenys, Knyght, Lorde Saye, — England, Tresourer of, Lorde Say, 208, 210.
Engleterre, Tresorer de, Johan Evesque de Hereford, 25.
Engleterre, Tresorer de, Walter Seigneur de Hungyrford', 129, 131, 132.
Engleterre, Tresorer de, Willielmus Kynwolmersshe, 110.
Engleterre, Tresorer de, Johan Evesque de Saresbirz, 42.
Engleterre, Tresourer de, Sire de Scrop, 167.
England', late Tresourer of, Lord Rauf Sudeley, 209, 255.
(*See also Anglia, &c.*)
Ermoniæ, Rex, 47.
Erpyngham, Thomas, 63, 115.
Escoce, 43, 55.
Espaigne, 38, 39.
Essex', 47, 125, 222, 316, 322.
Essex', Willielmus, 217, 224.
Estcourt, Johannes, 95, 99.
Estfeld', Sir William, Knyght, 255, 256.
Estfeld of London', William, 168, 175, 202.
Esturmy, Willielmus, 68.
Euere, Rauf de, 55.
Eugenius Papa, Dominus, 227.
Everwyk, 27.
Everwyk, Duc de, 40.
Exon', 160.
Exon', Dux, 112.
Exon', Episcopus, 3, 66.
Exon', Episcopus, Thomas, 5, 8.
Exton', Nicholaus de, Mair de Londres, 23, 25.
Eyre de Padeley, Robertus, 112.
Eyre, Simon, Civis et Aldermannus London', 232.
Eyston' de Istelworth, Willielmus, 169.

F.

Faunhop', Faunhope, Lorde,—Johannes nuper Dominus, 207, 208, 209, 210.
Fawnhope, Lorde, Executors of the, 257.
Fawland', 80.
Faxflete, Johannes de, 44.
Felbrigg', Georgius, 22, 24.
Felde, Feelde, Thomas, 74, 76, 83, 88, 94, 98.
Felde, Thomas, Episcopus Norwic', 84.
Felton', Robertus, 102, 103.
Felton', Thomas de, 40.
Felton', Thomas de, et Johanna uxor ejus, 13.
Fenes, Robertus, 18.
Fenne, Hugo, 204.
Fenys, Jacobus, Miles, Dominus de Saye, Thesaurarius Angliæ, —Jamys Fenys, Knyght, Lorde Saye, Tresorer of Englond', 210, 212.
Fermer, Lambertus, 28.
Ferriby, Thomas de, 12.
Filia Nicholai le Taillour de Yeuele, Johanna, 90.
Filii Hugonis de Normanton', Hugo filius Johannis, 31, 32.
Filius Adæ Pounde, Johannes Pounde, 44.
Filius et heres Johannis Hunt, Willielmus, 5.

Filius Henrici, Willielmus, 33, 34.
Filius Jacobi de Radcliff, Johan, 137.
Filius Johannis de Stretton', Ricardus, 44.
Filius Ricardi de Weston', Willielmus, 32, 33.
Filius Willielmi de Normanton', Johannes, 34.
Filius Willielmi de Weston', Johannes, 34.
Filius Willielmi de Weston', Nicholaus, 32, 33, 34.
Fife, Comes de, 89.
Fillipot, Johannes, 4.
Fisher, Busshop, 324.
Fitz Harry, Thomas, 239.
Fitz Hugh, Henricus, Thesaurarius Angliæ, 97.
Fitz Lowes, Philipp', 222.
Fitz Nicholai, Thomas, 187, 188.
Fitz Roberti, Johannes, 129.
Fitz Wauter, Willielmus, et Alicia uxor ejus, 12.
Flandria, 67, 68, 80, 82, 95, 99, 113, 192, 200, 203, 204, 248.
Flaxflete, Manerium de, 6.
Flemmyng, Ricardus, 98.
Flemyng', David', 69.
Flemyng', Ricardus, nuper Episcopus Lincoln', 149, 151.
Flete, Willielmus, 160.
Florence, Florencia, 37, 96, 227.
Florencius Comes de Holand', 200.
Florymundus, Franciscus, 27.
Foitz, Foix, Comes de, 16, 34, 105, 194.
Foljambe, Jacobus, 48.
Fordham, Johannes, Clericus Privati Sigilli, 2, 5, 81.
Fournyvall', Dominus de, 71, 72.
Fox, Ricardus, 95.
Franceys, Adam, 25.
(*Fraunce*, *France.*)
France, Frauncis King of, 333.
Francia, 30, 31, 49, 63, 67, 68, 77, 110, 131, 135, 154, 156, 157, 159, 163, 191, 194, 195, 196, 197, 198, 201, 217, 299, 327.
Franciæ, Ambassiatores, 65, 66, 67, 68, 80, 197.
Franciæ, Arma, 98, 117, 120, 140, 150.
Franciæ, Cancellarius, Episcopus de Tyrwyn, 154, 159, 169.
Franciæ, Commissarii, 196, 197, 198.
Franciæ, Rex, 27, 43, 45, 46, 61, 62, 66, 67, 77, 91, 92, 104, 110, 136, 141, 147, 195, 196, 198, 333.
Franciæ, Rex, Carolus, *vel* Francorum, Karolus Rex, 99, 109, 147, 194, 198.
Franciæ, Rex, Johannes, 65, 98, 179.
Franciæ, Isabella filia Karoli Regis, 60, 62.
Francia, Sanctus Lodowycus de, 216.
Fraunceys, Adam, 51.
Frauncis Kinge of France, 333.
Fratrum Minorum, Domus, in Villa Salop', 108.
French territories, 324.
Frere, Johannes, de Blakenay, 45.
Fry, Frye, Robertus, 20, 56, 65, 66, 67, 71, 74, 76, 86, 87, 92, 93, 121.
Fryse, 64.
Fryseby, Johannes de Yngham de, 45.
Fulborne, Willielmus, 28.
Furnevale, Dominus de, 70.
Fuxi, Comes, Thesaurarius Angliæ, 104.
Fylongeley, Richard, 43.
Fynes, James, 208.

G.

Galandre, Willielmus, 42.
Gales, 40.
Gales, Principaltee de, 133.
Gales, Prince de, Edward, 43.
Gallicus, Rex, 64.
Garnsey et Jerseye, 319.
Gascoine, 327.
Gaunstede, Simon', 57, 188.
Gedyngton', Ricardus, 42.
Gelre, Gelrie, Duc, Duk', Dux de, 25, 26, 81.
Geleriæ, Gelieræ, Dux, Willielmus, 22, 24.
Georgius, Sanctus,—George, Saint, 119, 143, 164, 183, 185, 202, 204, 253, 254, 256, 257, 260, 271, 272.
Gerberg', Thomas, 40, 42.
Gernade, Roy de, 38.
Geyton', Ecclesia de, 237.
Glancestr' de Sutton', Johannes de, 32, 33.
Gloucestr', 77.
Gloucestr', — Mineræ auri et argenti in Comitatu, 22.
Gloucester, Statutes of, 317.
Gloucestriæ, Dux, 93, 110, 133, 161, 165, 214, 215, 254.
Gloucestriæ, Dux, Humfridus, 115, 181.
Gloucestriæ, Dux, Thomas, 48, 114.
Godford', Johannes, 5.
Goldbeter, Bartholomeus, 122.
Gornay, 45.
Goston, Francis, 306, 309.
Gotehurst, Tenementa de, 178.
Gourney, Matheus de, et Philippa uxor ejus, 45.
Graciis juxta Turrim London', Abbas et Conventus Beatæ Mariæ de, 57.
Grame, Johannes, Comes de Monteth', 234.
Gray, Dominus de, 7.
Grecorum, reductio ad Ecclesiam Catholicam, — Grecorum, Sigilla aurea, 227.
Gregorius Papa, 70.
Gressethorp', 34.
Gresthorp', Campus de, 31.
Griffyth', Henricus ap, 239.
Grill', Reginaldus, 63.
Grymesby, Willielmus, Armiger, Subthesaurarius Angliæ, 238.
Grymeston', Gerardus de, 45.
Guernsey, 320.
Guyene, 52, 181.
Guyene, Duchy de, 133.
Guyene, Principalte de, 38.
Guynes in Marchia Cales', 122.
Gwyn, Morys, 42.

H.

Haddeley, Johannes de, 23.
Hadlegh', Tenementa in, 203.
Hals, Johannes, 160.
Halswell', Willielmus, 178.
Hamme uppon Kyngeston', Manerium de, in Comitatu Surr', 95.
Hampdon', Stoke under,—Manerium de, 192.
Hampton Court, 321.
Hance, Hanss', Hans, Homines de Prucia sic vocati, 170, 193.
Hankeford', Willielmus, 161.
Hardyng', Johannes, de Kyme, 225, 234, 235.
Harecourt, Willielmus de, Comes de Tankerville, 224.
Hareflete, 100.
Harlyng, Thomas, 187, 189.
Harpeden', Johannes, 57.
Harry, Thomas fitz, 239.
Haryngton', Willielmus, 103.

Hastynges, Edwardus, 69.
Hatclyff, Willielmus, 192.
Hateleyfeld', Campus vocatus, 78.
Hatton' Grange, 12.
Haudenstank', 59, 71.
Haukesworth', Johannes, 162.
Haukford', Willielmus, 188.
Hauley, Thomas, 140.
Haverford', Villa de, 42.
Hawele de Dertem', Johannes, 28.
Hay de Lochorwart, Willielmus de, 89.
Hayton', Daiquin de, 18.
Hayton', Willielmus, 141.
Heen, Johannes, 188.
Heende, Johannes, Civis et Aldermanus London', 126.
Hemyrford', Henricus, 90.
Henrici, Willielmus filius, 34.
Henricus Cardinalis Angliæ et Episcopus Wynton',—Henri Cardinal d Engleterre, Evesque de Wynchestre, — Herry Byschop of Wynchestre and Cardynal of Yngeland, 115, 136, 142, 145, 146, 154, 163, 164, 183, 187, 201, 202.
Henricus Princeps Walliæ, 65.
Henricus II., 316.
Henricus III., 318, 329.
Henricus IV., 3, 7, 9, 20, 26, 27, 55, 58, 59, 60, 61, 63, 64, 65, 66, 67, 68, 69, 70, 71, 72, 73, 74, 75, 76, 77, 78, 79, 80, 81, 82, 83, 84, 85, 86, 92, 108, 112, 195, 221.
Henrici IV., Philippa filia Regis, 65.
Henricus V., 76, 83, 84, 85, 86, 87, 88, 89, 90, 91, 92, 93, 94, 95, 96, 97, 98, 99, 100, 101, 102, 103, 104, 105, 108, 109, 110, 122, 137, 138, 139, 140, 141, 154, 156, 159, 161, 179, 180, 183, 194, 195, 203, 213.
Henricus VI., 1, 56, 82, 85, 89, 93, 96, 98, 105, 109, 110, 113, 114, 115, 116, 117, 120, 121, 122, 123, 124, 125, 126, 127, 128, 129, 130, 131, 132, 133, 134, 135, 136, 137, 138, 139, 140, 141, 146, 147, 148, 149, 151, 152, 153, 154, 155, 156, 157, 158, 159, 160, 161, 162, 163, 169, 170, 172, 175, 178, 179, 181, 186, 189, 190, 191, 192, 193, 194, 195, 196, 197, 198, 199, 200, 201, 202, 203, 204, 207, 210, 212, 213, 214, 216, 217, 221, 223, 224, 226, 227, 228, 229, 230, 231, 232, 233, 234, 236, 238, 239, 248, 253, 255, 321, 332.
Henricus, Henry, VII., 321, 323, 333, 334.
Henricus, Henrye, VIII., 305, 306, 316, 318, 321, 323, 325, 327, 328, 333, 334.
Herburgh', Henricus, 77.
Hereford, Arma de, 207.
Hereford', Comitissa, Johanna,—Johanna de Bohun Comitissa, 85, 187, 188.
Hereford' Episcopus, Johannes, 21.
Hereford', Evesque de, Johan, Trésorer d Engleterre, 252.
Hermesthorpe, Johannes de, 5, 8, 15, 22, 24, 28, 30, 41.
Hermesthorp', Willielmus de, 3.
Hertford', 160.
Hertham, Johannes, 60.
Heruorst, Hugo de, 58.
Hetou', Daykyn de, 18.
Heud, Johannes, 78.

Hibernia, 3, 4, 27, 31, 49, 58, 75, 90, 130, 198, 199, 327.
Hibernia, Privilegia Regis in, 121.
Hiberniæ, Dux, 52.
Hirtz Horn', Johannes, 59.
Hispania *vel* Ispania, 19, 20, 53, 88, 92, 93, 94, 99, 197.
Hispania *vel* Hyspania, Petrus de, 21.
Hispanniæ *vel* Ispanniæ, Rex, Alfonsus, 94.
Hobbesgrove, 51.
Hoke, Johannes, 61.
Hokelyng', Robertus, 12.
Holand', Johannes, Comes Huntingdon', 72, 85.
Holand', Karolus de, 76, 83.
Holand', Thomas de, — Comes Kanc', 10.
Holand', Comes de, Florencius, 200.
Holbache, David', 187.
Holdanby, Rogerus, 65.
Holdirnesse, 115.
Holgot, Hugo Burnell', Miles, Dominus de, 95.
Holt, J. Beauchamp de, 25.
Holtzhein, Wynandus de, 58.
Hoo, Thomas, 193.
Hotoft, Johannes, Thesaurarius Hospitii Regis, 114, 129, 130, 131, 160.
Houdenstang, 73.
Howme of Barwycke, George Lorde, 299.
Hubbard', Sir Henry, Attorney Generall, 325.
Hughloc, Willielmus, 28.
Hugo filius Johannis filii Hugonis de Normanton', 31, 32, 34.
Hugonis, Robertus filius, 32.
Hull', Kyngston' super, 44.
Humbr', Barton' super, 44.
Humfridus Dux Gloucestriæ, 115, 181.
Hundeslowe, Prior et Conventus Sanctæ Trinitatis de, 12.
Hungerford', Hungyrford', Dominus, Thesaurarius Angliæ, — Hungerford', Le Sire, Thesorer d Engleterre, — Hungreford', Walterus Dominus, Thesaurarius Angliæ, 110, 111, 123, 124, 125, 127, 128, 129, 130, 131, 132, 133, 134, 135, 136, 137, 138, 139, 140, 141, 178.
Hunt, Rogerus, 192.
Hunt, Thomas, 11.
Huntyngdon', 62.
Huntingdon', Comes, Johannes, 105.
Huntingdon', Comes, Johannes Holand', 72, 85.
Huntyngdon', filia Comitis, 62.
Huntingdon', Willielmus filius et heres Johannis, 5.
Hyntylsham, Tenementa in, 203.

I.

Iclyngton' *vel* Iklenton Coler, 129, 165, 184.
Inglond and France, Armes of, 250, 251.
Inglond', and Bisshop' of Wynchestre, Herry Cardynall' of, 128.
Inglond', Tresourer of, 167, 168, 169, 170, 175, 177.
Inglond', Tresorer of,—Rauf Lord Cromwell', 182.
Innocent, Johannes, 29, 48, 50, 51, 55, 56, 59, 63.
Innocentius Papa III., (*Lotharius Cardinal Bishop of Ostia*,) 3.

Innocentius Papa IV., (*Sinebaldo de' Fieschi,*) 2.
Irby, Johannes, 101.
Ireland', 17, 299, 334.
Irlond', Ricardus, 188.
Isabella Ducissa Burgundiæ, 203.
Isabella Regina Angliæ, 64, 192.
Isabella filia Karoli Regis Franciæ,—filia Regis Franciæ, 60, 62.
Isabella uxor Ricardi Magotson', 33.
Isabella uxor Willielmi de Byngham, 49.
Islip Abbot of Westminster, 334.
Istelworth', 169.
Istelworth', Willielmus Eyston' de, 169.

J.

Jacobus Comes de Douglas, 228.
Jacobus Comes d'Ormon', 130.
Jacobus Comes Wiltes', Thesaurarius Angliæ, 237, 239.
Jacobus Dominus de Say, Thesaurarius Angliæ et Camerarius Scaccarii Regis Westmonasterii, 204, 214, 216.
Jacobus Rex, James I., 299, 306, 309, 333.
Jacobus Rex Scociæ *vel* Scottorum, 120, 121, 133, 172, 201, 213, 235.
Jamie, Johannes, 44.
Janua, Mercatores de, 58, 63.
Janua, Ludovicus de Valle de, 239.
Januæ, Baptista Mercator, 6.
Januæ, Treuga, 240.
Januens', Civitas, 21, 103.
Januens', Dux, 103.
Jersey et Garnsey, 319, 320.
Jerusalemitanorum, Domus Theutonica, 81.
Johan Evesque de Saresbirz; Tresorer d Engleterre, 42.
Johan Roy, 165, 166.
Johane, Quene, 254.
Johanna Comitissa Hereford', 85.
Johanna filia Nicholai Taillour de Yeuele, 90.
Johanna uxor ac executrix testamenti Willielmi Bardolf, 153.
Johanna uxor Ricardi Buckland', 191, 192.
Johanna uxor Thomæ de Felton', 13.
Johanna uxor Johannis Pauely, 49.
Johannes Archiepiscopus Cantuar', 209, 225, 330.
Johannes Camerarius de Dalburgh', 59.
Johannes Cancellarius Angliæ, 109.
Johannes Cardinalis, Archiepiscopus Cantuar', Sanctæ Balbinæ Episcopus, 229.
Johannes Cardinalis Eborum, 195.
Johannes Comes de Alencon', 84.
Johannes Comes de Foitz, 105.
Johannes Comes Huntingdon', 105.
Johannes Comes Salop', 198.
Johannes Comes Wygorniæ, Angliæ Thesaurarius, 85, 227, 228, 230.
Johannes Dominus de Beauchamp, Thesaurarius Angliæ, 222, 223.
Johannes Dominus Fawnhop',—John late Lorde Fawnhop, 207, 208.
Johannes Dominus Lescrop, 182.
Johannes Dominus Stourton, 230, 232.
Johannes Dominus de Tiptot', 172, 180, 192.
Johannes Dux Bedford', 122, 147, 152, 156.
Johannes Dux Bituriæ et Alvern', 84.

Johannes Dux Britann',—Johan' Duc de Bretaign', 2, 30, 92, 190.
Johannes Dux Burbon', 84.
Johannes Dux Burgundiæ, 115, 179.
Johannes Dux Lancastr', 12.
Johannes Dux Norffolk', 177.
Johannes Episcopus Bangoren', 20.
Johannes Episcopus Bathon', 110.
Johannes Episcopus Dunolm', 19.
Johannes, Johan, Episcopus Hereford',—Evesque de Hereford', 21, 25.
Johannes Episcopus Norwici, 187, 188.
Johannes Episcopus Roffen', 65.
Johannes filius Willielmi de Normanton', 34.
Johannes filius Willielmi de Weston', 31, 32, 33.
Johannes fitz Robert, 129.
Johannes Rex Angliæ, 3, 113, 121, 332.
Johannes Rex Castellæ et Legionis, 91, 98.
Johannes Rex Castellæ et Legionis, Dux Lancastr', 1.
Johannes Rex Castellæ, Legionis, et Toleti, 20.
Johannes Rex Franciæ, 65, 98, 179.
Johannes Rex Portugaliæ, 88.
Johannes Thesaurarius, 115.
Johannes Vicecomes de Beaumont, 221.
Johannis Baptistæ, Sancti, Capella, 78.
Johannis filii Hugonis de Normanton', Hugo filius, 31, 32.
Johannis Montagu nuper Comitis Sarum, Matillda uxor, 74.
Johannis de Pauely, Johanna uxor, 49.
John Baptiste, Seint, 111, 118, 168.
John the Evangeliste, Seint, 273.
Joynour, Ricardus, Civis et Grocerus London', 216, 217, 220, 223, 224.
Juliacen' Dux, Willielmus, 24.
Juyl, Rogerus, 28.

K.

(*Kanc'*, *Kent.*)

Kanc', Kent, 23, 30, 47, 79, 80, 179, 218, 219, 319.
Kent', Comes de, 20.
Kanc', Comes, Thomas de Holand', 10.
Kent, Kente, Thomas, 82, 192, 197, 198, 199, 200, 213, 221, 228.
Kent, Robertus, 82, 214.
Karliol', Episcopus,—Thesaurarius Angliæ, 152.
Karlioli, Episcopus, Marmaducus, — Thesaurarius Angliæ, 201.
Karlioli, Episcopus, Thomas, 59.
Karlioli, Episcopus, Willielmus Styrkland, 81.
Karolus Dominus de la Brytte, 179.
Karolus Dux Aurelien', 84.
Karolus, Rex Franciæ, Carolus, 60, 99, 109, 147, 194, 198.
Karolus primogenitus Johannis Regis Franciæ, 98.
Karolus Rex Navarræ, 46.
Katherine, Quene Dowager, 334.
Katerina Regina Angliæ, — Katerine the Quene, 102, 103, 164, 254.
Katerine, Seint, 117.
Kentewode, Reynald', 133.
Kermerdyn, 40.

Keston', Rogerus, 102.
King's Bench, 332.
Kirkeby, 28, 75.
Kirketon', Manerium de, 13.
Knebill', Thalpinus, 59.
Knolles, Robertus, 4, 13, 15.
Kyme, Johannes Hardyng de, 234.
Kynalton, 49.
Kynbell', Johannes, 41.
Kyngeston', Manerium de Hamme upp', 95.
Kyngston' super Hull', 44.
Kyngton', Johannes, 68, 81.
Kynuolmarch', — Kynwelmerch', —Kynwolmerssh', Willielmus, 86, 96, 97.
Kynwolmersshe, Kynuolmarch', Kynwelmerch', Willielmus, —Deputatus Thesaurarius Angliæ, Tresorer d Engleterre, 86, 96, 97, 99, 101, 103, 110, 112, 113, 187, 188, 189.
Kyrketon', Rogerus de, 7.

L.

Laghern', Thomas, 42.
Lambheth', 84.
Lamport, Ricardus, 221.
(*Lancastre*, *Lancastria*.)
Lancastre, 1, 2.
Lancastre, Armes de, 119.
Lancastriæ, Comitatus, 326.
Lancastriæ, Ducatus, 19, 81, 94, 95, 96, 105, 149, 150, 152, 156, 157, 160, 162, 163, 170, 172, 179, 181, 182, 190, 191, 192, 193, 194, 195, 196, 197, 198, 199, 200, 201, 203, 204, 213, 214, 217, 221, 222, 227, 228, 231.
Lancastria, Lancastre, Duc de, 19, 26, 27, 35, 117, 160.
Lancastriæ, Johannes Dux, 12.
Lancastre, Tablet of, 257.
Landes, Batable, 226.
Landon', Johannes, 138.
Langele, 28.
Langeley, Tenementa in, 79.
Langle, 80.
Langley, Thomas, 66.
Langport, Ricardus, 82, 214.
Lannoy, Johannes, 90.
Larchier, Thomas, 6.
Lardener, Katerina, 123.
Large, Robertus, 168.
Lary, Robertus, 72.
Lascels de Bristuyt, Johannes de, 22.
Lasyngby, Alexander, 102.
Latimer, Willielmus de, 16.
Launde, Robertus, 4.
Lavardyn, 200, 201.
Lazaro, Baptista, Mercator de Janua, 6.
Leeton', Rogerus Yeve de, 78.
Leget, Helminus, 9.
Legionis et Castellæ, Rex, 19, 46, 88, 92.
Legionis, Johannes Rex Castellæ et, 20, 91, 98.
Leicestr', Leycestr', 124, 125.
Leicestr', Comitatus, 72.
Leneve, Peter, 320.
Lenne, 132.
Lental, Reynald', 131.
Lentale, Rolandus, Miles, 134.
Lenton', Johannes, 194.
Leons, Roi de, 27.
Lescrop', Ricardus, 3.
Lescrop', Stephanus, 13.
Lescrop', Willielmus, 61.
Lescrop, Dominus Johannes, 181, 182.
Lesparre, Bernardus de,—Dominus de la Barda, 109.
Leuesham, Thomas, 122.

Leulyngham, 67, 68, 80.
Leventhorp', Johannes, Johann, 149, 150, 152, 188.
Lewes Priory, 326.
Leyot, Ricardus, 116.
Leyre, Rector Ecclesiæ de Dodyngton', Johannes de, 11.
Libri de Remembrances, 157.
Liddale, Robertus, Armiger, 228.
Lincoln', 324.
Lincoln', Comitatus, 22, 41, 50, 229, 322, 325.
Lincoln', Episcopus, 82, 105.
Lincoln', Episcopus, Willielmus, 170.
Lincoln', nunc Episcopus, Willielmus nuper Episcopus Norwicen', 181.
Lincoln', Episcopus, Ricardus Fleming, 149, 151.
Littelton', Thomas, 229.
Lochorwart, Willielmus de Hay de, 89.
Lodewycus, Dominus, Comes Palatinus Rheni, 69.
Lodowycus de Francia, Sanctus, 216.
Lollardus Lollardorum, Johannes Oldecastle, 102.
Lollyngham, 66.
(*London, Londres.*)
London', 9, 23, 46, 50, 51, 75, 91, 108, 170, 197, 318, 319, 320, 326.
London', Portus, 78, 162.
Londres, Seint Poule de, 133.
London', Turris, 10, 57, 62, 86, 105, 122, 196, 222, 299, 306, 309.
Londres, Wodewarf de, 25.
London', Aldermannus, Johannes Heende, 126.
London', Aldermannus, Simon Eyre, 232.
London', Aurifaber, Johannes Rus, 134.
(*London, Londres — continued.*)
London', Civis, Johannes Sherborne, 44.
London', Civis et Pannarius, Nicholaus Yoo, 253.
London', Civis et Grocerus de, Ricardus Joynour, 216, 223.
London', Episcopus, 30, 75, 148, 230.
London', Episcopus, Robertus, 48.
Londres, Mair de, Nicholas de Exton', 25.
London', Major et Communitas, 66.
London', Major, Ricardus Merlowe, 81.
London', Vicecomites et Aldermanni Civitatis, 21.
London, William Estfeld of, 175.
London', William Milrede of, 172.
London', Willielmus Vannere de, 58.
London', Henricus, 75.
Longevile, Johannes, 141.
Longlondes, le, 34.
Lopham, 58.
Lorde Cardynall' of England, 177.
Lote, Stephanus, 50.
Lovell', Armes du Seigneur, 128, 129.
Lowe, John, 333.
Lowes, John, 222.
Lowes of Essex, Philipp fitz, 222.
Lowys, Rogerus, 28.
Lubicen', Civitas, 170, 231.
Lucia uxor Willielmi Napper, 90.
Lucy, Walterus, 225.
Ludlowe, Willielmus, 188.
Luke, George, 180, 181.
Lumbard', 11.
Lumbardestrete, 72.
Lumlyne, Bartholomeus, 162.
Lusshingbourn', Johannes, 154.
Lyborne, 37, 38, 39.
Lyndeseye, Manerium de Kirketon' in, 13.

Lyndewode, Willielmus, 182.
Lynsz, Tilmannus de, 190.
Lynwode, Custos Privati Sigilli, Willielmus, 170.
Lyskyrde, 72.

M.

Macmaghon', Bernardus, 130.
Macmurghe, Onell', 198.
Madhowe, Johannes del Wod de, 13.
Magdalenæ, Capella in honore Sanctæ Mariæ, 79.
Magno Consilio Regis, Domini de, 75.
Magotson', Isabella quondam uxor Ricardi, 33.
Maienburgh', 81.
Malet, Manerium de Cory, 192.
Malet, Walterus, 45.
Malpas, Henricus, 47.
Malpas, Philippus, 220.
Manfeld', Robertus, 196.
Manus, Johannes, 53.
Mapilton', 91.
Mapurley, Thomas, 157.
March' Cales', Guynes in, 122.
Marchal, The Erle, 250.
Marche, Conte de, 149.
Marescall', Comes, 151.
Marescalli, filius Comitis, 62.
Margareta Regina Angliæ, 215, 216.
Margareta uxor et executrix Laurencii Seybrok', 46.
Maria Virgo, Beata, 21.
Mariæ, Beatæ, Liber de Concepcione, 97.
Mariæ, Beatæ, de Graciis juxta Turrim London', Abbas et Conventus, 57.
Mariæ, Beatæ, Henricus de Plalvo Frater ordinis, 81.
Marie, the Quene, 318.
Marka, de partibus Alemanniæ, Gerardus de Clivis Comes de, 182.
Markham, Johannes, 229.
Marmaducus Episcopus Karlioli, Thesaurarius Angliæ, 201.
Martham, Robertus, 238.
Martyn', Johannes, 115.
Massy, Johannes, 73.
Massy, Willielmus, 55.
Matilda uxor Johannis Montagu Comitis Sarum, 74.
Matilda uxor Thomæ Comitis Sarum, 74.
Mauncell', Maunsell', Thomas, 201, 202, 210, 211.
Mavan', Petrus, 138.
Melcombe, Portus de, 61.
Melcombe, Villa de, 60.
Melkesham, Foresta de, 6.
Melton', Willielmus, 13.
Menevensis, Cathedralis Ecclesiæ, 51.
Menevensis, Episcopus, Guy, Guido, Mone, 53, 54.
Menteth', Comes de, 89.
Menteth, Johannes Grame Comes de, 234.
Mereduth', Owen' app', 173.
Merlawe, Manerium de Parva, 29.
Merlawe, Ricardus, nuper Thesaurarius Villæ Cales', 82.
Merlowe, Ricardus, Major London', 81.
Mersh', Ricardus Wilkokes de, 44.
Merston', 110, 113, 223.
Merston', Henricus, 115.
Merston', Marston', Johannes, Custos jocalium Regis, — Merston', John, Keeper of the Jewels, 114, 116, 123, 126, 127, 128, 129, 130, 131, 132, 134, 135, 138, 139, 141, 148, 151, 182, 204, 205, 207, 214, 215, 216, 222, 255.

Merwyck', Isbrandus de, 182.
Meryng', Franciscus de, 32, 33.
Meryng', Willielmus, Miles, 135.
Meux, 155.
Michael, Seint, 258.
Middelton', Johannes, 44, 177.
Milrede, William, of London', 172.
Minorum in Villa Salop', Domus Fratrum, 108.
Mitau, Fridericus de, 59.
Mitford, Johan' de, 55.
Moleneux, Adam, 179, 180.
Molyns, Adam, 179, 181, 190, 193.
Mone, Guy, — Mone, Guido, Episcopus Meneven', 53, 54.
Montague, Charles, Esquier, Chanceler of the Exchequer, 333.
Montague, the Earle of, 324.
Montague, Johannis nuper Comitis Sarum, Matilda uxor, 74.
Monte Acuto, Johannes de, nuper Comes Sarum, 63.
Moore, Edmundus, 238.
Moore, Thomas, 47.
More, Simon atte, 20.
More, Sir Thomas, 324.
Morende, Castrum de, 11.
Morende, Manerium de, 11.
Mortimer, Hugo, 77.
Morton', Robertus, 95.
Mortymer, Johannes, 218, 219.
Mountjoy Priory, 322.
Moyses Yerde, 264.
Muerse, Comes de, 58.
Munketon', Tenementa de, 178.
Murehede, Willielmus, 69.
Muscham, Willielmus de Bacheley de, 31.
Muskham, Johannes, 7.
Muskham, Robertus, 1.
Mylewater, Johannes, 239.

N.

Nansumer, Henricus, 90.
Napper, Willielmus, et Lucia uxor ejus, 90.
Navarr', Rex, Roy de, 37, 38.
Navarr', Rex Carolus, 46.
Navern', Arma de, 104.
Nessefeld', Willielmus de, 44.
Neuton', 49.
Neve, Peter le, 333.
Nevill', Johannes de, 41.
Nevill', Thomas, 233.
Nevill' de Raby, Johannes de, 15.
Newe Pallace at Westminster, 312.
Nicholai, Thomas fitz, 187, 188.
Nicholaus Bathon' et Wellen' Episcopus, 180.
Nicholaus filius Willielmi, 32, 33, 34.
Norbury, Johannes, 58, 62, 63, 76, 85.
Norffolk, 229, 238, 316, 322, 326.
Normannia, Normandy, 98, 141, 163, 191, 231.
Normanniæ, Ducatus, 163.
Normanniæ, Thesaurarius, Johannes Stanlowe, Armiger, 193.
Normanton', Campus de, apud Dalthorndik', 31.
Normanton', Hugo filius Johannis filii Hugonis de, 31, 32.
Normanton', Johannes filius Willielmi de, 34.
Normanton' Mersshe, 34.
Normanton', Outegong' de, 34.
Normanton', Robertus de Camera de, 32.
Normanton' super Trentam, 31.
Northalle, Manerium de, 58.
Northampton', 11, 26, 320, 325.
Northbury, Johannes, 43, 60.
Northumbr', 24, 320.

Northumbr', Comes,— Northumberland, Earle of, 29, 66, 327.
Northumbr', Henricus de Percy Comes,—Northumbr', Henry Percy Conte de, 15, 27, 81, 172.
Northwales, 320.
Norton', Ricardus, 188.
Norwic', Civitas, 132.
Norwic', Ecclesia Cathedralis SanctæTrinitatis, 233, 237.
Norwic', Episcopus, 70, 98.
Norwic', Episcopus, Johannes, 187, 188.
Norwic', Episcopus, Thomas Feld', 84.
Norwic', Episcopus, Willielmus, 120.
Norwic', Episcopus, Ricardus,— Norwicen', Ricardus Courteney Episcopus, — Norwicen', nuper Thesaurarius Cameræ Regis Henrici Quinti, Ricardus Courtenay nuper Episcopus, 104, 106, 111, 127, 128, 131, 135, 181.
Norwicen', nuper Episcopus, Willielmus, nunc Episcopus Lincoln', 181.
Norwich', Busshoprik of, 327.
Not', Thomas, 59.
Notingham, 62.
Notingham, Johannes, 29.
Nottingham, Comitatus, 33, 48.
Nottingham, Lorde Admyrall of Englande, Charles Erle of, 299.
Novi Collegii sive Cantariæ in cimiterio juxta Ecclesiam Cathedralem Menevensem, Magister et Capellani, 51.
Novum Castrum super Tynam, 24.

O.

O'Bryn', Donatus, 130.
O'Tothill', Dermoin', 130.
Oeffeldia, Johannes de, 182.
Okeborne, Prioratus de, 36.
Oldecastell', 89.
Oldecastell', Thomas, 53.
Oldecastell', Johannes, Lollardus Lollardorum, 89, 102.
Olgis, Mouster de, 37.
Oliverus, Petrus, de Barselonia in Catelonia, 74.
Omnium Sanctorum in London', Parochia, 108.
Oneyll', Euvegenius, 130.
Ordialis, Castrum de, 39.
Orealensis, Dux, 224.
Orgrave, Thomas, 3, 4, 5, 10, 14.
Orlien', Dux,—Orliaunce, Duke of, 161, 181.
Ormond', Comes de,—Ormond, Conte de, 4, 5, 17.
Ormond', Comes de, Jacobus, 130.
Oudeby, Johannes, 9, 20, 60, 66, 80, 81.
Outegong' de Normanton', 34.
Outhorp', 49.
Overey, Prioratus Sanctæ Mariæ de, 187.
Owen' app' Mereduth', 173.
Oxford, Cardinall Colledg in, 329.

P.

Padeley, Robertus Eyre de, 112.
Palays, Johannes, 17.
Palmer, Elizabeth, 32.
Paralipomenon, Liber vocatus, 97.
Parke, Henricus, 203.

Parker, Johannes, 51.
Parva Merlawe, Manerium de, 29.
Parys, Civitas, 59.
Parys work, 173.
Patesle, Johannes, 153.
Pauele, Johannes, 48.
Pauely, Johanna uxor Johannis, 49.
Paulet, Willielmus, 178.
Pauli, Comes Sancti, 5, 36.
Paynour, Willielmus, 188.
Pecche, Willielmus, 203.
Pelegryn, Reimundus, 9.
Pembroch', Comes, 34.
Penycok', Johannes, 151.
Percy, Henricus de, 79.
Percy, Henricus de—Comes Northumbriæ, 15, 26, 172.
Percy, Thomas, 18, 35, 41.
Pereguert, Comes de, 53.
Perers, Alicia, 8.
Perret, Oliverus, 231.
Petro, Roy Don, 38, 39, 40.
Petrus Rex Castellæ,—Don Petro Roy de Castell', 37, 93.
Peverell' Evesque de Wycestr', Thomas, 130.
Philip', Johannes, 104.
Philip and Mary, 318, 323.
Philip fitz Lowes of Essex, 222.
Philip—Philippus Dux Burgundiæ, 153, 200, 204.
Philippa uxor Mathei de Gourney, 45.
Philippa filia Regis Henrici Quarti, 65.
Picardiæ, Partes, 192.
Pilkyngton', Johannes, 140.
Plalvo, Henricus de, Frater ordinis Beatæ Mariæ, 81.
Plumpton, Robertus de, 13.
Plumptre, 49.
Pobelewe, Robertus, 187, 189.
Pole, Petrus, 112.
Pole, Michael de la, 32, 33, 41, 44.
Pole, Michael de la, Cancellarius Angliæ, 17.
Pole, Michael de la, Comes Suff', 31, 36.
Pole, Willielmus de la, Comes Suffolk', 158.
Pomfreit, 71.
Pomiers, Gill' Sire de, 3.
Pontrell', Johannes, 123.
Ponynges, Blanchia Domina de, 52.
Ponynges, Thomas, Seigneur de Seint Johan, 57.
Poole, Cardinall, 334.
Popyngeay, Robertus, 123.
Port, Guy de, 70.
Port, Porte, William, Willielmus, 167, 168, 169, 175, 177, 186, 187, 201, 241.
Portebrig', Manerium de, 47.
Porter, Willielmus, 135.
Portugalia, Portyngal, 20, 88, 89, 159.
Portugaliæ *vel* Portingaliæ Rex, 19.
Portugaliæ, Rex Alfonsus, 89.
Portugaliæ, Rex Edwardus, 159.
Portugaliæ, Rex Johannes, 88.
Poule de Londres, Seint, 133.
Poule, Counte de Seint, 19.
Pounde, Adæ, Johannes Pounde filius, 44.
Pounde, Thomas, 168, 176, 180, 181, 231.
Pountfreit, 69, 73, 77.
Pouterell', Johannes, 134.
Poutrell', John, 180, 181.
Powys, Edwardus de Cherlton Dominus de, 188.
Poyane, Seigneur de, 40.
Prest, Galfridus, 50.
Preston', Christoforus, 112.
Profet, Johannes, 9.
Prophet, Johannes,—Custos Privati Sigilli, 74.
Prucia, 68, 81, 82, 118, 163, 170, 193, 213, 221.

Prucia, Homines de, vocati Hance, 193.
Pudsey, Johannes, Armiger, 132.
Pye, Georgius, 32.

Q.

Queyte, 39.

R.

Raby, Johannes de Nevill' de, 15.
Radcliff, Johannes filius Jacobi de, 137.
Radclyf, Johannes, 102.
Radyngton', Baldewynus, 42.
Randolf, Johannes, 108, 112.
Raucestre, 6.
Redeston', Willielmus, 104.
Redford, Henricus, 224.
Redmayn, Richard, 55.
Relleston', Robertus, 97.
Rempston', Thomas de, 48, 49.
Reni *vel* Rheni, Lodewycus Comes Palatinus, 69.
Reni *vel* Rheni, Rupertus Comes Palatinus, 59.
Reydon', Tenementa in, 203.
Ricardi, Willielmus filius, 32, 33.
Ricardus Comes Arundell', 14, 57.
Ricardus Comes Sarum, 230.
Ricardus Comes Warrewyci, 230.
Ricardus Dux Eborum,—Richard, Rychard, Prynce *or* Duk' of York', 170, 171, 191, 193, 226, 229, 230.
Ricardus Episcopus Norwicen', 128, 131, 135.
Ricardus filius Johannis de Stretton', 44.
Ricardus I., 329, 331, 332.
Ricardus II., 1, 2, 3, 4, 5, 6, 8, 9, 10, 11, 13, 14, 15, 17, 18, 19, 20, 22, 23, 24, 25, 26, 31, 34, 35, 36, 40, 41, 42, 45, 46, 47, 48, 50, 51, 52, 53, 54, 55, 57, 58, 59, 60, 63, 72, 81, 88, 108, 124, 125, 136, 190, 195, 323, 325, 330, 331.
Ricardus Rex Angliæ, (*i. e.* Ricardus II.,) 12, 20, 21, 30, 43, 56, 61, 62, 66, 180.
Richemund', 1.
Richemund' *vel* Richemond', Comes, 54.
Rixston', Nicholaus, 66, 67, 68, 80.
Roberti, Johannes fitz, 129.
Robertus Dominus de Wylughby, 115.
Robertus Episcopus London', 48.
Robertus filius Hugonis, 32.
Robertus Rex Scociæ, 89, 90, 234.
Robesart, Canon', 3.
Rocheford', Radulphus, 122.
Rodes, Robertus, 160, 161.
Roffen', Episcopus, 61.
Roffen', Episcopus, Johannes, 65.
Rogerus, Magister, 79.
Rokell', Galfridus, 73.
Rokes, Thomas, 110.
Rokesburgh', 221, 226.
Rolleston', Robertus, 101, 162, 182, 194, 196.
Rollyngswerd', John, Marchaunt of Almayne and Servaunt of the Erchebisshop' of Cologne, 255.
Romana Curia, 193, 194.
Romanorum Rex, 9, 66, 111, 162.
Romanorum, Rex, Rupertus, 69.
Romanorum semper Augustus, Rex, Sigismundus, 138, 161, 179, 180, 225.

Romanorum, Rex Vinceslaus, 11.
Rome, Johannes, 84.
Roos, Dominus de, Thesaurarius Angliæ, 70.
Roos, Johannes, Armiger, de Chirburgh', 158.
Rotel', 11.
Rotel', Edwardus Comes, 59.
Rothesayæ, David Dux, 56.
Rotheuale, Johannes, Miles, Thesaurarius Angliæ, 101, 217, 220, 226.
Rothomag', 193.
Rouland', 135.
Roulles, Johannes atte, 24.
Rous, Robertus, 5.
Rupellà, 98.
Rupertus Comes Palatinus Reni et Dux Bavariæ, 59.
Rupertus Rex Romanorum, 69.
Rus, Johannes, Aurifaber London', 134.
Rusderf, Dominus, Paulus,—Magister ordinis Beatæ Mariæ Teuthonicorum, 163.
Rutland', 62.
Ryholmestrete, 34.
Rykedon', Robertus, 188.
Ryman', Willielmus, 188, 189.
Ryston', Richard, 110.

S.

Sak', Johannes, 154.
Salesbury, Johannes, 57.
Salesbury, Nicholaus, 29.
Salisbury, Countisse of, 324.
Salisbury, Bisshop' of, Richard Beauchamp', 236.
Salop', Comitatus, 78, 321.
Salop', Domus Fratrum Minorum in Villa, 108.
Salop', Comes, Johannes, 198.
Salop', Comes, Johannes Talbot Thesaurarius Angliæ, 234.
Salvatoris juxta Shene, Domus Sancti, 97.
Salvatoris Trajecten', Ecclesia Sancti, 24.
Sanctæ Balbinæ, Episcopus, Cardinal', Archiepiscopus Cantuar', Johannes, 229.
Sanctæ Mariæ de Overey, Prioratus, 187.
Sanctæ Trinitatis Norwici, Ecclesia Cathedralis, 233, 237.
Sanctæ Trinitatis de Hundeslowe, Prior et Conventus, 12.
Sancti Andreæ, Costa, 273.
Sancti Andreæ Colon', Ecclesia, 182.
Sancti Augustini Cantuar', Abbas et Conventus, 51.
Sancti Florini Confluen', Ecclesia, 190.
Sancti Johannis Baptistæ, Capella, 78.
Sancti Ludgeri, Monasterien' Ecclesia, 182.
Sancti Pauli, Comes, 5, 36.
Sanctorum, Parochia Omnium, in London', 108.
Sandes, Johannes, 4.
(*Sandewich', Sandewic'.*)
Sandewich', 142.
Sandewici, Robertus Audemer nuper Scrutator Regis in Portu Villæ, 157, 158.
(*Sarum, Saresbirz, &c.*)
Sarum, 236.
Sarum, Ecclesia Cathedralis, 113.
Sarum, Comes, Johannes Montagu, 74.
Sarum, Comes, Ricardus, 230.
Sarum, nuper Comes, Johannes de Monte Acuto, 63.
Sarum, Episcopus, Robertus, 180.

(*Sarum, Saresbirz, &c.—cont.*)
Sarum, Thomas nuper Comes,—Saresberis, Thomas Count de, 138, 194.
Sarum, Thomas filius Comitis, 74.
Sarum, Episcopus, J.—Johan Evesque de, 41, 51.
Saresbirz, Evesque de, Tresorer d Engleterre, Johan, 42.
Sauncey, 305.
Saundes, Johannes, 20.
Saus, Gilliam, Sire de Pomiers, 3.
Say *vel* Saye, Jacobus Fenys, Miles, Dominus de, Thesaurarius Angliæ,—Say, Jacobus Dominus de, Thesaurarius Angliæ, &c.—Say, Dominus de, Thesaurarius Angliæ, 156, 204, 207, 208, 210, 212, 214, 216, 240.
Say, Johannes, Subthesaurarius, 240.
Scarburgh', Johannes, 36.
Scardebrow, Villa de, 13.
Scarle, Johannes, 61.
Schakull', Johannes, 16.
Sclygh', Johannes, 17.
(*Scocia, &c.*)
Scocia, Scotlande, 54, 60, 62, 71, 80, 89, 90, 120, 146, 147, 172, 200, 213, 222, 225, 227, 234, 235, 299, 305.
Scociæ, Ambassiatores, 69, 226.
Scociæ, Camerarii et Justiciarii, 234.
Scociæ *vel* Scottorum, Commissionarii Regis, 226, 228.
Scociæ, Gubernator, 80, 89.
Scotland and England, Leagues between, 334.
Scotica Lingua, 73.
Scociæ, Parliamentum, 234, 235.
Scociæ, Tractatus, 71.
Scociæ, Scottorum, Rex, 56, 62, 63, 69, 71, 82, 113, 133, 200, 221, 226, 227, 228.
(*Scocia, &c.—continued.*)
Scociæ, David Rex, 234, 235.
Scociæ *vel* Scottorum, Rex Jacobus, 120, 121, 133, 172, 201, 213.
Scociæ, Rex Robertus, 89, 90.
Scocia, David' de Bruys de, 15.
Scociæ, David primogenitus Regis, 59.
Scoteneye, Sutton', 69.
Scrop', Sire de, Tresourer d Engleterre, 167.
Scrop', Johannes le, Thesaurarius Angliæ, 141.
Scrop', Ricardus, 114.
Scrop', Willielmus le, 14, 19, 20, 59.
Seint Albones, 110.
Seint Cristofre, 173, 273.
Seint David, l'Evesque de, 70.
Seint David, Johan Evesque de, 41.
Seint George, 119, 143, 164, 183, 185, 202, 204, 253, 254, 256, 257, 260, 271, 272.
Seint George and Seint Michael, Orders of, 327.
Seint Johan Baptiste, 111, 118, 268.
Seint John the Evangeliste, 273.
Seint Johan, Thomas Ponynges S[r] de, 57.
Seint Michael, 258.
Seint Poule, Counte de, 19.
Seint Poule de Londres, 133.
Seint Thomas, 119.
Seint Thomas of Canterbury, 272.
Selby, Radulphus, 52.
Sellyng, Ricardus, 153.
Seman, Robertus, de Duryngton, 57.
Sevenhamton', Manerium de, in Comitatu Somers', 14.
Seybrok, Laurence, 46.
Seymor, Sir Edward, 327.
Shadworthe, Johannes, 126.
Shakirston', Villa de, 72, 73.

Sharneffeld', Nicholaus, 5.
Shene, 225.
Shene, Domus Sancti Salvatoris juxta, 97.
Shepey, Johannes, 56.
Sherborne, Civis London', Johannes, 44.
Sholden', Thomas, 148.
Shotesbrok', Robertus, 199.
Shyrley, Radulphus, 106, 107.
Siciliæ, filius Henrici Regis Angliæ, Edmundus Rex, 152.
Sigismundus Rex Romanorum, 138, 161, 179, 180, 225.
Simon, 28.
Sintre, Villa de, 160.
Skelton', Johannes, 76, 80, 83, 92, 93, 139, 141.
Skipse, Castrum et Manerium de, 115.
Skydmore, Johannes, 104.
Slegge, Stephanus, 207.
Slegh', Johannes, 51.
Smith, John, Esquire, 333.
Somer, Henricus, 77, 78, 80.
Somer, Henricus, — Cancellarius Scaccarii, 85.
Somer, Johannes, 23.
Somerset, 14, 22, 90, 177.
Somerset, Comes, 190.
Soto, Petir de, 40.
Southampton', Comitatus, 69.
Southdykes, le, 33, 34.
Southwales, 320.
Southwhetlee, 36.
Southwodehous, 36.
Sparham, Johannes, 233, 237, 238.
Sparrays, Castellania de la, 100.
Sparre, Castellania de la, 100.
Sparre, Bernardus de la, Dominus, 14, 97, 100, 181.
Spayne et Aragon, 327.
Spayne, Palet de, 126.
Spayne, le Spey de — Spayne, the Swerd of, 53, 144, 146, 167, 183.
Spencers, father and sonne, 326.
Spreber, Willielmus, 199.
Sprucia, 214.
Squiercroft, Terra de, 33.
Stafford', Cancellarius Angliæ, Johannes, 146.
Stafford', Custos Privati Sigilli, Johannes, 109.
Stafford', Johannes, Thesaurarius Angliæ, 110, 113, 114, 115, 117, 120, 123, 124.
Stafford', Episcopus Bathon', Thesaurarius Angliæ, Johannes, 122.
Stanley, Thomas, 43, 59.
Stanlowe, Johannes, Armiger, — Thesaurarius Normanniæ, 193.
Staple, Johannes, 44.
Stapulæ Villæ Cales', Major, 518.
Staverton', Johannes, 108.
Steenbergen', Henricus de, 24.
Stellata Camera, — Sterre Chambre, 25, 148, 149, 194, 227.
Stepyngdon, Johannes, 169.
Stocker, Johannes, 82.
Stokdale, Thomas, 114, 120.
Stoke Cursy, Tenementa de, 178.
Stoke under Hampdon', Manerium de, 192.
Stokes, Alanus de, 8.
Stokes, Johannes, 94, 133.
Stokker, Johannes, 221.
Stokker, Wauter, 181.
Stopyngton', Johannes, 147, 190.
Storthwayt, Johannes, 182.
Stourton, Johannes Dominus, 230, 232.
Strabolgy, David, Comes de Athell', 234.
Strangways, Jacobus, 115.
Stretton', 36.
Stretton', Ricardus filius Johannis de, 44.
Strivelin, 213.
Strode, Manerium de, 6.
Stury, Ricardus, 48.

Styrkland', Willielmus, Episcopus Karlioli, 81.
Sudeley, Rauf late Lord, Tresourer of England',—Sudeley, Radulphus Dominus de, Thesaurarius Angliæ, 195, 197, 209, 255.
Suffolk', Comitatus, 203, 316, 326.
Suffolk', Comes, Michael de la Pole, 31, 36.
Suffolk', Erle of, Thomas, Lord Chamberleyne of the Kynges Householde, 299.
Suffolk', Comes, Willielmus, 155, 212.
Suffolk', Comes, Willielmus de la Pole, 158.
Suffolk', Comes, Willielmus de Ufford' nuper, 47.
Super Hull', Kyngston', 44.
Super Humbr', Barton', 44.
Super Trentam, Normanton', 31.
Super Twedam, Castrum de Berewico, 123.
Surr', 42, 95.
Surr', Comes, Johannes de Warenna, 100.
Sussex', 326.
Suthant', Custumar' de, 161.
Suthcote, Walterus, 161.
Sutton', Johannes de Glancestre de, 32, 33.
Sutton' Scoteneye, 69.
Sutton', Dionisia uxor Willielmi de, 5.
Swalclyve, Georgius, 163.
Symme, Johannes, de Wrytelmersh', 30.

T.

Taillour de Yeuele, Nicholaus, et Emma uxor ejus, et Johanna filia eorundem Nicholai et Emmæ, 90.
Talbot, Dominus de, 198.
Talbot Comes Salop', Johannes,—Thesaurarius Angliæ, 234.
Talbot, Ricardus, 57.
Talbot, Willielmus, 127.
Tankerville, Willielmus de Harecourt Comes de, 224.
Tarent, Willielmus, 45.
Temestrete in London', 108.
Templehurst, Manerium de, 6.
Templeneusom, Manerium de, 6.
Teuthonicorum, Dominus Paulus Rusderf, Magister ordinis Beatæ Mariæ, 163.
Teye, Robertus, 126.
Theodericus Coloniensis Archiepiscopus, Sacri Romani Imperii per Italiam Archicancellarius, Westfaliæ et Angariæ Dux, 190.
Theologicæ Veritatis, Liber vocatus Compendium, 97.
Theutonica Jerusalemitanorum, Domus, 81.
Thirwall', Willielmus, 115.
Thomas of Canterbury, Seint, 172.
Thomas Comes Arundell', Thesaurarius Angliæ, 84.
Thomas Comes de Bukyngham, 11, 12.
Thomas Comes Devon', 226.
Thomas nuper Comes Sarum, 194.
Thomas Count de Sareberis, 138.
Thomas Dux Clarenciæ, 131.
Thomas Dux Glouc', 48, 114.
Thomas Episcopus Bathon' et Wellen', 199.
Thomas Episcopus Dunolm', 187, 188, 189.
Thomas Episcopus Exon', 5.
Thomas Episcopus Karlioli, 59.
Thomas Erle of Suffolke, Lord Chamberleyne of the Kynges Householde, 299.
Thomas filius Matilldæ et Comitis Sarum, 74.
Thomas fitz Harry, 239.

Thomas fitz Nicholai, 187, 188.
Thomas, Seint, 119.
Thortyngton', Manerium de, 14.
Throkmarton, Johannes, Clericus Thesaurariæ, 158.
Thurstan', Johannes, 41.
Tiptot, Typtot, Dominus, 139, 140, 170.
Tiptot, Tiptote, Dominus Johannes de, 7, 172, 180, 181, 190, 192.
Tiptot, T., Thesaurarius Angliæ, 78.
Tirell', Thomas, 217, 218, 219, 220.
Tirwyn', Tyrwyn', Episcopus de, — Cancellarius Franciæ, 154, 159, 169.
Toleti, Rex Castellæ, Legionis, et, 88.
Toleti, Johannes Rex Castellæ, Legionis, et, 20.
Toly, Willielmus, Secretarius Domini Cardinalis Angliæ, 152, 153.
Tone, Ricardus, 195.
Tour de Loundres, Turris London', Tower of London, 57, 62, 86, 105, 122, 196, 222, 299, 306, 309.
Trajecten', Ecclesia Sancti Salvatoris, 24.
Trane, Sandic de la, 9, 10.
Trent, 316.
Trentam, Normanton' super, 31.
Tresilian, Robertus, 16, 28.
Trinitatis de Hundeslowe, Prior et Conventus Sanctæ, 12.
Tunica inconsutilis, 164, 186, 215.
Turcays, Gerardus de, 40.
Turon', 197.
Twedam, Castrum de Berewico super, 123.
Tygre, le, 138, 145, 146, 147.
Tynam, Novum Castrum super, 24.
Tyne, River of, 316.

U.

Ufford', Willielmus de, nuper Comes Suffolk', 47.
Umfravill', Robertus, 55.
Upham, Ecclesia de, cum Capella de Cherlton', 113.
Upme Graue, Johannes, 182.
Urbanus Papa VI., (*Bartholomeo Prignani, Archbishop of Bari,*) 4.

V.

Vale d'Anande, Dominus de, 200.
Valesci de Almadana, Johannes, 88.
Valle Dei, Conventus de, 50.
Valle, Ludovicus de, 239.
Van Clux, Hertauk', 180.
Vandale, Tudericus, 7.
Vandom, Lodewicus de Burbon' Comes de, 96.
Vannere de London', Willielmus, 58.
Vasconia, 7, 125.
Vasconiæ, Judex, 178.
Veele, Johannes Bykenore de Claveryng' dictus la, 47.
Veer, nuper Dux Hiberniæ, Robertus de, 52.
Vendom, 86.
Vendom, Comes de, 97.
Venecia, 77.
Venicia, Mercatores de, 122.
Vermeo, Chastel et Lieu de, 39.
Victory, Mercator Florenciæ, Johannes, 96.
Vinceslaus Rex Romanorum, 11.
Virgo Maria, Beata, 21.
Visen', Johannes Aluarus Decanus, 88.
Vulre, Gervasius de, 169.

W.

Wakefeld', Ricardus, 48.
Wakeryng', Johannes, 76, 81, 83, 84.
Wakeryng', Johan, Gardein du Prive Seal,—Custos Privati Sigilli, 130, 132.
Walden, Rogerus, 52, 53.
Wales, Princes of, 247, 317.
Walford, Willielmus, 79.
Waller, Ricardus, 217, 218, 219, 220.
Wallia, 4, 157.
Walliæ, Clerici, 328.
Walliæ, Ducatus, 113.
Walliæ, Principatus, 59, 98, 99, 103, 109, 115, 120, 121, 122, 125, 133, 136, 138, 147, 180, 193.
Walliæ, Princeps, Edwardus, 125, 140.
Walliæ, Princeps, Henricus, 65.
Waltam, Willielmus, 130.
Walter Seigneur de Hungyrford, Treserer d Engleterre, 111, 124, 125, 127, 128, 130, 131, 133, 134, 135, 136, 137, 138, 139, 140, 141.
Walterus Episcopus Dunolm', 64.
Waltham, Johannes, 5, 13, 14, 22.
Waltham, junior, Johannes de, 22.
Walton', Thomas, 12.
Walwen', Thomas, 53.
Walweyn', Makeney, Scutifer Domini Typtot, 139, 140.
Warde, Willielmus, 122.
Warder, Mr Gidiok, 315.
Ware, Roger Seigneur de la, 40.
Warre, Dominus le, 50.
Warrenna, Comes Surr', Johannes de, 100.
Warrewyk', Castrum de, 54.
Warrewyk', Comes, Ricardus, Camerarius Scaccarii, 230.
Warrewyk', Warwick', Comitatus, 35, 178, 325.
Warwick Landes, 321.
Warrewyk', Johannes, 48.
Wasshbroke, Tenementa in, 203.
Watford', Tenementa in, 160.
Watreford', Cite de, 17.
Watton', Robertus, 76, 81, 83.
Wauter, Willielmus fitz, et Alicia uxor ejus, 12.
Wellen', Episcopus Bathon' et, 66, 180, 199.
Welles, 177.
Wellyngbourne, J., 20.
Wellyngburgh', Johannes, 29.
Welton', Thomas, 93.
Wendum', Comes de, 86.
Wenhyngburgh', Johannes, senior, 11.
Wenlok', Johannes, John, 207, 208, 209, 210, 211.
Westbury, Willielmus, 177.
Westmerland', Comitatus, 24, 326.
(*Westmonasterium, Westminster, &c.*)
Westmonasterium, Westmoustier, 6, 28, 31, 41, 49, 56, 58, 60, 75, 91, 142, 149, 150, 199, 210, 212, 230, 238.
Westmonasterii, Abbacia, Conventus, &c.,—Abbas, Abbas et Conventus, 41, 46, 52, 61, 111, 124, 126, 127, 156.
Westminster, Islip the Abbot of, 334.
Westminster, Henry the 7th's Chappell at, 333.
Westmonasterium, Camera Stellata apud, 194.
Westmonasterium, Consilium Regis apud, 225.
Westmonasterii, Scaccarius Regis, 204, 214.
Westmonasterium, Thesauraria apud, 123, 132, 135, 136, 137, 138, 180.

(*Westmonasterium, Westminster, &c.—continued.*)
Westmonasterii, Thesauraria in Abbatia,—Westminster, Treasury of, — Westmynster, Kynges Tresory within, — Westmynstre, Tresoury de, — Thesauraria Regis in Claustro Abbatiæ, 70, 106, 159, 167, 168, 177, 311.
Westmynstre, Grete Tresoury of, 241.
Westminster, seacond Threasaurie of, 332.
Westminster, the third Threasaury in the Chapter House of the Abbay of, 329.
Westminster, fourth Threasaurie in the Cloyster of the Abbay of, 312, 316, 332.
Westminster, Newe Palace at, 312.
Weston', 31, 32.
Weston in the Clay, 32, 33.
Weston' juxta Baldok', 321.
Weston', Willielmus de, et Johannes filius ejus, 31, 32, 33.
Wetton', Ricardus, 200.
White, Willielmus, 94.
Whityngton', Ricardus, 75, 78.
Whytheued', Alanus, 71, 72.
Whytyngton, Johannes, 239.
Wigorn', Comes, 225.
Wigorniæ, Comes, Johannes, Thesaurarius Angliæ, 85, 226, 227, 228, 230.
Wilkokes de Mersh', Ricardus, 44.
William the Conquerer, 316.
Willielmi, Nicholaus filius, 32, 33, 34.
Willielmus Comes Suffolk', 155, 212.
Willielmus de la Pole Comes Suffolk', 158.
Willielmus Dux Geleriæ, 22, 24.
Willielmus Episcopus Lincoln', 170.
Willielmus Episcopus Norwic', 120.
Willielmus nuper Episcopus Norwicen', nunc Episcopus Lincoln', 181.
Willielmus filius et heres Johannis Hunt', 5.
Willielmus filius Henrici, 33, 34.
Willielmus filius Ricardi, 32, 33.
Willielmus fitz Wauter, 12.
Wiltes', Comitatus, 321.
Wiltes', Jacobus Comes, Thesaurarius Angliæ, 237, 239.
(*Winchester, Wynton', &c.*)
Winchester, Statute of, 317.
Wyncestr', 107.
Wynton', Episcopus, 34, 117, 123, 201.
Winchestre, Wynchestre, Herry Byschop of, and Cardynal of Yngeland',—Wynchestre, Henri Cardinale d'Engleterre, Evesque de, 136, 142, 143, 144, 182.
Winton', Wynton', Episcopus, Henricus, Cardinal Angliæ, 145, 146, 154, 187, 201, 202.
Winton', Episcopus, Willielmus de Wykham, 14, 34, 117, 123, 201.
Windsor, 321.
Windsor, Dean and Canons of, 328.
Wod de Madhowe, Johannes del, 13.
Wode, Johannes, Clericus Thesaurarii Angliæ, 226, 227.
Wodehous, Johannes, 132, 188, 233, 237, 238.
Wollsey, Cardinalis, 318, 322, 326, 329.
Worcester, Master of the Horse, Edwarde Erle of, 299.
Wroghton', T., 42.
Wrytelmersh', Johannes Symme de, 30.
Wycestre, l'Evesque de, Thomas Peverell', 130.

Wyche, Ricardus, 90.
Wydeslade, Johannes, 161.
Wygmore, Johan, 170.
Wykes, Abbaye de, 322.
Wykham, Willielmus de, Episcopus Wynton', 14.
Wylton', Stephanus, 248.
Wylughby, Constantyn', 172.
Wylughby, Henricus, 157.
Wylughby, Robertus, 163.
Wylughby, Robertus Dominus de, 115.
Wymbush', Nicholaus, 83.
Wyngefeld', Johannes de, 44.
Wyngham, Robertus, 8.

Y.

Ybernia, 5.
Yelverton, Willielmus, 203.
Yerde, Willielmus, 105.
Yeuelchestre, 90.
Yeuele, Emma uxor et Johanna filia Nicholai Taillour de, 90.
Yeuele, Tenementa in, 90.
Yevele, Henricus, 50.
Yngeland, Herry Byschop of Wynchestre and Cardynal of, 136.
Yngham, Johannes de, de Fryseby, 45.
Yoo, Nicholaus, Civis et Pannarius London', 253.
Yorke, 229.
Yorke, Prynce Richard' Duk' of, 170.
Yorkshire, 322, 324.
Yve, Rogerus, de Leeton, 78.

END OF VOL. II.

London: Printed by George Eyre and Andrew Spottiswoode, Printers to the King's most Excellent Majesty. 1836.

Lightning Source UK Ltd.
Milton Keynes UK
UKHW02f0659140918
328884UK00012B/824/P

9 780260 304940